D1330013

Translating Slavery, Volume I

TRANSLATION STUDIES
BRIAN J. BAER, EDITOR
Albrecht Neubert, Gert Jäger, and Gregory M. Shreve, Founding Editors

Translating Slavery

Volume I

Gender and Race in
French Abolitionist Writing,
1780–1830

Edited by
Doris Y. Kadish
and
Françoise Massardier-Kenney

The Kent State University Press
KENT, OHIO

© 2009 by The Kent State University Press, Kent, Ohio 44242
All rights reserved
Library of Congress Catalog Card Number 2009021365
ISBN 978-1-60635-008-9
Manufactured in the United States of America

Permission to print "A Black Woman and a White man" and "A White Woman and a Black Man," Liverpool Online Series. Permission to print excerpts from The Saint Domingue Plantation, Louisiana State University Press. Permission to print excerpts from "Translating Abolitionist Poetry and Theatrical Works." Interview, Doris Y. Kadish and Norman R. Shapiro. *ATA Chronicle*. November/December 2008. 26–31.

Library of Congress Cataloging-in-Publication Data
Translating slavery / edited by Doris Y. Kadish and Françoise Massardier-Kenney. — [rev. and expanded ed.]
    p.   cm. — (Translation studies ; 5)
Vol. 1. Gender and race in French abolitionist writing, 1780–1830 —Vol. 2. Ourika and its progeny.
Includes bibliographical references and index.
ISBN 978-1-60635-008-9 (v. 1 : pbk. : alk. paper)—ISBN 978-1-60635-020-1 (v. 2 : pbk. : alk. paper) ∞
1. French literature—Women authors—History and criticism. 2. French literature—19th century—History and criticism. 3. French literature—18th century—History and criticism. 4. Slavery in literature. 5. Race in literature. 6. Sex role in literature. 7. French literature—Translations into English—History and criticism. 8. Duras, Claire de Drufort, duchesse de, 1777–1828. Ourika. 9. Duras, Claire de Durfort, duchesse de, 1777–1828—Translations into English. 10. Translating and interpreting—Philosophy. I. Kadish, Doris Y. II. Massardier-Kenney, Françoise.
PQ288.T73 2009
840.9'9287'09033—dc22   2009021365

British Library Cataloging-in-Publication data are available.

13 12 11 10 09   5 4 3 2 1

Contents

Preface

Doris Y. Kadish

We are publishing this revised edition of *Translating Slavery* in response to requests received over the years for paperback editions that would be accessible and useful to students and teachers in the fields of translation and French slavery studies. We have attempted to take into account the notable strides that have been made in those fields in the years since the publication of the first edition and to update sources and other materials accordingly. Because the number of translated works in the revised edition has been substantially expanded, we have chosen to present most of the original texts online rather than as appendices. See www.uga.edu/slavery.

Translation, gender, and race, the main topics of this volume, have often been relegated to a marginal status. In recent years, however, they have begun to receive the serious attention they deserve. Each of these topics stands at the frontier of much of the most challenging theoretical, linguistic, and historical activity occurring in the humanities and social sciences today. However, the important ties among these three topics have been insufficiently explored, leaving a gap in the treatment of the complex interrelationships that exist among them. *Translating Slavery* attempts to fill that gap by focusing on the French revolutionary period in the late eighteenth and early nineteenth centuries in France, from 1780 to 1830, a paradigmatic period during which a number of French women spoke out against the oppression of slaves and women. As the dates in the subtitle indicate, our focus is no longer limited to the period during which three women writers (Olympe de Gouges, Germaine de Staël, and Claire de Duras) wrote. Instead, we have chosen to broaden our focus to encompass the entire decade of the 1820s, a period that was especially rich in material by women and about gender and that we have only gradually begun to uncover.

Antislavery writings by French women have tended to be overshadowed by the far more negative, repressive works produced by French men writing in the second half of the nineteenth century. Those works functioned to crystallize and legitimize a fictive Africanist discourse that served, as Christopher Miller has shown (*Blank Darkness* 14–15), like Orientalism, to generate a set of mythic concepts and categories that stood as a screen between European subjects and the reality of the Other. Although it is true that antislavery works by women in the late eighteenth and early nineteenth centuries contributed to the creation of that discourse, it is also true that those works contributed significantly to a tradition of resistance against that discourse. Admittedly it is a mistake, as David Brion Davis points out, to glorify early antislavery writers, to overestimate their contribution, or to fail to acknowledge that their writings were motivated by a variety of economic, religious, humanitarian, and other considerations, not all of which were noble and disinterested.[1] But it is also a mistake, as Raymond Williams states, "to overlook the importance of works and ideas which, while clearly affected by hegemonic limits and pressures, are at least in part significant breaks beyond them, which may again in part be neutralized, reduced, or incorporated, but which in their most active elements nevertheless come through as independent and original" (114). This volume discovers in French women's writings of the revolutionary and post-revolutionary periods evidence of those significant breaks and independent, original elements.

For the purposes of this volume, 1780 and 1830 have been chosen as convenient and representative boundaries not only because they mark the dates when the principal works translated in this volume were written or published but also because they delineate an especially active period during which French women resisted the joint oppression of slaves and women. However, for more than a century before 1780, and for decades after 1830—even after 1848, when slavery was officially abolished once and for all in the French colonies—the interrelationships of gender and race continued to run through the fabric of French culture.

This volume focuses on translation, with a specific emphasis on gender and race. In addition to the marginalization that they typically undergo in literary and historical studies, translation, gender, and race all entail the same kind of mediating process. Looking closely at what happens when translators translate and when writers treat gender and race, we can see that literature is not an objective expression of universal values, as has been traditionally assumed, but an ideological expression of local values. *Ideology* is defined broadly here as the process by which particular groups produce meanings, beliefs, and values that are central to the social and political order of their time.[2] When translators translate works and women writers write works about the highly charged issues of gender and race, the processes of mediation and ideology that occur need to be made visible to critical scrutiny through analysis.

A crucial component of telling the story of translating gender and race entails looking at what happens when persons of color write about the subject of slavery or translate works about that subject. Unfortunately, little on this topic has been unearthed or explored in depth. The voice of the racial Other is not yet as readily available in French during the period highlighted in this volume as is the voice of the feminine Other. However, various ways of trying to hear that voice from the past, which has been largely silenced, have been adopted in this volume. Whenever possible, there will be mention of specific persons of color who have spoken about this period and who may have thus perhaps given a voice to those who remain silent: for example, the political leader Toussaint Louverture, the critic and historian C. L. R. James, the modern writers Caryl Phillips and Patrick Chamoiseau, the model for the nineteenth-century writer Claire de Duras' character Ourika, and other victims of the institution of slavery. Also, as translators and critics, we have attempted to sustain a dialogue that shows at least the willingness to listen in order to produce echoes today of that distant, muted voice. The dialogue that appears in chapter 8 and that tries to bring into the open some of the ways in which translators' racial and cultural backgrounds affect their translations is the result of just such an attempt.

This volume argues, then, that the processes of mediation and ideology are essential for understanding translation and, accordingly, that translation should not be taken as rising above or standing outside those processes. For translators in the twentieth and twenty-first centuries, as for writers or translators of an earlier time, ideological factors inevitably affect the treatment of issues of gender and race. The purpose of the analyses of translation provided in this volume is to identify some of those factors and to provide an occasion for reflecting upon the way they affect translators, critics, and readers of literary and historical works. Rather than allowing silence to surround the problems encountered in producing translations of gender and race, this volume seeks instead to identify such problems and thereby increase our awareness of the constraints of ideology. Rooted in the choices that translators make regarding gender and race, it is a method that scrutinizes works of literary translation textually, linguistically, and ideologically.

The numerous literary and expository texts dealing with slaves and slavery that women produced, especially those works by French women in the late eighteenth and early nineteenth centuries singled out for close consideration here, deserve to be better known. By making them better known, this volume foregrounds the existence of a French tradition of women's antislavery writing—Moira Ferguson similarly identifies "a gynocentrically-oriented discourse on slaves" (133) that existed in England from the seventeenth through the nineteenth centuries—that plays a significant but often overlooked role in French literature and history. This volume provides as well a selection of modern translations that will make some of the works in that feminine tradition available to English-speaking readers interested in issues of translation, gender, and race. This volume attempts to highlight key issues in the theory of translation as well as essays on the practical issues involved in translating gender and race. The translations produced for *Translating Slavery* were originally produced collaboratively by a group of women of French, American, and African American origin. Working as a team, this group of women attempted to make accessible the work of women writers of the past and thereby to maintain in some measure the tradition of women's resistance to those hegemonic cultural and social practices that have adversely affected women and persons of color. For the revised edition, we have expanded our group to include other translators, who have made it possible to incorporate new antislavery material.

Translating Slavery opened the door to an inquiry into the interwoven issues of race, gender, and translation some fifteen years before Christopher Miller's recent reassessment of those issues in *The French Atlantic Triangle*. Following the lead of our book, which he examines in detail, Miller "adopts" our focus on translation, which he considers essential for understanding the slave trade, and, acknowledging the centrality of gender for understanding abolitionist history, he "adapts" our separation between women and men in structuring the two central parts of his book (102). Miller's book differs from ours, however, in seeking to deconstruct clear divisions between genders. As Miller states, "Gender, like any boundary, is a line of demarcation that can be crossed, tripped over, or even transcended through acts of translation," and he asks, "Why are men who participated in the same intellectual project of abolitionist 'translation' not considered as part of the same picture? I will nominate counterexamples: several men who conform to the intellectual definition of a 'woman' that seems to be at work in *Translating Slavery*" (100). Although our revised edition does, for reasons of comparison and contrast explained below, include male writers, we do not propose adding them as "women." Perhaps in another place and time we can debate the deep-seated and far-reaching theoretical differences between our feminist project and Miller's deconstructive objectives.[3]

However, Miller raises one specific issue that we wish to address here. It is the limited selection of writers in the 1994 edition. Unearthing silenced voices in abolitionist history, with a special focus on women, has been central to our project from the start. Now, fifteen years later, having discovered more materials and made editions of primary texts available, we are able to add Sophie Doin, Marceline Desbordes-Valmore, and others to those voices in *Translating Slavery*. Although Miller's questioning of the exclusion of more widely accessible authors such as Grégoire and Lambert is understandable, he perhaps misunderstands the importance that we have attributed and continue to attribute to making little-known writers available to students and scholars of French and world literatures and history. It is telling that Miller resorts to a dismissive, aestheticizing language in his discussion of Doin and abolitionist poets, calling both "well intentioned and noble in purpose but mediocre by any standard of literary quality" (*French Atlantic Triangle* 216). Ironically, this is the same language that Flaubert and others used to dismiss *Uncle Tom's Cabin* and that has blocked the entry of so many historically significant writers into the literary canon. Miller's enthusiasm for hearing the "voices from below" of persons of color who have been silenced in the past and present does not seem to be as great when it comes to lesser-known women authors, for whom gaining a voice has presented and continues to present considerable challenges.

Chapter 1 presents a theoretical framework for the issues of translating slavery that are raised in this volume. Drawing on the contributions of a number of recent translation theorists, this chapter articulates an approach that has among its goals to textualize and contextualize translation, to produce a collaborative patchwork of textual components, to de-essentialize race and gender, and to practice a "creole translation" that distances itself from claims of universality and monolingualism. It is also an approach that attempts to be self-reflective and to address openly the ideological and linguistic limitations of its own theory and practice. In addition, chapter 1 dwells on some of the strategies adopted in order to maintain or restore the resistant elements of the works translated in this volume. Further discussion of those strategies and of specific problems encountered in translating particular authors occurs in later chapters.

Chapter 2 establishes the kind of broad historical context that is necessary for dealing adequately with the specific topic of translating gender and race in the period highlighted in this volume. In order to set the stage, the chapter begins by moving back before 1780 and taking up an example that illustrates especially well how the processes of mediation and ideology at work in translation affected a work about slavery. That example is the translation into French by a French male writer, Pierre Antoine de La Place, of what is commonly acknowledged as the seminal novel about slavery, *Oroonoko,* by the English woman writer Aphra Behn.[4] Although Behn's novel dates from the late seventeenth century and La Place's translation from the mid-eighteenth century, the issues surrounding the translation of *Oroonoko* provide a highly relevant context for discussing those issues about gender and race that resurface in the production of translations of works from the period examined in this volume. After the discussion of *Oroonoko,* the second chapter then takes up the period from 1780 to 1830 in order to provide the historical and literary context necessary to understand more fully the significance of the works by writers translated and analyzed later in the volume. The second chapter comes to a close with careful consideration of a second example, which again stands outside the specific period of interest in this volume but, like the first example, is part of the broad context necessary for understanding the intricate ties among translation, gender, and race in the revolutionary period. This second example consists of the translation into French by the Irish writer Louise Belloc, in collaboration with Adélaïde de Montgolfier, of what is undoubtedly the best-known work about slavery, Harriet Beecher Stowe's *Uncle Tom's Cabin.* By contrasting that translation by a woman, which Stowe singled out for praise, claiming that "I am convinced that a feminine mind can more easily mould itself to my own" (Belloc vi),[5] with the translation of the novel by a man, Emile de La Bédollière, we are able to shed further light on the complex historic interaction among translation, gender, and race.

Parts 2 and 3 focus on two specific women writers.[6] The first, Olympe de Gouges, wrote about the subject of slavery directly before and during the early years of the revolution at a time when overtly abolitionist sentiment was prevalent. The second, Germaine de Staël, wrote about that subject at the same time as Gouges, as well as at the end of the Napoleonic period, when pressure from England to end the international slave trade was being exerted. The introductory essays in parts 2 and 3 provide a context for understanding the particular nature of these women's contributions and for understanding the differences among them. Produced by members of a collaborative team who have different backgrounds and who were dealing with authors having a greater or lesser degree of direct connection to translation per se, these introductory essays sketch different kinds of contexts, in some cases focusing more on literary history; in others, more on biography and translation practice. Parts 2 and 3 then go on to provide representative translations. Each translation is followed by a translation analysis that looks at the issues of gender and race that those translations bring to the fore. Like the introductory essays, these analyses adopt very different approaches, according to the disparate backgrounds and interests of their authors. In the case of Gouges, the translator comments on her intentions and the decisions that she made. In the case of Staël, two of the translators engage in a dialogue aimed at identifying, however tentatively and preliminarily, the ways in which the existence of different cultural and linguistic backgrounds affect translation, especially for the highly sensitive and ideologically charged issue of race. The purpose of these different kinds of analysis is to provide examples of ways to address the ideological issues that inevitably arise in translation. Each of these analyses, like the translations themselves and other textual components included here, has its limitations. The process of reflection upon those limitations, begun by the contributors to this collaborative project within the pages of this volume, needs to be continued by its readers.

Part 4 provides translations of a group of authors—Marceline Desbordes-Valmore, Sophie Doin, Victor Chauvet, M. Dumesnil, Charles de Rémusat—whose works have been added to this revised edition. To reflect the literary breadth and depth of antislavery writing from the 1820s, we have chosen to include new material in the genres of poetry, narrative, and theater in chapter 9. Although *Translating Slavery* remains focused throughout on women's writings, some of this new material consists of translations of works by male authors: Charles de Rémusat, the author of the play *L'habitation de Saint-Domingue, ou L'insurrection,* and Victor Chauvet and M. Dumesnil, the authors of two widely acclaimed abolitionist poems. Gender was central to the writings of these men, as it was to French abolitionism generally. By including their works in *Translating Slavery*, we seek to illuminate through comparison and contrast some of the distinctive features of women's writings against slavery. In addition, in chapter 10 we include an interview with Norman R. Shapiro, who has joined the team of women translators represented in this book. His expertise in translating poetry and theater considerably enriches the revised edition, as do his reflections on what translating antislavery writing has meant to him.

This volume is intended for a variety of readers, both bilingual and monolingual. It is hoped that bilingual readers will want to go back to the original texts provided online after reading the translations and that their own reading will be informed by the translators' theory and practice. It is hoped that bilingual readers will scrutinize those texts for the interventions of the translators and assess what was done or could have been done. It is further hoped that, as a result of the kind of scrutiny practiced by the translators here, monolingual readers will be more aware in reading translations that translation has occurred, and that they will be reminded that translation is a kind of cultural mediation that we need to explore and examine, all the more so since we live and write under conditions of cultural protectionism that act to exclude languages and values other than our own.

This volume is also intended to serve a variety of academic purposes. Some readers may wish to focus on the translations as applications of the theoretical principles that this volume develops. Other readers may wish to focus on the women whose work as writers and translators is highlighted in this volume. Still other readers interested primarily in literature or history may wish to focus on the texts, which are difficult to obtain either in French or in translation. The authors of this volume hope, of course, that most readers will want to read the book in its entirety and that a comprehensive reading will make the important point that translation, literature, and history are all most clearly illuminated when their inextricable links are acknowledged and understood.

Part One

Theory, Practice, and History

CHAPTER 1

Translation Theory and Practice

Françoise Massardier-Kenney

As the title indicates, *Translating Slavery: Gender and Race in French Abolitionist Writing, 1780–1830* links theory and practice. The contributors to this volume are not speaking of literary and cultural translation in general, nor are they essentializing race and gender. Translating "gender and race" suggests that race and gender are already textualized. "Translating" race and gender implies a transitive operation that is necessarily contextualized. The translators who worked on the pieces by women writers—Olympe de Gouges, Germaine de Staël, Sophie Doin, Marceline Desbordes-Valmore (volume 1), and Claire de Duras (volume 2)—have doubled these authors' common discourse, a discourse that iterates that race, class, gender, and culture are figures of difference that are essentialized as causes of differences rather than as effects of a specific power imbalance. The texts presented here include analyses of the contribution during a specific period primarily of French women and of some male authors who wrote about people of color at a time when race was starting to be defined in essentializing terms,[1] and who have not been part of the canon of French literature. They also include translations of the French texts and comments on the translations by the translators themselves or by translators of other pieces. This collaborative patchwork of texts, comments, and translated texts deliberately fuses/defuses the differences between text and translation, between translating and writing, between reading and critiquing, and brings attention to translation as a critical gesture.[2] The consequence of this attempt to present translation and commentary, theory and practice, and gender and race as inextricably linked in a kind of hybrid text is that this presentation will inevitably require a discourse that cannot, that will not, neatly separate these strands, that will only leave gender to come back to it via a discussion of race, that will describe cultural difference only to question it in the practice of translation.

The displacement of writing and translation implied in a patchwork is especially apparent in the sections of the book devoted to Gouges, Staël, and Duras. In those sections, the translators reproduce the authors' own practices and awareness of the importance of translation for the representation of race and gender. Each of these three authors was directly involved in translation. Olympe de Gouges wrote in French, not her native language, so that for her the very act of writing was a translation. It is therefore not surprising that her writing-in-translation produced results that pushed the limits of the genre of French theater. Germaine de Staël's involvement with translation was more mediated, but no less central. She was a practitioner of translation, a theorist of translation, and her story "Mirza," presented here, fuses the three key elements of translation, race, and gender. Similarly, Claire de Duras practiced translation, criticized it, and created a powerful Senegalese heroine who represents the colonized subject as a "translated being," as someone who is seen and sees herself through the lens of the colonizing dominant culture.

In *Siting Translation* Tejaswini Niranjana has said about translators' prefaces that "the work from which they seem to exclude themselves (i.e., the translation) is constituted by the traces of their historicity, and the gesture of exclusion they perform makes possible the presentation of the text as a unified and transparent whole" (49). Here the contributors to this volume wish to come out into the open, to move, so to speak, from the preface to the surface, to face, and perhaps "deface," these texts in a movement that acknowledges that translation practice is always a practice of a "theory" or a working out of an ideological position, but also that translation theory inevitably emerges out of a specific practice. As Antoine Berman has shown, "There is no translator without translating position" (75).

This attempt at a self-reflecting translating practice follows in the steps of the most recent and interesting theoretical discussions of translation that have appeared in English. These discussions emphasize the ideological position implied by translation practices, the inevitable "refraction," to use André Lefevere's term, that occurs when a foreign text enters another culture.[3] One of these positions, as Lori Chamberlain has demonstrated, involves the traditional representation of translation in gendered terms. This representation implies a hierarchical relation (translation is like woman, i.e., secondary) that Chamberlain proposes to challenge by advocating a translating practice that asserts the role of the translator as that of an active textual producer. Barbara Godard is also struggling against the ancillary, feminine conception of translation when she advocates a conception of translation within the context of the theory of feminist discourse as "production not reproduction," and within "a logic of disruptive excess in which nothing is ever posited that is not also reversed" (90).

Rather than accept the opposition that Godard retains between production and reproduction, an opposition that goes back to the notion of the origin, authority, and superiority of the one who produces, translators could perhaps reclaim "reproduction" for translation as that operation that produces, through labor, something issued of something else, of an Other something. Thus reproduction as gendered production, as the labor of childbirth, of bringing forth a text out of another text, is a metaphor rich in implications for our understanding of translation as a linguistic mediation rather than as a linear source/target movement that reinscribes the notion of writing as origin.[4]

Of course, since translation is also a legitimizing process for a writer—a writer takes on the authority implied in being an author insofar as he or she becomes translated—a translator can become an active textual producer in the very process of choosing who will be translated, a choice that does not have to be left to the editors of commercial publishing houses or even to the academic establishment. Translation may not be a form of discourse encouraged by the cultural hegemonic powers in this country, but its very obscurity gives its practitioners a certain amount of freedom.[5]

It is because of this awareness that translation is a way to bring a certain authority to texts, a way to alter specific cultural power structures,[6] that the contributors to this volume have chosen works by authors who stand in some cases in the margins of French literature, and whose texts are often hard to obtain in English, if not in their native language. European women attempt to make us hear colonized voices at a time when such voices were barely audible. Translating authors such as Gouges, Staël, Doin, Desbordes-Valmore, and Duras means that their attempt at revoicing the colonized will be heard again. Significantly, their voices are part of a tradition of political opposition that expressed itself, among other things, as an opposition to the politics of slavery and racism. Our choice of authors, which points to the intersection of gender, race, and translation at the level of practice, reflects the increasing number of translations of noncanonical and older texts, many made by women translators and editors.

That the work of translation can be the process of creating meaning and restoring literary reputation is clear within the context of these writers: for example, Gouges' work in French has been dismissed as "bad," Staël's "Mirza" was dismissed as "awkward" and her essay on translation ignored, Desbordes-Valmore's writing was dismissed until recently, Doin has remained largely unknown, and Duras' *Ourika* was often forgotten until recently. The translations of the works presented in this volume, by pushing on the texts' resistant features, provide critical readings that follow the hidden threads of female agency and show that women authors of this period were, perhaps because of their cultural position, sensitive to the plight of Africans and opposed slavery textually in ways that their male counterparts (canonical writers such as Hugo and Mérimée) did not or could not (see, for example, Hugo's *Bug-Jargal* and Mérimée's *Tamango).*

The practice of translation can be conceived of as a kind of "archeology of knowledge": translation can reconstitute traditions that have been ignored because of their radicalness or their difference, or it can show how isolated voices could be seen as constituting traditions. As Pascale Casanova has brilliantly demonstrated in *La république mondiale des lettres,* the space of literature has been an international space for several centuries and translators have been essential creators of literary "value" in this world literary market (31). By translating, one participates in the constitution of culture, and the very gesture of translating can create pockets of resistance in the cultural hegemony. Translation does not necessarily have to be market driven and geared to producing easily digested versions of compliant texts that mirror American cultural values, which is how Lawrence Venuti defines the major output of translations into American English.

However, translating a text is more complex than just choosing a text, since it puts into play not only gender and race, but the issues of social class and nationality as well, and it is the very complexity of translation that the translators and critics of these volumes foreground here. These issues directly confront the translator as a woman who has to mediate between her desire to be visible in all it implies in terms of her own ideological investment and the necessarily different ideological positions of the text she translates. Any attempt to bring into another language or another culture the racial or cultural Other—women or persons of color—inevitably implicates the translator-mediator in the exploitative conditions that link Otherness to a specific power structure. Because of the specific historical and social circumstances in which women writers such as Gouges, Staël, Doin, Desbordes-Valmore, and Duras wrote, their texts present characteristics that the modern reader is likely to view as compliant with the dominant culture rather than as "radical," in spite of the fact that these authors were generally progressive (Staël, for example) or revolutionary (in the case of Gouges). For instance, Staël writes to urge the abolition of the slave trade, not the abolition of slavery itself, and in "Mirza" uses a male narrator who stereotypes African blacks in what may be offensive terms to present-day readers. At the same time, Staël's story valorizes her Jolof heroine and gives her access to language in a movement that was certainly resistant at the time.[7] What can the translator do to make this resistant gesture apparent? Is it sufficient to acknowledge this resistance in the "margins" of the translation, in the preface, or can this gesture be included in the translation itself? Since the goal of the collaborators of this volume is to reconstitute a tradition of women writing in a specific historical context, any intervention of the translator for the benefit of the modern reader could scramble the very voices the translator sought to bring back. Instead of stemming from an attention to the French author's particularity, adapting the radical gesture of the text could very well be another way of making the text "culturally fluent," of making it fit our own contemporary expectations of what constitutes "resistant" writing, or, to use Antoine Berman's expression, to impose one's own poetics. Making Staël politically correct could be far more compliant than producing a text whose mixture of radical and compliant elements makes us see the struggle involved against the dominant patriarchal discourse of the time and the inevitable limits that ideology places upon any writing, our own included—if not always acknowledged. As Gayatri Spivak has observed about the translation of Indian works into English, the translator "must be able to confront the idea that what seems resistant in the space of English may be reactionary in the space of the original language" ("The Politics of Translation" 186), and we may add that the reverse is true: what may appear compliant in English might have been resistant in the original language, and the translator-reader needs to decide how to handle the discrepancy between the two cultures.

This choice (unconscious as well as conscious) of whether to radicalize the text or not is scarcely gender free. A question one might ask about some of the translation practices discussed in chapter 2, "Translation in Context," is whether they are the result of a historical shift in translation theory (after the 1800s, the concept of translation as something "faithful" displaced the concept of translation as adaptation),[8] or whether the kinds and the number of liberties that translators take with their texts may also have to do with gender. For instance, Louise Belloc, who translated Harriet Beecher Stowe's *Uncle Tom's Cabin* in 1853, produced a translation that was very close to the American text and contained very few added or deleted elements, while Emile de La Bédollière, in his translation of that same text in 1852, produced a freer adaptation. We must notice that Belloc, a woman translating another woman, very carefully listened to the voice of her text, whereas the male translator La Bédollière felt free to rewrite Stowe's work to fit the expectations of his audience or his own expectations of what male and female characters could say. These examples may or may not be representative, but they bring out the question of whether the range of the translator's textual intervention is linked to gender positions.

The global strategies used by the different translators who worked on the texts presented here seem to follow parallel patterns. While the translators all refrain from adapting the French authors' politically and racially radical positions to the new Anglo-American context, and thus seem to produce linguistically conservative versions, they nonetheless do what Godard describes as "feminist discourse as translation." For Godard, "translation is one among many ways of rewriting within literary systems, pushing them in a certain direction through canonization" (92).

First, the translators have attended to the specific linguistic experiments, to the stylistic difference of the authors they were translating, in that the translators were furthering their agenda of reconstituting forgotten voices, looking toward their French texts rather than their audience. Maryann DeJulio's translation of Olympe de Gouges, for instance, emphasizes the polemical, rhetorical tone of the author, a tone that contributed to the creation of a new kind of ideologically engagé (i.e., politically committed) theater that has been largely ignored. The translator emphasizes the legal aspect of Gouges' writing by adding expressions from the language of contracts.

Staël's pieces, in turn, are translated with an attention to word choice that stresses the male/female opposition and valorizes the female in an effort to emphasize Staël's position as a woman writer, in conformity with the view that "the task of the feminist translator is to consider language as a clue to the workings of gendered agency" (Spivak, "The Politics of Translation" 177). Similarly, the translation of *Ourika* (in volume 2) by Claire Salardenne and Françoise Massardier-Kenney purposefully heightens the eloquence of the black female character in an effort to make heard a female voice that reaches the modern reader muted, already in translation (since Ourika does not know her mother tongue, she does not know the tongue of her mother). Here Ourika's fluency is not a way to satisfy the demands of the intended reader but a strategy that emphasizes the strength of a voice formed and perhaps deformed by the colonizing culture. It satisfies the demands of the translators as readers. It should be added that the two contributors, working on different pieces of *Ourika,* both purposefully effaced what sometimes appeared to them as the whining undertones of the character Ourika. This decision was made because of their common intention to produce a text that presents an oppressed but dignified woman of color. Specific lexical choices were thus made on the basis of the impression that the translators wanted the whole text to make. Our project of presenting these authors as exemplary presences who gave voice to forgotten subjects (women and blacks) made the translators aware of the patronizing implications of presenting a woman and a colonized subject strictly as a victim.

These contributors' own desire as women translators to empower the female characters dictated a number of their choices. In this regard, as the feminist translator Susanne de Lotbinière-Harwood points out about feminist translation in general, they recognize that "context determines translation strategies" (114) and that this particular context (women authors, women translators, a university press, and a sympathetic audience) made it possible for us to make the feminine visible in the text and valorize it.

Translation, as a self-reflective activity that contributes to the construction of a specific gender position, does not necessarily need to work on texts already, transparently, "feminist." As the examples presented here show, the translator can bring to the surface elements that specific historical and cultural modes of discourse bury. The translator can bring out in specific parts of the text the hidden or implied gender identification of the text as a whole. They can bring it out or subvert it in the case of sexist male writers, in the sense of bringing out a version of the text that is there only implicitly, as Suzanne Jill Levine argued about her own translation of Latin American works.

However, unlike Lotbinière-Harwood, because of the very nature of our project, we refused to consider gender as a factor overriding all others, gender as a unified context that determines all translation strategies. The translators attempted to attend to the interrelationship of all the factors—gender, race, or class—that were present in the texts. The translators of this volume reacted to the texts in ways that suggested that race, gender, and class were equally important ideological issues. For instance, Sharon Bell's translation of Staël's essays "Appel aux souverains" and "Préface pour la traduction d'un ouvrage de M. Wilberforce" was the result of conflicting responses to the texts. On one hand, in her position as a woman translator, Bell reported her appreciation for Staël's tactful use of logic to convince her audience. She was drawn to Staël's conciliatory tone and her effortless passage from logic to feelings, a quality she attributed to her being a woman. As a result, Bell's translation reflects an author-centered strategy, a strategy that expresses the translator's respect for the author's achievement. On the other hand, Bell is also African American and Staël's use of words like *primitive* and her mention of slavery as an African practice offended her. Because of these "details" in the text, she experienced a racial, a historical, and a class distance from Staël. To handle that distance in her translation, she stayed very close to the French text, a closeness here that paradoxically expressed her alienation, her lack of intimacy with Staël. Thus, the same strategy of translating very closely the French text, of not attempting to make it "transparent," resulted from both respect and repulsion, reactions that fell along specific ideological identifications.

Bell's strong reactions to specific words that had to do with the description of race helped certain of the other European American translators become more sensitive to the translation of these terms, helping them to attend to race as much as to gender issues in the texts. The sensitivity thus acquired is apparent, for example, in Maryann DeJulio's discussion of her reasons for not translating *primitif* as "primitive" in Gouges' play *L'esclavage des noirs*. For specific words like *noir* and *nègre*, much of the translators' work was collaborative.

A major working decision for certain of the translators' handling of race was to find out what kinds of connotations these words had at the time when they were used. By consulting dictionaries of the times, we found that *nègre* often tended to be synonymous with *slave*, and that *noir* became associated with abolitionist politics. As William Cohen claims, "It was no accident that, at its founding in 1788, the abolitionist society took on the title Société des Amis des noirs" (*French Encounter* 132). It must be added that a modern French dictionary like the *Larousse* gives *nègre* as synonymous of "slave" but also defines *nègre* as "a person of black race," a revealing definition, since the concept of a black *race* has been discredited as having little scientific validity.[9] But even dictionaries of the period hide the complexity of this semantic issue, a complexity linked to specific historical changes, as Serge Daget shows in his statistical study of the use of the words *esclave, nègre,* and *noir* in French abolitionist literature from 1770 to 1845. Although there was no strict consensus on usage, an analysis of abolitionist writings shows that until 1791 the term *esclave* tended to be avoided (the disappearance of the term being linked to a push for the disappearance of slavery), while *nègre* was still used, but since some of its uses were pejorative, *noir* came to be the preferred term. Daget argues that since in seventeenth-century literature, *noir* was rarely capitalized, capitalizing it was a significant innovation (as in the Société des Amis des Noirs). This use stemmed from a desire to give a moral lesson to proponents of the slave trade. The use of *noir* led to strong violent reactions, which proved that changing the word was indeed perceived as a way to work for abolition. However, even Clairière, the president of the abolitionist Société des Amis des Noirs, used traditional vocabulary (i.e., *esclave* or *nègre*) as well as *noir* to "convince everyone and not only people already devoted to the abolitionist cause" (Daget 524). Furthermore, specific historical events triggered changes in usage. For instance, the word *nègre* was widely used during the rebellion in Saint Domingue in 1791, while, paradoxically enough, the 1792 suppression of subventions to the slave trade led to the disappearance of the word *noir* as free people of color "categorically rejected nègre or Noir" (Daget 525). But after the 1794 decree abolishing slavery, *noir* regained favor in France. With the restoration of slavery by Napoleon in 1802, *noir* lost ground to *nègre,* which again became the preferred term. After Napoleon's fall in 1814, the term *noir* came back into favor. Daget's study shows that translating terms connected with race is complex and that even typographical markers like a capital letter are significant. An author's use of *nègre* instead of *noir* is thus linked to specific times and to the kinds of audience the author had in mind.

The dictionary equivalent for *nègre* is "Negro," but its use in our translations was debatable, since today it is rejected by African Americans. Geneva Smitherman's description of the changing use of the word *Negro* shows the complexity of its use, a complexity that parallels that of French usage. According to Smitherman, in colonial America, whites used *negroes, slaves,* and *niggers* to designate African Americans. *Negro* and *nigger* were used interchangeably, and "it was not until the twentieth century that whites began to semantically distinguish 'negro' and 'nigger,' with the latter becoming a racial epithet" (36). At that time *Negro* was not capitalized, as in the original Spanish form it was an adjective. However, in colonial America, blacks used the term *African,* which was abandoned in the nineteenth century. At that time, some blacks began to use the white man's term *negro* as well as *colored*. In the 1920s black leaders advocated the capitalization of *Negro*, and a number of blacks adopted it. Although *Negro* was never totally acceptable or universally used by blacks themselves (Smitherman 40), it was widely used in its capitalized form until the 1960s.

Since our translations are sited as historical texts and since *Negro* was used until the 1960s by blacks themselves, we chose to keep the term in certain cases. Bell's knowledge of the current vocabulary of race sensitized the native French translators to the many connotations that terms describing race have in the United States and helped us make our decision, not because of any "intuition" based on race, but because of her familiarity with several types of black culture in the United States. The collaboration of several translators working from different cultural backgrounds helped us balance our specific ideological interest. The mixture of black, white, American, and French translators produced what we hope are translations in which all the factors of race, gender, and nationality intersect.

A specific challenge was presented by the translation of *Ourika*, since this is the only case where there exist other translations. To emphasize translation as process, and as ideological mediation, we did not consult the existing translations; we wanted to be able to verify whether our attempt to work could self-consciously produce a translation different from the two others, which we assumed had been written without the kind of attentiveness to racial or gender context that we had. The analysis by Doris Kadish of the three translations in volume 2 allows the reader to see how this situation of translation consciousness has worked out. Normally, a final version of a new translation of any work would only come after the translators consulted the existing versions and modified their own version to include particularly felicitous items from the others, or to clarify in their texts what the other versions do effectively. However, here the translators skip this final step because they want to use the translation of *Ourika* as a kind of "control" that indicates whether their experiment with race and gender can produce a different kind of translation. The translators also acknowledge that one of the translations is by the British writer John Fowles and that one of the best ways not to be swayed by the language of the canonical writer is to not read or hear him or her.

That translation is a powerful cultural activity for the construction of race as well as gender has been argued in its most negative consequences, most pointedly by Niranjana. She argues about the translation of Indian texts into English (and this specific context will be particularly important) that translation, by presenting specific versions of the colonized subject in coherent and transparent texts, contributes to the repression of difference and is part of the process of colonial domination. Niranjana's argument that translation practices are overdetermined by religious, racial, sexual, and economic discourses—in other words, that they are a significant component of cultural hegemony, to use Gramsci's terms (12)—is both a criticism and a reminder of the power of translation, since translation not only legitimizes specific authors but also gives a seal of authority to certain versions of entire cultures or races. Although Niranjana's examples deal specifically with the way British translation is implicated in the construction of the colonized Indian, her observations pertain generally to translations of culturally and racially different texts. Race can therefore be seen as a key issue in translation. The implications of Niranjana's work for our project are many and force us to ponder the following questions: Is her description of the translation process when it involves a first-world culture and a third-world culture applicable to the translating situation when the power balance seems to be even, such as when two Western first-world languages such as French and English are involved? Is translation's constitutive power over the colonial subject the same kind of power as for the colonizing (i.e., French) subject? Next, how can Niranjana's call for a need to "translate, that is [disturb or displace] history," be applied to texts that present beings already in translation, that is, African voices available only through the French colonizer's language?[10]

Although the texts considered in these volumes are coherent, and certainly transparent texts that represent characters of color and do minimize differences between cultures and races, their representation of race and difference is embedded in a specific historical situation that produces an opposite effect to that described in general terms by Niranjana. The authors considered here do construct images of women and people of color, but they do not necessarily "repress" difference. Instead, they de-essentialize it; they displace it: they present people who are different not because of an essential, inherent Otherness, but because of specific historical conditions. For example, the violence of Gouges' black hero Zamor is not shown as a trait of his race, but as the only resource available to a slave who has to protect his honor and his life.[11] Moreover, Gouges does not naively indulge in a romantic view of the Other. She also represents another Other, a Native American, a cruel man who is opposed to the lofty Zamor.

Similarly Staël's "Mirza" contrasts the situation of the white male narrator to that of her three West African characters, but she carefully distinguishes between them. These characters belong to different tribes who are at war (here Staël expresses her distance from the myth of "the" African), and these characters are individualized. For example, the women characters react very differently to authority: Ourika is presented as a beautiful and dutiful wife, while Mirza is a solitary thinker. Gouges and Staël do, in some instances, minimize difference by suggesting that blacks and whites are not essentially different. What is different is their specific circumstances and their relation to power. In these instances, Gouges and Staël are writing against their own culture, which stakes its political, economical, and moral superiority on the belief that people of color are essentially different, that is, so unlike oneself that one does not have to treat them as one would oneself. In this context, if the translator were to affirm difference, a practice that Niranjana recommends as "enlightened," it would be a racist strategy. The lesson for us is that any theory of translation must be embedded in a specific practice. It must be theoretical, but it must not be universalizing. In this, we could argue that translation is like creoleness as it is defined by Bernabé, Chamoiseau, and Confiant in "In Praise of Creoleness": "Creoleness is an annihilation of false universality, of monolinguism, and of purity" (892).

In *Ourika* Duras takes the de-essentializing of difference a step further, since she recounts the excruciating experience of difference by a character who is precisely like the members of the hegemonic culture. *Ourika* exposes a situation described by Fanon, and, more recently, by Caribbean writers Bernabé, Chamoiseau, and Confiant, as "a terrible condition to perceive one's interior architecture, one's world, the instants of one's days, one's values with the eye of the other" (886). For Duras, racism, which makes an outcast of the Senegalese Ourika in French culture, is precisely that which insists on essential differences. So while the presentation of characters can seem to "repress" difference, it can as well be seen as an effort to deconstruct the notion that a different shade of complexion is essential, rather than a detail used by a powerful group to facilitate the repression of a less powerful group. This holding at bay of difference, of color, that acknowledges its existence is a central paradox of translation. Translation is a linguistic mediation conducive to creoleness. By setting up all the factors of race, gender, class, and culture for a kind of "creole translation practice," translators can produce a text that claims its hybridity,[12] that distances itself from the claims of universality, monolinguism, and purity.

Significantly, the original French texts on which the translations presented here are drawn heighten the problematic link between difference and translation. They represent race (i.e., exemplary difference) in a language that negates that difference: literally, all the West African characters speak and think in French (and English in the translations). So translation starts from a desire to give voice to the Other but can only do so under erasure, as it were. Staël's characters are West Africans but their representation is monolingual, and some readers may be too. These characters come to us already in translation, a translation that inscribes a specific power balance: a French version of the West African colonized for a French reader. Although Staël's goal of promoting antislavery sentiments is antihegemonic, the text replays the historical and cultural imbalance, and so will the translation in English, unless some gesture is made to restore that balance in the direction of the absent language.

It is at this moment perhaps that the radicalization of the text that we discussed earlier can be done: not in the direction of the English-speaking reader, but in the direction of the language that was never there, in the direction of multilinguism, of an intersection of several languages, and this gesture would not be a fluent, compliant strategy. A localized linguistic intervention can defamiliarize the text and make the readers experience directly the absent Otherness in its disquieting foreignness. For instance, the West African characters in "Mirza" reach us already in translation, a fact hidden by the white narrator, whose "guide" is really an interpreter who makes it possible for him, and for us as readers, to communicate with the Senegalese characters. Perhaps then, the translator can present a version of the missing voice and emphasize that all the French author has given the reader is a translation of a translation. The translator can recover Ourika's speech in Wolof and make clear that the interpreter's version in French is a sign of the narrator's and the reader's linguistic weakness. By translating from French into Wolof, rather than from French into English, in strategic parts of the text, the translator can momentarily "withhold translation"[13] to make the translation apparent, to restore multilinguism. The strategic use of Wolof could also be paired with "code mixing," that is, the regular interspacing of words of one language in sentences from another language spoken in a multicultural environment.[14] Although such code mixing is considered an interference, in an interpreting situation, the translator could rather claim it as an "intersection" where languages can meet.

Since code mixing is most often used in speech, using it in a written text would also have the advantage of emphasizing the "orality" of the translated text, an orality that is an important component of the texts considered here, as the analyses provided in the following chapters will make clear. Moreover, orality is an especially important component for the cultural survival of the people of color who were enslaved in a number of West African countries as well as the West Indies.[15] Attending to the orality of the texts we present here is thus a necessity; as Bernabé, Chamoiseau, and Confiant convincingly argue, the "nonintegration of oral tradition was one of the forms and one of the dimensions of our alienation" (895).

Orality is situated at the intersection of gender and race, and as translators, editors, and critics, we needed to attend to it. Although the strategy of code mixing was very appealing, our lack of familiarity with the specifics of code mixing in French and Wolof made us refrain from using it. However, if code mixing was not possible in the translation of "Mirza," its use was still possible in the comments following the translation. Thus, the critical essay that was supposed to follow the translation of "Mirza" became a dialogue between two translators of Germaine de Staël. The code mixing became a text mixing between the language of writing and that of speaking, between translating and analyzing. The momentary withholding of translation in the English version of "Mirza," however, is not possible for the translation of *Ourika* because the very issue presented in the novel is that there is nothing to translate back to. The Senegalese character's only language is French, the language of the slave traders who took her away from her family, and that of the man who brought her back to France to save her from slavery. Duras presents an extremely pessimistic view of cultural translation as that which presents the cultural Other as deprived of her own language. Duras presents an indictment of translation conceived as monolinguism, as the presence of the discourse of the master. Translating a text that so deeply points to the repressive aspect of cultural translation can be daunting; but if we remember that what is condemned is translation as erasure of the language of departure, the producer of the English version can ensure that, at least, traces of that language are left in the text. In this case, since the translators of *Ourika* were both French, moving from their mother tongue into the foreign language, their translation is inevitably marked by Gallicisms, which are not signs of linguistic weakness, but a reminder to the reader that *Ourika* is a translation of a French text, which, far from being absent, is but a few pages away. The fact that a French text is translated into English by French natives contributes to a shift in the balance of cultural power, since their version of *Ourika* is then partially dependent on their identification with the culture of departure rather than with the dominant values of American culture.[16]

Similarly, texts strongly marked by race and gender would probably need to be translated by people who are concerned with these issues. That is not to say that only a woman can translate a woman author, or that only a person of color can translate an author of the same color, but that a translator aware of issues of the construction of gender and race will be better equipped to pick up in the texts the strands that are significant in terms of gender, or of race.

Obviously, the conscious valorization of gender or race can better be done by translators who have a stake in it and who can read the intertexts present in the text they translate, as Lotbinière-Harwood has demonstrated about feminist works (126–31). Since this is the case, the ideological investment of the translator determines the kinds of practice the translator engages in, although ideally (or perhaps utopically) this investment should not lead to the absence of questioning of the very notions he or she seeks to promote. Thus, while the collaborators of this volume want to investigate the interrelations of gender, race, and translation, they also recognize that it is important to problematize these very notions of gender and race, or at least avoid forgetting to be sensitive to other issues such as social class and nationality. In this regard, Christopher L. Miller's recent *The French Atlantic Triangle,* which broadens our subject by including male authors, is a welcome gesture.

The very authors we present here lead us to consider many such issues, since their texts bring together all these ideological formations—race, gender, social class, nationality—and de-essentialize them. Their female characters at times act in ways conventionally defined as manly, the authors often seem to identify with their black characters, the rigid class structure they represent is frequently questioned, and they iconoclastically blur differences between French and Senegalese. In brief, their representations of race, class, gender, and nationality suggest that these are figures of difference that are essentialized as causes of differences to mask the real gap, that is, a power gap. It is this gap that the translator straddles. Because of its very nature as language mediation, translation can only exist in a situation of difference, but the work of translation consists precisely in de-essentializing and recontextualizing this difference. That some translation practices attempt to erase difference, be it linguistic or cultural difference, is but an extreme example of the process of translation as the necessary inclusion of both sameness and difference. The translations and the critical comments presented in this volume are an attempt to practice translation as a coexistence of sameness and difference, as a kind of situation of *créolité* that privileges a discourse on race and gender.

CHAPTER 2

Translation in Context

Doris Y. Kadish

The importance of translation and women's antislavery writing during the period from 1780 to 1830 needs to be situated within a broad historical context. To achieve the necessary breadth, this chapter begins and ends by stretching the boundaries of that period: at the beginning, with the example of Pierre Antoine de La Place's 1745 translation of Aphra Behn's 1696 *Oroonoko,* and at the end, with the example of Louise Belloc's 1853 translation of Harriet Beecher Stowe's 1852 *Uncle Tom's Cabin.* These two examples provide detailed illustrations of the ideological nature of translation, of the importance of women writers' relation to antislavery, and of the inextricable links among translation, gender, and race.

To record the trajectory from *Oroonoko* to *Uncle Tom's Cabin,* and from La Place to Belloc, is also to record a significant shift that occurred in translation theory and practice in the eighteenth and nineteenth centuries.[1] Although that shift in no way eliminates or even lessens the ideological nature of translation, it is an integral component in the historical context of the period and works under consideration in this volume. Unlike Germany, where a tradition of "faithfulness" in translation existed, other countries, especially France, adhered to the neoclassical notion of translation as a *belle infidèle* (a lovely but unfaithful woman). In the French tradition, it was the accepted standard for translators to change the original substantially in order to "improve" it and enhance its beauty.[2] Indeed, changes were necessary in order to achieve the chief goals of pleasing and, concomitantly, not offending a French audience. Adaptations, modifications, corrections, and additions for a variety of reasons were considered acceptable. When Voltaire translated the celebrated monologue from *Hamlet* in 1734, he added a denunciation of the hypocrisy of the clergy ("nos prêtres menteurs") on moral and political grounds, and when Helen Maria Williams translated Bernardin de Saint-Pierre's *Paul et Virginie* in 1789, she added eight sonnets, presumably to enhance the novel's lyrical and pastoral tone, and eliminated many philosophical dialogues on the grounds that they would be uninteresting to English readers (Robinson 846, 852–53).

By the time in the mid-nineteenth century of Belloc's very close and careful translation of *Uncle Tom's Cabin* containing no major adaptations or modifications, a shift in thinking about translation had occurred. Fundamental to that shift was a newly developed belief, which the various women writers, translators, and abolitionists discussed in this chapter played a significant role in developing and implementing, that national and racial particularities needed to be acknowledged through translation and other forms of cultural mediation. Acknowledging those particularities required shifting the focus of translation to the source-language text and culture and away from the earlier, more exclusive focus on the conventions and expectations of the target-language society. As this chapter attempts to show, women writers and translators played a role in implementing that shift and even in articulating its principal bases, as is clear in Staël's 1816 essay "The Spirit of Translations," discussed and translated later in this volume.

A number of lessons about the workings of translation can be learned from a close look now at La Place's translation of Behn's *Oroonoko*. To begin with, the substantial changes that La Place made help put the concept of fidelity into an instructive historical perspective, reminding us that standards for what constitutes a legitimate translation vary over time. As noted above, in La Place's time, it was the accepted standard for translators to change the original substantially. Summing up the attitude of his time, La Place states in the preface to *Oroonoko* (spelled *Oronoko* in his translation), "My intention was not to produce a literal translation, nor to adhere scrupulously to my author's text. *Oronoko* was popular in London dressed in English clothes. To be popular in Paris, I believed that it needed French attire. This way of translating works of pure entertainment may well be the best" (1:viii). La Place explains that many changes were necessary to preserve "good taste," and he expresses his wish that the enjoyment thus procured for his refined readers will compensate for "what may be lacking in terms of precision" (1:x). Although readers today may be tempted to think of the French *Oroonoko* more as an adaptation than a translation, eighteenth-century readers accepted it as a translation, La Place's substantial additions and deletions notwithstanding.[3]

Oroonoko and La Place's translation also provide a useful lesson about the need to give serious attention to literary translation and women's writing, both of which have been frequently marginalized in French literary and historical studies. Such marginalization is especially surprising in the case of *Oroonoko*, whose importance in France has been recognized by a few literary historians. Stressing the central role in French eighteenth-century literature and thought played by the seven immensely popular editions of *Oroonoko* in translation, Seeber explains that

> in this early English novel we can find the substance and technique of much of the *littérature négrophile* of the eighteenth century, a period when the Negro emerges from his despised condition and takes on heroic qualities and possibilities. . . . This English story, of which the purpose might well have been didactic, written by "the first literary abolitionist . . . on record in the history of fiction," as Swinburne called Mrs. Behn, was to have far-reaching consequences in French humanitarian thought. . . . Thus did a strong current of English abolitionist thought pass into France three years before Montesquieu published in his *Esprit des lois* the first formal and concise arraignment of slavery in the French language. ("*Oroonoko* in France" 28)

Seeber goes on to observe that *Oroonoko* was among the most widely read English novels in France in the middle of the eighteenth century, exceeded in popularity only by Richardson's and Fielding's novels, and that its popularity even exceeded that of most celebrated French novels of the time. Citing Seeber, Philippe Van Tieghem even claims that this book was "largely the cause of the suppression of slavery in 1794" (77), a claim that forms a curious echo of similar claims often made about *Uncle Tom's Cabin*. One is surprised to note, then, that French literary historians often fail to acknowledge fully Behn's role, focusing instead on male writers—Jean-François Saint-Lambert, Victor Hugo, Prosper Mérimée[4]—who extended the vogue of stories about African slaves that she launched.[5] And although Behn's work unquestionably contains strong ambivalences and ambiguities regarding slavery, as Ferguson has demonstrated (27–49), it also contains a select but significant number of abolitionist and resistant elements that are typically not found in the works of those male writers. Readers are thus often left with the impression that most writing about slavery by Europeans was negative, if not altogether racist. This volume attempts to correct that impression by showing, starting with Behn, the existence of a more positive and emancipatory intertextual tradition of women writing about slaves.

Further marginalization and devalorization of this tradition of women's writing and of important works in translation such as La Place's occurs among critics who, failing to adequately relativize or contextualize their aesthetic judgments about works of literature, often relegate translations and works about gender and race to an inferior position. Thus, for example, Jürgen von Stackelberg fails to come to grips with the abolitionist thrust of either Behn's or La Place's texts by essentially dismissing Behn's achievement altogether. He describes *Oroonoko* derisively at one point as "an English text that generates disorder on all sides, that is constructed without rules or taste, and that notwithstanding the existence of certain narrative elements is overwhelmed by exoticism" (238), and he speaks dismissively of the "legend of the revolutionary importance attributed to this novel" (247). Along similar lines, William B. Cohen asserts that "while not often depicted in the first-rate literature of the nineteenth century, the black man and the African continent were more wont to be the subject of second- and even rather third-rate literature" ("Literature and Race" 181), which he further characterizes as "often mediocre works by unoriginal writers" ("Literature and Race" 181–82). Although Cohen acknowledges that these works have historical importance, he still indirectly affirms the existence and superiority of certain presumably fixed universal aesthetic criteria. The application of those criteria often has the deleterious effect of placing works about gender and race, works by women, and literary translations outside the mainstream of literary history. The criteria for what constitutes "first-rate" literature need to be reexamined and expanded to include not only narrowly aesthetic standards but broadly cultural, historical, and political criteria as well.

Further lessons to be learned from *Oroonoko* and La Place's translation concern the ideological aspect of translation and the close connection between gender and race, to which translators need to pay special attention. Because La Place's translation mediates so visibly the treatment of gender and race in Behn's novel, his translation serves to illustrate, writ large as it were, the profoundly ideological nature of translation, as a brief summary of the plot and the major differences between Behn's and La Place's texts can serve to illustrate.

The major difference in the first half of the novel is that when Oroonoko, an African prince and the favored grandson of his country's autocratic ruler, is trained to be a brave warrior and enlightened gentleman, the general who trains him is African in Behn's work, whereas he is European in La Place's. Since Oroonoko's love for Imoinda, the daughter of that general, provides the dominant romantic element in both Behn's and La Place's texts, it is clearly significant that Imoinda is a black woman in Behn's novel, whereas La Place never addresses the issue of her racial identity explicitly. The second half of the novel contains numerous substantial modifications. In both Behn's and La Place's texts, Oroonoko and Imoinda are sold into slavery, having been renamed Caesar and Clemene, and transported to the colony of Surinam. Purchased by a kindly owner, Trefry, they are reunited and, despite Trefry's willingness to liberate them, are unable to obtain their freedom from the absent governor, who alone has the power to authorize the emancipation of slaves. Oroonoko's desire for freedom, the dominant plot line in Behn's novel, competes in La Place's translation with romantic subplots introduced through page-long digressions concerning other contenders for Imoinda's affections. In those digressions La Place departs from the abolitionist logic of Behn's novel to create scenes of jealousy, confession, and outraged honor in the French seventeenth-century style of Corneille or Mme de La Fayette. The most substantial differences occur at the end. In Behn's text, as the time approaches for Imoinda to give birth to a child, Oroonoko becomes desperate that he has failed to obtain his freedom and chooses to kill his beloved wife rather than see her and their child continue to live in slavery. This violent and relatively precipitous conclusion to Behn's novel is changed to a happy and very long, drawn-out concatenation of events in La Place's translation, the result of which is that both slaves and their child eventually return to their African homeland, where Oroonoko assumes his rightful place as king. (An American translation of *Paul et Virginie* in 1824 similarly gave that novel a happy—and abolitionist—ending as well, by inventing a black slave, the son of a king, who saves Virginie and then gains his freedom by this proof of heroism [Robinson 844, 851].) A major part of the ending in La Place's text consists of some twenty-five pages in which Imoinda recounts her version of the concluding drama.

These substantial differences between Behn's and La Place's texts can be accounted for, up to a point, in terms of literary and linguistic conventions, as a number of translation critics have demonstrated (Hoffmann 244–45), but without an emphasis on the important extent to which those conventions feed into and become inextricably linked with ideology. At issue specifically in the case of Behn's and La Place's texts is the systematic application of French neoclassical conventions, which resulted in La Place's edulcorating of an English work that a French eighteenth-century audience would have found excessively direct, descriptive, and violent. Consider, for example, the opening lines of the address made by Oroonoko (aka Caesar) to his fellow slaves: "Caesar, having singled out these men from the women and children, made an harangue to them, of the miseries and ignominies of slavery; counting up all their toils and sufferings, under such loads, burdens and drudgeries, as were fitter for beasts than men; senseless brutes, than human souls. He told them, it was not for days, months or years, but for eternity; there was no end to be of their misfortunes" (Behn, *Oroonoko* 190). La Place provides the following translation of this passage:

> César, ayant trouvé le moyen de tirer les hommes à l'écart, tandis que les femmes et les enfants continuaient à se réjouir, leur fit un discours touchant, sur la misère, et l'ignorance de leur condition. Il leur représenta, avec les couleurs les plus vives, les travaux attachés à l'esclavage: Espèce de travaux, ajouta-t-il, plus convenables à des bêtes, qu'à des hommes! Encore, criait-il avec feu, si c'était pour quelques jours, pour quelques mois, pour quelques années mêmes? . . . Mais c'est pour toujours! (2:75)

To mention just a few of the ways in which La Place softens and attenuates the abolitionist thrust of Behn's text, as he does consistently throughout his translation: he translates "harangue" as "discours touchant," a less political and more sentimental choice of expressions, and he renders with the single, ideologically neutral term of "les travaux" (work) what in the original appears as the highly charged repetition of such terms as "toils, sufferings," "loads, burdens and drudgeries." Structural or stylistic features of translation thus assume ideological content in their application.

It must also be pointed out that the rest of Oroonoko's address to the slaves is left out altogether. In the section that is omitted, Oroonoko reproaches the slaves for putting up with their condition

> like dogs, that loved the whip and bell, and fawned the more they were beaten . . . and were become insensible asses, fit only to bear: nay, worse; an ass, or dog, or horse, having done his duty, could lie down in retreat,

and rise to work again, and while he did his duty, endured no stripes; but men, villanous, senseless men, such as they, toiled on all the tedious week . . . and then, whether they were faulty or meriting, they, promiscuously, the innocent with the guilty, suffered the infamous whip, the sordid stripes, from their fellow-slaves, 'till their blood trickled from all parts of their body; blood, whose every drop ought to be revenged with a life of some of those tyrants that impose it. (Behn, *Oroonoko* 190–91)

This passage, which La Place omits, is characterized by a number of features of Behn's work that the neoclassical style eschewed: highly concrete language ("whip and bell," "dogs," "asses," "horse") as well as violent and indelicate expressions ("stripes," "blood trickled from all parts of their body"). Style functions ideologically in translation here. With respect to political content too, La Place unquestionably weakens the abolitionism of the original by omitting some of the accusations leveled against slave owners in this passage and, most notably, the cry for revenge at the end.

A similar ideological process involving both style and content applies to La Place's far less direct or concrete treatment of African women, one of the ways in which the translation differs most markedly from the original. As noted earlier, Imoinda is changed from a black woman in Behn's novel to a woman of indeterminate race in La Place's translation, and to a certain extent, this change may reflect a characteristically neoclassical unwillingness to deal openly with issues of race. Accordingly, as Léon-François Hoffmann has perceptively observed, the translation fails to translate the reference to color in such descriptions of Imoinda in the original as "the beautiful black Venus" (Behn, *Oroonoko* 137) and "the most charming black" (Behn, *Oroonoko* 171) by omitting those passages altogether. In other instances, such passages are translated but modified so that color is not an issue. Thus the phrase "he was infinitely surprized at the beauty of this fair queen of night" (Behn, *Oroonoko* 137) is translated as "il fut vivement frappé de sa beauté" (La Place 1:22). La Place also omits the kind of detailed physical descriptions of Africans generally, and Imoinda as an African woman especially, that are so unique in Behn's work. On one occasion, for example, Behn describes Imoinda's body as "being carved in fine flowers and birds," and she goes on to explain: "I had forgot to tell you, that those who are nobly born of that country, are so delicately cut and raised all over the fore-part of the trunk of their bodies, that it looks as if it were japanned, the works being raised like high point round the edges of the flowers" (*Oroonoko* 174). That a European woman writer chose to dwell, albeit imaginatively, on the physical beauty of an African woman in this truly amazing description, for which there are few if any precedents, suggests a sympathetic response to a woman by a woman that is an important ingredient in the abolitionist meaning of Behn's novel. *Oroonoko* can even be imagined as a translation of a text by a black woman in the sense that it is an attempt on Behn's part to give voice to a feminine presence that was silenced at that historical moment.

The profoundly ideological aspect of translating *Oroonoko* observed above leads to a number of conclusions that will have significance throughout the pages of this volume. The first is that it is necessary to judge literary works and literary translation from the past according to the criteria of their time, not only our own. Hoffmann rightly observes that La Place's changes reflect the slower development of abolitionism in France than in England, and he concludes that if La Place diminished the abolitionist force of the original, "we should undoubtedly not blame him for it, for he was obliged to submit to the taste of his time" (62). In a similar vein, Laura Brown observes that "even though Behn can see colonialism only in the mirror of her own culture, that occluded vision has a critical dimension" (61), as of course does La Place's translation, which captures the critical image of Behn's work in the mirror of eighteenth-century French culture. In contrast with Hoffmann and Brown, however, Stackelberg downplays the abolitionism of both Behn and La Place by judging them according to twentieth-century standards. It is true, as Stackelberg points out, that Behn views Oroonoko's color as detracting from his otherwise uniformly beautiful European appearance (243), and that by describing his willingness to trade slaves for his release, she points a finger at African complicity in the European slave trade (247–48). What Stackelberg fails to appreciate fully, however, is that Behn's adherence to the ideological values of her time, even ones that to us today may seem offensively Eurocentric, does not obviate her abolitionism according to seventeenth- or eighteenth-century standards. Brown rightly explains that "the obvious mystification involved in Behn's depiction of Oroonoko as a European aristocrat in blackface does not necessarily damage the novella's emancipationist reputation: precisely this kind of sentimental identification was in fact the staple component of antislavery narratives for the next century and a half, in England and America" (48). To fail to acknowledge the emancipationist significance of *Oroonoko,* in the original and in translation, is tantamount to blurring the distinction between pro- and antislavery writers and to diminishing the literary and historical significance of contributions made by women writers and by literary translators to the antislavery movement.

A second conclusion is that it is essential that translators, and of course critics and general readers as well, not lose sight of the vital connections between gender and race. Brown indicates a number of bases of this connection, claiming, indeed, that "*Oroonoko* can serve as a theoretical test case for the necessary connection of race and gender" (43), and she goes on to explain that the two are connected in *Oroonoko,* among other ways, through Behn's treatment of race according to the generic conventions of French heroic romance, conventions developed by seventeenth-century women writers such as Mlle de Scudéry and produced largely for a feminine aristocratic audience. "Behn's novellas, like other English prose works of the Restoration and early eighteenth century, draw extensively upon this French material, and the foregrounding of female authorship in *Oroonoko* through the explicit interventions of the female narrator signals the prevalent feminization of the genre" (49–50). Significantly, in Caryl Phillips's *Cambridge,* about nineteenth-century slavery in the English West Indies, the black author chooses to tap into the strongly feminine tradition that marks *Oroonoko* and other abolitionist novels of the past by creating two narrative voices, one of a European woman and the other of a male slave. Such an understanding of the close connection in literary history between gender and race is similarly reflected in La Place's addition of Imoinda's story at the end of his translation. Like the authors of *Oroonoko* and *Cambridge,* La Place used the nondominant voice of a woman to double and reinforce the similarly nondominant voice of a slave. The fact that such close connections between gender and race have existed historically is clearly not understood by Stackelberg, who draws only negative conclusions about La Place's choice to tap into the intertextual tradition of the French heroic romance. Thus, he is dismayed that "the translator integrates the English text into the narrative tradition of his country and makes Mrs. Behn into a Mlle de Scudéry!" and he blames La Place for having "pushed gallantry to the limit" (247) by elevating the status of women in the novel, letting Imoinda speak far more in his translation than she does in the original text.

Gender and race in *Oroonoko* are connected in other ways that translators and translation critics need to appreciate. Admitting that "the treatment of slavery in *Oroonoko* is neither coherent nor fully critical" (52), although still distinctly emancipationist for its time, Brown explains that Behn's novel operated both within the feminized aristocratic code of heroic romance and within the similarly feminized bourgeois code of imperialism, in which women were imagined to be the chief beneficiaries of colonial commerce: "Dressed in the products of imperialist accumulation, women are, by metonymy identified . . . with the whole fascinating enterprise of trade itself" (55). It is not enough simply to point out, as does Stackelberg, that aristocratic allegiances are evident in Behn's novel. Dismayed that "this novel by a Tory sympathizer displays a thoroughly aristocratic plot" (246), Stackelberg adduces such traces of aristocracy as further evidence against Behn's abolitionism. Brown provides a far more nuanced and illuminating explanation of the relevance of class for *Oroonoko*. She enables us to see that because Behn's class allegiances are complex and subject to conflict, and be-cause they intersect with her emancipatory attitudes toward gender and race, *Oroonoko* creates a site—a perspective and a conceptual framework—from which the author can call colonialism into question and resist the forces of opposition. Brown explains the creation of that site in terms of the special role that Behn grants to women:

> But though they have no independent place to stand in, in their me-diatory role between heroic romance and mercantile imperialism, they anchor the interaction of these two otherwise incompatible discourses. They make possible the superimposition of aristocratic and bourgeois systems—the ideological contradiction that dominates the novella. And in that contradiction we can locate . . . a point of critique and sympathy produced by the radical contemporaneity of issues of gender with those of romance and race. (54–55)

It is clearly not only possible but absolutely essential to develop an ap-proach to translation that strives to integrate the multifarious forces of gender, race, and class as well as the broad range of linguistic, literary, and historical determinants that come into play in works such as Behn's and La Place's. It is also essential in both the analysis and the translation of the antislavery literature produced by women to explore the numerous links connecting women and slaves. As Brown observes in her concluding re-marks, it is enlightening to juxtapose "the figure of the woman—ideological implement of a colonialist culture—with the figure of the slave—economic implement of the same system." She adds, "Though Behn never clearly sees herself in the place of the African slave, the mediation of the figure of the woman between the two contradictory paradigms upon which her narrative depends uncovers a mutuality beyond her conscious control" (54–55). A century after *Oroonoko,* French women will see themselves very clearly "in the place of the African slave" and will push the mutuality between women and slaves to new emancipatory lengths.

TRANSLATING ANTISLAVERY, 1780–1830

The survey of the period from 1780 to 1830 provided in this section is intended to supply the historical background necessary for understanding the specific topics and allusions that will be encountered later in the translations and analyses in this volume. In addition, this historical survey situates translation as one kind of mediation within a broad spectrum of mediating linguistic and political activities, the purpose of which is to bring about communication or compromise between disparate social groups. This period from 1780 to 1830, during which linguistic and political mediation played such a noteworthy role, can be divided into three abolitionist phases and illustrated through the activities of the writers translated in this volume. During the first phase, from 1780 to 1799, abolitionist activities were visible and direct, as can be seen by a general survey of the wide variety of political and literary activities that occurred at that time, including the diverse endeavors that Gouges and Staël undertook in the political and literary arenas. During the second phase, from 1800 to 1820, abolitionist activities were more limited and sporadic, as examples from that period illustrate. The third phase occurred during the Restoration regimes of Louis XVIII and Charles X. Events contributing to the interest in the subjects of slavery and abolition demonstrated by the authors considered in this volume were the resumption of abolitionist activity by the Société de la morale chrétienne in 1821, the choice of the subject of abolition by the Académie française as the subject of the poetry prize in 1823, and Charles X's recognition of Haiti's independence in 1825. During all three phases, however, women writers typically joined with other liberal writers and thinkers in adopting what we would today consider a moderate reformist position that failed to call into question the economic infrastructure underlying the system of slavery. They argued, instead, that the amelioration of the slaves' lot was compatible with the preservation of European commercial interests, and they avoided addressing the issue of eventual emancipation. Acts of linguistic and political mediation functioned during both phases to affirm and advance that moderate position.

In order to appreciate fully women writers' activities as linguistic and political mediators during the first phase, it is important to take note of the exceptionally important role played at that time by the type of mediation that is of most concern to us in this volume: translation. Translation's significance at the time represents the culmination of several decades during which French Enlightenment works that denounced the abuses of slavery were translated into English to further abolitionist causes in Britain and America. This period coincides with the shift in translation practice noted earlier whereby national and racial particularities began to be taken seriously, and translators refrained, especially in political and philosophical works, from the kinds of modifications that occurred in *Oroonoko* and other neoclassical literary translations in the eighteenth century. Early French works that had a decisive impact when translated into English include the Baron de Montesquieu's 1748 *L'esprit des lois,* translated into English as *The Spirit of the Laws* in 1751, and the Abbé Raynal's *Histoire des deux Indes* (*History of the Two Indies*), which was first published in 1770 and then subsequently reprinted in thirty-eight French and eighteen English editions during the following decades.[6] These and other works from the French Enlightenment attacked the cruelty and injustice of slavery, warned of such dangers as desertion (*marronage*) or revolt by slaves, and pleaded for more enlightened colonial policies and enforcement of the *Code noir,* instituted in 1685 under Louis XIV to ensure humane treatment of slaves but never strictly observed. Although Raynal's work does on occasion address the need for the eventual abolition of slavery and even, in later editions, calls for violent revolt led by a black leader, for the most part his and other works of this period take the moderate reformist position adhered to by liberal writers in the period from 1780 to 1830. Translation from French into English and from English into French of works that adopted this position contributed substantially to setting the tone and the objectives of eighteenth- and nineteenth-century abolitionism in France, England, and the United States.

The importance of translation for the abolitionist cause continued to be acknowledged during the revolutionary period itself. Translations of works that would further the agenda of antislavery, widely acknowledged among abolitionists to be an international cause that transcended narrow national interests, were actively sponsored by abolitionist societies in Paris, London, Philadelphia, and elsewhere, including the French Société des Amis des Noirs, which was founded in 1788 by Brissot de Warville, and whose other leaders included the Marquis de Condorcet and the abbé Grégoire. The Amis des Noirs were responsible for obtaining translations of key works by such English abolitionists as Thomas Clarkson, whose *Essay on the Slavery and Commerce of the Human Species,* published in England in 1786, was translated by Gramagnac and published in French in 1789 (Sypher 99; Mercier, *L'Afrique noire* 174). Seeber records that "immediately after the organizing of the Amis des Noirs, Brissot wrote to James Philips, a Quaker and an original member of the English abolition society, to inform him, among other things, that the new French society had decided to translate and publish English anti-slavery works" and also provides a list of the more than thirty-five such works supplied by the Amis des Noirs (*Anti-slavery Opinion* 161, 197–99). To understand the importance that Staël will later attribute to translation, one needs to remember that her parents, Jacques and Suzanne Necker, were members of the Amis des Noirs and that Necker's publication in 1784 of *De l'administration des finances de la France,* which expressed outrage over the fact that twenty thousand Africans were being carried away from their homeland each year and subjected to inhumane treatment during the transatlantic passage and subsequently under slavery, was one of the works that was translated into English; it appeared in England in 1787 as *Treatise on the Administration of the Finances of France* (Sypher 99). Staël's interest in translation and her concerns about slavery expressed in "Mirza," written in 1786 and published in 1795, like the related interests and concerns of Gouges around the same time, need to be understood in the context of the importance that Staël's parents and French society of the time attributed to the wide range of related political and linguistic mediations to which translation belongs.

The importance of translation during the first phase from 1780 to 1799 is not limited to political or theoretical works such as those written by Montesquieu, Raynal, Clarkson, and Necker, however. Literary works that would further the agenda of antislavery were also of interest to abolitionists, as Seeber records: "Brissot's correspondence makes clear also the early determination of the Amis des Noirs to disseminate anti-slavery thought through literature" (*Anti-slavery Opinion* 160–61).

Olympe de Gouges provides an especially salient illustration of women's role as linguistic, cultural, and political mediator during the French Revolution. Although not a translator per se, Gouges embodies the mediating position between two cultural and linguistic groups that the translator occupies. She herself constantly had to mediate between the official use of the French language and her own regional use of Occitan. The fact that her works were typically dictated rather than written (see Gouges, *Oeuvres* 16, 20) suggests a curious parallel between Gouges and Toussaint Louverture, the black military and political leader of Saint Domingue, who also dictated speeches and statements that were rewritten and revised in standard French by secretaries (see James 197–98). To some extent, then, a comparison can be drawn between the disempowerment of the persons of color about whom she wrote and Gouges' own linguistic disempowerment as a speaker of Occitan. (The matter of Gouges' relation to language is considered more fully in chapter 3.) As Vèvè Clark observes: "When the ruling French elite succeeded in diminishing the importance of a provincial language such as the *langue d'oc*, and, moreover, standardized correct speech through the offices of academies and dictionaries, they subjected the lower classes to a form of internal colonization" (237). Standing as she does between regional and official languages as well as between the language of the cultural elite and the language of the masses or the downtrodden, Gouges dramatizes what Clark identifies as the problem of "the bilingual landscape of the Revolution and the history of communication between colonials and African slaves beginning in the seventeenth century" (241–42). It is against the background of that bilingual landscape that Gouges' writing and thinking about gender and race need to be understood.

Gouges' literary and political activities, which will also be discussed in greater detail later, provide a number of further indications of her role as a mediator. In literature she straddled, on one hand, the high culture of theater as practiced at the Comédie-Française, a cultural domain from which women writers were typically excluded, and, on the other hand, the popular culture of pamphlets, speeches, and melodrama, the intended audience of which included members of the lower classes and the downtrodden. (Curious parallels exist also between Gouges and Behn, who were among the few female dramatists of their times and were similarly imprisoned at some time. Both complained that their authority as writers was insufficiently recognized and that they were considered suspect with respect to their paternal origins and the authenticity of their writings.) In addition to straddling these two disparate cultural domains, Gouges sought to mediate between them. While persisting in attempts to gain acceptance by those in positions of power at the Comédie-Française, a bastion of conservatism, Gouges also advocated the mediating structure of an alternative national theater that would perform works by women. More generally, as Joan Wallach Scott has explained, Gouges stands at the juncture of two conflicting cultural positions: "De Gouges at once stressed her identity with the universal human individual and her difference" ("French Feminists" 9). Gouges' literary works consistently bespeak the desire to reconcile high and low, conservative and radical, masculine and feminine, universal and particular.

Gouges sought the same kind of reconciliation, compromise, and mediation in the political realm as in the linguistic and literary arenas. She was an ardent abolitionist. Not surprisingly, then, she was the only woman among the seventy French writers and political figures that Grégoire named in his 1808 *De la littérature des nègres,* translated in 1810 as *An Enquiry concerning the Intellectual and Moral Faculties and Literature of Negroes,* which he dedicated to "all the courageous men who have pleaded the cause of the unfortunate blacks."[7] She was not, however, a political extremist. On the contrary, her moderate Girondin politics, which she shared with Brissot and the other Amis des Noirs, placed her between the right-wing proponents of the ancien régime and colonialism, who gathered at the Club Massiac, and the left-wing Jacobin proponents of radical change and republican government. Those on the far Right viewed her as one of the rabble-rousers responsible for the violent events in Saint Domingue in 1791, when rebellious slaves took the lives and destroyed the property of white planters. Members of the Club Massiac denounced and attacked her, unconvinced by her protestations that her writings about slavery were intended, as she states in the preface to *L'esclavage des noirs,* to preserve for the colonists "their properties and their most cherished interests." The fact that the hero of her play is a black man who kills a white man and is ultimately exonerated for his crime surely did not sit well with her critics on the Right. Those on the Far Left found her politics equally offensive, however, because of her unwavering monarchism, which she retained until the end, when she was guillotined as a counterrevolutionary in 1793. It must be remembered, however, that her monarchism was shared not only by the Third Estate generally but also by Toussaint Louverture and his black followers in Saint Domingue at that time (Lacour 43; James 124). For Gouges, monarchism and antislavery were compatible, as is evident in her signing of her letter to the actors at the Comédie-Française, "The most committed royalist and mortal enemy of slavery" (*Oeuvres* 145). (That she similarly saw monarchism and feminism as compatible is evident in her dedication of her celebrated *Déclaration des droits de la femme* to the queen.) Unlike members of the Far Left, moreover, she rejected and denounced violence in all its forms, whether in France under the Terror or in Saint Domingue during the slave revolts. Above all, she differed profoundly from Marat and from Robespierre and other Jacobins who contributed to widening the rifts among the various factions on the Left and who failed to adhere unanimously or consistently to an antislavery position. Her great dream, in contrast, was reconciliation of difference, compromise, and mediation, a dream in which the end to the oppression of slaves was a primary and recurrent component.

Politically there is much common ground between Gouges' *L'esclavage des noirs* and Staël's "Mirza." In these works both authors seek to resolve the problem of slavery by proposing compromise solutions, which they saw as successfully mediating the differences between the colonizers and the colonized, but which today seem fraught with contradictions. Both women writers deplore the abuses of slavery, and both seek to discover nonviolent solutions to improve the lot of slaves, while cautiously refraining from calling for any radical measures that would jeopardize the economic interests of planters in the immediate future. Gouges offers such moderate reformist proposals as providing instruction for slaves; promoting kindness and generosity on the part of colonists; and relying on faith, hope, and love. Staël is more concrete in favoring a proposal developed by Dupont de Nemours and others, and articulated by literary figures such as Bernardin de Saint-Pierre, La Vallée, and Saint-Lambert, whereby Africans would be taught to cultivate sugar and engage in free trade themselves in order to gradually render unnecessary the use of slaves in the West Indies (Grégoire, *An Enquiry* 145–46; see also Seeber, *Anti-slavery Opinion* 190). To us today it, of course, seems contradictory to wish to empower blacks economically while at the same time wishing to preserve the planters' economic interests, but moderates at the time believed that such apparent contradictions would disappear with time. (Numerous contradictions can also be discovered in Staël's life: in 1791 her guests included such members of the Amis des Noirs as Condorcet and Brissot as well as such spokesmen for the Club Massiac as Barnave and the

Lameth brothers, whom she helped save in 1792; she also helped save her lover Narbonne, whose fortune derived from his wife's sugar plantations in the West Indies [Berchtold 173], and she herself was given a slave, baptized as Robert Jean Marie Chaumont.)[8] Further contradictions in Gouges' and Staël's works derive from the authors' firm belief in the benevolent influence and mediating function of the patriarchal figures of fathers, governors, and above all the king. Although Gouges' and Staël's belief in the necessity for patriarchal authority may seem to us today to contradict their belief in the necessity for racial or sexual equality, both sets of beliefs tended to prevail among French abolitionists until the execution of Louis XVI in 1793 and the dramatic events that occurred subsequently during the Terror and the Directory, when abolitionism as an active movement virtually disappeared. Clearly the moderate, mediating solutions envisioned by Gouges, Staël, and others early in the revolutionary period were inadequate, ineffectual, and probably premature; it is not clear that they had any real effect on the eventual abolition of the slave trade or slavery. The same is true, however, of the more radical solution, the abolition of slavery, which occurred in 1794 but was revoked by Napoleon in 1802. Neither moderate nor radical solutions were adequate to bring about emancipation, which would only occur many decades later in the nineteenth century.

To look now at the second phase of our history—from 1800 to 1820—is to look at a period that held far fewer opportunities for the kinds of mediation that flourished during the revolutionary period. Although antislavery opinion continued to exist, it was largely silenced under repressive proslavery governments. Quoting Chateaubriand's famous statement in *Le génie du christianisme*—"Who would still dare to plead the cause of blacks after the crimes they have committed?" (2:149–50)—Seeber reminds us that this statement

by no means belies his sympathy for the negro so clearly expressed in this work and in *Les Natchez*. It is symptomatic, rather, of the decline of overt opposition to slavery during the decade and a half following 1802, when slavery was reinstated by Bonaparte as a supposedly necessary adjunct to his vigorous colonial program. . . . Neither does the citation from *Le Génie du christianisme* reflect a general condemnation of the excesses committed by the revolted Santo Domingan slaves. On the contrary, the rebel leader Toussaint Louverture was regarded as a sort of glamorous hero, the incarnation of the numerous literary progeny of Oroonoko. (*Anti-slavery Opinion* 194)

Authors were reluctant to plead "the cause of blacks" overtly. But many enlightened individuals continued to believe in the necessity of doing away with the slave trade and eventually slavery itself. That Staël sustained that belief to the end is evident in her *Considérations sur la révolution française,* written in 1816 and published posthumously in 1818, in which she evokes her heartfelt commitment to freedom for slaves in the closing paragraph. In that work she responds to Chateaubriand by comparing the black slaves in Saint Domingue to the French people during the Terror, stating that if the former "committed more atrocities, it was because they had been oppressed more" (178).

Although frequently only covert or sporadic, the work of mediating the competing interests of antislavery and proslavery factions did continue during the period from 1800 to 1820, however, and translation, both from French into English and vice versa, continued to constitute an important component of that work. Its chief impetus was what David Turley has called "internationalizing the argument" (49), that is, using the arguments or achievements of one country to further the abolitionist goals of another. The most notable achievement, which was emphasized by the few French abolitionists such as Grégoire and Staël who spoke out publicly during the Napoleonic era, was the abolition of the slave trade in England in 1807 and in the United States the following year. In his 1808 *De la littérature des nègres,* Grégoire deplores France's failure to follow the English and American example and draws his French audience's attention to some of the noteworthy antislavery arguments that had been set forth by abolitionists in England. His role, then, resembles that of the translator, who similarly transposes ideas originating in one culture and makes them available to readers in another culture. The translation of Grégoire's work into English further extends the same process whereby abolitionists in England and especially America drew upon and disseminated the arguments developed in France and other countries. As the preface to the 1810 American translation makes clear, the translator's intention is to use the compelling case that Grégoire makes to demonstrate the intelligence and intellectual achievement of Negroes in order to move beyond the abolition of the slave trade in England and to achieve the goals of "universal emancipation" (*An Enquiry* 13–14).

Internationalizing the antislavery argument necessitated various kinds of mediations, as can be seen in the translations in this volume of the two short works written by Staël in 1814. In those works she strives to mediate between France and England, and between what was perceived as more radical French liberal thought and more moderate English abolitionism, urging broad general support among the French for the English example. The key figure in her mediating efforts was Wilberforce, whom she described as "the most beloved and respected man in all of England" (qtd. in Wilberforce and Wilberforce 4:159), and to whom she wrote that "no purer glory has ever been given to any man" (qtd. in Wilberforce and Wilberforce 4:217). Such elevated praise needs to be understood in the context of the opinion voiced by Chateaubriand and undoubtedly held by Staël and others during the period from 1800 to 1820, when France possessed no leader who, like Wilberforce, was free of association with the radical Jacobin politics of the 1790s, an association that for most of the French marred the earlier abolitionist activities of the Amis des Noirs. Chateaubriand wrote that "the principal defender of abolition among us is a regicide" (qtd. in Wilberforce and Wilberforce 213), presumably referring to Grégoire's failure to oppose the execution of Louis XVI in 1793 by absenting himself at the time of the vote.

Staël's efforts at mediating between France and England, and between French and English attitudes toward abolition, are apparent in the "Préface pour la traduction d'un ouvrage de M. Wilberforce sur la traite des nègres" and in "Appel aux souverains réunis à Paris pour en obtenir l'abolition de la traite des nègres," In the "Préface," Staël presents to the French public Wilberforce's 1807 *Letter on the Abolition of the Slave Trade, addressed to the freeholders and other inhabitants of Yorkshire,* a work that "consolidated and summarised all the arguments that the Abolitionists had been using since they began their crusade" (Furneaux 248–49). In this work she calls attention to such prominent English legislators as William Pitt and Charles Fox, who, like Wilberforce, were instrumental in achieving the abolition of the slave trade in England, as well as to the writings and efforts of such other major English abolitionists as Clarkson and Thomas Macaulay. She also counters the argument that the English motive in pushing for international abolition of the slave trade is to weaken France and enhance England's own economic position. As Staël states in the "Appel," she views England as "the richest and most fortunate nation in the universe," a country where "enlightenment is so widespread, and the circulation of ideas so free" that the pursuit of truth and justice regarding slavery can be wholly disinterested. And if it is true that most historians today would view such anglophile views as excessive and would accept David Brion

Davis's argument that both economic and humanitarian factors motivated the British in seeking to obtain the abolition of the slave trade by the French and other European countries (52–66), it is also true that many enlightened French thinkers in Staël's time shared her view of England as a model that could serve to facilitate the development of an acceptable compromise between the opposing proslavery and antislavery factions in France.

Staël's mediating efforts in the two short works from 1814 also have a certain number of specific goals. One is to influence the newly restored Louis XVIII—"a monarch . . . enlightened by religion"—and convince him to abandon the negrophobic policies of Napoleon, whom she calls "the oppressor who lay like a pall over the human race." Another goal, as indicated in the title "Appel aux souverains réunis à Paris pour en obtenir l'abolition de la traite des nègres," is to influence other European leaders to join with France in following England's example of abolishing the slave trade. Her other goals were to influence public opinion and to enlist Talleyrand's and Wellington's support for getting a measure to abolish the international slave trade passed at the Congress of Vienna.[9] Other efforts to influence political leaders and French opinion about slavery were widespread in England at the time. As Davis explains, "In 1814 the country was alive with public meetings; hundreds of petitions demanded the universal abolition of the slave trade. Reformers appealed to the humanitarian sentiments of the pope, the czar of Russia, and of the treaty-making dignitaries of Europe" (68). These efforts in England, which were taking place already during Staël's stay in London in 1813 when she encountered Wilberforce, met with mixed success. Ironically, it was Napoleon who, after his downfall, abolished the slave trade during his hundred days in 1815 in an attempt to gain British support. Although that abolition was maintained by the restored Bourbon monarchy following the Congress of Vienna in 1815, no provisions for enforcement were made, and it was only effectively eliminated in France after 1830.

There were other important arenas for Staël's activities as a political, cultural, and linguistic mediator. As her descendant the comtesse de Pange writes in 1934, Staël's contributions to abolition in France were intricately related to her opposition to Napoleon in general and to his negrophobic policies in particular. Pange writes: "In 1803 . . . she emerged definitively as Bonaparte's adversary. Under the Consulate her salon soon became the center of the liberal opposition and of overt war against the First Consul" (434). Pange thus underlines one of the chief vehicles for mediation in Staël's time:

the salon. As historians have observed, the salon enabled women to mediate between the public and private spheres, between diverse social classes, and between men and women. Although not engaged directly themselves in policy-making activities, women often influenced and helped form those activities in the salon. By today's standards, influential women like Staël may seem to stand on the sidelines of history, but their effect on society generally and the history of antislavery specifically should not be underestimated. Consider the case mentioned earlier of Abbé Raynal's call for a black leader in the highly influential *Histoire des deux Indes,* which, according to James, had a direct impact on the course of history when "it came into the hands of the slave most fitted to make use of it, Toussaint Louverture" (25). Regarding women's roles in relation to antislavery, it is enlightening to learn that Raynal's work is considered to have been composed collectively in the salon, where women, writers, and philosophers joined together to exchange ideas, letters, manuscripts, and a variety of other intellectual and political materials, and to learn, moreover, that "he wrote his book in the Necker salon, according to those he spoke to at the time" (Goodman 340–45).

Ultimately, however, none of Staël's diverse activities as a political, cultural, and linguistic mediator overshadows those activities pertaining to her overriding interest in literature and literary translation, as several of the translations provided in this volume illustrate. Her treatment in "Mirza" of noble, sensitive, even poetically inspired African men and women in their native African land contributed to the establishment of an intertextual tradition tapped by writers during the Restoration, as is clear from Duras' adoption of the name of one of Staël's heroines, Ourika, for the protagonist of her novel. Edith Lucas even goes so far as to maintain that Staël's return to Paris in 1815 actually brought about a rebirth of negrophile literature during the Restoration (15). Staël also made a major contribution to bridging the gap between diverse national, cultural, and political groups by promoting the study of comparative literature, most notably in her celebrated *De l'Allemagne* in 1813. The goal of the numerous translations that she provides in that work was to introduce new elements that would enrich French culture, a goal that she and her followers at Coppet pursued actively, in her case, for example, by translating Italian poems by Minzoni and Filicaja and German works by Goethe and Schiller into French.[10]

Special mention needs to made of "De l'esprit des traductions," which, as noted earlier, crystallizes many of the newer ideas about translation theory and practice developed during the course of the nineteenth century. The Italian translation by Pietro Giordani, published in January 1816 in the *Biblioteca italiana*, provoked both lively debate and hostility among Italians. Some were insulted by Staël's exhortation to them, as to the French in *De l'Allemagne*, to enrich their culture through translation of works from other cultures (Balayé 224–25). Others were invigorated by Staël's celebration of Italian culture and call for romanticism in Italy (Luzzi). Among the important ideas expressed in "De l'esprit des traductions" is the notion that "one should not follow the French, who give their own color to everything they translate," a very clear and, for the time, very modern rejection of the kind of translation practiced by La Place and others in the eighteenth century. Staël also rejects a narrow notion of literal translation, which she claims is inadequate for producing literary meaning in anything but the most mechanical and prosaic of ways; in her words, "translating a poet is not like taking a compass and measuring the dimensions of a building. It is making a different instrument vibrate with the same breath of life as the one we normally hear." Indeed, to practice literal, mechanical translation is tantamount to treating language as a slave, as is clear from the recurrence in her essay of words pertaining to translation such as *conquest, submission, imprisonment,* and *liberation.* It is also clear from her repeated use of a vocabulary of commerce, profit, wealth, and value that Staël conceives of translation as an active social and economic process, as well as an active process that rejuvenates and enriches the foreign and translated literature. In numerous ways, then, translation represents for Staël the prototypical mediating activity, a paradigm of the social, economic, and cultural mediation that is central to her life and her published works.

The third phase of our history—from 1820 to 1830—represents a period replete with representations of blacks as victims of oppression and with calls for the abolition of the slave trade. They include such texts produced by women as the narrative and poetic works by Sophie Doin and Marceline Desbordes-Valmore. Their writings and the other texts provided in chapter 9 indicate how the agenda of antislavery was advanced during this period through the kinds of linguistic and political mediations of which translation has been seen to be one form. To sketch the background for this corpus of texts from the 1820s, a few words are needed about the loci through which antislavery activity developed—the salon, the theater, the Société de la morale chrétienne, and the Académie française—and about the individual authors whose works are translated here as representative samples of antislavery writing. Although some of the texts in question were produced through predominantly male institutions or by male writers, they too will be seen to have profound gender ramifications.

The feminine-centered salon continued during the Restoration to be an important venue for antislavery activity and for women's mediating function with respect to both politics and language. As Steven Kale explains, with the creation of the Charte and the shift to constitutional government, the court no longer functioned as the center of political power. Instead, the salons became one of the chief arenas for partisan politics, serving as "sounding boards that registered the deliberations of the Chambers" (107). Staël's death in 1817 marked neither the end of the influence of women in the salon nor the end of the salon as a locus for liberal thought. Although many of the conservative habitués of her salon, including Chateaubriand, migrated to the salon of Mme Récamier, liberals, including Constant, attended the salon of Staël's daughter Albertine de Staël Holstein, duchesse de Broglie (1797–1838). In her salon, as Kale observes, "Women with austere political and religious principles performed an educative and mediating function by presiding over and participating in reasoned and critical debate" (121). Slavery was central to that debate. In 1814, Albertine had translated one of Wilberforce's short works on the slave trade (Berchtold 173), and her husband, Victor de Broglie, was a committed abolitionist who vigorously pursued the antislavery cause in the legislative arena.

It comes as no surprise, then, that the Broglie salon was one of those in which Charles de Rémusat, who embodies the liberal thought of the 1820s and who was one of the founders of the Société de la morale chrétienne, chose to read his antislavery play *L'habitation de Saint-Domingue, ou L'insurrection.*[11] Never intended to be performed, this play was one of many such literary, historical, or political writings that were read in salons where authors could fashion a reputation and publicize their works. The Broglie salon was especially appropriate venue for the expression of Rémusat's antislavery ideas, since he was profoundly influenced by Germaine de Staël's *Considérations sur la révolution française,* published shortly after her death in 1817. One of his first published writings, "De l'influence du dernier ouvrage de Madame de Staël sur la jeune opinion publique," published in the *Archives philosophiques, politiques et littéraires* in 1818, explained in detail his intellectual affiliation with Staël and placed him firmly in the orbit of the Staël and Broglie families. The attitude toward slave insurrection expressed in *L'habitation,* and most notably the view that obdurate ultraconservatives unwilling to change are responsible for the uprisings produced by oppressed people, can be traced back to views about the French Revolution expressed by Staël.

As with Staël, political and linguistic mediation went hand in hand for Rémusat. Having spent a year from 1817 to 1818 in the Ministry of the Navy's Office of the Direction of the Colonies, Rémusat acquired a solid knowledge of colonial affairs. He was thus well qualified to write summaries of British newspaper articles, letters, and brochures about the slave trade and slavery for the *Journal de la Société de la morale chrétienne* and *Le Globe* (Goblot xi–xxxiii). The linguistic mediation he performed with respect to antislavery, which consisted of bridging the gap between British abolitionism and efforts to develop comparable activities in France, parallels the political mediation that he performed in advocating British-style constitutional monarchy in France. Also following in Staël's footsteps, Rémusat was keenly aware of the extent to which political change could be brought about in France through translation, which he himself practiced by translating Goethe and Cicero and by actively collaborating in the project that began in 1822 to publish the *Chefs d'œuvre des théâtres étrangers*. The political importance he attributed to going beyond the constraining limitations of French classical theater is apparent in his writings about Shakespeare, who embodied for Rémusat and others of his generation the freedom to look back at their country's national past and to represent that past in the form of tragedy, as Rémusat does in *L'habitation de Saint-Domingue*. To do so was to reject the Bourbon policy of *union et oubli*, whereby national unity (*union*) required forgetting the past (*oubli*), in particular the revolutionary and republican past.

Mediation in the period of 1820s concerned not only politics and language but gender as well, as Rémusat's example illustrates. The mediating role that women are called upon to play in *L'habitation de Saint-Domingue* was undoubtedly inspired by his mother, Claire, whose success in balancing her competing allegiances to the royalist and imperial regimes is detailed in the several volumes of her memoirs. Claire also conceived of education for women as a way to empower them to exercise the roles of social, political, and moral mediators that she herself had played and that women in *L'habitation de Saint-Domingue* are called on to play. Viewing education as the best form of mediation—a bridge between the lower and upper classes and between women and men—she detailed her pedagogical principles in her *Essai sur l'éducation des femmes*, which Charles published shortly after her death, around the same time that

he wrote *L'habitation de Saint-Domingue.* Echoes of her belief in the importance of educating both daughters and mothers are distinct in *L'habitation de
Saint-Domingue.* As Célestine, the young daughter in the Valdombre family,
struggles to understand the abuse of slaves that she sees occurring around her
on the plantation, she turns to her mother for moral and intellectual guidance,
which Mme Valdombre is ill equipped to provide. Further echoes of Claire de
Rémusat's ideas regarding the moral empowerment of women can be heard
in the scenes of the play excerpted in chapter 9, in which it is a black woman,
Hélène, who is called upon to play a mediating role. Having been raped earlier by Célestine's brother Léon, Hélène stands up to her abuser in act 3 and
denounces the crime that he has committed, thus demonstrating her strength
as a moral agent. Later, in act 5, Hélène confronts the insurgent slaves who
threaten to rape Célestine in retaliation for Léon's crime. She is the one who
positions herself between the opposing forces of masters and slaves to preach
a lesson of humanity and to serve as a moral compass for the black insurgents.
The moral superiority she demonstrates is one of the key topoi concerning
women in the abolitionist writing of the time.

Turning now to the example of Marceline Desbordes-Valmore, we again
find the theater as a locus for an author's attempts to mediate the linguistic
and political issues related to slavery, but in this case the context is the socially
marginalized world of theatrical performance, as opposed to the elite world of
theatrical readings within the salon. Having traveled to Guadeloupe in 1802
as a young actress, and having been stranded there when her mother died
from yellow fever at the time of the slave uprisings on that island, Desbordes-
Valmore acquired a firsthand awareness of issues related to slavery. That
awareness is reflected in a small but significant number of her published
works: a series of poems and the novella *Sarah,* all published in the early
1820s.[12] Although the circumstances of the trip that Desbordes-Valmore
made with her mother, who put her daughter on the stage at age eleven, are
vague, the history of theater in France and the French Caribbean suggests that
the two women may have been seeking theatrical employment in a colonial
context. The marginalized world of the theater, in which Catherine Desbordes
passed on her lessons of strength and survival to Marceline, was a favored
locus for feminine independence and empowerment, a locus that offered
great resources for persons, male and female, whose familial disturbances
required that they rely on themselves. In addition to enabling women from
destabilized personal backgrounds to lead independent lives, the world of

the theater placed them in contact with the urgent political and social issues of their time: "Ever since the closing of churches, the theater was the only place where people could assemble in sufficient number to form a sounding board whose political significance did not go unnoticed" (Ambrière 70–71). Although economically and geographically unstable, this world also enabled Marceline as a young girl to be immersed in literature through learning parts and performing roles from dramatic texts on the stage.

As a woman whose entry into the world of antislavery can be traced to her involvement in the world of the theater, Desbordes-Valmore occupies a mediating position with respect to language that bears distinct links to that which Olympe de Gouges was seen earlier to hold. Like Gouges, Desbordes-Valmore was not a monolingual speaker of the French language. Although Douai, the capital of Flanders, where she was born, had been incorporated into France since 1667, Desbordes-Valmore was nostalgically attached to Flemish customs and the Flemish patois that appears in several of her poems. Later, when she was stranded in the Caribbean, she learned what she called a "patois créole," which she mastered sufficiently to be able later to publish poems in a Creole/French hybrid. A translated example, "Creole Awakening," is provided in chapter 9. (The original, "Le réveil créole," appears in the appendix along with the French originals of her other translated poems.) Throughout her life, then, Desbordes-Valmore found herself in a position that required her to mediate between regional and official languages as well as between the language of the cultural elite and the popular language of the majority.

Like other women writers of the 1820s such as Claire de Duras, Desbordes-Valmore approaches the problem of slavery indirectly by linking issues of love, marriage, and the family to the condition of slaves. Writing in the sentimental style that had gained popularity since the end of the eighteenth century, Desbordes-Valmore links the white reader and the enslaved African in the construction of family built on such common building blocks as maternity, paternal authority, filial devotion, romantic love, and family bonds. The problem of identification is paramount in a genre that asks readers to see themselves as African families torn asunder and suffering at the hands of inhuman slave traders. In contrast with her much maligned aristocratic counterpart, the bourgeois woman was rhetorically summoned through sentimental discourse to heed the voice of the heart and to illustrate through her beneficent conduct how essential humanity can transcend social hierarchies. The discourse of feeling encompasses narratives of misfortune that portray the humanity of suffering heroes and heroines. It propels the formerly excluded to center stage. Antislavery topoi such as pitting virtue against villainy and innocence against persecution enabled sentimental fiction to reach a popular audience unreceptive to Enlightenment discourse of reason and argument. Discussions of race entered less erudite cultural genres such as melodrama and popular fiction to bring readers into the text. Sentimental literature ends with a leveling of social classes: "One of the structural requirements of the process of sentimentalization is a more or less explicit denial of the importance of social hierarchy. It is where social barriers are transgressed, when some kind of *déclassement* occurs, when a shift down the social ladder takes place, that true sentimental epiphany is provoked" (Denby 96).

A third representative author from the 1820s, Sophie Doin, bears a strong resemblance to Marceline Desbordes-Valmore as a writer of sentimental literature.[13] As the daughter of a wealthy family and thus a member of a privileged social class, however, she stood closer than Desbordes-Valmore to the center of intellectual and political life in the 1820s. Of special importance is the fact that she had access to the information that was generated by the Société de la morale chrétienne, a member of which was her husband, Guillaume Tell Doin, a Protestant doctor. Since he was the one who belonged to the Société, one might initially assume that her position in the family or in relation to antislavery was less important than his. But to make such an assumption would be to disregard the complex ways in which antislavery functioned in France in the 1820s and the crucial mediating role that women played in relation to it. For one thing, it was Sophie, not Guillaume Tell, who supported the family and sponsored their philanthropic and political activities. And for another, although both were published authors, Sophie is the one who assumed a major role on the abolitionist stage in the 1820s. Like other couples whose work touched on colonial issues, the Doins came together in their commitment to and knowledge of social issues. Such collaborations were not uncommon.[14] Even when they were not confined to the home, nineteenth-century women typically stood at the center of a domestic circle that informed their identity. As for Germaine de Staël, the network of a woman's closest contacts within the family was an enabling condition for the spread of abolitionist ideas for Sophie Doin.

As for other writers of the period, mediation is central to Sophie Doin's antislavery activities. Although she did not herself produce translations like Rémusat or stand on the cusp of two linguistic worlds like Desbordes-Valmore, she was a translator in the broad sense of having as a mission to "translate" abolitionist texts into forms that made them available to diverse audiences. Having contact with the Société de la morale chrétienne and the translations of English publications about slavery that they provided in their journal and special library, she saw her role as disseminating antislavery lessons to readers, and especially to women, who would not otherwise have had access to them. She specifically sought to extend the reach of the elitist French abolitionist movement to the common people, an objective that had met with greater success in England than in France. At the beginning of her didactic novel *La famille noire*, Doin explains that her purpose is to "instill in all ranks of society a feeling of horror for the slave trade" by conveying information about the misfortunes to which Africans have been subjected for centuries. She goes on to claim that "no work has yet made known to the masses in our country the true position of blacks; I do that here," and she specifies that, by using the "light form" of literature, she will ensure that "truth will shine through for all classes" (6). She goes on in that novel to draw on translations of works by such British authorities as Thomas Buxton and, most importantly, Thomas Clarkson, the author of *Cries of Africa*, translated into French as *Cri des Africains* in 1822.[15]

Doin's task of extending the reach of antislavery texts broadly also concerned works by Haitian writers of color. In *La famille noire*, Doin refers to *Histoire de la catastrophe de Saint-Domingue*, published in 1824 by the former naval officer Bouvet de Cressé. The author of that work was Juste Chanlatte, one of a number of French-educated *anciens libres* of Saint-Domingue who served in the governments of independent Haiti. Chanlatte first served Henry Christophe in his black-dominated monarchy in the north, then Pétion in the mulatto-dominated republic in the south, and finally Boyer, who created a unified Haitian republic in 1820. Detailing a litany of horrors perpetrated by whites during slavery, Chanlatte reaches the conclusion, which Doin makes hers as well, that the violence that occurred during the Haitian Revolution had as its root cause the culpable conduct of whites. Conveying this message clearly mattered to Doin, as it similarly did for Rémusat. Again, Doin's role was that of an intermediary, someone who could reach out to women and other readers by translating abolitionist writings into touching stories. Interestingly, Bouvet de Cressé makes a point of saying in his preface that women should not read the work he is publishing: "They would be too painfully affected; there would be too much danger for them even in glancing at this long series of crimes against humanity" (vi). This sentence suggests the role that an enlightened mediator such as Doin could have seen herself called upon to perform by indirectly exposing women to the truth of past events.

Doin's awareness of the politics of Haiti and the active political role of persons of color can undoubtedly be linked to an aspect of her mediating activities that sets her apart from more moderate antislavery writers. That aspect is her endorsement of interracial relationships in "Noire et blanc" and "Blanche et noir." Both stories end with the implication that black and white partners will eventually wed, an outcome that is extremely rare in nineteenth-century literary writings about blacks. It can be understood in a number of ways. One is as an echo of the calls for interracial marriage in Haiti made by Henri Grégoire at around the same time that Doin was writing. His goal, as a member of the Catholic clergy, was to do away with arrangements of concubinage between women of color and white colonists and to replace them with the religious and legal bond of marriage. Doin's willingness to envision interracial relationships in her literary works can also be understood as symbolic. From such a perspective, the unions between the races in Doin's stories represent the harmonious relations between blacks and whites that Doin and others saw as central to the unification of Haiti under the mulatto President Boyer. Although the two stories close with the suggestion that the black and white characters will marry, the prospect of their physical union is not what matters to Doin. Although she does not explicitly rule out the possibility of mixed-race children, as Claire de Duras does in *Ourika,* she chooses not to dwell within the pages of her works on interracial marriage as a means of bringing forward a next generation of mixed-race children. As the titles of the stories indicate, black and white ultimately remain distinct and separate. But the separation in no way implies hostility or indifference. On the contrary, by uniting whites and blacks within the innermost space of the family unit, Doin articulates the primacy of racial equality, commitment, and loyalty as the bases of the moral and political future of Haiti and the French colonies.

A fourth institution that fostered antislavery writing in the 1820s, along with the salon, the theater, and the Société de la morale chrétienne, was the Académie française. The academy's poetry contest on the subject of the abolition of the slave trade in 1823 elicited fifty-four responses, of which the winning poem was Victor Chauvet's *L'abolition de la traite des noirs.* That poem, along with another submission, M. Dumesnil's *L'esclavage,* is included in chapter 9 as a representative example of abolitionist poetry that illuminates through comparison and contrast the issues of gender that are central to *Translating Slavery*. Although all the submissions were by male authors,[16] many of the poems, and the contest itself, functioned as forms of political and linguistic mediation. Politically, the academy chose to exercise a moderating influence on ultraconservative former colonists and their supporters, as the Société observed: "Honor to those members of our literary body who proposed such a subject, who got it accepted by the Academy, despite the oppositions of their fellow members."[17] With respect to language, the poems strike a middle ground between the poetic innovations of romanticism, which was developing in France in the early 1820s, and the classical motifs and neoclassical style that found favor with the academy. Although these poems differ from the simple, lyrical poems about slaves written by Desbordes-Valmore, they also contain sentimental motifs, lexical components, and other literary features that indicate the mediating position that antislavery poetry occupied.

Chauvet's and Dumesnil's poems convey the message of antislavery largely through sentimental stories about African women. Specifically, both poets draw upon the touching figure of Nealee, as does Sophie Doin in *La famille noire*. Nealee (variant spellings include Néali and Néala) was first described by Mungo Park, the celebrated late eighteenth-century explorer sent by the British African Association to trace the course of the Niger River. His *Voyages to the Interior of Africa*, published in 1799, was used as the basis of arguments against slavery set forth by Thomas Clarkson in *Cries of Africa*. The indirect approach of drawing on sentimental stories such as the Nealee story, which clearly was favored by the academy, differed from the more direct approach of documenting violations of the ban against slave trading that the Société de la morale chrétienne adopted in its own contest in 1824. In that contest, writers were invited "to present the difficulties of abolishing the slave trade in its true light; to discuss them without yielding to exaggeration, attenuation, or reticence; to carefully document them; to propose solutions."[18]

To compare Chauvet's and Dumesnil's versions of Nealee to black women figures found in antislavery works by women writers is to reveal considerable overlap as well as significant differences. Like Germaine de Staël in "Mirza," Chauvet approaches his African subject through the construction of a Eurocentric frame narration. In his case, the frame narrator is a traveler following in the traces of Mungo Park. Like Park, Chauvet's traveler visits Africa and offers an eyewitness report of his exploration ("I see shuddering whites wrench from his misery the African"). Like other travelers and missionaries, his purpose is to educate and enlighten Africans; but, in the process, he is appalled to learn that his fellow Europeans are exporting suffering and exploitation rather than Christian morality. Upholding the same principle of the peaceful cohabitation of colonizers and African slaves advanced by Staël and other antislavery writers, Chauvet's narrator implores the French, all Europeans, and their kings or other leaders to develop Africa and to end the practices of the slave trade that are inimical to achieving colonial development. In the case of Dumesnil, a comparison can be drawn between his Néala and Sophie Doin's character of the same name in *La famille noire*. Both African women are models of self-sacrifice: Dumesnil's character sacrifices herself in a vain attempt to bury her father, whom inhuman slave traders have killed; Doin's Néala sacrifies herself in a similarly vain attempt to exchange her freedom for that of an older woman. Dumesnil's Christian perspective on antislavery can also be compared more generally to that held by Staël, her family, and the Société de la morale chrétienne. Not surprisingly, his poem was praised in the Société's journal for highlighting the salutory effects of Christianity and, in particular, the opposition voiced by Popes Leon X and Paul III against slavery.[19]

There are notable differences, however, between the abolitionist poems written by male poets and works produced by women writers at the same period of time. Whereas in "Noire et blanc," Doin describes in detail Charles's physical attraction to Nelzi, in *L'esclavage*, Dumesnil justifies the beauty of his Néali by commenting in a footnote that she has "neither the broad nose, the thick lips, nor the kinky hair of other Negresses" (34). And whereas Doin is willing to place blame on the colonists for the violence that occurred during the slave uprisings, as is Rémusat, Dumesnil puts actions by blacks and whites on the same plane: "Modern history is filled with atrocities caused both by oppression and by rebellion, two equally criminal practices." Chauvet's poem also differs significantly from the perspective found in women's antislavery texts. Like Victor Hugo in *Bug-Jargal* and Prosper Mérimée in *Tamango*, and even Rémusat in *L'habitation de Saint-Domingue* to a certain extent, Chauvet emphasizes the rivalry between two men for the body and the affection of a black woman, as opposed to the dramas of loss of freedom, disrupted families, and sentimental bonds enacted by women writers. It may not be the case that antislavery writings by men and women contain different sets of literary, political, and philosophical components. But it is true that differences exist in the emphases that are placed on those components in male- and female-authored texts. It may be best to envision antislavery writing of the 1820s as a continuum: at one end stand writers, typically women, who try to understand the black perspective on the slave uprisings and to call attention to the personal tragedies experienced by enslaved women and children; at the other end stand writers, typically male, whose perspective is more clearly Eurocentric and whose emphasis is on violence and sexual rivalry.

We can sum up by emphasizing that it is clearly a mistake to glorify antislavery writers or to fail to acknowledge that European writers' concern for slaves was inevitably fraught with contradiction, ambiguity, and ambivalence. It is also necessary to acknowledge that the abolitionist efforts that they directly or indirectly promoted may even have had negative effects. Winthrop Jordan notes that "by concentrating on elimination of inhumane treatment, the humanitarian impulse helped make slavery more benevolent and paternal and hence more tolerable for the slaveowner and even for the abolitionist" (368), but at the same time he emphasizes that abolitionist efforts helped turn attention toward the slave trade. As Davis states, "If there had been no abolitionists, the injustices of slavery, which mankind had tolerated for several millennia, would hardly have seemed a serious problem" (*The Problem of Slavery* 163). This volume will show that, in addition to those limited but significant forms of direct participation in abolitionist activities by French women writers of the revolutionary period noted above, these women used literature to call attention to that serious problem of the injustice of slavery.

TRANSLATING *UNCLE TOM'S CABIN*

The concluding example of Harriet Beecher Stowe's celebrated *Uncle Tom's Cabin,* published in March 1852, can help to reemphasize the main points developed in this chapter: that translation is profoundly ideological; that translation, gender, and race are inextricably linked in ways that translators and translation critics need to recognize; and that women writers maintained over time a special relationship to antislavery. Specifically, this section will consider the reception and production of *Uncle Tom's Cabin* in relation to gender, a consideration that will set the stage for a comparative analysis of Louise Belloc's and Emile de La Bédollière's translations of that novel. The ideological limitations of Belloc's translation as well as the attempts made in it to resist oppression can help us as translators and translation critics to reflect upon the similar limitations and attempts that we grapple with in the present.

Literary history undoubtedly contains few more striking examples of a major work that has been identified with women and that has continued to interest and inspire women critics and readers than *Uncle Tom's Cabin.* Abraham Lincoln's celebrated remark on meeting Stowe—"So this is the little woman who made this big war"—draws attention to the feminine stamp that from her lifetime to the present time has marked the author and her work. (It also brings to mind the similarly strong claims about a woman writer's influence that have been made about Behn's novel.) Emphasizing Stowe's feminine status, John Lemoine wrote in the autumn of 1852 in the *Journal des débats* that *Uncle Tom's Cabin* "levels against the unholy institution of slavery perhaps the most severe blow it has ever received; and this blow has been struck by the hand of a woman" (qtd. in La Bédollière 1). Other accounts similarly show that at the time of its publication, critics and general readers worldwide perceived the book as having special relevance or appeal to women: "Women responded to Mrs. Stowe from all over the world—George Sand from France, Jenny Lind and Frederika Bremer from Sweden, Anna Leonowens on behalf of a Siamese court lady, impelled to free all her slaves. Queen Victoria's friend, the Duchess of Sutherland, Lady Byron, Mrs. Browning and a half million other women in Europe and the British Isles filled twenty-six folio volumes with their greetings and signatures—and protests against slavery—and forwarded this Affectionate and Christian Address to Mrs. Stowe" (Papishvily 74). It is significant not only that Sand, a celebrated French woman writer and prominent humanitarian voice, chose to promote *Uncle Tom's Cabin* in her article about the novel that appeared in *La Presse* in December 1852, thereby contributing to its success in France, but also that she did so by emphasizing its feminine qualities. She states that "mothers, young people, children, and servants can read and understand" what she calls "an essentially domestic novel," going on to observe that even "superior men" will be touched by Stowe's unique descriptive and sentimental talents, which she compares to Walter Scott's and Honoré de Balzac's. Asserting the superiority of moral over aesthetic values, heart over mind, and female saints over male writers, she eulogizes her American fellow novelist by attributing to Stowe "the most maternal soul that has ever existed" (320–25).

Uncle Tom's Cabin stands as a striking example, furthermore, of the collaborative and overlapping efforts of women in the production, translation, and criticism of literature. Stowe's sister-in-law is credited with having urged her to write the book, and Mrs. Weston Chapman, an author and abolitionist, with ensuring its translation into French by the Irish writer Louise Belloc in collaboration with Adélaïde de Montgolfier. Stowe, in praising that translation, which is distinguished from most others in its willingness to grapple with the translation of the black dialect used in the novel, called attention, as noted earlier, to the issue of feminine gender, stating: "I am convinced that a feminine mind can more easily mould itself to my own" (qtd. in Belloc vi). (Stowe's novel can itself be read as a translation inasmuch as it strives to translate black language and culture into an idiom that white readers of her time could appreciate and understand.) That women identify with Stowe's sympathetic treatment of racial and sexual Others is evident from the attention that women critics have given to her work. Sand, as noted earlier, helped to ensure Stowe's popularity in France, seeing in the American writer's social, humanitarian, and religious thought an echo of her own. Another especially noteworthy woman critic for our purposes here is Edith Lucas, whose *Littérature anti-esclavagiste au dix-neuvième siècle: Etude sur Madame Beecher Stowe et son influence en France* provides a thorough analysis of translations of Stowe's novel. Other important critical works by women include Elizabeth Ammons's "Heroines in *Uncle Tom's Cabin*," which dwells on the feminine, Christlike figures of Tom and Eva and highlights the resistant thrust of Stowe's advocacy of maternal over patriarchal values, and Jane Tompkins's "Sentimental Power: *Uncle Tom's Cabin* and the Politics of Literary History," which explores the crucial links among sentimental literature, religion, and the political empowerment of women in Stowe's novel and nineteenth-century American literature.

The strong involvement or association of women with *Uncle Tom's Cabin* raises the thorny issue of the ideological implications that can be drawn from those women's attempts to deal with the issues of gender and race. Needless to say, those attempts do not always appear from a modern perspective to display sufficient sensitivity to racial issues or sufficient self-awareness of their ideological limitations.[20] Sand's essay on Stowe, for example, like many other similar nineteenth-century texts, could be accused of complacency, of allowing middle-class whites to congratulate themselves for their pity and compassion while failing to call into question the system that produced and sustained slavery. Sand wrote about Stowe in the early 1850s under Napoleon III's repressive imperial regime, which Sand chose not to oppose; indeed,

Stowe's success in France, to which Sand contributed, can be attributed at least in part to the censorship of French works addressing social issues that existed at that time and the tolerance of discussion of such issues in foreign books (Lucas 239–42). Among the many objections that have been raised against *Uncle Tom's Cabin*, at least some have stemmed from a suspicion that complacency, complicity, and hypocrisy were common denominators among popular authors producing antislavery works, general readers avidly consuming those works, and figures of power in France encouraging discussion of social issues abroad yet censoring discussion of such issues at home.

The best-known accusation against Stowe herself for lacking sufficient sensitivity to racial issues is undoubtedly to be found in James Baldwin's article "Everybody's Protest Novel," published in the *Partisan Review* in 1949. Baldwin is suspicious of Stowe's appeal to the emotions of her reading public. Accordingly, he states acrimoniously, "*Uncle Tom's Cabin* is a very bad novel, having, in its self-righteous, virtuous sentimentality, much in common with *Little Women*. . . . The wet eyes of the sentimentalist betray his aversion to experience, his fear of life, his arid heart; and it is always, therefore, the signal of secret and violent inhumanity, the mask of cruelty" (28). Baldwin's article has the merit of challenging modern readers, critics, and translators to consider seriously the underlying complicity that Stowe and other antislavery writers may have had with those responsible for the cruelty practiced by whites against blacks during slavery. However, by labeling the sentimental literature that nineteenth- and twentieth-century women typically produced and read as categorically inferior, Baldwin repeats the kind of undervaluing of feminine genres and literary conventions noted earlier in this chapter with respect to Behn's intertextual ties to French women in the tradition of heroic romance. By addressing solely the issue of race, and by failing to see it in relation to gender, Baldwin ends up substituting, if not sexism, then gender insensitivity for racism, and he thereby ends up failing to perceive the complexity and multifariousness of resistance to oppression in nineteenth-century literature by women. Many elements of that resistance found in *Uncle Tom's Cabin* are precisely those that other antislavery writings by women also developed: emphasis on white women's sympathetic response to black women; on the voice of the Other; on the mental, spiritual, or creative strengths of persons of color.

Gustave Flaubert provides another example of a male critic who applies aesthetic criteria that effectively function to dismiss the legitimacy of women's writing. In a letter to Louise Colet dated December 9, 1852, he states his negative reaction to Stowe's novel based on two closely related sets of criteria. The first set, a combination of metaphysical and aesthetic considerations, serves to relegate women's writing to an inferior status because that writing is typically concerned with pragmatic concerns or domestic issues. Flaubert objects, for example, that *L'oncle Tom* is too narrow and too topical. Limited to the current situation of slavery, it fails to aspire to "eternal truth" and "pure beauty." His second set of criteria focuses on the abstract narrative principle of objectivity, a principle that, if adopted by women writers, would effectively function to silence their voices as women. Claiming to be "incessantly irritated" by Stowe's reflections about slavery, Flaubert asserts that the novel should "cancel out the author," and he goes on to say that "the author in his work should be like God in the universe, present everywhere, and visible nowhere," and that the author should manifest "a hidden and infinite impassibility" (2:203–4). Ironically, Flaubert maintained close personal and artistic relationships with women writers such as Colet and Sand and was writing to a woman to express these views, which can be interpreted as excluding women's voices. Clearly there was a gender-based conflict between the kind of socially oriented literature that appealed to women writers and readers and his own more masculine belief in art for art's sake.

As we turn now to an analysis of how gender and race function both as ideological limitations and as sites of resistance in translations of *Uncle Tom's Cabin,* it is important to point out the unusual facts surrounding the translation and publication of Stowe's novel in France. Due to its unprecedented popularity—in its first year alone, 120 editions and 300,000 copies in the United States, and 40 editions and an estimated 1.5 million copies in Great Britain—there was a tremendous rush to translate and publish *Uncle Tom's Cabin,* which, when it appeared, enjoyed an unprecedented success for a foreign book. Within ten months, eleven different French translations were published (Lucas 67). (A fictitious story published in the humorous periodical *Charivari* describes ten translators who arrive at Mrs. Stowe's hotel during her visit to Paris in 1853. Unable to speak any English, they resort to speaking to her in a black dialect of French. Puzzled and frightened, she calls the police and they end up in jail [Birdoff 170–72].) The flurry of competing translations stirred debates over such issues as the relative merits of translating "Uncle Tom" as *l'oncle Tom* or *le père Tom,* or of translating "cabin" as *case* or *cabane.* Among the various translations, the one by Belloc, which, as noted earlier, was singled out for praise by Stowe herself, represents an attempt to reproduce the original text without major deletions or additions. It thus can stand as an example of the kind of translation envisioned by Staël and developed in the nineteenth century, which strives to respect national and racial particularities. An instructive contrast can be made with the first and perhaps the best-known translation of *Uncle Tom's Cabin,* produced by La Bédollière and published in 1852. That translation, which dramatically shortens the novel and leaves out much of the descriptive detail in order to enhance its dramatic effect, is closer to the example examined at the beginning of this chapter of La Place's *Oroonoko,* which focuses more on the translated-language text and culture than on the text and culture of the foreign language.

It is a complex and difficult matter, however, to try to discover appropriate criteria for justifying the relative superiority of Belloc's full-length translation over La Bédollière's more abbreviated version, as one can see from Lucas's attempts to evaluate the various translations of Stowe's novel. Interestingly, she does not adopt the criterion of "faithfulness" as a way to justify the superiority of one translation over another. Lucas subscribes to the notion, which seems to have been shared by all the translators, that Stowe's style could profit from stylistic corrections, and that the need for such correction would override the need to remain faithful to the original. Speaking of the translation by Alfred Michiels, Lucas states: "Mrs. Stowe's English is not even always correct. The French version is superior to the original text in distinctness and precision" (75). The anecdote mentioned earlier also relates Stowe's having learned that her translators were coming to call and, not yet questioning their competence in English, politely sending them a note acknowledging "that the French often improved upon the original style, and that they had a finer appreciation of the subtle shades of meaning than the English" (Birdoff 170). Lucas, the translators, and in this anecdote even Stowe herself thus end up agreeing essentially with Flaubert, who complained that the success of *Uncle Tom's Cabin* was not attributable to its literary merit, and who firmly adhered to the position that that there are objective criteria for judging artistic value. It is only a short step from that position to the related position that the translator should improve rather than faithfully render the original.

A countervailing position would consist of justifying the superiority of Belloc's full-length translation on the grounds that it respects and preserves distinctive features of women's writing, notably women's narrative voice and narrative traditions, rather than erasing those features in the name of such universalist aesthetic criteria as Flaubert's objectivity and narrative omniscience. And although it is true that neither Belloc nor such sympathetic women critics as Sand and Lucas articulated this position per se, it is implicit in their writings about Stowe and about translation. In her preface, Belloc takes strong exception to the exclusively aesthetic criteria applied by Flaubert and others of his time, stating, "To judge this work from a purely literary point of view would in our opinion be sacreligious" (viii). Belloc's conviction that women's writing such as Stowe's cannot be judged according to universalist aesthetic criteria is echoed by Sand, who demonstrates a highly modern awareness of the relativity of aesthetic values and the importance of the relativity in judging works by women writers. Sand states in this vein,

> If the best compliment that can be given to authors is liking them, the truest compliment that can be given to books is liking them for their defects. Those defects should not be shrouded in silence; discussion of them should not be avoided; and you should not be bothered when people tease you for crying naively over the fate of victims in stories about simple, true events.
>
> Those defects only exist in relation to artistic conventions that have never been and will never be absolute. If critics who are enamored of what they call structure discover tedious passages, repetitions, awkwardness in this book, look carefully, in order to reassure yourself about your own judgment, and you will see that their eyes will not be perfectly dry when you read them a chapter taken at random. (320)

Although the issue of translation does not arise here specifically, these comments demonstrate the respect for differences based on gender that translators and translation critics need to possess. Sand's awareness that artistic conventions vary, and that women's writing does not always follow the same conventions as men's, constitutes the kind of understanding that translators and critics need to have in dealing with works like *Oroonoko* and *Uncle Tom's Cabin,* both of which have been seen to have profound ties with feminine intertextual narrative traditions. Lucas too seems to have sensed that Belloc, as a woman translator, was especially sensitive to preserving Stowe's feminine voice, echoing thus Stowe's own response. Although, writing in the 1930s, Lucas does not possess the awareness of ideological issues that one finds among critics today, her praise for Belloc's treatment of stylistic elements such as lively portraits, comic effects, descriptive detail, and clear style reveals her awareness of the special attention to Stowe's distinctive style and voice that characterizes Belloc's translation.

It is worth turning now to comparisons of a few passages from the original and from the translations by La Bédollière and Belloc to look at the ideological limitations as well as the resistant features of those texts. One of the most noteworthy differences involves the emphasis that both the original and Belloc's translation place on the feminine gender of the authorial voice. That emphasis begins with the author's preface, not included in La Bédollière's translation, which highlights feminine agency from the outset. Although Belloc transposes indications of gender and authorship from one paragraph to another according to the linguistic dictates of the French language, she creates an equivalent effect. In the original, for example, two successive paragraphs contain the phrases "Experience has shown *her*" and "What personal knowledge *the author* has had, of the truth of incidents such as here are related, will appear in its time" (Stowe vi). In the translation, those two paragraphs contain the equivalent phrases "*L'auteur* le sait par expérience" and "Ce que *l'auteur* a vu et su par *elle-même* des événements racontés paraîtra en son temps" (Belloc xviii).

The concluding chapter, which, like the author's preface, places a strong emphasis on gender and authorial voice, is especially illustrative of the difference between the two translations. Belloc follows Stowe in acknowledging the author's feminine gender, although specific linguistic markers of gender in French such as *elle* or *elle-même* do not appear in the opening paragraphs as they do in the original. La Bédollière, in contrast, chooses to erase both the presence of the author and her feminine gender by adopting the gender-neutral pronoun *we* (*nous*). Consider the two translations of the following sentence from the original: "*The author* hopes *she* has done justice to that nobility, generosity, and humanity, which in many cases characterize individuals at the south" (Stowe 470). Belloc translates this sentence as "*Elle* espère avoir rendu justice à la noblesse, à la générosité, à l'humanité qui distinguent parfois les habitants du Sud" (585), whereas La Bédollière's translation reads : "*Nous* espérons avoir rendu hommage à la générosité, à la grandeur d'âme, à l'humanité, qui caractérisent un grand nombre d'habitants du Sud" (319). He thereby fails to capture the feminine agency that is crucial not only to *Uncle Tom's Cabin* but to abolitionism and antislavery literature as well. He also overstates her claim that "in many cases" Southerners respond in ways that are noble, generous, and humane: whereas Belloc presents those responses as occurring "parfois" (sometimes), La Bédollière attributes them to "un grand nombre" (a great number) of people in the South.

With respect to race, matters are less clear cut, however. In some cases Belloc's greater respect for Stowe's voice results in a resistance to oppressive notions of both gender and race. In the preface, for example, Stowe feminizes Africa and thereby suggests the related oppression of women and slaves, which, as noted earlier, was a recurrent theme in women's antislavery writing. She writes:

> In this general movement, unhappy *Africa* at last is remembered; *Africa*, who began the race of civilization and human progress in the dim, gray dawn of early time, but who, for centuries, has lain bound and bleeding at the foot of civilized and Christianized humanity, imploring compassion in vain.
>
> But the heart of the dominant race, who have been *her* conquerors, *her* hard masters, has at length been turned towards *her* in mercy. (v)

The three occurrences of feminization in the original are not only preserved but greatly intensified in Belloc's translation, which reads:

> Dans ce mouvement général, on s'est enfin rappelé *la malheureuse Afrique, elle* qui, *la première,* ouvrit aux clartés douteuses et grisâtres du crépuscule la carrière de la civilisation et du progrès; *elle* qui, après des siècles entiers, *enchaînée* et *saignante* aux pieds de l'humanité chrétienne et civilisée, implore en vain la compassion.
>
> Mais la race dominatrice s'est laissé fléchir; le cœur des maîtres, des conquérants s'est amolli. (xviii)

That there are eight occurrences of feminization in Belloc's translation, as opposed to three in Stowe's original, is attributable in part to the morphological properties of the French language, in which gender appears in articles and adjectival forms as well as pronouns and possessive adjectives. However, Belloc also appears to wish to accentuate the resistant thrust of relating gender and race in this passage about Africa; feminine gender appears in association with Africa six more times subsequently in her text, whereas it does not reappear in the original. At times Belloc also uses footnotes to intensify the abolitionist thrust of the novel (e.g., 172, 572) and on occasion strengthens the abolitionist tone through translation itself, as, for example, in her translation of a passage in which Stowe states that Africans have won from the Anglo-Saxon race "only misunderstanding and contempt" (v), which Belloc translates by writing that the African race, which "n'a pu se faire comprendre de ses oppresseurs, reste prosternée sous le poids de leur mépris" (xvii).

There are as many instances, however, in which Belloc actually intensifies the implicit racist overtones of the original. Whereas she strives to render what Stowe presents as black dialect in the original, Belloc at times makes that dialect more ungrammatical, as for example in her translation of "Ah, master trusted me, and I couldn't" (Stowe 13) as "Oh! moi, pas pouvoir: maître s'être fié à Tom" (Belloc 3). As this example illustrates, Belloc consistently employs unconjugated infinitives as the mark of black speech, with the result that the wide variety of grammatical and lexical features of that speech in Stowe's novel is narrowed and rendered more stereotypical in Belloc's text. Predictably, then, a phrase such as "How easy white folks al'us does things!" (Stowe 32) becomes "Comme petit blanc faire tout bien!" (Belloc 28). Belloc also introduces the semantic feature of animality, in some cases by adding an element that is altogether absent in the original ("le malin singe" [52]; "ces chiens de nèg" [259]), and in other cases by translating a less racially charged expression with a more offensive one, as in the translation of "what a young un" (Stowe 14) as "voilà un curieux petit singe" (Belloc 5).

There are other times when Belloc's commitment to respecting the tone and voice of the original seems to backfire and to add a racist element that is missing in La Bédollière's more neutral and shorter version of the novel. Consider the following passage, in which the nominal and pronominal references to black children have been italicized:

> "Now, Augustine, what upon earth is this for?" said Miss Ophelia. "Your house is so full of *these little plagues,* now, that a body can't set down their foot without treading on 'em. I get up in the morning, and find *one* asleep behind the door, and see *one black head* poking out from under the table, *one* lying on the door-mat,—and they are mopping and mowing and grinning between all the railings, and tumbling over the kitchen floor! What on earth did you want to bring this *one* for?" (Stowe 259)

Belloc's translation of this passage seems to revel in the multiplication and intensification of racial terms:

—Or ça, Augustin, qu'est-ce que cela signifie? dit miss Ophélia. La maison regorge déjà de *ces petites pestes:* on ne saurait marcher sans mettre le pied dessus. Ce matin, je me lève, *un négrillon* roule endormi de derrière ma porte; *une tête noire* se dresse de dessous la table; je heurte *un troisième moricaud* couché sur le paillasson. De tous côtés, sur les balcons, sur les balustrades, on voit grimacer *quelque face de suie;* partout *moricauds, moricaudes, négrillons, négrillonnes,* dorment, rient, pleurent, cabriolent, se roulent à terre, et fourmillent sur le plancher de la cuisine. Au nom du ciel, pourquoi nous embarrasser d'*une* de plus? (313–14)

Not only does Belloc retain the reference to "plagues" ("pestes") and "black head" ("tête noire"); she adds a reference to a "face de suie" (a sooty face), three occurrences of the French terms for Negro children in the masculine and feminine ("négrillon," "négrillonne"), and three more occurrences of a pejorative term for persons of color, also in both the masculine and feminine forms ("moricaud," "moricaude"). In contrast, La Bédollière's translation, in striving less to capture the tone and detail of the original, appears less racially offensive. "—Augustin, dit miss Ophélia, qu'est-ce que cela signifie? votre maison est si remplie de *ces petites pestes,* qu'on ne peut faire un pas sans marcher dessus. Le matin, en me levant, je trouve *un négrillon* sur le paillasson; je vois *une tête noire* sortir de dessous la table. Au nom du ciel, pourquoi m'avoir amené *cette fille?*" (173). It is worth noting that Stowe's passage of 94 words is reduced to 61 in La Bédollière's translation, whereas it is expanded to 108 in Belloc's. In this instance, as in many others, one can see that the kind of attention to descriptive detail and comic effect that Lucas praises in Belloc's translation and interprets unproblematically in stylistic terms has significant ideological effects.

In short, it is clear from Belloc's translation, as it was from La Place's and others referred to in this chapter, that ideological pitfalls surround translation at every turn. Whether translators shorten or expand, whether they correct the original or choose to remain faithful to it, whether they emphasize gender or race, they make choices that ultimately have profound effects on the meaning that they give to an original text that they present to another audience, often, as in the translations contained in this volume, at another, very different moment in time. To understand fully those original works in translation entails the complex interweaving of theoretical, practical, and historical considerations that this chapter has attempted to provide. Only within the interwoven fabric of those considerations can we as contemporary readers and translators discover ways to appreciate the literary contributions made by nineteenth-century antislavery writers and to reflect intelligently upon the ideological implications of their works.

Part Two

Olympe de Gouges, 1748–1793

CHAPTER 3

Olympe de Gouges, Feminism, Theater, Race: *L'esclavage des noirs*

Marie-Pierre Le Hir

For nearly two hundred years, Olympe de Gouges' drama was nearly forgotten: in the absence of new editions, her plays were no longer read and few scholars commented on her work. To specialists, this neglect seemed hardly exceptional: it was the common fate of plays written during the French Revolution, a voluminous body of works more frequently studied by historians than by literary critics.[1] But for the feminist critics who rediscovered Olympe de Gouges in the 1980s, and who subsequently reedited her work,[2] her literary destiny had been sealed by another factor as well: up to then, commentaries on her writings had been "usually negative and characterized by an incredible misogyny" (Thiele Knobloch, in Gouges, *Théâtre politique* 8).[3] Predominantly biographical in nature and penned by male critics, these early assessments of Gouges' work, feminist critics showed, had been so strongly influenced by negative biases against the person of Olympe de Gouges, the revolutionary activist and militant feminist, that even the comments of a famous historian like Michelet could not pass as serious criticism.[4] In the decades that have elapsed since Olympe de Gouges' work became the subject of serious critical attention, many essays and books have been written about her, her contributions to the French Revolution, and her publications. As part of the continuing effort to highlight the significance of her literary and political contributions, this essay examines her conception of theater and her role as an activist playwright before the Terror. More specifically, it presents her best-known play, *Black Slavery, or The Happy Shipwreck* (*L'esclavage des noirs, ou L'heureux naufrage;* 1792),[5] as a powerful drama committed to a double agenda of sociopolitical and dramatic reform.

RECOVERING A LOST AESTHETIC

In *The Sentimental Education of the Novel,* Margaret Cohen remarks that "physical access is not the last nor certainly the least of the difficulties in working with literature *hors d'usage,*" works that have been out of circulation for a long time. The real problem, she explains, is how to approach works that were shaped by an aesthetic that defies the reader's expectations: "Without understanding that forgotten works are shaped by a coherent, if now lost, aesthetic, one simply dismisses them as uninteresting or inferior in terms of the aesthetics that have won out" (21). Although Cohen is referring to novels that were written by women during the revolutionary period, her comments apply to revolutionary theater as well. They also aptly describe the greatest difficulty encountered in Olympe de Gouges' drama: her plays are bound to seem foreign to readers no longer attuned to the aesthetic that prevailed during the revolutionary period.

Indeed, even the best-intentioned contemporary critics, those who admire the political pamphleteer and the feminist activist, have expressed serious reservations about Gouges' talent as a playwright. Perturbed by the "constant digressions" and "inflated lyricism" (20) characteristic of her drama, Benoîte Groult hardly conceals that, in her view, Olympe de Gouges was a terrible playwright.[6] Similarly, Roland Bonnell—in an article documenting the playwright's passion for her career—finds serious flaws in her writings for the stage: "A play by Olympe de Gouges is a piece of prose that is neither polished nor proofread" (83). Though Bonnell's comment is difficult to refute, observations of this kind can only reinforce the already considerable barrier separating contemporary critics from the works of a largely self-taught and self-published playwright like Gouges, who lived through a period of considerable cultural and political upheaval. Indeed, without a true appreciation for revolutionary aesthetics, critics have found it difficult to counter the notion that her dramatic style was awkward and inappropriate for the stage, and consequently to refute the misconception that she was a bad and failed playwright. My point here, and the purpose of this essay, is not to argue that Gouges was a good playwright by contemporary standards, but to try to make it easier for contemporary readers to understand her play by examining it in its own context, on its own aesthetic and historical terms.

Foremost among the contemporary critical biases on revolutionary drama is the prevailing tendency to read these texts through the distorting prism of two dichotomies that were not pertinent two hundred years ago: the opposition between the realms of politics and arts, and the opposition between high and low culture. As an illustration of the first point, one can mention Groult's critique that Gouges' style "was much more appropriate for her rousing patriotic pamphlets than for the plays she took into her head to write" (Gouges, *Oeuvres* 41), an assessment that implies a distinction between arts (plays) and politics (pamphlets) that was not pertinent during the Revolution.[7] As illustration of the second point, one must point to the general rejection of Gouges' drama on the basis of its melodramatic style, a value judgment that recycles a largely unquestioned bias against the melodrama and the so-called popular stages dating back to the genesis of romantic drama (see Le Hir, *Le romantisme* 93–113). Popularized in the nineteenth century, this bias consists in separating form and content; in holding that both sentimentality and emphasis on moral or political content preclude literary quality; and, as a result, in relegating these modes of expression to the realm of a popular culture gendered as feminine in the case of sentimental fiction and drama, and (mistakenly) associated with lower classes, in the case of the melodrama. To assess the quality of Olympe de Gouges' drama on the basis of her sentimental, melodramatic style is therefore to evaluate her work on the basis of "the aesthetics that have won out" (Cohen, *The Sentimental Education* 21). It is also to disregard the fact that the melodrama, as a codified genre, did not exist until 1800,[8] and that the popular stages came into existence only in January 1791, when the National Assembly, abolishing privileges formerly granted to royal theaters, declared that "any citizen was free to establish a public stage and have plays of any genre represented on it" (Renouard 315–16). Olympe de Gouges herself was an active participant in the struggles that led to these important changes in copyright legislation[9]—to wit, the pamphlet *Les comédiens démasqués*, which she addressed to the National Assembly when it was debating reform in literary property. Although Gouges did not benefit from it herself—since her career as a playwright took place before the legislation took effect—it is fair to say that she lived through a period of unprecedented cultural upheaval, and of mixed, messy rules and codes—in short, the period of transition between the monopoly system of the Old Regime, to which the Comédie-Française[10] was clinging, and the democratic culture (however short lived it was to be) that Gouges envisioned and fought for, and participation in which she saw as her right as a citizen.

HISTORY OF THE PLAY

Olympe de Gouges penned as many pamphlets, prefaces, and postscripts documenting the difficulties she encountered in having her *drames* performed as she wrote plays. To the extent that many of them provide an account of the genesis of *Black Slavery, or The Happy Shipwreck,* these texts are of interest not only to historians of literary property but also to literary scholars. In "Reflections on Negroes" (1788), a postface to *Zamore et Mirza,*[11] Gouges attributed her initial interest in the issue of race to an encounter with a black woman that occurred when she was a child, as well as to the unsatisfactory responses adults provided when she inquired about color difference: "They called those people brutes, cursed by heaven." She also linked her initial interest in writing for the stage to her desire to denounce slavery: "Convinced for a long time of this truth—that it was force and prejudice that had condemned them to that horrible slavery—and troubled by their dreadful situation, I dealt with their story in the very first work I wrote." In the preface to the 1792 edition of *Black Slavery,* she also provided a brief history of her play, stating that it had been "accepted in 1783 by the Comédie-Française, printed in 1786, and performed in December 1789,"[12] thereby making it clear that she viewed all existing versions as one and the same work.

Up to now, critics saw no reason to question Gouges' statements on these two points, but doubts have recently been cast about their accuracy. Arguing that scant critical attention has been paid to *Zamore et Mirza* in the past, Gregory S. Brown and Christopher L. Miller have emphasized "significant" differences between the 1788 and 1792 editions[13] and used them to express reservations about Gouges' account of her initial interest in slavery[14]—and by extension her commitment to the abolitionist cause—as well as her claim that she wrote just one play about slavery, of which the 1792 edition was the definitive version.[15] In both cases, the bone of contention is the play's geographical setting: in the "East Indies" in *Zamore et Mirza,*[16] and in the French island colonies of the West Indies in *L'esclavage des noirs.* In "Abolitionism and Self-Fashioning," Brown paints Olympe de Gouges as an opportunist more interested in her own self-promotion as a literary figure than in the abolition of slavery.[17] Directly contradicting Gouges' claim that she "dealt with their story [the story of black slaves] in the very first work [she] wrote," he asserts: "Only . . . in late 1788 or early 1789, did Gouges make substantial revisions which transformed the play from a fantastic, sentimental melodrama about a loving French family's reconciliation in the utopian setting of the 'East Indies [Indes orientales]' in which the characters, Zamore and Mirza, are 'slaves' who are South Asians rather than Africans."[18] Christopher L. Miller agrees to a large extent with Brown on Gouges' ulterior motives in denouncing black slavery,[19] but he is less sanguine on the issue of self-promotion.[20] He nonetheless interprets her "Reflections on Negroes" as a pamphlet meant to promote her play.[21] "It was first and foremost a plea addressed to the Comédie: 'Ladies and Gentlemen, put my play on'" (*French Atlantic Triangle* 117). In both Brown's and Miller's views, in short, *Zamore et Mirza* was never about black slavery until it was performed in 1789, and the reason Gouges changed her characters from Asian Indians to black slaves was to better ride the rising abolitionist wave—the Société des Amis des Noirs was created in 1788.

The flaw in this interpretation is that it is based on the assumption that the 1788 version of the play, *Zamore et Mirza,* was the play that Gouges had originally submitted to the Comédie in 1783.[22] But according to Gouges herself, and to Chalaye and Razgonnikoff, who examined it, the 1783 version was situated in the West Indies and dealt with black slavery.[23] Gouges has given a detailed account of the developments that led to the 1788 version of her play: the Comédiens asked her to modify the text of her play[24] as a precondition for performing it. Gouges refused to comply and held steady for several years: implementing the changes the Comédiens wanted would, in her view, change the nature of her play and diminish its impact. What was the crux of their disagreement? The original play required actors to play the roles of black slaves, or more precisely, in the absence of black actors in France, to paint their faces black.[25] The Comédiens deemed this face painting an inconvenience and an attack on their professional dignity: the public would not see their facial expressions.[26]

By 1788, having waited five years to see her play performed, Gouges seemingly complied with the Comédie's demands: she transposed the plot of *Zamore et Mirza* from the West to East Indies[27]—thus making the issue of black makeup a moot one—and she published this amputated version of *Zamore et Mirza.* But she had not yet given up the hope of seeing her play performed the way she wanted to (i.e., as a play on black slavery), and she used the opportunity provided by the publication of *Zamore et Mirza* to go public over her disagreement with the Comédie, to make the public a witness to her protest over the modifications imposed by the Comédiens. This protest is voiced in the two texts that frame the published play: its preface and her pamphlet that follows the play, "Reflections on Negroes." In the preface, Gouges disavowed the version of the play she was publishing: "I conclude this preface by informing the reader that this drama is about the story of Negroes that the Comédie forced me to disfigure in costume and color, and that I had no choice but to substitute savages for [the Negroes]" (*Zamore et Mirza,* in *Oeuvres* 21)—and again in the postscript, "Reflections on Negroes": "But let us not talk about my Play any longer. *The way it was approved for performance,* I present it to the Public" (emphasis added). And to set the record straight, to make clear what her play was really about, she denounced black slavery in "Reflections" instead of in *Zamore et Mirza.*[28]

It thus makes sense to view the simultaneous publication of these three texts—preface, play, and postscript—as the last of the strategies devised by Gouges to have her play performed as a play on black slaves. Having failed, over a long period of time, to convince the Comédie, she turned to the public, making it the witness of her trials and tribulations, and denouncing the Comédie's power to blackmail playwrights into submission. "Reflections" indeed shows that she had by no means given up on seeing her play on black slavery performed as such:

> I have only one piece of advice to give to the actors of the Comédie-Française, and it is the only favor I will ask of them, that is to wear the color and costume of the Negro race. Never has the occasion been more opportune, and I hope that the Play will have an effect in favor of these victims of whites' ambition.
>
> The costume will contribute greatly to the interest of this play, which will inspire the pens and the hearts of our best writers. My goal will thus be attained, my ambition satisfied, and the Comédie-Française will be honored rather than dishonored by the issue of color.
>
> My happiness would be too immeasurable if I were to see my play performed as I wish.

In the end, Olympe de Gouges' persistence paid off: when her play was finally performed on December 28, 1789, at the Comédie-Française it was as a play about black slavery, *L'esclavage des nègres.*

REVOLUTIONARY DRAMA

Renamed Théâtre de la Nation during the Revolution, the Comédie-Française played the leading role in the politicization of culture that was to become the hallmark of the period. Marie-Joseph Chénier's *Charles IX,* performed on November 4, 1789, a month before *L'esclavage des noirs,* is considered a turning point in that regard. It is precisely because Chénier's play "was a political tragedy of a type hitherto unknown in French literature," because "it introduced revolutionary propaganda into the tragic genre," that it was well received at the Comédie (Bingham 8). Its success therefore illustrates that it was possible to write politically committed plays and to be considered a good playwright. How then can we explain that following *Charles IX* Chénier became "the foremost poet of the French Revolution" (Bingham 8), while Gouges, with *L'esclavage des noirs,* allegedly only proved her "uncanny ability for writing unsuccessful plays on apparently foolproof subjects" (Carlson 55)? Leaving misogyny aside, the contrast between these two critical appraisals might partially be explained by Chénier's choice of a "foolproof" genre, tragedy in verse, and by comparison, Gouges' choice of a more recent genre, drama in prose; but also, more strikingly, by the contrast between their respective treatments of their political subject matter and their divergent political views. Chénier used the St. Bartholomew Massacre to attack the monarchy, a "foolproof subject," since the topic was "used all during the eighteenth century by the philosophes in their concerted attack on the fanaticism of the Catholic Church" (Bingham 8). Gouges openly advocated monarchist views and vehemently denounced slavery, another controversial and politically touchy issue.

   L'esclavage des noirs is a *drame,* and as such, it belongs to an ambitious project developed during the second half of the eighteenth century that aimed at reforming French theater and at imposing the new genre at the Comédie-Française. As the endless quarrels on rules of unity and *bienséances* demonstrate, French classical tradition—as embodied in the works of Corneille and Racine—emphasized form and "good taste." Proponents of the *drame,* who rejected the aesthetics of classical theater and the premises on which it was based, had quite a different agenda. For Gouges and many contemporary playwrights, drama was not a remote aesthetic domain; it was part of "nature," of life. This continuity of life was expressed in the conception of the *drame* as a bridge over the division between comic and tragic genres and in the choice of a language accessible to all: prose, as opposed to poetry—which only selected audiences of connoisseurs could appreciate. With the *drame,* theater lost its primary aesthetic function to take on a new social role: to turn spectators into better men, women, and citizens.

Denis Diderot, Louis-Sébastien Mercier, and Gouges shared a perhaps naive assumption about the dynamics of drama performance: they thought that through the powerful emotional communion with their characters' sufferings, the spectators' true nature, their "humanity," would surface, allowing them to shake off prejudices and be better human beings. The proper way to convince was to reach the heart first, or, to quote Mercier, to make "cold, shrunken, souls" feel again (7). Without this emotional preparation, Mercier argued, spectators would not readily receive the grave lessons in "honesty and virtue" (7) a playwright had to offer. To that effect, sentimental and bourgeois drama resorted to various techniques. Tableaux, usually at the end of an act, presented characters in a state of emotional upheaval, with teary eyes to convey their heartfelt emotions. Melodramatic style, which combined both sentimental, flowery language and grandiloquent phrases; sometimes music; and even dance were used for the same purpose.

All of this, tableaux and melodramatic language, is found in *L'esclavage des noirs.*[29] The redundant qualifiers ("scoundrel," "wretch," "barbarian"), exclamatory comments ("How we are to be pitied!" "How I pity him, this unhappy man!" "How their misfortune renders them interesting!"), lengthy monologues, and affected *aparté* clearly belong to the melodramatic register. For proponents of the *drame,* style no longer was the aesthetic cornerstone and sole measure of achievement. The play's lesson and the playwright's effectiveness in conveying it became the proper criteria by which to determine the value of a play. Gouges adhered to this principle: "The author and friend of the truth, who has no interest but to remind men of the charitable principles of Nature, who respects laws and social conventions no less, is still an estimable mortal, and if her writings do not produce all the good that she had hoped for, she is to be pitied more than blamed." Gouges' own declarations concerning her lack of stylistic and literary talents have to be considered in that context. They have often been taken at face value, or at best, as indications of her feminine modesty—with a few critics rightly arguing that, judged by contemporary standards, her allegedly terrible style was by no means any worse than her contemporaries' (see Manceron, in Blanc 5). Both interpretations, however, fail to take into account the specific function of Gouges' emphasis on her alleged stylistic deficiencies: to stress them was her way to distance herself from a classical tradition that valued above all the beauty of poetic language and to direct the reader or spectator to what she considered the salient feature of her writings: their ethical dimension. "Literary merit," she wrote in "Response to the American Champion, "amounts to very little when it is stripped of these two advantages": "honor and integrity." And defending her play, L'esclavage des noirs, she contrasted again, in the preface, literary talent and ethics: "This work may lack talent, but not morals." More than "simply request understanding in light of the larger issues that were at stake" (Miller, *French Atlantic Triangle* 110–11), Gouges established a clear scale of priorities for herself as a writer: some things were essential for an author (honor, integrity); others (the painstaking details of the writer's craft) were not as important. Her persistence in defending the causes she embraced and the sense of urgency that presides over her writings attest to these priorities, priorities that originate in part in the belief commonly held during the Enlightenment that humans know right from wrong by instinct, and that proximity to nature makes for better ethics and sounder judgement. This, in any case, is what Gouges, the child of nature, tells her readers in the preface of her play, that her judgment is sounder than that of scholars, who lose themselves in petty detail: "The Learned may dwell upon and lose themselves in these metaphysical observations. I, a woman, who have only studied the good principles of Nature, I no longer set forth man's nature; my rude learning has taught me to judge things only after my soul." Hence the crucial importance she attached to "convinc[ing] the Public and the detractors of my Work of the purity of my maxims."

Her choice of a melodramatic style as the appropriate means to stage the moral issues at stake in her plays was also no coincidence. Today, we often fail to appreciate how widely popular melodramatic style was in revolutionary France: melodrama was a dominant mode of expression that pervaded the entire public sphere, including the stage, the political assemblies, and, as historian Sarah Maza has shown, the legal and political writings of the time. To use melodramatic forms of expression, including demonstrative gestures and body language, was thus to speak the language of politics and thereby assert theater's place within the political sphere. Turning away from the rules and regulations of classical theater, Gouges opted for this highly politicized mode of expression that was also the language of the inventors of the *drame*.

Thematically, *L'esclavage des noirs* is linked both to Diderot's *drame bourgeois* and Mercier's *drame civique,* but it goes further, insofar as it represents an attempt to merge the two. In his theoretical writings as well as in his plays, Diderot focused on the private sphere in an attempt to redefine relationships within the family and to replace the feudal family model, based on the absolute authority of the father, with a bourgeois model, still patriarchal, but based on love and understanding. With Diderot's *Le fils naturel,* for instance, *L'esclavage des noirs* shares a common theme: the recognition by fathers of all their children, even those born out of wedlock. In Gouges' play, Sophie's recognition by her father illustrates Diderot's ideal of family relations centered on love and equality among children. Politically, both plays argue against *droit d'aînesse*—the Old Regime right of the firstborn son to be considered sole heir—since in both cases, illegitimate children inherit from their fathers. Gouges, however, goes a step further than Diderot, since Sophie is not only illegitimate but also female. She thereby exemplifies her refusal to exclude women from any redefinition of family relationships.

As frequently stated in her biographies, Gouges had a personal interest in defending the cause of illegitimate children, since she claimed to be, and probably was, the illegitimate daughter of Lefranc de Pompignan, himself a playwright. Yet it is difficult to argue that in defending the cause of illegitimate daughters, Gouges was only pleading her own case (i.e., making a direct appeal for recognition to her father): Lefranc de Pompignan died before the play was written. This filiation was apparently of great importance to Gouges, but more so in its symbolic than biological dimension. Her obstinate efforts to have her first play performed where her father had been acclaimed, at the Comédie-Française, indicate that she was determined to be his literary daughter. In trying to establish this literary filiation, she took the burden of proof on herself: to show herself worthy of him, she had to succeed without his help and in spite of her mixed social status; like her friend Mme de Montanclos, she had to gain literary recognition on her own merits. This symbolic filiation would then bring her what her illegitimacy had deprived her of—social recognition and perhaps financial rewards—since to have a play performed successfully at the Comédie meant both literary recognition and financial security. In that regard, Gouges' literary endeavours help characterize her as feminist in two ways: her vindication of daughters' rights is doubly exemplified in her determination to be a successful playwright and in the arguments put forward in the play.

L'esclavage des noirs is also related to Mercier's *drame civique.* In *Du théâtre* (1773), Mercier had written about the "slave trade, this hateful public violation of natural rights" (261), and although he did not write a play himself on that topic, he thought that it would make an excellent subject for a *drame*. For him as well as for Diderot, drama's function was didactic and political, but for the former, drama's primary vocation was to produce good citizens. His *drames* therefore focus not only on the family but on the social and political sphere as well. Centered on both private and public life, *L'esclavage des noirs* illustrates Gouges' conviction that private life is part of a larger political context.

STAGING SLAVERY

The plot of *L'esclavage des noirs* can be summarized in a few sentences: two fugitive slaves, Zamor and Mirza, are wanted for the murder of a slave-master who tried to seduce Mirza. On the desert island where Zamor and Mirza have found refuge, they rescue Valère and Sophie, a young French couple in search of Sophie's father, from a shipwreck. But Zamor and Mirza are captured and condemned to death. Only the governor of the colony they have fled, who turns out to be Sophie's father, can save them. Thanks to him, Valère and Sophie are able to save their new friends' lives. At the end of the drama, the two slaves are freed and married.

As a political narrative *L'esclavage des noirs*' importance lies in its examination and redefinition of gender and race relations in a radically new society based on democratic principles. In the opening scene, the topos of the desert island signals the allegoric dimension of the play. Gouges proceeds the same way as Marivaux in *L'île des esclaves* (1725): in both cases, the island serves to establish a sociopolitical context that differs greatly from contemporary society. But whereas Marivaux's island harbors a utopian society in which former slaves hold the political power, no organized society is found on Gouges' island: her desert island symbolizes nature at first. Stranded on a desert island, Zamor and Mirza are beings in and of nature. What does "nature" mean for Gouges? For her, nature exists at two levels: on the surface, it is complex, "bizarre et variée," but at a deeper level, it is also one. Late in the play, Zamor illustrates Gouges' conception of nature through the following remarks: "Nature seems to stand in contrast with herself in this spot. Formerly she smiled upon us: she has lost none of her attractions, but she shows us both the image of our past happiness and the horrible fate to which we shall be victim" (3.2). Nature, without changing, can be perceived differently according to circumstances. For Gouges, the same holds for human nature: human nature does not only exist at the level of perception, where it is "bizarre" and "variée." Like others at the time, Gouges invokes "nature as the origin of both liberty and sexual difference" (Scott, "A Woman" 104), but for her, liberty and sexual difference are not equally weighted: nature is invoked as the origin of liberty and equality first. According to her, human nature is first revealed in that which distinguishes men from animals, not men from women, blacks from whites, or masters from slaves: in the same blood that flows in human veins. This primary distinction between humans and animals is introduced in act 1, scene 9, when Sophie rejects the opinion that blacks "are born to be savages" and should therefore be "tamed like animals" as the origin of racial prejudice ("What frightful prejudice!"). Failure to stress human commonality is at the origin of racial, but also sexual and class, prejudice.

It is therefore important to view the desert island in *L'esclavage* not solely as a symbol of (primitive) nature, but also as a symbol of liberty: the island is the site of resistance to political oppression. Zamor, after murdering the governor's "confidential agent," has fled from and rejected the sociopolitical order of the colony. Mirza, as the indirect cause of the murder, exemplifies the potential danger woman represents for that existing order. For the two runaway slaves, the island clearly means freedom from slavery. But similarly, and as we will see shortly, despite Gouges' support for the king, the island also represents freedom from the prevailing feudal order for Valère and Sophie. This idea is embodied in the metaphor of the shipwreck and directly expressed through a comparison: the parallel situations of the French people (Valère and Sophie) "groaning under the despotism of Ministers and Courtiers" (1.7) and of the black people (Mirza and Zamor) groaning under "the frightful despotism" of "barbaric masters" (1.1). Unlike Marivaux, whose play can be read as advocating a reversal of master and slave relations, Gouges' ideal is to abolish this type of relations, to promote social equality. This notion is clearly expressed in the second act by Coraline, who declares: "We lack but liberty. Let them give it to us, and you will see that there will no longer be masters or slaves" (2.2). It is already illustrated in the first act through the harmonious relations between the islands' four inhabitants. Gouges does not deny that differences exist in nature. On the contrary, her choice of characters stresses differences of race (black and white), gender (man and woman), and social class (slaves, bourgeois). In the touching scene where Mirza and Sophie study each other's beauty, they recognize each other as humans, and therefore as equal, and yet as different. Liberty and equality are therefore the first characteristics of Gouges' ideal society, the third being solidarity. Better than fraternity, solidarity expresses the main characters' natural propensity to want the best for fellow human beings: in Gouges' play this form of altruism is far from restricted to "brothers"; it characterizes all humans, not only men. A woman, Mirza, is the first to express that it is "sweet . . . to soothe the misfortunes of others" (1.2), a notion repeatedly expressed by other characters throughout the play. Empathy, compassion, the instinctual desire to recognize others as human and to help them, is for Gouges what constitutes Mirza, Zamor, Valère, and Sophie as human beings. This ideal of solidarity is expressed through the recurrent motive of "saving someone else's life" and illustrated through the characters' actions: Valère attempts to save Sophie from drowning; Mirza actually saves Valère's life, and Zamor, Sophie's. It is because human nature transcends difference that equality and solidarity are possible: the desert island is for all of them; they share it in spite of their differences. "All men are born free and equal" therefore doesn't mean "all men as opposed to women," but "all human beings as opposed to animals." In summary, the island serves to establish a new ideal sociopolitical framework founded on the republican principles of liberty, equality, and solidarity.[30]

In this context, it is particularly striking that Gouges' ideal society, as presented in act 1, is elaborated in the absence of a male figure of authority. Unlike Diderot, who, in *Le père de famille*, centered on the father in his redefinition of private relations, and Marivaux, who, in *L'île des esclaves*, granted political power to a male slave in his reversal of social hierarchy, Gouges presents as ideal a society that is not founded on the authority of a father-king. In act 1, the concept of sovereignty of the people, symbolized by the free association of the four equal young men and women, replaces that of patriarchal authority as the foundation of society. The father, however, is not altogether absent from the play. In act 1 already, Sophie and, to a certain extent, Zamor are searching for him, and in acts 2 and 3, he figures prominently as father and governor in the person of M. de Saint-Frémont. The important role granted to the father in acts 2 and 3 therefore seems to cancel the democratic ideal presented in act 1 and to indicate a return to the patriarchal order. This important issue calls for an examination of gender relations in the play.

Joan Wallach Scott rightly argues that for Gouges "the union of man and woman replace[s] the single figure of the universal individual, in an attempt at resolving the difficulty of arguing about rights in univocal terms" ("A Woman" 111). For Scott this notion of union is "ambiguous": "It could be read as an endorsement of functional complementarity based on sex, but also as an attempt to dissolve and transcend the categories of sexual difference" ("A Woman" 114). But for Gouges, it is and can be both, complementarity and transcendence of the categories of sexual difference, because complementarity is not fixed: in freely consented unions, unions based on love, complementary roles are not ascribed to a specific gender. There is no typical female character in *L'esclavage*, no typical couple, no typical relationship between man and woman. In the relationship between Zamor and Mirza, Mirza seems to accept the passive role, domesticity: when Zamor asks her to "go and gather some fruit," she obeys. Yet Zamor and Mirza's relationship is only one among other possible configurations. In other words, the division of labor is arbitrary; the roles of man and woman vary in every couple. Sophie, for instance, plays a more "masculine" role than Mirza: she makes common cause with the slaves and is ready to die for the sake of her ideal. Since Mirza is a slave and Sophie a *bourgeoise*, the different roles they fulfill as women could be construed as resulting from their different social origins. But Gouges' careful selection of her two other couples shows this interpretation to be inaccurate. In act 2, for instance, it is an educated slave woman, Coraline, who exposes Gouges' political views, while Azor, a male slave, listens; in the Saint-Frémont couple, not only does the wife have the economic power, but she has also given her name to her husband. With regard to gender relations, Gouges' position is consistent with the position outlined in her general social framework: equality prevails in couples in spite of sexual difference, not in a fixed complementarity, which ascribes certain functions to a certain sex, but in a flexible complementarity. Unlike many women writers later on, Gouges does not subscribe to a kind of complementarity that would dictate gender-specific roles in the couple; she does not advocate the myth of two separate spheres. Her conception of complementarity helps her sustain an egalitarian doctrine. Gender equality, however, seems curiously at odds with the prominent role granted to the father figure, M. de Saint-Frémont, in the play. By placing the play in its historical and political context, however, we can account for this apparent contradiction.

L'esclavage des noirs was retitled to better serve the cause of abolition, but its original political scope was wider. As a political narrative, the play comments on France's political options at the time of the 1789 revolution, and it conveys Gouges' vision of the society to come. The fact that Gouges referred specifically to the views expressed in the play and in the political pamphlet entitled *De l'esclavage des noirs* during her own trial in 1793 demonstrates that she attached a great deal of personal significance to them. Accused of antirepublican sentiments, Gouges countered "that for a long while she had professed only republican sentiments, as the jurors would be able to convince themselves from her work entitled *De l'esclavage des noirs*" (Levy, Applewhite, and Johnson 257).[31] So far, act 1 seems to corroborate Gouges' claims, but is this the case in the rest of the play?

As a dramatic theme, the quest for the father allows the play to move from utopia (the ideal society) to reality—to the colony and, by extension, to contemporary France in acts 2 and 3—and at that point to engage with sociopolitical rather than philosophical issues. If act 1 illustrates Gouges' ability to conceive of a truly democratic society, acts 2 and 3 exemplify her rejection of this ideal model as utopian. As a political theme, the quest for the father has another function: it enables Gouges to articulate her political preference for a monarchy, but for a monarchy based on republican principles, a constitutional monarchy. Gouges' political views have often been interpreted as inconsistent. Many critics find it difficult to reconcile her self-proclaimed republicanism and her royalism. There is no doubt that *L'esclavage des noirs* advocates monarchy—and if there were, we would still have to account for her vain but persistent efforts to provide legal council for the king and queen at their trials. What needs to be stressed, however, is that the opposition between monarchy and republic is not particularly useful for defining Gouges' political stand. That her preference was for monarchy *and* at the same time a democratic ideal can only be appreciated from her historical vantage point: in 1789, France was still a monarchy, not a republic; the French were still trying to regenerate their monarchy, to rebuild it on democratic principles. *L'esclavage des noirs* provides not only evidence of the continuity in Gouges' political thought over a period of years—since the play was written in 1783 and performed in 1789—but also material of particular importance to understand her political views and to establish their consistency: it stands as an illustration of the general consensus, which, in 1789, still made monarchy seem compatible with the democratic ideal proclaimed that same year in the *Declaration of the Rights of Man*.[32]

Acts 2 and 3 focus on this issue, and in particular on what Gouges considers the king's duty in transforming the old feudal monarchy into a constitutional monarchy. As the governor of the colony, M. de Saint-Frémont exemplifies the ideal of the citizen-king envisioned by the National Assembly, the father of the nation, dedicated to the freedom and happiness of all his subjects. M. de Saint-Frémont loves and recognizes all his children, daughters and slaves included. Rejecting tyranny and its "barbaric laws," which contradict his natural goodness and his sense of justice, he struggles with and triumphs over institutions (justice, police) that oppress the slaves and only serve the most powerful (here, the colonists). In short, he shares the same ideal as Coraline, the slave woman who envisions a society based on freedom, education, and work, with no masters or slaves. Struck by the similarity between Coraline's republican views and M. de Saint-Frémont's, Azor exclaims: "You speak like a man! You sound like the Governor" (2.2). As if good example were not enough, M. de Saint-Frémont directly appeals to Louis XVI to abolish all forms of oppression:

> Sovereigns render their People happy: every Citizen is free under a good Master, and in this country of slavery one must be barbaric in spite of oneself. Hey! how can I help abandoning myself to these reflections, when the voice of humanity cries out from the bottom of my heart: "Be kind and sensitive to the cries of the wretched." I know that my opinion must displease you: Europe, however, takes care to justify it, and I dare hope that before long there will no longer be any slaves. O Louis! O adored Monarch! would that I could this very moment put under your eyes the innocence of these condemned souls! (2.6)

Even though M. de Saint-Frémont's speech comes as a response to proslavery arguments advanced by the judge, the address to the king of France indicates that the message has to be lifted out of this particular context: the king is being asked to abolish not only slavery but all forms of political oppression. It is, in other words, a plea for the recognition of popular sovereignty. The hope that "before long there will no longer be any slaves" expresses the new creed that "all men are born free and equal." The sovereign people call on the father-king to choose between the old feudal order—tyranny symbolized in the play as the violent rule of weaponry—and the new egalitarian order based on freedom, nonviolence, and work.[33] To live up to his new role, the king has to become a patriot-king, "the father of the French, the King of a free people" (Schama 424). Gouges' conception of the monarchy and of the role of the monarch thus represents a departure from the old feudal model in which the king was seen as sacred.[34] The opposition she makes in the play between the old and new kind of king is also found in *Les comédiens démasqués* when she mentions "the huge distance among kings between those who are tyrants and those who are fathers to their people" (1).

M. de Saint-Frémont's plea is also a direct appeal for the abolition of slavery. In that respect, however, Gouges' position might appear more timid. Even though the play advocates the education of slaves, hints that slaves should be free to farm their own land, and openly promotes the abolition of slavery as a practice unworthy of the human race—"A commerce of men! o Heaven! humanity is repulsive" (2.2)—M. de Saint-Frémont's speech clearly indicates that for Gouges the abolition of slavery depends upon the generosity of a "benevolent and enlightened Government" (3.13). Far from advocating political empowerment by slaves, Gouges seems to postpone the abolition of slavery to a not foreseeable future: Zamor refuses to defend his own cause, and he later intervenes to end the slave rebellion he has indirectly caused: "Never deliver yourselves into excess to escape slavery. Fear breaking your irons with too much violence" (3.11). With hindsight, then, Gouges' demands might appear modest: the end to the slave trade, humane treatment of slaves. Miller underscores the similarities between Gouges' views on the abolition of slavery and those of Condorcet—who published his *Reflections on Black Slavery* in 1781—in the following manner: in both cases, "slavery is deplored; emancipation is called for, although it may be dangerous;[35] in the meantime, both say, the slaves' conditions must be 'softened.' Both are concerned with the slaves' potential behavior in the wake of emancipation" (*French Atlantic Triangle* 119).

In fact, and in spite of a report of slave unrest in her play, Gouges rejected as unfounded the colonists' accusations and the Comédiens' fears that *L'esclavage* would cause the slaves to revolt: "But, sirs, we are in Paris; my drama won't be performed in front of Negroes and I insist that [if it were] it would incite them to submission; I maintain that everything in it breathes morality and obedience to the laws. How can this drama be considered dangerous today when you accepted to perform it eight years ago, and when, under a despotic government, censors approved of it?" (*Les comédiens démasqués* 48). Both Gouges' moderation with regard to the slavery issue[36] and her insistence on retaining the monarchy originate in her conception of freedom as socially binding. A great number of situations in the play make it clear that for Gouges, the right of the individual should not be viewed independently from the collective good, which in turn implies preservation of some form of governing structure to legitimize the communities' claims. The notion that to free slaves would destroy the economy of the colony, that their individual freedom would be detrimental to the good of the colony, is rejected by Coraline in the play: "Let the Masters give liberty; no Slave will leave the workshop. Imperceptibly, the rudest among us will instruct themselves, recognize the laws of humanity and justice" (2.2). This declaration is only conceivable to the extent that even slaves are seen as part of the community—independently from the fact that they are mistreated and poorly rewarded for their labor: they are not the Other ("our enemies"), they play an important role in the community, they are "nos cultivateurs" ("our farmers"). Even when men are free, it is in their best interest to contribute to the good of the community (the nation or the colony); even when they are free, it is their responsibility to live by society's rules, a notion clearly expressed by Zamor in his address to the rebelling slaves and to the colonists: "Slaves, Colonists, listen to me: I have killed a man; I deserve to die. Do not regret my punishment; it is necessary for the good of the Colony" (3.11). In all instances, relinquishing individual rights for the good of society, making sacrifices for the benefit of others, is presented as an ideal: when Mme de Saint-Frémont encourages her husband to search for his daughter at the risk of finding his ex-wife, when Sophie throws herself in front of the firing squad to defend Zamor and Mirza, when slaves offer to eat less and work more in exchange for Zamor's and Mirza's lives, their generosity, which cuts across all differences of class, gender, and race, defines them as human beings.

Gouges has accordingly little to say about individual rights in the play. It is true that she grounds the right to be free in nature—Valère speaks of "rights under Natural Law" (1.7)—but this right can also be lost in nature (Zamor mentions "giv[ing] man back the rights that he has lost in the very bosom of Nature" [1.1]). More to the point, Valère's prediction that the *people* will "resum[e] all . . . rights" (1.7) confirms Gouges' conception of the rights of individuals as derived from their belonging to the same collective entity, from their citizenship. In other words, in 1789, Gouges still took the *Déclaration des droits de l'homme et du citoyen* to apply to all citizens, including women and slaves. When she wrote the *Déclaration des droits de la femme et de la citoyenne* two years later, her position had changed; she had come to understand that her interpretation of "man" would not prevail.

The importance Gouges attached to the father figure of the king can be seen as representing a guarantee that the claims of the community at large would prevail against the claims of the individual: as the "father of all," the king symbolized all his people. In *L'esclavage*, it is the king, through M. de Saint-Frémont, who sets the social tone for the nation, who advocates tolerance. It is also not by chance that M. and Mme de Saint-Frémont represent the most untraditional couple in *L'esclavage*. Through this unorthodox relationship, in which the husband takes his wife's name and accepts to share her fortune, Gouges further advances her political agenda: poised at the intersection of private and public spheres, the "royal" couple serves to articulate the political dimension of private relations and to point to new social configurations different from the traditional patriarchal order.

As evidenced in the happy ending of the play, Gouges was confident that the "republican monarchy" she had envisioned would prevail. When the play was performed in 1789, her original political message had lost some of its topical interest, since the new order she had envisioned was being realized. Later, her desperate attempts to save the king's and queen's lives show how consistent these efforts were with the political creed professed in *L'esclavage des noirs:* deprived of a royal couple's symbolic guidance, Gouges assumed, the revolutionaries would only meet her political agenda halfway. Leaving issues of gender and race unaddressed, they would be unable to achieve "perfect equality."[37]

FIGHTING FOR JUSTICE: GOUGES' POLITICAL STRUGGLES

According to Howarth, the degree of commitment of a playwright can be measured by his or her willingness to defend causes that have not yet gained general approval (99). By that standard, *L'esclavage* offers a perfect example of a truly committed play. In 1789, the abolition of slavery was such a cause. Brissot and Mirabeau had just created the Société des Amis des Noirs,[38] and it is very likely that this abolitionist society played a role in ensuring the representation of *L'esclavage* at the Théâtre de la Nation. Opinions differ as to whether Olympe de Gouges was herself a member of the Société.[39] She had contacts with Mirabeau, to whom she had sent her play,[40] and, according to others, with Condorcet.[41] The Société des Amis des Noirs relied on pamphlets and newspaper articles to promote abolition, but as Daniel P. Resnick has shown, because of its "narrow base of recruitment" (561) and its failure to provide an economic instead of a purely moral critique of slavery, it was relatively powerless in countering the diplomatic maneuvers of the proponents of slavery, who met at the Hôtel Massiac. According to Gabriel Debien, the "Club Massiac's influence through other friendly-minded clubs" (111) was "a particularly noticeable activity . . . from December 1789 onward . . . , when the Club's main struggle against Amis des Noirs and free people of color begins" (119). L'esclavage des noirs was performed during this period of intense confrontation between the pro- and antislavery camps.

From the colonists' perspective, the danger of Gouges' play was not so much its content, but rather the fact that it brought attention to and openly discussed the issue of slavery at a time when their political strategy was to silence it. Indeed, by stressing France's vital economic interests in the West Indies,[42] the colonists were able to prevent successfully the issue of slavery from being directly raised at the National Assembly, with the result that "subsidies to investors in the slave trade were not halted until the fall of 1793" (Resnick 564). This strategy was also successfully applied to silence Gouges: when overrating the didactic powers of her drame, she set out to convince an audience with vested interest in preserving the colonial system that slavery was both immoral and cruel. There is no question that the colonists had a strong interest in opposing the performance of L'esclavage des noirs and that they acted to prevent the Comédie-Française from performing it. As it turned out, the abolitionists won the first round: the play was performed in its entirety on December 26. But in this highly politicized context, it was very difficult, if not impossible, for Gouges to obtain a clear success on the stage.

Success in 1789 was largely determined by two factors: the affinities between the play's message and the political views of the audience, and reception in the press. Chénier, for instance, whose two previous plays had failed at the Comédie and who was determined to succeed with Charles IX, made sure he had strong, influential political supporters in the audience: "Several deputies of the National Assembly attended, headed by Mirabeau who led the applause from his box. Danton, Desmoulins, and the 'future nucleus of the Cordelier Club' were on hand as the play proceeded, right to the end, amid shouting, stamping of feet, bravos, and without the slightest murmur of disapproval being heard" (Bingham 13; emphasis added). Unlike Chénier, who preached to the converted only, Gouges' audience was, at best, divided along the lines of the slavery issue.

Accounts of whether *L'esclavage* failed or not diverge, however, with most critics arguing that it was a failure. Carlson, for instance, writes that "despite the appropriateness of its subject matter to the sentiment of the times and superlative interpretations by Molé and Suin, the play was hissed from the stage" (148). Welschinger, who otherwise stresses the importance of *L'esclavage des noirs,* which he calls "one of the most important plays, together with the works of the *philosophes,* in the fight against slavery," also asserts that the play failed: "The famous Olympe de Gouges . . . could find no solace after *L'Esclavage des Nègres* failed" (15). These assessments are problematic in several regards. First, they rely on reviews in the press without considering the partiality of the press on slavery.[43] Welschinger's comments on the play's reception are characteristic in that respect. His review is presented as an objective evaluation based on a study of the press ("according to newspapers"), when it is, in fact, just a quote—as the quotation marks indicate—taken from a single unnamed newspaper:

> According to newspapers "this play failed on the first night. We know of few performances as stormy as that one. Outcries from both parties have nearly ended it twenty times. People shouted, harangued, laughed, whispered, whistled. . . . Very poor style, patched-up plot, far-fetched situations, trite, outdated dramaturgy. . . . Someone stood up and said the author was a woman, but this did not make the audience more indulgent." (303-4)

Defamation was a strategy frequently used by the Club Massiac to silence abolitionists (Quinney, "Decisions on Slavery" 122), and Gouges' reputation as "an eccentric old lady" (Carlson 88) or as "half-mad" (Carlson 154) originates to a large extent in these biased accounts. But as Gabriel Debien has shown, many newspapers were partially financed by or at the service of the colonists. In the *Gazette de Paris,* for instance, Rozoi, "who made himself useful to the club [Massiac] by directly attacking books, pamphlets and plays in favor of abolition," denounced, after the performance of *L'esclavage des noirs,* "the 'indirect link' between theater audience and National Assembly as a way of preparing public opinion to blame or confirm decisions of vital interest" (Debien 128). Second, critics have frequently evaluated the literary merits of the play on the basis of its alleged failure: the play failed; it was therefore a bad play. Summarizing Gouges' career as a playwright, Carlson clearly establishes a link between the two when he mentions her works to prove that "pièces de circonstance were not necessarily successful even in the receptive surroundings of Revolutionary Paris" (148). Last but not least, critics have largely ignored Gouges' own testimony: according to her, the play was a success.[44] Pitting one opinion against another does not help, however. A more useful and neutral way to assess the success or failure of *L'esclavage des noirs* is therefore to consider the following: according to the rules of the Comédie-Française, had the play failed to bring in at least 1,500 livres on opening night, it would not have been performed a second time. Since *L'esclavage* was performed three times, there is no reason to question Gouges' testimony: the play succeeded on opening night.[45]

In *Les comédiens démasqués,* Gouges accused the actors, Molé in particular, of having done all they could to ensure the failure of *L'esclavage.* According to her, colonists had used their influence to warn that if the play succeeded, they would voice their protest by canceling forty subscriptions for loges at the Comédie; they had also used their money to buy actors, she said: those who played poorly were financially rewarded (45). These accusations have usually been treated with sarcasm by critics—Welschinger views them as yet more proof of Gouges' paranoia ("délire de la persécution" [297])—as proof of Gouges' inability to concede defeat and to admit simply that her play was bad. But since critics such as Carlson and Welschinger have wrongly argued that the play failed on opening night, serious consideration should be given to Gouges' account of the fate of her play in December 1789. Why, if the play succeeded at first, did it cease to appear after January 1790?

According to Gouges, her efforts to defer the second performance of *L'esclavage* and to make proper revisions to her manuscript were rejected by Molé, who convinced her not to adjourn the second representation. She soon realized, however, that Molé's eagerness to go on with the performances of *L'esclavage* was meant to ensure its failure (*Les comédiens démasqués* 46). Granted, this accusation sounds absurd at first: why would an actor insist on performing a play, if he wanted it to fail? Gouges was far from raving, however. There was a good reason, alluded to in *Les comédiens démasqués,* and later clearly exposed by Le Chapelier at the National Assembly in 1791: it was a question of literary property (see Renouard 309–13). A royal ruling for the Comédie, still enforced in 1789, stated that a play had to be performed twelve times during the winter months (or ten in the summer) and bring in

1,500 livres per performance to remain the property of the author. If it did not, it "fell into the rules"; that is, it became the property of the Comédie (Renouard 216–217, 220). When a play failed to bring in that amount twice, the author no longer could ask to have it performed, and he or she also lost his or her property rights. This is precisely what happened to *L'esclavage*. Gouges lost her rights to her play because the second and third performances failed to bring in 1,500 livres.[46]

The Comédiens' practice of making a play fail in order to legally become the owners of that play was widespread and often denounced by playwrights. Their outrage led to the measures that gave France her first "copyright" legislation, the Le Chapelier law of 1791. Summarizing playwrights' complaints, Le Chapelier justified the new law with the following arguments: "But to crown it all, playwrights are told: if actors perform your play in a cowardly manner, on a day when other entertainments will attract audiences; if they choose to put on the program another play which keeps spectators away; all these *ifs* which foul play and interest make not only likely, but very common: you've lost your property" (Renouard 311). Gouges' complaints about the Comédiens were identical: "They'll pick bad days, they'll perform my play three times in the same week and cut it crudely, they'll put the most outdated play the repertory has to offer on the program with it; they'll choose days when the audience is sure to be absent . . . : and as a result of these gentle precautions, my drama will fall into what the Comédie calls its rules, which is another way of saying that they will own it, simply because the takings will not have reached the fixed minimum" (*Les comédiens démasqués* 46). In her case, however, the Comédiens truly won: not only did they become the owners of the play, but it is more than likely that they were paid for it. The Club Massiac was known for having offered or given money to political figures in exchange for their influence on similar occasions; it is probably no coincidence that, for some "unaccounted" reason, the treasury of the Club Massiac was empty in December 1789, precisely at the time of the first performance of *L'esclavage des noirs*. According to Debien, "the account of the position on December 26 [1789] shows a deficit of [unknown] origin" but one that "must be important" (115), a statement confirmed by Lucien Leclerc: "It is doubtful that *all* revenues and expenditures appear on the books and registers located in the archives. We know, however, that in November 1789 expenditures were such that the treasurer had to remind club members of their obligation to pay their dues" (348).

Failure to take into account the historical circumstances under which *L'esclavage des noirs* was performed has led to Gouges' reputation as a failed and bad playwright. As we saw, this reputation had actually little to do with the literary merits of her play, but much to do with the unpopular political views she defended. Gouges, however, was proud of her achievements as a playwright, and she had good reasons to be. Shortly before her death, she abandoned the modesty characteristic of earlier statements concerning her alleged lack of talent. In *Testament politique,* she compared herself to Chénier, whom she had admired but bitterly envied, insinuating that political correctness, rather than literary talent, was the source of Chénier's success on the Parisian stages. To make it clear that she considered her achievements to rank at least as high as his, she wrote: "I bequeath . . . my creative genius to playwrights, they can use it [il ne leur sera pas inutile], and to the famous Chesnier in particular, my know-how in drama [ma logique théâtrale]" (11). The comparison with Chénier is not out of place. Gouges' willingness to experiment certainly exceeded Chénier's, but as a result, her staging innovations—such as having the Comédiens "adopt Negro color and clothing" to portray *L'esclavage's* black slave characters—were often viewed as too daring and too dangerous at the time. She was aware that she was breaking new ground in stage realism, and proud of it,[47] and she fully deserves recognition for her originality and creativity. Finally, regardless of the soundness of her political views, her pleas for tolerance and her courage have to be acknowledged. As opposed to Chénier, Gouges had no constituency ready to support her: not on the woman question, which she embodies in her determination to be a successful playwright; not on her vision of the ideal form of government for France; and also not on the issue of slavery—however moderate her demands might seem today. This lack of support from contemporary audiences is precisely what characterizes her plays, and *L'esclavage des noirs* in particular, as true politically committed drama.

CHAPTER 4
Translations of Gouges

"REFLECTIONS ON NEGROES"[1]

Sylvie Molta

I have always been interested in the deplorable fate of the Negro race. I was just beginning to develop an understanding of the world, at that age when children hardly think about anything, when I saw a Negress for the first time. Seeing her made me wonder and ask questions about her color.

People I asked did not satisfy my curiosity and my reason. They called those people brutes, cursed by Heaven. As I grew up, I clearly realized that it was force and prejudice that had condemned them to that horrible slavery, in which Nature plays no role, and for which the unjust and powerful interests of whites are alone responsible.

Convinced for a long time of this truth and troubled by their dreadful situation, I dealt with their story in the very first work I wrote. Several men had taken an interest in them and worked to lighten their burden, but none of them had thought of presenting them on stage in their costume and their color as I would have tried, if the Comédie-Française had not been against it.

Mirza had kept her native language; nothing was more touching. It added a lot to the interest of the play. All the experts agreed, except for the actors at the Comédie-Française. But let us not talk about my play any longer. The way it was approved for performance, I present it to the Public.[2]

Let us go back to the dreadful lot of the Negroes. When will we turn our attention to changing it, or at least to easing it? I know nothing about the Politics of Governments, but they are fair. Now the Law of Nature was never more apparent in them. People are equal everywhere. Fair kings do not want any slaves; they know that they possess obedient subjects, and France will not abandon the wretched in their suffering, ever since greed and ambition have inhabited the most remote islands. Europeans, thirsting for blood and for this metal that greed calls gold, have made Nature change in these happy lands. Fathers have repudiated their children, sons have sacrificed their fathers, brothers have fought, and the defeated have been sold like cattle at the market. What am I saying? It has become a trade in the four corners of the world.

Trading people! Heavens! And Nature does not quake! If they are animals, are we not also like them? How are the whites different from this race? It is in the color. . . . Why do blonds not claim superiority over brunettes who bear a resemblance to mulattos? Why is the mulatto not superior to the Negro? Like all the different types of animals, plants, and minerals that Nature has produced, people's color also varies. Why does not the day argue with the night, the sun with the moon, and the stars with the sky? Everything is different, and herein lies the beauty of Nature. Why then destroy its Work?

Is mankind not its most beautiful masterpiece? Ottomans exploit whites in the same way we exploit Blacks. We do not accuse them of being barbarian or inhuman, and we are equally cruel to people whose only means of resistance is their submissiveness.

But when submissiveness once starts to flag, what results from the barbaric despotism of the Islanders and West Indians? Revolts of all kinds, carnage increased with the troops' force, poisonings, and any atrocities people can commit once they revolt. Is it not monstrous of Europeans, who have acquired vast plantations by exploiting others, to have Blacks flogged from morning to night? These miserable souls would cultivate their fields no less if they were allotted more freedom and kindness.

Is their fate not among the cruelest, and their labor the hardest, without Whites inflicting the most horrible punishments on them, and for the smallest fault? Some speak about changing their condition, finding ways to ease it, without fearing that this race of men misuses a kind of freedom that remains subordinate.

I understand nothing about Politics. Some predict that widespread freedom would make the Negro race as essential as the white race, and that after they have been allowed to be masters of their lives, they will be masters of their will, and able to raise their children at their side. They will be more exact and diligent in their work. Intolerance will not torment them anymore, and the right to rise up like others will make them wiser and more human. Deadly conspiracies will no longer have to be feared. They will cultivate freely their own land like the farmers in Europe and will not leave their fields to go to foreign Nations.

Their freedom will lead some Negroes to desert their country, but much less than those who leave the French countryside. Young people hardly come of age with the requisite strength and courage before they are on their way to Paris to take up the noble occupation of lackey or porter. There are a hundred servants for one position, whereas our fields lack farmers.

This freedom will produce a large number of idle, unhappy, and bad persons of any kind. May each nation set wise and salutary limits for its people; this is the art of Sovereigns and Republican States.

My instincts could help, but I will keep myself from presenting my opinion, for I should be more knowledgeable and enlightened about the Politics of Governments. As I have said, I do not know anything about Politics, and I freely give my observations, both good and bad. I, more than anyone, must be interested in the fate of these unfortunate Negroes, since it has been five years since I conceived a play based on their tragic History.

I have only one piece of advice to give to the actors of the Comédie-Française, and it is the only favor I will ask of them, that is to wear the color and costume of the Negro race. Never has the occasion been more opportune, and I hope that the Play will have an effect in favor of these victims of whites' ambition.

The costume will contribute greatly to the interest of this Play, which will inspire the pens and the hearts of our best writers. My goal will thus be attained, my ambition satisfied, and the Comédie-Française will be honored rather than dishonored by the issue of color.

My happiness would be too immeasurable if I were to see my Play performed as I wish. This weak sketch would require a poignant group of scenes for it to serve posterity. Painters ambitious enough to paint the tableau would be considered Fathers of the wisest and most worthwhile Humanity, and I am convinced that they would favor the subject of this small Play over its dramatic expression.

So, Ladies and Gentlemen, act out my Play: it has waited long enough, and, to tell you the truth, probably much longer. As you have wanted, it is now published. I join every Nation in asking for its production, and I am convinced they will not disappoint me. This feeling that could be considered pride in others results from the impact that the public outcry in favor of Negroes has had on me. Any reader who appreciates my work will be convinced of my sincerity.[3]

But with you, Ladies and Gentlemen, I must justify myself, since you have tried to ridicule me with regard to Molière and M. Mercier, who enjoys my affection and respect in many ways, since, before me, he was treated so poorly by you. But he is a perfect gentleman. He knows nothing about adulation or the lowly jealousy of unimportant literary figures. I am not surprised that you were unable to appreciate him. Despite all my grievances against you, I have no doubt that you are able to render justice if you want to. But you must agree that you often do not want to. Falseness is pleasing to your character, and well-turned phrases to your talent. Dramatic expression escapes you, even though that is what should matter to you the most.

Forgive me these last statements; they are painful to express, but therein lies my right to them. Farewell, Ladies and Gentlemen, act my play as you see fit; I shall not attend the rehearsals. I turn over all rights to my son; may he make good use of them and protect himself from becoming a writer for the Comédie-Française. If he believes me, he will never pick up a pen to write literature. However, I was unable to prevent him from giving in to the general impulse. *Noyon's Daughter* suddenly made him an author.[4] The worthy exploits of Monseigneur the duc d'Orléans inspired his pen. I admit that I contributed to some of the anecdotes and that, other than the outcome of this frivolity, the production would be hard to justify and I would have left it anonymous. But convinced that it is poorly written, I am putting it at the end of my last volume. There are authors who always surround themselves in mystery unless they succeed. But I see no dishonor in a mediocre work. This one merits indulgence, as much for its objective as for its time. But he worked on the outline that Noyon's daughter gave him and, with one of his friends, made a comic opera that I think could have some success. I want the author's public to know and accept that the worst things in it are mine. I only spent an hour at most on it, and I gave it little thought. My son was hardly wiser, and my mediocrity in this genre only weakened his first effort. I thus ask indulgence for him, and for me the greatest rigor. I apologize in advance. And to gain my reader's pardon, I ask him to remember *Zamor and Mirza* and *Le siècle des grands hommes*. He will soon forget that I acted as a cruel stepmother in trying to be a good mother.

BLACK SLAVERY, OR THE HAPPY SHIPWRECK[5]
Maryann DeJulio

PREFACE[6]

In the Dark Ages men made war; in the most Enlightened Age, they want to destroy themselves. Will there ever be a science, a regime, an epoch, or an age when men will live in peace? The Learned may dwell upon and lose themselves in these metaphysical observations. I, a woman, who have only studied the good principles of Nature, I no longer set forth man's nature; my rude learning has taught me to judge things only after my soul. My works, therefore, bear but the color of human nature.

Here, at last, is my Play, which avarice and ambition have proscribed, but of which just men approve. What must my opinion be of these varying opinions? As an Author, I am permitted to approve this philanthropic work, but as an ear-witness of the disastrous accounts of the troubles in America, I should abhor my Work, if an invisible hand had not performed this revolution in which I did not participate except to prophesy its occurrence. However, you blame me, you accuse me without even having seen *Black Slavery*, accepted in 1783 by the Comédie-Française, printed in 1786, and performed in December 1789. The Colonists, whose cruel ambition was effortlessly satisfied, won over the Comédiens, and you can be sure . . . that the interception of my Play did not hurt their receipts, but it is neither the Comédiens nor the Colonists whom I wish to put on trial; it is rather myself.

I denounce myself publicly; here I am under arrest: I am going to plead my own case before this august Tribunal, frivolous . . . but redoubtable. I deliver myself to a vote of conscience; I shall win or lose by the majority.

The author and friend of the truth, who has no interest but to remind men of the charitable principles of Nature, who respects laws and social conventions no less, is still an estimable mortal, and if her writings do not produce all the good that she had hoped for, she is to be pitied more than blamed.

It is, therefore, important for me to convince the Public and the detractors of my Work of the purity of my maxims. This work may lack talent, but not morals. It is by means of these morals that public opinion must reconsider my case.

When the Public has read my Play, conceived in a time when it was to appear as a Novel drawn from an old Fairy tale play, it will recognize that it is the faithful tableau of the current situation in America. I give you, today, in the fourth year of the Republic, my Play such as it was approved under the despotism of the press. I offer my Play to the Public as an authentic document, which is necessary for my vindication. Is my work inflammatory? No. Is it insurgent? No. Does it have a moral? Yes, without doubt. What, then, do these Colonists want from me when they speak of me in such unsparing terms? But they are wretches. I pity them and shall respect their deplorable fate; I shall not even permit myself to remind them of their inhumanity: I shall permit myself only to mention all that I have written to preserve their properties and their most cherished interests: my Play is proof thereof.

I shall now address myself to you, slaves, men of color; perhaps I have an incontestable right to blame your ferocity: cruel, you justify tyrants when you imitate them. Most of your Masters were humane and charitable, and in your blind rage you do not distinguish between innocent victims and your persecutors. Men were not born in irons, and now you prove them necessary. If force majeure is on your side, why exercise all the fury of your fiery lands? Poison, irons, daggers—they say you invent the most barbarous and atrocious tortures with no effort. What cruelty! what inhumanity! Ah! How you make them moan, they who wanted to prepare you, by temperate means, a kinder fate, a fate more worthy of envy than all those illusory advantages whereby the authors of the calamities in France and America have misled you. Tyranny will follow you just as crime clings to depraved men. Nothing will reconcile you with yourselves. Fear my prediction, you know whether it be well founded or not. My pronouncements are based on reason and divine justice. I retract nothing: I abhor your Tyrants, your cruelties horrify me.

Ah! If my counsel reaches you, if you recognize its worth, I dare believe that your untamed wits will be calmed and that my counsel will restore harmony, which is indispensable to the colonial commonweal and to your own interests. These interests consist only in social order, your rights within the wisdom of the Law; this Law recognizes that all men are brothers; this august Law that cupidity had plunged into chaos has been finally extricated from the dark. If the savage, a ferocious man, fails to recognize this Law, then he is made for irons, to be tamed like a brute.

Slaves, people of color, you who live closer to Nature than Europeans, than your Tyrants, recognize these gentle laws and show that an enlightened Nation was not mistaken to treat you like men and give you rights that you never had in America. To draw nearer to justice and humanity, remember, and never lose sight of this, your Fatherland condemns you to a frightful servitude and your own parents put you up for sale: men are hunted in your frightful climes as animals are hunted elsewhere. The true Philosophy of the enlightened man prompts him to snatch his fellow man from the midst of a primitively horrible situation not only where men sold one another, but where they still ate each other. The true man has regards for all men. These are my principles, which differ greatly from those of these so-called defenders of Liberty, these firebrands, these incendiary spirits who preach equality and liberty with all the authority and ferocity of Despots. America, France, and perhaps the Universe will owe their fall to a few energumen that France has produced, the decadence of Empires, and the loss of the arts and sciences. This is perhaps a fatal truth. Men have grown old; they seem to want to be born again, and according to the principles of Brissot, animal life suits man perfectly. I love Nature more than he, she has placed the laws of humanity and wise equality in my soul; but when I consider this Nature, I often see her in contradiction with her principles, and everything then seems subordinate. Animals have their Empires, Kings, Chiefs, and their reign is peaceable; an invisible and charitable hand seems to conduct their administration. I am not entirely an enemy of M. Brissot's principles, but I believe them impracticable among men: I have treated this matter before him. I dared, after the august Author of *The Social Contract,* to provide *Man's Original Happiness,* published in 1789. I wrote a Novel, and never will men be pure enough, great enough, to recover this original happiness, which I found only in a blissful fiction. Ah! If it were possible for them to achieve this, the wise and humane laws that I establish in this social contract would make all men brothers, the Sun would be the true God that they would invoke; but always fickle, the *Social Contract, Original Happiness,* and the august Work of M. Brissot will always be chimerae and not a useful instruction. Imitations of Jean-Jacques are defaced in this new regime; what, then, would those of Mme de Gouges and M. Brissot be? It is easy, even for the most ignorant, to make revolutions in paper notebooks; but, alas! every People's experience, and now the French experience, teaches me that the most learned and the most wise do not establish their doctrines without producing all kinds of troubles.

I stray from the aim of my Preface, and time does not permit me to give free reign to philosophical reasons. It was a question of justifying black Slavery, which the odious Colonists had proscribed and presented as an incendiary work. Let the public judge and pronounce; I await its decree for my justification.

DRAMATIS PERSONAE

ZAMOR, educated Indian

MIRZA, young Indian, Zamor's lover

M. DE SAINT-FREMONT, Governor of an island in the Indies

MME DE SAINT-FREMONT, his wife

VALERE, French gentleman, Sophie's husband

SOPHIE, M. de Saint-Frémont's illegitimate daughter

BETZI, Mme de Saint-Frémont's maid

CORALINE, slave

INDIAN, M. de Saint-Frémont's slave steward

AZOR, M. de Saint-Frémont's valet

M. DE BELFORT, major from the garrison

JUDGE

M. de Saint-Frémont's MANSERVANT

OLD INDIAN

SEVERAL INDIAN PLANTERS of both sexes, and SLAVES

GRENADIERS and FRENCH SOLDIERS

The scene in the first act is a deserted island; in the second, a large neighboring city in the Indies; and in the third, a nearby Plantation.

BLACK SLAVERY, OR THE HAPPY SHIPWRECK
Act I

Shore of a deserted island, surrounded by steep cliffs, from which the high sea is visible in the distance. On one side in front is the open door of a hut surrounded by fruit trees from the region: the entrance to a seemingly impenetrable forest fills the other side. Just as the curtain rises, a storm agitates the waves: a ship has just broken to pieces on the rocks. The winds die down and the sea becomes calm.

SCENE I

ZAMOR, MIRZA

Zamor: Dispel your fears, my dear Mirza. This vessel is not sent by our persecutors: as far as I can judge, it is French. Alas! it has just broken to pieces on these rocks. None of the crew has escaped.

Mirza: Zamor, I fear only for you; punishment does not frighten me. I shall bless my fate if we end our days together.

Zamor: O my Mirza! How you move me!

Mirza: Alas! What have you done? my love has rendered you guilty. Without
the unhappy Mirza, you would never have run away from the best of all
Masters, and you would not have killed his confidential agent.

Zamor: The barbarian! he loved you, and that made him your tyrant. Love
rendered him fierce. The tiger dared charge me with the chastisement that
he inflicted upon you for not wanting to respond to his unbridled passion.
The education that our governor had given me added to the sensibility of
my rude manners and rendered the frightful despotism that commanded
me to punish you even more intolerable.

Mirza: You should have let me die; you would be beside our Governor, who
cherishes you like his child. I have caused your troubles and his.

Zamor: Me, let you perish! Ah! Gods! Hey! Why remind me of the virtues
and kindnesses of this respectable Master? I have performed my duty to
him: I have paid for his kindnesses with the tenderness of a son rather
than the devotion of a slave. He believes me guilty, and that is what renders my torment more frightful. He does not know what a monster he
had honored with his confidence. I have saved my fellow men from his
tyranny; but, my dear Mirza, let us destroy a memory too dear and too
fatal: we no longer have any protectors, save Nature. Benevolent Mother!
You know our innocence. No, you will not abandon us, and this deserted
spot will hide us from all eyes.

Mirza: The little that I know, I owe to you, Zamor. But tell me why Europeans
and Planters have such advantage over us poor slaves? They are, however,
made like us: we are men like them: why, then, such a great difference
between their kind and ours?

Zamor: That difference is very small; it exists only in color. But the advantages that they have over us are huge. Art has placed them above Nature:
instruction has made gods of them, and we are only men. They use us
in these climes as they use animals in theirs. They came to these regions,
seized the lands, the fortunes of the Native Islanders, and these proud
ravishers of the properties of a gentle and peaceable people in its home,
shed all the blood of its noble victims, sharing among themselves its bloody
spoils, and made us slaves as a reward for the riches that they ravished,
and that we preserve for them. These are their own fields that they reap,
sown with the corpses of the Planters, and these crops are now watered
with our sweat and our tears. Most of these barbaric masters treat us with

a cruelty that makes Nature shudder. Our wretched species has grown accustomed to these chastisements. They take care not to instruct us. If by chance our eyes were to open, we would be horrified by the state to which they have reduced us, and we would shake off a yoke as cruel as it is shameful; but is it in our power to change our fate? The man vilified by slavery has lost all his energy, and the most brutalized among us are the least unhappy. I have always shown the same zeal to my master, but I have taken care not to make my way of thinking known to my comrades. God! Divert the presage that still menaces these climes, soften the hearts of our Tyrants, and give man back the rights that he has lost in the very bosom of Nature.

Mirza: How we are to be pitied!

Zamor: Perhaps our fate will change before long. A gentle and consoling morality has unveiled European error. Enlightened men gaze compassionately upon us: we shall owe them the return of this precious liberty, man's primary treasure, of which cruel ravishers have deprived us for so long.

Mirza: I would be happy to be as well instructed as you, but I only know how to love you.

Zamor: Your artlessness charms me; it is the imprint of Nature. I leave you for a moment. Go and gather some fruit. I am going to take a walk down to the shore to collect the debris from this shipwreck. But what do I see? A woman who is struggling against the waves! Ah! Mirza, I fly to her rescue. Must excessive misfortune excuse us from being humane? (*He descends toward the rock.*)

SCENE II

Mirza: (*alone*) Zamor is going to save this poor unfortunate soul! How can I not adore such a tender, compassionate heart? Now that I am unhappy, I am more conscious of how sweet it is to soothe the misfortunes of others. (*She exits toward the forest.*)

SCENE III

Valère, alone, enters from the opposite side.

Valère: Nothing in sight on the agitated waves. O my wife! You are lost forever! Hey! Could I survive you? No: I must be reunited with you. I gathered my strength to save your life, and I have only escaped the fury of the waves. I breathe but with horror: separated from you, each instant redoubles my sorrow. I search for you in vain; in vain do I call out your name. Your voice resounds in my heart, but it does not strike my ear. I fly from you. (*He descends with difficulty and falls at the back of the Theater propped up against a boulder.*) A thick cloud covers my eyes; my strength abandons me! Almighty God, grant me strength that I may drag myself as far as the sea! I can no longer hold myself up. (*He remains immobile from exhaustion.*)

SCENE IV
VALERE, MIRZA

Mirza: (*rushing up and catching sight of Valère*) Ah! God! Who is this man? Suppose he were coming to lay hands on Zamor and separate me from him! Alas! What would become of me? But, no, perhaps he does not have so evil a scheme; he is not one of our persecutors. I am suffering. . . . Despite my fears, I cannot help myself from coming to his aid. I cannot see him in this state much longer. He looks like a Frenchman. (*To Valère*) Monsieur, Frenchman. . . . He does not respond. What to do! (*She calls out.*) Zamor, Zamor. (*with reflection*) Let us climb upon the rock to see if he is coming. (*She runs up to it and immediately climbs down.*) I do not see him. (*She returns to Valère.*) Frenchman, Frenchman, answer me! He does not answer. What help can I give him? I have nothing; how unhappy I am! (*taking Valère's arm and striking his hand*) Poor stranger, he is very ill, and Zamor is not here: he has more strength than I; but let us search in our hut for something that will revive him. (*She exits.*)

SCENE V
VALERE, ZAMOR, SOPHIE

Zamor enters from the side by the rock, carrying Sophie, garbed in a white dressing-gown, belted, and with her hair disheveled, who appears to have fainted in his arms.

Zamor: Regain your strength, Madame. I am only an Indian slave, but I shall help you.

Sophie: (*in a dying voice*) Whoever you may be, leave me. Your pity is more cruel to me than the waves. I have lost what was most dear to me. Life is odious to me. O Valère! O my spouse! What has become of you?

Valère: Whose voice is that I hear? Sophie!

Sophie: (*noticing Valère*) What do I see. . . . It is he!

Valère: (*getting up and falling at Sophie's feet*) Almighty God! You have returned my Sophie to me! O dear spouse! Object of my tears and my tenderness! I succumb to my suffering and to my joy.

Sophie: Divine Providence! you have saved me! Complete your work, and return my father to me.

SCENE VI

VALERE, ZAMOR, SOPHIE, MIRZA

Mirza, bringing some fruit and water, enters running, and surprised to see a woman, she stops.

Zamor: Approach, Mirza, there is nothing to fear. These are two unfortunates like us; they have rights on our souls.

Valère: Compassionate being to whom I owe my life and my spouse's life! You are not a Savage; you have neither the language nor the manners of one. Are you the master of this Island?

Zamor: No, but we have been living here alone for several days. You seem like a Frenchman to me. If the company of slaves does not seem contemptible to you, they will gladly share the possession of this Island with you, and if destiny wills it, we shall end our days together.

Sophie: (*to Valère*) How this language interests me! (*to the slaves*) Generous mortals, I would accept your offers, if I were not going farther to look for a father whom I shall perhaps never find again! We have been wandering the seas for two years, and we have found no trace of him.

Valère: Well then! Let us remain in this spot: let us accept the hospitality of these Indians for awhile and be persuaded, my dear Sophie, that by dint of perseverance we shall find the author of your days on this Continent.

Sophie: Cruel destiny! We have lost everything; how can we continue our search?

Valère: I share your sorrow. (*to the Indians*) Generous mortals, do not abandon us.

Mirza: Us, abandon you! Never, no, never.

Zamor: Yes, my dear Mirza, let us console them in their misfortunes. (*to Valère and Sophie*) Rely upon me; I am going to examine the entire area by the cliff: if your lost goods are among the debris from the vessel, I promise to bring them to you. Enter our hut, unhappy Strangers; you need rest. I am going to try to calm your agitated spirits.

Sophie: Compassionate mortals, we must repay you for so much kindness! You have saved our lives, how shall I ever acquit myself toward you?

Zamor: You owe us nothing; in helping you, I obey only the voice of my heart. (*He exits.*)

SCENE VII

MIRZA, SOPHIE, VALERE

Mirza: (*to Sophie*) I like you, though you are not a slave. Come, I shall care for you. Give me your arm. Ah! what a pretty hand, so different from mine! Let us sit here. (*gaily*) How happy I am to be with you! You are as fair as our Governor's wife.

Sophie: Yes? You have a Governor on this Island?

Valère: It seems to me that you told us that you live here alone?

Mirza: (*with frankness*) Oh! It is quite true, and Zamor has not deceived you. I spoke to you of the Governor of the Colony, who does not live with us. (*aside*) I must be careful of what I am going to say, for if he knew that Zamor has killed a white man, he would not want to remain with us.

Sophie: (*to Valère*) Her ingenuousness delights me; her countenance is sweet, and prejudices in her favor.

Valère: I have not seen a prettier Negress.

Mirza: You mock me. I am not for all that the prettiest. But tell me, are all French women as fair as you? They must be so, for Frenchmen are all good, and you are not slaves.

Valère: No, Frenchmen have a horror of slavery. One day more free they will see about tempering your fate.

Mirza: (*with surprise*) More free one day—how so, are you not free?

Valère: We are free in semblance, but our irons are only the heavier. For several centuries the French have been groaning under the despotism of Ministers and Courtiers. The power of a single Master is in the hands of a thousand Tyrants who trample the People underfoot. This People will one day break its irons, and resuming all its rights under Natural Law, it will teach these Tyrants what the union of a people too long oppressed and enlightened by a sound philosophy can do.

Mirza: Oh! Dear God! There are then evil men everywhere!

SCENE VIII

ZAMOR, on the cliff, SOPHIE, VALERE, MIRZA

Zamor: The worst has happened, unhappy Strangers! You have no hope. A wave has just swallowed up the remains of the equipage, along with all your hopes.

Sophie: Alas! What shall become of us?

Valère: A vessel can land on this Island.

Zamor: You do not know, unhappy Strangers, how dangerous this coast is. There are only unfortunates like Mirza and me, who have dared to approach it and overcome all perils to inhabit it. We are, however, only two leagues from one of the bigger towns in the Indies, a town that I shall never see again unless our tyrants come and tear us away from here to make us suffer the punishment to which we are condemned.

Sophie: Torture!

Valère: What crime have you both committed? Ah! I see; you are too educated for a slave, and the person who gave you your instruction has paid a high price, no doubt.

Zamor: Monsieur, do not hold your fellow men's prejudices against me. I had a Master who was dear to me: I would have sacrificed my life to prolong his days, but his Steward was a monster whom I have purged from the land. He loved Mirza, but his love was scorned. He learned that she preferred me, and in his fury he had me suffer frightful treatment; but the most terrible was to demand that I become the instrument of his vengeance against my dear Mirza. I rejected such a commission with horror. Irritated by my disobedience, he came at me with his naked sword. I avoided the blow that he wanted to give me. I disarmed him and he fell dead at my feet. I had but the time to carry off Mirza and to flee with her in a longboat.

Sophie: How I pity him, this unhappy man! Though he has committed murder, this murder seems worthy of mercy to me.

Valère: I am interested in their fate. They brought me back to life; they saved yours: I shall defend them at the cost of my days. I shall go myself to see his Governor: If he is a Frenchman, he must be humane and generous.

Zamor: Yes, Monsieur, he is a Frenchman and the best of men.

Mirza: Ah! If all the Colonists were like him, we would be less unhappy.

Zamor: I have belonged to him since I was eight years old; he took pleasure in having me educated and loved me as if I had been his son, for he never had one, or perhaps he was deprived of one: he seems to regret something. Sometimes you hear him sighing; surely he strives to hide some great sorrow. I have often surprised him in tears: he adores his wife, and she him in kind. If it depended only upon him, I would be pardoned; but they need an example. There is no hope of a pardon for a slave who has raised a hand against his Commander.

Sophie: (*to Valère*) I do not know why this Governor interests me. The account of his sorrows lies heavy on my heart. He is generous, clement; he can pardon you. I shall go myself and throw myself at his feet. His name? If only we could leave this Island.

Zamor: His name is M. de Saint-Frémont.

Sophie: Alas! This name is unknown to me, but no matter; he is a Frenchman: he will hear me, and I hope to move him to mercy. (*to Valère*) If with the longboat that saved them, we could guide ourselves into port, there is no peril that I would not brave to defend them.

Valère: I admire you, my dear Sophie! I approve of your plan: we have only to make our way to their Governor. (*to the Slaves*) My friends, this step barely discharges us of our obligation to you. Happy if our entreaties and our tears move your generous Master! Let us leave, but what do I see? Here are some slaves who are examining us and who are hurrying toward us. They are carrying chains.

Sophie: Unhappy lovers, you are lost!

Zamor: (*turns around and sees the Slaves*) Mirza, the worst has happened! They have found us.

SCENE IX

THE SAME, AN INDIAN, several SLAVES who are running down from the rock

Indian: (*to Zamor*) Scoundrel! At last, I find you. You will not escape punishment.

Mirza: May they put me to death before him!

Zamor: O my dear Mirza!

Indian: Put them in chains.

Valère: Monsieur, listen to our entreaties! What are you going to do with these Slaves?

Indian: A terrible example.

Sophie: You are taking them away to put them to death? You will take away our lives before tearing them from our arms.

Valère: What are you doing? My dear Sophie! We can place all our hope in the Governor's indulgence.

Indian: Do not flatter yourself. The Governor must set an example for the Colony. You do not know this cursed race; they would slit our throats without pity if the voice of humanity spoke in their favor. That is what you must always expect, even from Slaves who have received some instruction. They are born to be savages and tamed like animals.

Sophie: What frightful prejudice! Nature did not make them Slaves; they are men like you.

Indian: What language do you speak, Madame?

Sophie: The same that I would speak before your Governor. It is gratitude that interests me in these unfortunates, who know better than you the rights of pity. He whose position you uphold was no doubt a wicked man.

Zamor: Ah! Madame, cease your entreaties. His soul is hardened and does not know kindness. It is his daily task to make this rigor conspicuous. He believes that he would not be performing his duty if he did not push rigor to cruelty.

Indian: Wretch!

Zamor: I fear you no longer. I know my fate and shall submit to it.

Sophie: How their misfortune renders them interesting! What would I not do to save them!

Valère: (*to the Indian*) Take us away with them, Monsieur. You will oblige us to withdraw from here. (*aside*) I hope to move the Governor to mercy.

Indian: I consent with pleasure, especially as the danger leaving this Island is not the same as that risked to reach it.

Valère: But Monsieur, how were you able to land here?

Indian: I risked everything for the good of the Colony. See if it is possible to pardon them. We are no longer the Masters of our Slaves. Our Governor's life is perhaps in danger, and order will be restored on the plantations once these two poor wretches are punished. (*to the Negroes*) Negroes, fire the cannon, and let the prearranged signal announce to the Fort that the criminals are taken.

Zamor: Let us go, Mirza; we are going to die.

Mirza: Ah! God! I am the cause of his death.

Zamor: Our good action in saving these Strangers will cast some charm on our last moments, and we shall taste at least the sweetness of dying together.

Zamor and Mirza are led away. The other characters follow them, and they are all about to embark. The next moment the ship carrying them goes past.

END OF ACT I

Act II

A Company Drawing-room with Indian furnishings

SCENE I

BETZI, AZOR

Betzi: Well, Azor, what do they say about Mirza and Zamor? They are searching for them everywhere.

Azor: There is talk of putting them to death on the rock by the plantation. I even believe that preparations for their punishment are being readied. I tremble that they may find them.

Betzi: But the Governor can pardon them. He is their master.

Azor: That must be impossible, for he loves Zamor, and he says that he never had any complaint with him. The whole Colony is asking for their death; he cannot refuse it without compromising himself.

Betzi: Our Governor was not made to be a Tyrant.

Azor: How good he is to us! All Frenchmen are the same, but the Natives of this country are much more cruel.

Betzi: I have been assured that we were not originally slaves.

Azor: Everything leads us to believe that. There are still climes where Negroes are free.

Betzi: How fortunate they are!

Azor: Ah! We are really to be pitied.

Betzi: And no one undertakes our defense! We are even forbidden to pray for our fellow men.

Azor: Alas! the father and mother of the unfortunate Mirza will witness their daughter's punishment.

Betzi: Such ferociousness!

Azor: That is how they treat us.

Betzi: But tell me, Azor, why did Zamor kill the Steward?

Azor: I was assured that it was out of jealousy. You know quite well that Zamor was Mirza's lover.

Betzi: Yes, it was you who informed me of it.

Azor: The Commander loved her too.

Betzi: But he ought not to kill him for that.

Azor: That is true.

Betzi: There were other reasons.

Azor: That may well be, but I am unaware of them.

Betzi: If we could let them escape, I am sure that M. and Mme de Saint-Frémont would not be angry.

Azor: I think that too, but those who would serve them would put themselves at great risk.

Betzi: No doubt, but there would not be a death penalty.

Azor: Perhaps, I still know that I would not risk it.

Betzi: We should at least talk to their friends; they could win over the other slaves. They all love Zamor and Mirza.

Azor: There is talk of arming the entire regiment.

Betzi: It is hopeless.

Azor: On the contrary, we must urge them to obey for the good of our comrades.

Betzi: You are right; do it if you can, for I would never have the strength for it.

SCENE II

THE SAME, CORALINE

Coraline: (*running*) O my dear comrades! What bad news I bring you! It is certain that cannon fire has been heard and that Zamor and Mirza are captured.

Azor: Come, that is not possible, Coraline.

Betzi: Almighty God!

Coraline: I was at the port when they announced this unfortunate news. Several Colonists were impatiently awaiting a ship that could be seen in the distance. It finally entered port, and all the planters surrounded it immediately. I ran away, trembling. Poor Mirza! unhappy Zamor! our tyrants will not pardon them.

Azor: Oh! You may take my word for it; they will soon be dead.

Betzi: Without a hearing? Without a trial?

Coraline: Trial! We are forbidden to be innocent and to justify ourselves.

Azor: What generosity! And in the bargain, they sell us like cattle at the market.

Betzi: A commerce of men! O Heaven! humanity is repulsive.

Azor: It is quite true: my father and I were bought on the Coast of Guinea.

Coraline: There, there, my poor Azor, whatever our deplorable fate, I have a presentiment that we shall not always be in irons, and perhaps before long. . . .

Azor: Well then! What shall we see? Shall we be masters in our turn?

Coraline: Perhaps. But no, we would be too wicked. Indeed, to be good, one must be neither master nor slave.

Azor: Neither master nor slave. Oh! Oh! And what do you want us to be? Do you know, Coraline, that you no longer know what you are saying, though our comrades assure us that you know more about this than we do?

Coraline: There, there, my poor boy, if you knew what I know! I read in a certain Book that to be happy one need only be free and a good Farmer. We lack but liberty. Let them give it to us, and you will see that there will no longer be masters or slaves.

Azor: I do not understand you.

Betzi: Neither do I.

Coraline: My God, how kind you both are! Tell me, was Zamor not free? And because of that, did he want to leave our kind Master? We shall all do the same thing. Let the Masters give liberty; no Slave will leave the workshop. Imperceptibly, the rudest among us will instruct themselves, recognize the laws of humanity and justice, and our superiors will find in our attachment, in our zeal, the reward for this kindness.

Azor: You speak like a man! You sound like the Governor. . . . Oh! One must have wit to retain everything that others say. But here is Madame.

Betzi: Here is Madame, let us be silent!

Coraline: We must not tell Madame that we fear that Zamor has been captured. That would grieve her too much.

Azor: Oh! Yes.

SCENE III

THE SAME, MME DE SAINT-FREMONT

Mme de Saint-Frémont: My children, I need to be alone. Leave me, and do not enter unless I call for you or you have some news to announce. (*They exit.*)

SCENE IV

Mme de Saint-Frémont: (*alone*) My spouse has gone out on account of this unfortunate matter: he went to one of the plantations where his attendance was requested. Since this catastrophe, revolt reigns in the minds of our slaves. All maintain that Zamor is innocent, and that he only killed the Commander because he saw himself forced to, but the Colonists have gathered to ask for the death of Mirza and Zamor, and Mirza and Zamor are being sought every-where. My husband really wanted to pardon Zamor, though he pronounced his judgment, as well as that of poor Mirza, who is to perish with her lover. Alas! Expectation of their punishment throws me into a profound sadness. I am thus not born to be happy! In vain am I adored by my spouse: my love cannot conquer the melancholy that consumes him. He has been suffering for more than ten years, and I cannot divine the cause of his sorrow. It is the only one of his secrets that he has not entrusted to me. When he returns, I must redouble my efforts to wrench it from him. But I hear him.

SCENE V

MME DE SAINT-FREMONT, M. DE SAINT-FREMONT

Mme de Saint-Frémont: Well, then! My dear, did your presence dispel this unrest?

M. de Saint-Frémont: All my slaves have returned to their duties, but they ask me to pardon Zamor. This matter is quite delicate (*aside*) and as a crown-ing misfortune, I have just received heartrending news from France.

Mme de Saint-Frémont: What are you saying, my dear? You seem to reproach yourself. Ah! If you are only guilty with regard to me, I forgive you so long as your heart is still mine. You look away. I see the tears in your eyes. Ah! My dear, I no longer have your trust. I am becoming tiresome to you. I am going to retire.

M. de Saint-Frémont: You, become tiresome to me! Never, never. Ah! If I could have strayed from my duty, your sweetness alone would have brought me back to your feet, and your great virtues would render me still more in love with your charms.

Mme de Saint-Frémont: But you hide a secret worry from me. Confess it to me. Your stifled sighs make me suspect so. France was dear to you; she is your Country. . . . Perhaps an inclination. . . .

M. de Saint-Frémont: Stop, stop, dear spouse, and do not reopen an old wound that had closed beside you. I fear distressing you.

Mme de Saint-Frémont: If I am dear to you, you must give me proof of it.

M. de Saint-Frémont: What kind of proof do you demand?

Mme de Saint-Frémont: The kind that reveals the causes of your affliction to me.

M. de Saint-Frémont: This is what you want?

Mme de Saint-Frémont: I demand it. Be forgiven, by this complaisance, for this secret that you have kept from me for so long.

M. de Saint-Frémont: I obey. I am from a Province where unjust and inhuman laws deprive younger children of the equal share that Nature gives
to children born of the same father and mother. I was the youngest of
seven; my parents sent me to the Court to ask for employment, but how
could I have succeeded in a country where virtue is a chimera, and where
nothing is obtained without intrigue and baseness. However, I made the
acquaintance of a worthy Scottish Gentleman who had come with the same
purpose. He was not rich and had a daughter in a Convent: he took me
there. This interview turned fatal for both of us. The father, after several
months, left for the army: He enjoined me to go and see his daughter and
even said that she could be entrusted to me when she wanted to go out.
This worthy friend, this good father, did not foresee the consequences
occasioned by his imprudence. He was killed in battle. His daughter was
all alone in the world, without family or friends. She saw only me and
appeared to desire only my presence. Love rendered me guilty. Spare me
the rest: I swore an oath to be her spouse; there is my crime.

Mme de Saint-Frémont: But, my dear, did you determine by yourself to
abandon her?

M. de Saint-Frémont: Who, me? to have abandoned such a fine woman?
Ah! The longest absence would never have made me forget her. I could
not marry her without the consent of my whole family. She became the
mother of a daughter. Our liaison was discovered; I was banished. They
procured me a commission as Captain in a regiment that was leaving
for the Indies and made me embark in it. Not long after, I received the
false news that Clarisse was dead, and that only my daughter remained.
I saw you every day; with time your presence weakened the impression
that Clarisse's image still made on my heart. I requested your hand, you
accepted my vows, and we were united. But by an over-refinement of
barbarity, the cruel relation who had deceived me informed me that
Clarisse was still living.

Mme de Saint-Frémont: Alas! At what fatal price have I the honor of being your spouse! My dear, you are more unhappy than guilty. Clarisse
herself would forgive you, if she were witness to your remorse. We must
conduct an intensive search, so that your property and mine may acquit
us toward these unfortunates. I have no other relations but yours. I am
making your daughter my heiress, but your heart is a treasure that it is
not in my power to surrender to another.

M. de Saint-Frémont: Ah! Worthy spouse, I admire your virtues. Alas! I see only Clarisse who was capable of imitating them. It is thus at opposite ends of the earth that I was destined to meet the fairest and the most virtuous of your sex!

Mme de Saint-Frémont: You deserve a companion worthy of yourself; but, my dear, consider that in marrying me, you consented to take the name of my father, who, by giving you his name, had no other aim save yielding his position to you as to an adopted son. You must write your relations, especially your most faithful friends, to renew the search and give us prompt news of these unfortunates. I believe, my dear, that I shall have the strength to leave you in order to seek the daughter whom you fathered. I already feel a mother's compassion for her, but at the same time I shudder. O my dear, my dear! If I had to separate from you! If Clarisse tore you from my arms! . . . Her misfortunes, her virtues, her charms. . . . Ah! Forgive, forgive my despair, forgive me, dear spouse; you are not capable of abandoning me and making two victims for one.

M. de Saint-Frémont: Dear spouse! O half of myself! Cease breaking this heart, which already grieves too much. No doubt Clarisse is no longer alive, as it has been two years now since all the funds that I sent to France for her and for my daughter were sent back to me. What has become of them is not even known. But someone is coming; we shall resume this conversation later.

SCENE VI

THE SAME, A JUDGE

Judge: Monsieur, I have come to inform you that the criminals are captured.

Mme de Saint-Frémont: What! So soon! Time would have erased their crime.

M. de Saint-Frémont: (*grieved*) What a frightful example I am obliged to give!

Judge: Remember, Monsieur, your father-in-law's disgrace in this instance. He was constrained to give up his position for having exercised it with too much kindness.

M. de Saint-Frémont: (*aside*) Unhappy Zamor, you are going to perish! I have thus raised you from childhood only to see you dragged off to be tortured. (*aloud*) That my good offices should become fatal for him! If I had left him in his rude manners, perhaps he would not have committed this crime. He had no vicious inclinations in his soul. Honesty and virtue distinguished him in the bosom of slavery. Raised in a simple and hard life, despite the instruction that he had received, he never forgot his roots. How sweet it would be for me to be able to justify him! As a simple planter, I would perhaps be able to temper his arrest; but as Governor, I am forced to deliver him to the full rigor of the law.

Judge: They must be put to death at once, more especially as two Europeans have incited a general revolt among the Slaves. They depicted your Commander as a monster. The Slaves listened avidly to these seditious speeches, and all have promised not to execute the orders that they were given.

M. de Saint-Frémont: Who are these foreigners?

Judge: They are French citizens who were found on the coast where these criminals had taken refuge. They claim that Zamor saved their lives.

M. de Saint-Frémont: Alas! These unfortunate French citizens were no doubt shipwrecked, and gratitude alone has produced this indiscreet zeal.

Judge: You see, Governor, sir, that there is no time to lose, if you want to avoid the total ruin of our plantations. There is hopeless disorder.

M. de Saint-Frémont: I do not have the good fortune of having been born in your climes; but what sway the unfortunate hold over sensitive souls! It is not your fault if the manners of your country familiarized you with these harsh treatments that you exercise without remorse on men who have no other defense save their timidity, and whose work, so ill recompensed, increases our fortunes by increasing our authority over them. They have a thousand tyrants for one. Sovereigns render their People happy: every Citizen is free under a good Master, and in this country of slavery one must be barbaric in spite of oneself. Hey! How can I help abandoning myself to these reflections, when the voice of humanity cries out from the bottom of my heart: "Be kind and sensitive to the cries of the wretched." I know that my opinion must displease you: Europe, however, takes care to justify it, and I dare hope that before long there will no longer be any slaves. O Louis! O adored Monarch! Would that I could this very moment put under your eyes the innocence of these condemned souls! In granting their pardon, you would render freedom to those too long unrecognized; but no matter: you want an example; it shall be done, though the blacks assure us that Zamor is innocent.

Judge: Can you believe them in this?

M. de Saint-Frémont: They cannot deceive me, and I know more than they the virtues of Zamor. You want him to die without a hearing? I consent with regret; but you will not be able to reproach me for having betrayed the interests of the Colony.

Judge: You must do it, Governor, sir, in this matter in which you see that we are threatened with a general revolt. You must give the orders to arm the troops.

M. de Saint-Frémont: Follow me; we shall see what decision should be made.

Mme de Saint-Frémont: My dear, I see you go in sorrow.

M. de Saint-Frémont: My presence is necessary to restore order and discipline.

SCENE VII

Mme de Saint-Frémont: (*alone*) How I pity these wretches! The worst has happened! They are going to die. What chagrin for my spouse; but a greater chagrin agitates me once more. All that bears the name of a French woman terrifies me! If it were Clarisse! Oh! Unhappy me, what would be my fate? I know the virtues of my spouse, but I am his wife. No, no! let us cease in our deception! Clarisse, in misfortune, has greater rights on his soul! Let us hide the trouble that agitates me.

SCENE VIII

THE SAME

Betzi rushes up.

Mme de Saint-Frémont: What news is there, Betzi?

Betzi: (*with exaltation*) The Governor is not here?

Mme de Saint-Frémont: No, he has just gone out. Speak!

Betzi: Ah! Let me regain my senses. . . . We were on the terrace; from time to time we glanced sadly at the plantation. We see Mirza's father arrive from afar with another Slave; amid them was a foreigner, her hair disheveled and sorrow coloring her face: her eyes stared at the ground, and though she walked quickly, she seemed very preoccupied. When she was near us, she asked for Mme de Saint-Frémont. She informed us that Zamor had saved her from the fury of the waves. She added: "I shall die at the feet of the Governor if I do not obtain his pardon." She wants to implore your assistance. Here she is.

SCENE IX

THE SAME, SOPHIE, followed by all the SLAVES

Sophie: (*throwing herself at the knees of Mme de Saint-Frémont*) Madame, I embrace your knees. Have pity on an unhappy stranger who owes everything to Zamor and has no other hope but in your kind actions.

Mme de Saint-Frémont: (*aside*) Ah! I breathe again. (*aloud, while lifting Sophie to her feet*) Rise, Madame, I promise to do all that is within my power. (*aside*) Her youth, her sensibility, touches my heart beyond words. (*to Sophie*) Interesting Stranger, I shall use every means to make my spouse grant the pardon that you demand. Believe that I share your sorrows. I sense how dear these unfortunates must be to you.

Sophie: Without Zamor's help, as intrepid as it was humane, I would have perished in the waves. I owe him the good fortune of seeing you. What he did for me earns him my heartfelt assurance of his natural rights; but these rights do not render me unjust, Madame, and the testimony that they render to your rare qualities shows well enough that Zamor and Mirza cannot be reproached with a premeditated crime. What humanity! What zeal in succoring us! The fate that pursues them was to inspire them with fear rather than pity; but, far from shunning peril, Zamor has dared all. Judge, Madame, if with these feelings of humanity, a mortal can be guilty; his crime was involuntary, and to acquit him as innocent is to treat him as he deserves.

Mme de Saint-Frémont: (*to the Slaves*) My children, we must unite with the Colonists and ask that Zamor and Mirza be pardoned. We have no time to lose: (*to Sophie*) and you, whom I am burning to know, you are a French woman, perhaps you could . . . but moments are dear to us. Go back beside these unfortunates; Slaves, accompany her.

Sophie: (*transported*) Ah! Madame, so many kindnesses at once! Alas! I should like, as much as I desire it, to prove my gratitude to you. (*She kisses her hands.*) Soon my spouse will come and acquit himself of his obligation to you. Dear Valère, what happy news I am going to tell you! (*She exits with the Slaves.*)

SCENE X

MME DE SAINT-FREMONT, BETZI, CORALINE

Mme de Saint-Frémont: (*aside*) I find a resemblance in the features of this Stranger . . . What a chimera! . . . (aloud) And you, Coraline, summon M. de Saint-Frémont's Secretary.

Coraline: Ah! Madame, you are unaware of what is happening: he has just commanded your doors closed by order of the Governor. Everything is ablaze. . . . Listen, Madame . . . There is the call to arms . . . and the sound of bells. . . . (*The alarm must be heard in the distance.*)

Mme de Saint-Frémont: (*going with fright to the back of the theater*) Wretched! What is to become of me? What does my husband do?

Betzi: I tremble for my comrades.

Mme de Saint-Frémont: (*having given way to the greatest sorrow*) God, my Spouse is perhaps in danger! I fly to his aid. . . .

Coraline: Set your mind at rest, Madame, there is nothing to fear for the Governor. He is at the head of the regiment. But even if he were in the midst of the tumult, all the Slaves would respect his life. He is too cherished for anyone to want to harm him. The Slaves bear ill will only against some planters: they reproach them for the punishment of Zamor and Mirza; they are certain that without these planters, Zamor and Mirza would not have been condemned.

Mme de Saint-Frémont: (*agitated*) What! They are going to put them to death.

Coraline: Alas! Soon my poor comrades will be no longer.

Mme de Saint-Frémont: (*with alacrity*) No, my children, they shall not perish: my husband will be moved by my tears, by this Stranger's despair, who, perhaps better than I, will know how to move him. His heart does not need to be incited to do good; but he can take everything upon himself. (*aside*) And if this French woman were to give him news of his daughter! Almighty God! he would owe everything to these victims who are being dragged off to torture. (*aloud*) Let us go, Betzi, we must join my husband, tell him. . . . But how to enter into an explanation just now? I must see him myself. Where is he now?

Coraline: I do not know precisely with which regiment he is: the entire army is en route. They say only that M. de Saint-Frémont restores calm and order wherever he passes. It would be very difficult to find him just now. We have but to return to the plantation, if we have not already been forestalled. But the roads are broken up or cut off. It is hardly conceivable that they could have done so much damage in so little time.

Mme de Saint-Frémont: No matter. I fear neither danger nor weariness when the lives of two unfortunates are at stake.

END OF ACT II

Act III

A wild spot from which two pointed hills are visible, bordered by clusters of shrubby trees for as far as the eye can see. On one side is a steep cliff whose summit is a platform and whose base is perpendicular to the forestage. All the characters come on stage from the side of one of the hills, so that the audience can see them enter. A few Negro huts are scattered here and there.

SCENE I

VALERE, ZAMOR, MIRZA

Valère: Free! Both of you are free! I hasten to your chief. It will not be long before my wife reappears before our eyes. She will no doubt have obtained your pardon from M. de Saint-Frémont. I leave you for a moment but do not lose sight of you.

SCENE II

ZAMOR, MIRZA

Zamor: O my dear Mirza, our fate is deplorable! It is becoming so frightful that I fear this Frenchman's zeal to save us will only harm him and his wife. What a devastating idea!

Mirza: The same idea pursues me: but perhaps his worthy wife will have succeeded in moving our Governor to mercy; let us not grieve before her return.

Zamor: I bless my death since I die with you. But how cruel it is to lose one's life a culprit! I have been judged such; our good master believes it. That is what makes me despair.

Mirza: I want to see the Governor myself. This last wish must be granted me. I shall throw myself at his feet; I shall reveal everything to him.

Zamor: Alas! What could you say to him?

Mirza: I shall make him know the cruelty of his Commander and of his ferocious love.

Zamor: Your tenderness for me blinds you: you want to accuse yourself to render me innocent! If you scorn life at this price, do you believe me miserly enough to want to preserve it at your expense? No, my dear Mirza, there is no happiness for me on earth if I do not share it with you.

Mirza: It is the same for me; I could no longer live without seeing you.

Zamor: How sweet it would have been for us to prolong our days together! This spot reminds me of our first encounter. It is here that the tyrant received his death; it is here that they are going to end our lives. Nature seems to stand in contrast with herself in this spot. Formerly she smiled upon us: she has lost none of her attractions, but she shows us both the image of our past happiness and the horrible fate to which we shall be victim. Ah! Mirza, how cruel it is to die when one is in love.

Mirza: How you move me! Do not distress me more. I feel that my courage abandons me; but this good Frenchman is returning to us. What shall we learn from him?

SCENE III

ZAMOR, MIRZA, VALERE

Valère: O my benefactors! You must run away. Avail yourselves of these precious moments that your comrades procure for you. They are blocking off the roads; respond to their zeal and their courage. They risk themselves for you; flee to another clime. It is quite possible that my wife will not obtain your pardon. Several troops of soldiers can be seen approaching: you have time to escape by this hill. Go and live in the forests: your fellow men will receive you in their bosom.

Mirza: This Frenchman is right. Come, follow me. He loves us; let us profit from his advice. Run away with me, dear Zamor; do not fear returning to live in the heart of the forest. You scarcely remember our laws, but soon your dear Mirza will recall their gentle impression for you.

Zamor: Well! I yield. It is but for you that I cherish life. (*He embraces Valère.*) Farewell, most generous of men!

Mirza: Alas! I must leave you, then, without the pleasure of throwing myself at your wife's feet!

Valère: She will share your regrets, you can be sure; but flee this fatal spot.

SCENE IV

THE SAME, SOPHIE, SLAVES

Sophie: (*rushing into Valère's arms*) Ah! my friend, thank Heaven: these victims shall not perish. Mme de Saint-Frémont promised me they would be pardoned.

Valère: (*with joy*) Almighty God! What supreme happiness!

Zamor: Ah! I recognize her fair soul in these proceedings. (*to Valère*) Generous foreigners, may Heaven gratify your wishes! The Supreme Being will never abandon those who seek his likeness in good works.

Valère: Ah! How happy you make our days!

Mirza: How fortunate we are to have succored these French citizens! They owe us much, but we owe them even more.

Sophie: Mme de Saint-Frémont has assembled her best friends. I have instructed her of their innocence; she exerts all possible zeal in saving them. I had no trouble interesting her on their behalf; her soul is so fair, so sensitive to the troubles of the unfortunate.

Zamor: Her respectable husband equals her in merit and goodness.

Sophie: I did not have the good fortune of seeing him.

Zamor: (*alarmed*) What do I see! A throng of soldiers arriving! Ah! All is over! You have been deceived, generous Frenchman; we are lost.

Sophie: Do not become alarmed; we must first find out. . . .

Valère: I shall risk my life to defend them. Alas! They were going to run away when you came to reassure them. I am going to ask the Officer in charge of this detachment what his mission is.

SCENE V

THE SAME, MAJOR, JUDGE, INDIAN, GRENADIERS and FRENCH SOLDIERS, several SLAVES

A Company of Grenadiers and one of French Soldiers line up in the back of the Theater, their bayonets extended. A troop of Slaves with bows and arrows stands in front of them; the troop is headed by the Major, the Judge, and M. de Saint-Frémont's Slave Steward.

Valère: Monsieur, may I ask you what matter brings you here?

Major: A cruel function. I come to execute the death sentence pronounced against these wretches.

Sophie: (*upset*) You are going to have them put to death?

Major: Yes, Madame.

Valère: No, this frightful sacrifice will not be carried out.

Sophie: Mme de Saint-Frémont promised me they would be pardoned.

Judge: (*harshly*) That is not within her power; the Governor himself could not grant them their pardon. Desist therefore in your stubborn wish to save them. You make their punishment more terrible. (*to the Major*) Major, sir, execute the order that you were given. (*to the Slaves*) And you, lead the criminals to the top of the rock.

Indian Commander: Draw your bows!

Valère: Stop! (*the Slaves listen only to Valère.*)

Judge: Obey. (*The Major signals to the Soldiers; they run with their bayonets, which they point at the Slaves' chests. Not one Slave budges.*)

Zamor: (*rushing up to meet them*) What are you doing? Only I deserve to die. What have my poor comrades done to you? Why slaughter them? Turn your arms against me. (*He opens his jacket.*) Here is my breast! Cleanse their disobedience in my blood. The Colony asks only for my death. Is it necessary that so many innocent victims who were not parties to my crime perish?

Mirza: I am as guilty as Zamor; do not separate me from him: take my life out of pity; my days are bound to his destiny. I want to die first.

Valère: (*to the Judge*) Monsieur, grant a stay of execution, I beg of you. I assure you they are to be pardoned.

Major: (*to the Judge*) Monsieur, we can take this up ourselves; let us await the Governor.

Judge: (*harshly*) I listen to nothing save my duty and the law.

Valère: (*furious*) Barbarian! Though your position makes the soul callous, your being even more cruel than the laws have prescribed degrades what you do.

Judge: Major, sir, have this impudent man taken away to the Citadel.

Major: He is a Frenchman: he will answer to the Governor for his conduct. I am not required to take orders from you in this matter.

Judge: Then execute those you were given.

Sophie: (*with heroism*) This excess of cruelty gives me courage. (*She runs and places herself between Zamor and Mirza, takes them both by the hand, and speaks to the Judge.*) Barbarian! Dare to have me assassinated with them. I shall not leave them; nothing can wrench them from my arms.

Valère: (*transported*) Ah! My dear Sophie, this act of courage makes you even dearer to my heart.

Judge: (*to the Major*) Monsieur, have this impudent woman removed: you are not fulfilling your duty.

Major: (*indignant*) You demand it, but you will answer for the consequences. (*to the Soldiers*) Separate these foreigners from these slaves. (*Sophie screams while clasping Zamor and Mirza to her breast.*)

Valère: (*furious, running after Sophie*) If there is the slightest violence against my wife, then I cannot be held responsible for my actions. (*to the Judge*) And you, Barbarian, tremble: you may be sacrificed to my righteous fury.

A Slave: Were they to put us all to death, we would defend them. (*The Slaves *line up around them, forming a rampart. The Soldiers and Grenadiers approach with their bayonets.*)

Major: (*to the Soldiers*) Soldiers, stop. (*to the Judge*) I was not sent here to order carnage and bloodshed, but rather to restore order. The Governor will not be long, and his prudence will best indicate what we must do. (*to the Foreigners and the Slaves*) Take heart; I will not use force; your efforts would be useless if I wanted to exercise it. (*to Sophie*) And you, Madame, you may stand aside with these wretches; I await the Governor. (*Sophie, Zamor, and Mirza exit with several Slaves.*)

SCENE VI

VALERE, MAJOR, JUDGE, INDIAN, GRENADIERS and SOLDIERS, SLAVES

Valère: I cannot abandon my wife in this state. Do your utmost to sway M. de Saint-Frémont. I do not need to recommend clemency to you; it must reign in your soul. Warriors have always been generous.

Major: Rely upon me; withdraw and appear when it is time. (*Valère exits.*)

SCENE VII

THE SAME, EXCEPT VALERE

Major: (*to the Judge*) There, Monsieur, is the fruit of too much harshness.

Judge: We are losing the Colony today because of your moderation.

Major: More exactly, moderation is what may save the Colony. You know only your cruel laws, but I know the art of war and human nature. These are not our enemies whom we are fighting; these are our Slaves, or rather our Farmers. You would have them put to the sword to drive them to defeat, but in this instance, imprudence would take us further than you think.

SCENE VIII

THE SAME, M. DE SAINT-FREMONT

M. de Saint-Frémont enters from one side of the stage, and Valère from the other. Two Companies of Grenadiers and Soldiers escort several Slaves in irons.

Valère: (*to M. de Saint-Frémont*) Ah! Monsieur, hear our prayers: you are a Frenchman, you will be just.

M. de Saint-Frémont: I approve of your zeal, but in these climes zeal becomes indiscreet. It has even caused much trouble. I have just witnessed the most frightful attempt on a Magistrate. I had to use violence, contrary to my nature, to stop the slaves in their cruelty. I know all that you owe to these wretched creatures, but you do not have the right to defend them, nor to change the laws and manners of a country.

Valère: I have at least the right that gratitude gives to all fair souls: whatever harshness you feign, my heart appeals to your heart.

M. de Saint-Frémont: Cease your entreaties; it pains me too much to refuse you.

Valère: Your worthy wife had made us hope against hope.

M. de Saint-Frémont: She herself, Monsieur, is convinced of the absolute impossibility of what you ask.

Valère: If it is a crime to have killed a monster who made nature shudder, this crime, at least, is excusable. Zamor was defending his own life, and that is his natural right.

Judge: You abuse the Governor's complaisance: you have already been told this. The laws condemn them as homicides; can you change the laws?

Valère: No. But the laws could be tempered in favor of an involuntary crime.

Judge: Do you really think that? Temper the law in favor of a slave! We are not here in France—we need examples.

M. de Saint-Frémont: The worst has happened; the general order must be executed.

Valère: These words make my blood run cold and lie heavy on my heart. . . . Dear wife, what will become of you? Ah! Monsieur, if you knew her sensibility, her misfortunes, you would be moved. She had placed all her hopes in your goodness; she even flattered herself that you would give her some particulars on the fate of a parent, her sole support, of whom she has been deprived since childhood, and who must be settled in some part of this Continent.

M. de Saint-Frémont: Be assured that I shall do everything in my power to help you; but, as for the criminals, I can do nothing for them. Unhappy Stranger! Go and console her: she interests me without my knowing her. Deceive her even, if need be, so that she does not witness this frightful torture: tell her that they want to interrogate these wretches, that they must be left alone, and that their pardon depends perhaps upon this wise precaution.

Valère: (*weeping*) How we are to be pitied! I shall not survive their loss. (*He exits.*)

SCENE IX

THE SAME, EXCEPT VALERE

M. de Saint-Frémont: How this Frenchman grieves me! His regrets on behalf of these unfortunates increase mine. They must die, and in spite of my leaning toward clemency. . . . (*with reflection*) Zamor saved this foreigner; she is a French woman, and if I believe her husband, she is searching for a parent who lives in these climes. Would he be afraid to explain himself? His sorrow, his searches, his misfortunes. . . . Unfortunate, if it were she. . . . Where is nature going to mislead me! And why am I surprised? This Foreigner's adventure is so much like my daughter's . . . and my cankered heart would like to rediscover my daughter in her. It is the fate of the wretched to cherish hope and to find consolation in the slightest connections.

Judge: Major, sir, advance your Soldiers. (*to the Indian*) Commander, sir, escort the Slaves, and line them up as customary. (*The Indian exits with the armed Slaves, while a troop of the others throw themselves at the feet of M. de Saint-Frémont.*)

SCENE X

THE SAME, EXCEPT THE INDIAN

Armed Slaves are replaced by unarmed Slaves.

A Slave: (*kneeling*) Monseigneur, we have not been among the rebels' number. May we be permitted to ask for the pardon of our comrades! To redeem their lives we would suffer the most terrible chastisements. Increase our arduous toil; reduce our food rations—we would endure this punishment with courage. Monseigneur, you are moved to tears, I see the tears in your eyes.

M. de Saint-Frémont: My children, my friends, what are you proposing? (*to the Judge*) How do you want me to respond to this act of heroism? Ah! Heavens! They show such greatness of soul, and we dare to regard them as the meanest of men! Civilized men! You believe yourselves superior to Slaves! From infamy and the vilest state, equity and courage raise them in one instant to the ranks of the most generous mortals. You see the example before your eyes.

Judge: They know your heart well, but you cannot yield to your inclination without compromising your dignity. I know them better than you; they promise everything in these moments. Besides, these criminals are no longer in your power; they are delivered to the rigor of the law.

M. de Saint-Frémont: Well, then, I abandon them to you. Alas! Here they are. Where can I hide? How cruel this duty is!

SCENE XI

THE SAME, INDIAN, ZAMOR, MIRZA

Zamor: There is no longer any hope; our benefactors are surrounded by soldiers. Embrace me for the last time, my dear Mirza!

Mirza: I bless my fate, since the same torment reunites us. (*to an old man and an old Slave woman*) Adieu, dear authors of my days. Do not cry for your dear Mirza; she is no longer to be pitied. (*to the Slaves of her sex*) Adieu, my companions.

Zamor: Slaves, Colonists, listen to me: I have killed a man; I deserve to die. Do not regret my punishment; it is necessary for the good of the Colony. Mirza is innocent, but she cherishes her death. (*to the Slaves, in particular*) And you, my dear friends, listen to me in my last hour. I leave this life; I die innocent, but fear rendering yourselves guilty by defending me. Fear especially this factious spirit, and never deliver yourselves into excess to escape slavery. Fear breaking your irons with too much violence. Time and divine justice are on your side; stand by the Governor and his respectable spouse. Pay them by your zeal and your attachment for all that I owe them. Alas! I cannot fulfill my obligation to them. Cherish this good Master, this good father, with a filial tenderness as I have always done. I shall die happy if I can believe at least that he will miss me! (*He throws himself at his feet.*) Ah! My dear Master, am I still permitted to name you thus?

M. de Saint-Frémont: (*with intense sorrow*) These words wring my heart. Wretched man! What have you done? Go, I no longer hold it against you; I suffer enough from the fatal duty that I fulfill.

Zamor: (*bows and kisses his feet*) Ah! My dear master, death holds nothing frightful for me. You still cherish me; I die happy. (*He takes his hands.*) May I kiss these hands for the last time!

M. de Saint-Frémont: (*full of pity*) Leave me, leave me, you are breaking my heart.

Zamor: (*to the armed Slaves*) My friends, do your duty. (*He takes Mirza in his arms and climbs upon the rock with her, where they both kneel. The Slaves aim their arrows.*)

SCENE XII

THE SAME, MME DE SAINT-FREMONT with her SLAVES, GRENADIERS, and FRENCH SOLDIERS

Mme de Saint-Frémont: Stop, Slaves, and respect your governor's wife. (*to her husband*) Mercy, my friend, mercy!

SCENE XIII

THE SAME, VALERE, SOPHIE

Sophie: *(to Valère)* You restrain me in vain. I absolutely want to see them. Cruel one! You deceived me. (*to Mme de Saint-Frémont*) Ah! Madame, my strength abandons me. (*She falls into the arms of the Slaves.*)

Mme de Saint-Frémont: *(to her husband)* My friend, you see this French woman's despair; would you not be moved?

Sophie: (*recovering herself and throwing herself at the feet of M. de Saint-Frémont*) Ah Monsieur! I shall die of sorrow at your feet if you do not grant their pardon. It is within your heart and depends upon your power. Ah! If I cannot obtain it, life no longer matters to me! We have lost everything. Deprived of a mother and of my fortune, abandoned at the age of five by a father, my consolation was in saving two victims who are dear to you.

M. de Saint-Frémont: (*aside, in the keenest agitation*) My memory . . . these features . . . that time . . . her age. . . . What confusion stirs my soul. (*to Sophie*) Ah Madame! Respond to my marked attention; may I ask you the names of those who gave you birth?

Sophie: (*leaning on Valère*) Alas!

Valère: Oh my dear Sophie!

M. de Saint-Frémont: (*more warmly*) Sophie . . . (*aside*) She was named Sophie. (*aloud*) What name did you utter. . . . Speak, answer me, for pity's sake, Madame, who was your mother?

Sophie: (*aside*) What confusion agitates him, the more I examine him. . . . (*aloud*) The unfortunate Clarisse de Saint-Fort was my mother.

M. de Saint-Frémont: Ah! My daughter, recognize me. Nature did not deceive me. Recognize the voice of a father too long absent from you and from your mother.

Sophie: Ah! My father! I am dying. (*She falls into the arms of the Soldiers.*)

M. de Saint-Frémont: O my daughter! O my blood!

Sophie: What did I hear? Yes, yes, it is he. . . . His features are still etched in my soul. . . . What good fortune makes me find myself in your arms once more! I cannot express all the feelings that agitate me. But these wretched creatures, O my father, their fate is in your hands. Without their help, your daughter would have perished. Grant to nature the first favor that she asks of you. Planters, Slaves, fall at the knees of the most generous of men; one finds clemency at the feet of virtue. (*All kneel, except the Judge and the Soldiers.*)

Slaves: Monseigneur!

Planters: Governor, sir!

M. de Saint-Frémont: What do you demand of me?

All: Their pardon.

M. de Saint-Frémont: (*moved*) My children, my wife, my friends, I grant it to you.

All: What happiness! (*The Grenadiers and soldiers genuflect.*)

Major: Brave warriors, do not blush at this show of sensibility; it purifies, rather than vilifies, courage.

Mirza: Bless me! You change our unhappy fate; our happiness runneth over. Manifestations of your justice never cease.

M. de Saint-Frémont: My friends, I give you your liberty and shall look after your fortune.

Zamor: No, my master. Keep watch over your kindnesses. The most precious kindness for our hearts would be to live in your midst along with all that you hold most dear.

M. de Saint-Frémont: What! I have found my daughter again! I clasp her in my arms. A cruel fate thus ends its pursuit of me! O my dear Sophie! How I fear to learn of your mother's cruel fate.

Sophie: Alas! My poor mother is no longer! But, dear father, how sweet it is for me to see you. (*to Valère*) Dear Valère!

Valère: I share your happiness.

Mme de Saint-Frémont: My daughter, see in me only a tender mother. Your father knows my intentions, and you will soon learn them yourself. Let us concern ourselves only with the marriage of Zamor and Mirza.

Mirza: We are going to live to love each other. We shall live happily ever after.

Zamor: Yes, my dear Mirza; yes, we shall live happily ever after.

M. de Saint-Frémont: My friends, I have just granted you your pardon. Would that I might also give liberty to all your fellow men, or at least temper their fate! Slaves, listen to me; if ever your destiny were to change, do not lose sight of the love of the public good, which until now has been unknown to you. Know that man, in his liberty, needs still to submit to wise and humane laws, and without disposing yourselves to reprehensible excesses, place all your hopes in a benevolent and enlightened Government. Let us go, my friends, my children, so that a general holiday may be the happy presage of this sweet liberty.

END

"RESPONSE TO THE AMERICAN CHAMPION"
Maryann DeJulio

Since we are no longer fighting in France, sir, I agree with you that we sometimes assassinate each other, that it is imprudent to provoke assassins. But it is even more indiscreet, more indecent, and more unjust to attack people of honor, to attack them in the most inept and yet the most calumnious way, by imputing a lack of courage to M. de La Fayette, whom you fear, perhaps, at the bottom of your heart. I shall tell you that I do not know this magnanimous hero as you claim. I know only that his reputation is intact, his worth known. Like Bayard's heart,[7] his is fearless and unimpeachable. We shall perhaps owe him France's good fortune and her power as a nation. I shall not undertake to justify the famous men whom you provoke; they are all military men and French, and this title suffices for me to believe them worthy.

But if I imitate you, Sir, by this kind of challenge, I stray a bit too far from my aim and blunder into the same gross error as you with respect to me. It is not the philosophers' cause, the cause of the Amis des Noirs, that I undertake to defend; it is my own, and you shall kindly permit me to use the only weapons that are within my power. We are going then to wage war, and this single combat, thanks to my *jeanlorgnerie*,[8] will not be murderous. Yet you grant me virtues and courage beyond my sex. I could acknowledge them without too much pride, but you do not credit me less gratuitously with the ambition to consult academicians, learned men and women of letters, and all the Muses, which protect more than one fool, and on which I set very little value, except for the writers, who have respected talent with honor and integrity, about language and my feeble productions. Literary merit amounts to very little when it is stripped of these two advantages: but let us pass on to that which is important for me to tell you, and of which you are completely unaware.

You claim, sir, that the Amis des Noirs used a woman to provoke the colonists. It is certainly much more extraordinary that a man who evinces some spirit, some aptitude, and even gallantry should charge a woman with being the bearer of a cartel and want, by a venture as singular as it is cowardly, to prove her courage. I can appreciate your merit only as a kind of Don Quixote and regard you as a slayer of giants and phantoms, which do not exist. Yet I want, by bringing you round to reason, to laugh with you at the troubles for which I see no remedy. You have to battle the Société des Amis des Noirs, and I, I have to confound something even more terrible, that is. . . . Time, which destroys everything, which changes the arts, manners, and human justice at will, shall never change the corporate feeling of those of whom I have very strong reason to complain.

For several months now in France, we have seen error, imposture, and injustice unveiled, and finally we have seen the walls of the Bastille fall; but we have not yet seen the fall of the despotism that I attack. I therefore see myself reduced to trying to overthrow it. Despotism is a tree in the middle of a thickly wooded maze, bristling with thorns and prickles: to prune its branches, I need all of Medea's magic. The retrieval of the golden fleece cost Jason less care and skill than the torment and snares it is going to cost me to avoid these poisonous branches that damage the celebrated tree and man's genius. To destroy them, I must lay low twenty dangerous dragons who, turning sometimes into zealous citizens, sometimes into supple serpents, creep everywhere and spread their venom over my works and my staff.

But, in my turn, must I not, sir, rightfully suspect you of putting yourself honorably forward in this rampant faction that protested against *L'esclavage des nègres*? With what do you charge this work? With what do you charge the author? Is it to have sought to have the colonists in America slaughtered and to have been the agent of men whom I know less than you, who perhaps do not value all my productions since I have shown that the abuse of liberty had borne much evil? You know me very little. I was the apostle of a sweet liberty in the midst of despotism. But a true French woman, I idolize my country: I have sacrificed everything for her. I cherish my king to the same degree, and I would shed my blood to restore all that to which his virtues and his paternal tenderness entitle him. I would sacrifice neither my king to my country nor my country to my king, but I would sacrifice myself to save them both together, persuaded as I am that the one cannot exist without the other. Man is known, so we claim, by his writings. Read me, sir, from my

Lettre au peuple to my *Lettre à la nation,* and you will recognize, dare I flatter myself, a heart and spirit that are truly French. Extreme parties have always feared and detested my productions. These two parties, divided by contrary interests, are always unmasked in my writings. My invariable maxims, my incorruptible sentiments, there are my principles. Royalist and true patriot, in life and in death, I show myself such as I am.

Since I have the courage to sign this written document, do likewise to show you are my equal and obtain my esteem, which is not perhaps indifferent to a gallant man: for I grant it with as much difficulty as Jean-Jacques. I may elevate myself to the level of this great man with respect to the righteous mistrust that he had of men: I have met few who are just and truly estimable. I do not reproach them minor faults, but their vices, their duplicity, and their remorseless inhumanity toward the weakest among us. May this revolution regenerate the spirit and the conscience of men and reproduce the true French character! Permit me a word more, please.

I am not well informed though it pleased you to bestow this glory upon me. One day, perhaps, my memory will be well known because of my ignorance. I know nothing, sir, nothing, I tell you, and I have learned nothing from anyone. Student of simple nature, abandoned to her care alone, she thus enlightened me, since you think me completely informed. Without knowing the history of America, this odious Negro slave trade has always stirred my soul, aroused my indignation. The first dramatic ideas that I set down on paper were on behalf of this class of men tyrannized by cruelty for so many centuries. This feeble production may suffer perhaps a little too much from its being a dramatic career's debut. Our great men themselves did not all begin as they finished, and an attempt always deserves some indulgence. I can thus bear witness, sir, that the Amis des Noirs did not exist when I conceived this subject, and you should rather assume, if prepossession has not blinded you, that this society is perhaps based on my drama, or that I have had the happy talent of nobly coming upon it. May they form a more general society and inveigle it more often with its own representation! I did not try to chain public opinion to my patriotism; I patiently awaited its felicitous return on behalf of this drama. With what satisfaction I have heard myself say on all sides that the changes that I had made generated widespread interest in this play, which can only increase when the public learns that, for four months now, I have dedicated this work to the nation, and that I have assigned its proceeds to the coffers of the patriots, whose establishment I presented in my *Lettre au peuple,* in print for eighteen months. This priority justifies perhaps my considering myself, without vanity, the author. This pamphlet caused quite a stir at the time, was likewise criticized, and the plan that it offered has not been the less successfully effected. I should inform you, as well as the public, of these deeds that characterize the love that I have for the true French character and the efforts that I make for its preservation. I do not doubt that the Comédie, moved by these zealous acts, conspires to give the most propitious days[10] to the performance of this drama; I cannot dissemble their boundless interest in my play. The Comédie has given me proof thereof, which I cannot call into question. While multiplying their pleasures, the author, the Comédie, and the public will all contribute to increasing the stock of the patriots' coffers, which alone can save the state, if all citizens recognize this truth.

I must further note that in these patriotic performances a number of persons have often paid beyond the price of their seats. If this one moves them in the same way, then we must distinguish between the patriots' profits and the Comédie's rights. An accurate list, remitted to the nation by the Comédiens, will give proof of these new citizens' zeal and fiat.

I hope, sir, and I dare flatter myself, that after my enlightening you on *L'esclavage des nègres,* you will no longer proceed against it, and that you will become on the contrary the zealous protector of this drama; in being performed even in America, it shall always bring black men round to their duties, while expecting the abolition of the black slave trade and a happier fate from colonists and the French nation. There are the attitudes that I have displayed in this work. I have not sought, under the circumstances, to make my play a banner of discord, a signal for insurrection; I have, on the contrary, since tempered its effect. If ever you doubt this assertion, read, I beseech you, *L'heureux naufrage,* in print for three years; and if I have made some allusion to men dear to France, these allusions are not at all harmful to America. The performance of my play will convince you of this, should you honor me by coming to see it. It is in this sweet hope that I beseech you to believe me, sir, in spite of our little literary discussion, in accordance with accepted convention, your very humble servant,

DEGOUGE

Paris, 18 January 1790.

Post-scriptum

I would have thought to have compromised myself, if I had responded in the body of this letter to all the filth that an infamous lampoonist has just spread about me in his mercenary rag. It is sufficient for me to remind the public, in order to confound this abominable calumniator, of *La lettre écrite à M. le duc d'Orléans, La motion,* or *Séance royale.* The public will recognize that I employed the voice of honor with this prince in order to bring him round to his duty, if he had strayed from it. But at the same time these writings did unmask him, if he was guilty. I do not know if he was in fact, but that of which I am convinced is that my son was sacrificed and has just lost his position in the house of this prince. There is my justification.

CHAPTER 5

On Translating Olympe de Gouges

Maryann DeJulio

Olympe de Gouges wrote the preface to *L'esclavage des noirs* to vindicate herself and her play. She hoped to convince the public that she had not produced an incendiary work in *L'esclavage des noirs,* and, furthermore, that the colonists and the Comédiens had sabotaged her play for financial and political gain. Like all good rhetoricians, Gouges relies upon "emotional persuasion to excite her public to pity, indignation, contempt, horror, and conviction."[1] She makes full use of the melodramatic potential of the contents of her own story in order to establish her rights as a citizen by explaining them to the judges and to the public. It is therefore not at all surprising that Gouges' writing recalls the *mémoires judiciares* of her day, printed versions of lawyers' defenses of their clients, which developed in the later eighteenth century into a highly popular form of pamphlet literature (Maza 1252–53).

My translation of the preface to *L'esclavage des noirs* emphasizes the legal conventions and the popular style of pamphletism, which influenced Gouges' writings; she herself wrote a number of pamphlets devoted to the Revolution (see Harth 214). Whenever possible, my portrait of Gouges stresses the fact that her ideas derive from sensations, a commonplace in an era impressed with Lockean epistemology, and that these sensations are particular to a woman writer and activist who seeks to accord public consciousness with her own experiences.

Key terms in my translation that relate to legal conventions include the following: *témoin auriculaire* ("ear-witness"); *en état d'arrestation* ("under arrest"); *plaider ma cause* ("plead my own case"); *Tribunal* ("Tribunal"); *au scrutin des consciences* ("a vote of conscience"); *pluralité des voix* ("majority"); *preuve* ("proof"); and *droits incontestables* ("incontestable right"). I have maintained the cognate *force majeure* and inserted terms such as "thereof" and "whereby" to effect a language of contract law, thus underscoring Gouges' bold appropriation of an idiom exercised by professionals openly hostile to women inasmuch as they found women "incapable of covenanting for want of sufficient reason or independence" (Maza 1261). Certain collocations such as *principes bienfaisants de la nature* ("good principles of Nature") and *douces lois* ("gentle laws"), which convey the ethos of an era heavily influenced by Rousseau's writings on nature and society, were relatively equivalent in English; however, the abstract noun *bonheur,* also reminiscent of Rousseau, and the phrase *belle âme* proved more problematic insofar as their elusiveness suggests a range of possible solutions. My decision to translate *bonheur* as "pleasure," "happiness," or "good fortune" depended upon its context, whereas I translate *belle âme* as "fair soul" to emphasize the judicious nature of woman, the "fair sex," as presented by Gouges.

In the preface to *L'esclavage des noirs,* Gouges creates a set of oppositions, which she hopes to resolve in her favor: she contrasts metaphysical observations with personal experience, and men with herself, a woman. Gouges stages her personal drama throughout the preface, always careful to cast herself as a woman writer, friend of the Truth, whose modest resources are but her soul and her words. She opens the preface with a comparison between the *siècle de l'ignorance,* the standard French expression for the Dark Ages, and *le siècle le plus éclairé,* a so-called Enlightened Age. By not translating *le siècle le plus éclairé* with the stock phrase "the Age of Enlightenment," I suggest that Gouges herself did not share conventional views about her century, and that the mixture of preconceived notions and originality in her use of language was calculated to shape public opinion to her own ends.[2]

Gouges links questions of gender and race in the preface by asserting that her works, that is, works written by a woman who does not figure among the Learned ("les Savants"),[3] bear but the color of human nature ("la couleur de l'humanité"). Gouges' use of the term *color* to evoke a range of human characteristics, which are observable through personal experience, thus serves two purposes: first, Gouges dissociates the term "color" from a strictly racial context; second, Gouges endows her own perspective with universality, a quality heretofore denied her as a woman writer. In this way, Gouges integrates notions of gender and race into what, for her, a French woman writing at the end of the eighteenth century, is a more natural point of view.[4]

My translation takes full advantage of the grammatical aspect of the gender question by feminizing all possessive adjectives and pronouns that relate to abstract notions of justice and compassion. Similarly, I have feminized the construct of Nature, but, unlike the Nature of convention, often presented in a feminine guise, Nature in Gouges' writing acquires universally reasonable principles: Nature "has placed the laws of humanity and wise equality in my soul." In addition, my translation feminizes the generic term *author,* along with the fruits of authorial productivity ("her writings"), in order to strike a clearer difference between Gouges, the writer whose gender here allies her with representations of virtue and goodness, and men, even men of color,[5] when they seek to imitate tyrants or are condemned to servitude by their "Fatherland." I have translated *patrie* as "Fatherland" rather than "Motherland" or "mother country" to emphasize the negative context in this instance.

Of course, Gouges' writings were also subject to literary conventions and influences, and these are felt especially in my translation of the dialogue from the play *L'esclavage des noirs.* The hyperbolic language, strong emotions, and moral polarization that characterized the melodramatic writing that first appeared in France in the 1750s and 1760s in the *drame* or *genre sérieux* of such writers as Denis Diderot, Pierre-Augustin Caron de Beaumarchais, and Louis-Sébastien Mercier (Maza 1257–58) convey the complex interplay of oppression and resistance throughout Gouges' work.

My translation of the title *L'esclavage des noirs* (*Black Slavery*) represents the moral polarization in Gouges' play: on one hand, her play asserts that the concept of slavery itself is reprehensible; on the other, it shows that the enslavement of blacks in the French colonies serves a particular financial and political purpose. By transposing the French noun *noirs* and the English adjective *black,* I am able to connote the evil consequences of slavery, as well as the fact that Gouges is a European writer who does not truly individuate black slaves as characters in her writing but rather uses them as vehicles for the expression of her ideas. At the time, it was not uncommon, in fact, to find a certain misrepresentation everywhere in antislavery writing, as is suggested by the British habit of calling yellow, brown, or red people "black."[6] The usage of the term *black* now has a long history that is sometimes tainted by racism; however, I have opted to use the term *black* in my fairly literal translation of Gouges' play because I do not believe that its effect in the eighteenth century was racist.[7]

Expressions and terms that indicate the historical moment in which the play was written provide other instances of moral polarization. My translation of *étranger* depends, for example, on varying perceptions of difference:

"stranger" connotes sensitivity to a character's otherness, whereas "foreigner" indicates a situation in which political distinctions prevail. Similarly, the general terms used to designate the protagonists—*ce bon Français* ("this good Frenchman"); *camarades* ("comrades"); *semblables* ("fellow men"); *habitants* ("planters"); *esclaves* ("slaves"); *cultivateurs* ("farmers")—position the characters one against the other, depending upon who is addressing whom. When the term *espèce*, pronounced by Mirza and Zamor, the two slaves, is translated as "kind" or "species," it is meant to be both objective and, for the modern reader or spectator, somewhat reminiscent of Darwinian genetics. In this way we see that Mirza and Zamor differentiate between themselves, people of color, and the Europeans and planters, whose advantage over them is clearly racist. I have translated *Négresse* as "Negress," though considered pejorative in current parlance, to show the bias and confusion regarding people of color in late eighteenth-century France. When Valère, a Frenchman, attempts to flatter Mirza, a slave from the Indies, by saying, "Je n'ai pas vu de plus jolie Négresse," it appears that he conflates Africans and Indians.

In order to elicit the range of strong emotions called for in Gouges' play, I have relied especially upon the translation procedure of componential analysis, namely, the comparison of "a source language word [in this instance, in French] with a target language word [in English], which has a similar meaning, but is not an obvious one-to-one equivalent, by demonstrating first their common and then their differing sense components" (Newmark 114).[8] My translation of *malheureux* as "wretch," "wretched creature," "wretched man," "unfortunate," and "unhappy," and of *supplice* as "punishment," "torment," and "torture," can illustrate this procedure. I use the term "wretch" in situations in which an empathetic speaker's social status is superior to that of those he or she addresses; the pejorative connotations of "wretch" in twentieth-century English underscore differences in social class. "Wretched creature" and "wretched man" are used similarly; however, they exact greater emotional intensity from the speaker and are allied with the speaker's sense of responsibility toward the victim. Both Sophie and M. de Saint-Frémont, her father, refer to the slaves in this manner. Sophie's description of Zamor and Mirza to M. de Saint-Frémont, "wretched creatures," recalls the themes of nature and natural rights associated with female personae throughout the play, whereas M. de Saint-Frémont's use of "wretched man" when addressing Zamor, one of his slaves who has just pledged undying loyalty to him, his master, suggests that to treat Zamor as anything less than a man greatly pains M. de Saint-Frémont.

My use of "unfortunate" and "unhappy" as translations for *malheureux* shifts emphasis from the more corporeal aspects of wretchedness to those aspects that relate to the heart or soul, the seat of feelings or sympathies. When Sophie declares that she had no trouble interesting Mme de Saint-Frémont on the slaves' behalf, she states that Madame is "so fair, so sensitive to the troubles of the unfortunate." Likewise, Mirza is "unhappy Mirza" when she confides to Zamor that her love has rendered him guilty.

In translating *supplice* as "punishment," "torment," or "torture," I have been especially attentive to the function of the word in the line as well as to the emotional tone that it conveys. Generally speaking, the move from "punishment" to "torment" to "torture" marks an increase in emotional intensity either on the part of a character or on the part of the reader or spectator. Characters may be reacting to a specific situation or to a series of situations that have accumulated during the course of the play, while the reader or spectator is then incited to react in turn. Thus, Mirza speaks to Zamor, her lover, of the "same torment [that] reunites" them; M. de Saint-Frémont tells Valère that he should not let Sophie witness "this frightful torture"; and the judge observes, without passion, that Sophie only makes "their punishment more terrible." By act 3, "torture" has become the most frequent translation for *supplice*, despite one instance in which I substitute a legal convention for the expression "Monsieur, suspendez, je vous prie, leur supplice" ("Monsieur, grant a stay of execution, I beg of you").

Questions of gender and race are formulated in the hyperbolic language of melodrama that Gouges uses throughout her play. The redundant qualifiers, exclamatory comments, and affected *aparté* represent an eighteenth-century melodramatic style whose very awkwardness attests to its emotional poignancy. Though all the characters speak in the same register, be they slave, governor, or French citizen, class differences based on race and gender are made apparent by means of social titles, a common practice of the period. In most cases, I have kept the French titles *Monsieur, Madame, Monseigneur*, and the like, to reflect the original context; however, I have been careful to use a juridical language in instances where the social relationship emphasizes its contractual nature, as, for example, when I have translated *époux* or *épouse* as "spouse" rather than "husband" or "wife."

Thomas Holcroft's translation of *Coelina* (1800) by Pixérécourt, the first play to be designated a bona fide melodrama, provided me with a parallel text or model in English for the many stock phrases, exclamations, and terms of endearment scattered throughout Gouges' play (see Holcroft, *A Tale of Mystery*). Though I do not use exactly the same expressions found in Holcroft's translation, my solutions approximate the affected tone of his language, which has a slight biblical tinge. I use such apostrophes as "Divine Providence!" "Almighty God!" and "Ah! Gods! Hey!" as well as the more secular "Dear spouse! O half of myself!" and "O Louis! O adored Monarch!" plus the phrases "Adieu, dear authors of my days" and "Our happiness runneth over." While I continue to represent Nature as female and compassionate ("Benevolent Mother!"), I have female characters blur gender distinctions in their speech. In the last two scenes of the play, for example, when Mme de Saint-Frémont entreats her husband to act judiciously and pardon Mirza and Zamor, she calls him *mon ami,* which I translate quite literally as "my friend" although it usually means "my dear" in a domestic context.

Of the many qualifiers in Gouges' play, her use of *sauvage* is among the most interesting. Each time she uses the word *sauvage,* she recalls nature and the origins of liberty and equality. Similarly, my translation of *sauvage* recalls nature with the epithet "rude," that is, primitive or natural. I only use the cognate "savage," which connotes bestiality, to emphasize misunderstood racial tensions: "Compassionate being to whom I owe my life and my spouse's life! You are not a Savage; you have neither the language nor the manners of one. Are you the master of this Island?" (Valère to Zamor [1.6])

My aim in the translation of "Réponse au champion américain" (1790) is to emphasize the connection between knowledge and equality for women. Although the occasion for Gouges' writing of "Réponse" is, of course, the slave trade, as she herself tells us: "It is not the philosophers' cause, the cause of the Amis des Noirs, that [she] undertake[s] to defend; it is [her] own." Likewise, in *Déclaration des droits de la femme,* Gouges feels compelled to "say a few words about the public disturbances supposedly caused by the decree in favor of men of color on our islands"; however, she closes her document with the image of man and woman "united, but equal in strength and virtue."

It is arguable that in both "Réponse" and *Déclaration des droits de la femme* Gouges moves from abolitionist remarks regarding the plight of slaves to analogous remarks concerning women's situation. In the one instance in "Réponse" in which Gouges uses the term *espèce,* my translation generalizes the slaves' plight by using the word "class" to designate them as a group, rather than a race, that has been "tyrannized by cruelty for so many centuries." In this way, it becomes easier to identify women as another group that has been similarly oppressed.

Throughout "Réponse," Gouges is keen on demonstrating the apparent contradiction of a situation in which one would accuse her of being well informed but not at all learned. In order to highlight the illogicality of her circumstances, I juxtapose the two contrary notions of knowledge and ignorance in the same line: "One day, perhaps, my memory will be well known because of my ignorance." There is, in fact, a pattern of alternating images in which Gouges insists that she has learned nothing from anyone and that she must enlighten her opponent on this matter, which my translation would stress. In the line "Since I have the courage to sign this written document, do likewise to show you are my equal," I introduce the principle of equality into a literate context.

In 1792, a year after Gouges' *Déclaration des droits de la femme,* Mary Wollstonecraft's *Vindication of the Rights of Woman* would champion women's rights and women's education. Though Wollstonecraft's and Gouges' political views differ considerably, they share similar opinions concerning a woman's right to prove herself intellectually equal to men.[9] Thus, it is helpful to compare Wollstonecraft's prose with Gouges', despite the fact that Wollstonecraft was supposedly unaware of her contemporary.[10]

As we have seen above, Gouges' writing is a mixture of received notions and originality, and she uses language to shape public opinion to her own ends. There is a parallel tendency in Wollstonecraft to rely on "personal observation, repetition, forceful comparisons (especially metaphors from ordinary life), and use of autobiographical reference, in a sentimental mode" (Siebert 352). If Wollstonecraft and Gouges were both accused at times of poor literary style and sometimes faulty grammar, closer inspection of their images reveals an urgency of conviction that transcends lack of formal education and the stress under which they wrote. In "Réponse," for example, in response to her challenger, Gouges modifies the standard expression *tomber dans l'erreur grossière* to turn it in her favor: "But if I imitate you, Sir, . . . I stray a bit too far from my aim and blunder into the same gross error as you with respect to me." Since Gouges insists that she is a student of simple nature, and that nature alone has enlightened her, I translate references to her own work with images drawn from the material world whenever possible. I have, at times, used figures of conception, birth, and generation to feminize Gouges' political and creative activities: "May this revolution regenerate the spirit and the conscience of men and reproduce the true French character!" Similarly, the changes that Gouges made to her play "generated widespread interest."

Part Three

Germaine de Staël, 1766–1817

CHAPTER 6

Germaine de Staël, Translation, and Race

Françoise Massardier-Kenney

Germaine de Staël (1766–1817) is the only major woman author of the nine-teenth century, with the exception of George Sand, who has managed to break through the silence in literary history surrounding women's writing during that time. Still, until recently, her reputation has rested mostly on her introduction of German romanticism in France in *De l'Allemagne* (1810), on her opposition to Napoleon, and on her affair with Benjamin Constant, which he fictionalized in *Adolphe*. Her works were hard to find, and her major pieces were not available in current reeditions. The last two decades have seen a flurry of revisionist studies, critical editions, and translations,[1] which bear witness to the considerable interest that Staël's oeuvre holds for anyone interested in nineteenth-century intellectual movements and literature. Yet her important connection to race and to translation has been largely ignored, although a few recent articles point to the crucial role of Staël in the conceptualization of translation and can provide an opening for considering the interaction of translation, gender, and race. Staël's relation to translation was first examined in Avriel Goldberger's pioneering article on the translation of *Corinne*,[2] and more recently in essays on Staël and Goethe or Shakespeare.[3] Kurt Mueller-Vollmer analyzes *De l'Allemagne* as a text of "discourse formation and of translation" (152) and describes the complex strategies Staël used to effect the transfer of new ideas and the new vocabulary of German romanticism into French, while Deidre Shauna Lynch's study of Staël and Shelley connects issues of gender to translation and notes that Staël locates "the reproduction of culture outside nature and the confines of the nation-state, in the circulation of languages among women" (217). Similarly, Maddalena Pennacchia concludes her study on Staël's urging Ital-ians to translate Shakespeare in "De l'esprit des traductions" by concluding that a link between women's conditions and the subjection of people runs throughout her work (20). In her essay "Germaine de Staël and Gayatri Spivak: Culture Brokers," translation scholar Sherry Simon opposes Spivak's questioning of the notion of nation to Staël's earlier support of translation as a way to create strong national cultures (thus strong nations),[4] but Simon rightly sees that for both Staël and Spivak, translation has sweeping cultural implications and that while it is influenced by "historical patterns of global exchange" (136), it is capable of disturbing these relations. Jane Elisabeth Wilhelm further demonstrates the central role that translation plays for Staël in opposing the nationalist and imperialist conceptions of Napoleon (notions that would lead to emerging concepts of nation and of racial identity).

Finally, the 1934 description of Staël's lifelong interest in the question of slavery by her descendant the comtesse Jean de Pange—"Mme de Staël et les nègres"—gives useful facts but does not analyze either her particular sensitivity as a woman author to the plight of slaves or her idea of culture based on differences and cross-influences. It is time for Staël's connection to race, gender, and translation to be examined.

Germaine de Staël is the quintessential figure of the translator; she embodies the ideal of translation. She is that "voice from the other side" who, throughout her life and works, forced her audience to become aware of their own culture through an appeal to the culture of others, be they German, English, or African. Her subtle but unrelenting questioning of the values of French culture through a discourse describing different discourses present in other cultures makes her an "exemplary intellectual" (11), as Pierre Barbéris has called her. She provides us with the point of view of one who is on the margin of mainstream culture and public life.

Staël and her family were, in a subtle way, outsiders. She was born in 1766 to Suzanne Curchod Necker, a highly educated Swiss-born woman who had visited Rousseau and Voltaire during her years as governess to the children of the Swiss pastor Moulton. Suzanne Curchod married the Protestant Swiss banker Jacques Necker, who became famous as finance minister under Louis XVI and as a financial innovator who used massive borrowings to restore French finances. Mme Necker's Parisian salon was one of the most famous of the times. Germaine Necker thus entered the world in a prominent family and from her earliest years benefited from the company of the most famous men; but the Neckers were Swiss and Protestant in a French Catholic society, and of course they were commoners.

The primacy of the spoken voice was to be a prominent feature of Staël's fiction. Suzanne Necker, a Rousseau disciple, devoted much time to her daughter's education and kept her with her in her salon. She was apparently unable to show her affection or approval, and her relations with her daughter were strained, both women focusing their love on Jacques Necker, the "patriarchal God of the household."[5] However, through her mother, Germaine Necker first encountered the life of the intellect in conversations, and she herself became a conversationalist well before she became a writer. The importance of the oral is obvious in the poetic improvisations of her famous heroine Corinne,[6] but also in the readings in this volume, in the early hymns of her Jolof character Mirza. Very early in her life and in her writing career, Staël abstains from valorizing the values of Western Europe, of "civilization." Her emphasis on the oral rather than on the written made her particularly suited to accept cultures from Africa and to appreciate their oral traditions. Her partial exclusion from written discourse because of her gender allowed her to be inclusive racially, and her early concern about the question of slavery would last throughout her life.

This privileging of the spoken voice also came as a transformation of an all-too-real denial of access to the written word. Germaine Necker's mother, Suzanne, had started a nonfictional work that she had to abandon at her husband's request. Jacques Necker disapproved of women writing. Later, when the Neckers' daughter began to write, both parents made light of her efforts, and the father reiterated that writing was to be the sole province of men. Between a father whom she adored but who disapproved of her writing, and a mother whom she disliked and who had suppressed her own writing, Staël would have little space in which to maneuver, and her literary strategies would tend to be indirect.

Staël's entry into the world of letters coincided with her gaining some distance from her father. In 1786 Germaine Necker married the Swedish ambassador to France, Eric-Magnus de Staël, and opened a Parisian salon that would soon become famous. Her first work, titled *Lettres sur les ouvrages et le caractère de Jean-Jacques Rousseau* (1788), was published anonymously, but everyone knew she was the author. This first act of writing already bore the marks of Staël's strategy: seeming to obey the paternal injunction not to write (she published the work anonymously, she was no longer Mlle Necker, and the work is a praise of another male role model), while nonetheless engaging in the act of writing (she did write and publish, and her authorship was known). This work was to attract a great deal of attention and be reedited a number of times. Composed of five letters (a borderline genre between the oral and the written), it is a defense of Rousseau and approves of his views on women (i.e., that they should not play a role in public life).[7] Thus in her first publication of nonfiction, Staël took a firm position as a liberal[8] (her subject is a philosopher who questions the most basic institutions of the monarchy), but she also endorsed the paternalistic views of her male model, an endorsement that prefigured the Revolution's relegatation of women to the private sphere. A radical activist like Olympe de Gouges could publish a *Déclaration des droits de la femme et de la citoyenne* (1791), and women formed clubs of their own (Les amies de la vérité, and Citoyennes révolutionnaires), but the Convention abolished them in October 1793, and Gouges' efforts on women's behalf were to end on the guillotine. What we can learn from comparing Staël to Gouges is that Gouges' efforts on behalf of women and of people of color were more direct and urgent, and immediately thwarted. Her play *L'esclavage des noirs* was immediately brought down by the powerful colonists' Club Massiac, while Staël's more timorous but perhaps more timely efforts (specifically her intervention on behalf of the Guadeloupean Pelasge in 1803,[9] her introduction to Wilberforce's essay against slavery in 1814) would go unimpeded.

Staël's paradox was to be that having accepted the paternal male denial of women's involvement in writing and in public life, she would, perhaps indirectly but steadily, write and make for herself a place in public life by using her writing differently from more radical figures like Gouges. A major strategy of Staël's (but by no means a conscious one) was the timing of the publication of her works so that she would avoid being silenced the way women like Gouges had been. It is perhaps not by chance that a work like *Lettres* (a work not concerned with gender or race) was the first piece she published. It gave her a public voice that she would later use to disseminate her more unsettling works, those sensitive to women, slaves, and cultural differences. Throughout her career she would interspace essays and works of fiction from which a dialogue of different voices would be heard. At the time she published *Lettres,* she had already written three short stories, the publication of which was delayed until 1795, with the "Essai sur les fictions" in a book titled *Recueil de morceaux détachés.* The short stories not published earlier were "Mirza, ou Lettre d'un voyageur," "Adélaïde et Théodore," and "Histoire de Pauline." In her preface to "Mirza," Staël indicated that the stories were written before the Revolution and when she "was barely twenty." Although these stories have not been dated with certainty, if we take Staël's word, we are led to conclude that they were written before she married and before she published *Lettres*. They can be read as a counterpoint to *Lettres*, or at least as another point of view, one Staël seemingly did not chose to make public when she was still Mlle Necker.

During the Revolution, Staël became politically active in a perhaps limited but real way. At the beginning of the Revolution, she returned to Paris with her parents, her father having been recalled to the Ministry of Finance by public acclaim. She stayed in Paris until 1792, when the Terror forced her to take refuge in Switzerland. She spent the rest of the Revolution in exile in England and in Coppet, the family estate in Switzerland that Necker had bought earlier. In 1794 the Convention freed slaves in the colonies, and that same year Staël returned to Paris, where she became active politically. She publicly espoused republicanism and in 1797 founded the Club constitution-nel with Benjamin Constant, among others. She soon became disenchanted with the government of Napoleon, who banned several of her works and exiled her from Paris. It was only in 1815 after the fall of Napoleon that she would be free to return to Paris.

During the years of the revolution, Staël experimented with a number of forms and developed a theory of literature grounded on the necessity of cross-influences from foreign literatures. She first published several plays (*Sophie, Jane Gray,* both written in 1786) depicting women's sacrificial love, as well as several newspaper articles: "Réflexions sur le procès de la reine" (1793), "Ré-flexions sur la paix" (published in 1794 in Switzerland, and in 1795 in France). At the same time, she published *Zulma,* another short story probably written a few years earlier, and an essay on politics entitled *De l'influence des passions* (1796). She expressed her views of literature both in the "Essai sur les fictions" (1795) and in *De la littérature considérée dans ses rapports avec les institutions sociales* (1800), where she argues that the Revolution changed the conditions in which literature was produced. It was no longer a matter of entertaining, of writing according to the rules and taste of a privileged class, but of expressing "the situation of the individual in modern society" (Coulet 646). Her ideal is one of the republican novel: "The novel, in republican France, shall depict personalities, personal feelings, teaching man about himself and his relations with his fellow men and with society [la collectivité]" (Coulet 651). This repub-lican novel will benefit from "graftings" from other foreign literatures. Such a program could not endear her to Napoleon, whose ambition was to forge a unified France that would be inwardly turned and would shun enemy influences coming from the countries around it (or "surrounding" it, as Napoleonic ideology would have phrased it).

Staël practiced in her own works the kind of intralingual translation that she advocated in her theoretical works. In 1802 she published *Delphine*, a fictional reworking of the themes of *De la littérature*, which rekindled the controversy created by that work, with the result that Napoleon forbade her to stay in Paris. As Pierre Barbéris has insightfully noted, Staël constituted the "legitimization of another language" (15). Her militant cosmopolitanism is but a way to question the unexamined values of French culture, what Barbéris calls "franco-centrism" and "voltairo-centrism" (12). Thus the Germany she appeals to in *De la littérature* is used not as a historical reference but as a utopian antidote to France, an open culture that, "because of its versatility, lends itself to antagonistic exchanges" (Macherey 34). This appeal to the foreign in order to acknowledge and question the limits of one's culture and language is original: Staël is not interested in describing the picturesque or the exotic. She focuses on the essential: how sentiments are expressed and how power is exercised. In order to do so, she moves between fiction and essays, between what is French and what is foreign in a movement that makes her an exemplary practitioner of intralingual translation. She is interested in the ways in which cultural hybridization can be apprehended as a gain for the culture that lets in influences from the outside. In fact, she seems to sense that culture is "cultural capital," to use Pierre Bourdieu's term,[10] but that it should not be immobilized by trade barriers.

During the years 1803–1813, Staël traveled to Germany and Italy and would write her major works. The outcome of her travels to Italy was the publication of *Corinne* (1807), which became an immediate success. In 1810 she published *De l'Allemagne*, which was immediately banned by Napoleon (before it was even distributed) and caused her to be sent back to her Swiss retreat at Coppet. *De l'Allemagne* finally appeared in 1813 in London (still in French). During this same decade, she published two antislavery pieces: "Préface pour la traduction d'un ouvrage de M. Wilberforce" (1814), written in London and translated into English by her daughter Albertine, and "Appel aux souverains" (1814), in which she went back in nonfictional form to the concerns expressed at the beginning of her career in "Mirza" and "Histoire de Pauline." Her abolitionist pleas had already been voiced in the opening of "Pauline," written some twenty years earlier: "These scorching climates where men, solely occupied with a barbaric trade and gain, seem, for the most part, to have lost the ideas and feelings which could make them recoil in horror from such a trade" (1:88).

She spent her last years actively fighting Napoleon's regime, and during these years of political opposition, perhaps not accidentally, she published her last work, "De l'esprit des traductions" (1816), in Milan, where it was to create a major debate and influence the development of Italian romanticism. In this essay Staël advocates translation as the condition necessary to keep national literatures alive. She conceives of translation not as an imitation of what is foreign but as a way to move free from obsolete literary conventions. She argues that it is through the influence of translation that a national literature can learn and develop new forms.[11] Staël's conception of translation is political or, rather, ideological, in that she perceives that literature is a cultural product that functions like a commodity. She herself uses the phrase "circulation of ideas" and links translation to "other forms of commerce." In a very modern way, she perceives that translation is the agent of change that acknowledges that culture is determined by the society and the times in which it thrives, and that translation is a sort of ideological distancing from and criticism of existing national modes of writing. Her repeated use of gold as a metaphor to represent literature emphasizes that literature is a form of capital, and like a good liberal, she wants that capital to circulate freely between countries.

Her survey of the situation of translation in different countries emphasizes that literatures, without or with little translation, are dead literatures, precisely because they are severed from the influence and the test of other literatures. For Staël, a literature can thrive only if it is part of the great chain of other signifying practices. In her conclusion she calls for the practitioners of Italian literature to turn outward and to let translation rejuvenate their writing.

When it has been mentioned at all, "Mirza" has been dismissed idly as "an awkward work" (Coulet 647) or patronizingly as "strictly a curiosity, of merely marginal interest" (Switzer 308). Yet the story's depiction of gender and race makes it an important text in the tradition of women's writing and antislavery. It may even be that it is this very conjunction of race and gender that has placed "Mirza" in the "margins," that space in established discourse that Staël was to use and appropriate to create a theory of cultural identity based on maintaining oppositions and differences, not on erasing them. As Pierre

Macherey has observed, "It became possible for her to think about cultures, not from within, but from the gaps that, separating them from themselves, projected them outside of their own constitution" (36). From this perspective, Switzer's charges that "she is incapable of reacting to any kind of beauty that is not strictly within the scope of Western European standards" (306), that she "indulges in the same kind of stereotypes adopted by Hugo in *Bug Jargal*" (304), are unfounded. Whereas *Bug-Jargal* presents stereotypical descriptions of people of color (i.e., as childlike, violent, or overly physical figures), the black characters in "Mirza" are intellectual, sensitive, and their sexuality is not emphasized. Moreover, the title character, Mirza, is endowed with qualities that historical accounts tell us characterize the author. This identification of the implied author with the black character is the opposite of what happens in a work like *Bug-Jargal*. Finally, these characters are not simply "African"; they belong to two different tribes, a distinction of importance.

Obviously, Staël does not depict "real" Africans any more than she would later depict "real" Germans. She is using the depiction of the Other, of the foreigner, to bring out particularities and deficiencies in her own culture. In a perhaps extremely perceptive and honest move, she seems to know that the Other's point of view can be used to place in question her own culture, but that its representation is inevitably mediated by the gender, the class, the culture—in brief, the ideology—of the author, that the recognition of the limits of such a representation is at the center of her refusal to endorse culture-centrism.

"Mirza" clearly links antislavery sentiments and women. First, the preface, written several years after Staël wrote the story, but before it was published in 1795, reclaims the narrative and its authorship. The presence of the preface provides a frame for the narrative, made by a male European to an unknown woman, so that, although the narrator is male, both the author and the addressee are women. This story of women and slavery is thus doubly gendered. Secondly, the title character, Mirza, the African heroine, is first presented as the eloquent voice of antislavery. The character Ximeo first hears her speak: "The love of freedom, the horror of slavery were the subjects of the noble hymns that filled me with a rapturous admiration." Moreover, it is made clear in the story that Mirza, an orphan member of the Jolof tribe,[12] opposes the male warriors' custom of selling their war prisoners as slaves. The female character is thus the only one not ideologically implicated in the slave system. Revealingly, after offering herself as a substitute slave to save

Ximeo[13] and after being saved by the French governor, Mirza chooses to die. The superficial reason is her broken heart over Ximeo's faithlessness; but another motive, more indirect but still significant, is the impossibility for the independent woman to owe her life and her freedom to a European colonialist, generous as he may be. Thus Mirza dies while Ximeo heads a European-style plantation, answering the naive and patronizing questions of the European narrator about his superior ability to speak French and to smoothly run a plantation. Ximeo only escapes the power structure of master/ slave, superior/inferior, European/African that links him to the European visitor through the retelling of Mirza's story (her story of abandonment and death, but also of rebellion): indeed, while the author carefully avoids using direct discourse between the European male narrator and Ximeo, thus sidestepping the question of using *tu* (the usual form for an intimate or an inferior) or *vous* (the form reserved for equality or formality), Ximeo finally addresses the narrator as *tu*, an astonishing *tu* that acknowledges the significance of telling Mirza's story as a way to undermine confidence in the value, let alone superiority, of the European.

Lest this significant use of *tu* be interpreted as a sign of Ximeo's lack of mastery of the French language (the enduring stereotype was that Africans spoke *petit nègre,* the French version of pidgin English), the narrator had earlier emphasized Ximeo's native command of French. One sees here that, although superficially correct, the charge of franco-centrism waged against Staël and other women writers for making their African characters speak perfect French needs to be reexamined. If a French author depicts foreign characters (be they Jolof like Mirza or Italian as in *Corinne*), their language will inevitably be a translation. The question is whether this translation will emphasize their lack of control of language through a stereotypical distortion of standard French or whether the translation will be transparent (i.e., emphasizing what they say rather than how inadequately they express themselves or how peculiar they sound).[14] Thus Staël shifts the difference of her characters away from the grammatical forms of their language (from *langue*) to voice, a more individual, less collectively determined language (to *parole*); she is engaged in the representation of different modes of thinking and speaking. And speak is precisely what Mirza does, unlike Ximeo, who is left speechless when Mirza improvises on the theme of freedom. Throughout the narrative, Staël emphasizes the power of Mirza's voice. When, at the end, she speaks up to the slave traders in favor of Ximeo, he is again speechless.

Staël is here suggesting that Mirza's kind of voice, the voice of passion, of antislavery, of female difference, of the spoken, can unsettle or even silence and counterbalance—for a moment—the discourse of the male, patriarchal, European colonialism and deceit. When asked by Ximeo to speak about love, Mirza opposes herself to the other tribe. She tells Ximeo: "Do not expect from me the art of the women of your country." Mirza opposes the "naturalness" of her speech, which is the sincere outpouring of feelings, to a language that is deceitful. Through Mirza, Staël criticizes the classical, regulated language of traditional French literature as well as the oppressive language of Ximeo. Mirza's language is a utopian language that is opposed to patriarchal language. At the same time, Staël refuses to create a mythical figure of an "African" who speaks a "pure" language; she distinguishes between Ximeo from Cayor and Mirza, the Jolof.

The link among patriarchy, political division, and deceit is made clear by Ximeo, who, after writing a letter to Mirza about his departure and his alleged trip, attempts to justify himself: "My father would never have called by the name of daughter a woman from the Jolof country." The inability of one culture to accept an exterior element is directly linked to the father's discourse. "Mirza" does present a series of oppositions—Mirza/Ximeo, Africa/Europe, woman/man, voice/written discourse, antislavery/patriarchy—but these oppositions are not static binary oppositions. Shifts occur, change is possible, the language from without can enter and rejuvenate the culture from within. The male Ximeo shifts from the weak listener and writer position to that of speaker: "But I have wanted to speak of her." The male character redeems himself by telling the woman's story, by learning to understand and speak her language. The link between race and gender is made once again.

Ximeo the African prince is to the European colonialist as woman is to man. Ximeo's feminization is suggested early in the story. The European male narrator describes him in ways that emphasize not so much his Europeanness, but his feminine aspect. His features are "ravissantes" (beautiful), he is "trop mince pour un homme" (too thin for a man); he has "beaux yeux" (beautiful eyes); he has more "délicatesse" (frailty) than "force" (strength)." Staël's description of Ximeo's physical appearance, which runs counter to the stereotype of the black man as threatening because of his size and his physicality, is in fact one of her indirect ways of connecting race and gender. Ximeo is black and thus feminine in the eyes of the European (and it is the narrator who comments on Ximeo's lack of the "defects of the men of his color").[15] Revealingly, the female heroine Mirza is hardly described at all; rather, she is situated in a utopian elsewhere outside the economy of static subject/object positions. The European male gaze of the narrator has not seen her, and Ximeo has been subjugated by her voice.

Staël's strong liberal position and the indirect strategies she used to link gender and race, and to present the oppression of Africans and women by the French male patriarchy, seem to be the salient features that would direct the "siting" of the translation of "Mirza." While Staël could not transcend the limits placed on her by her time and place, her opposition to franco-centrism, to slavery, and to patriarchy should not be minimized and decontextualized. In the same way that Staël used transparency yet allowed for the voice of difference, the translator translating "Mirza" for a modern American audience has to both work with a tone and a vocabulary that seem at home in English and give an indication that the text comes from a culture that is different from ours but that we can apprehend without "cannibalizing" the source text, without erasing its difference. Avriel Goldberger has similarly stated about her translation of *Corinne*, "The translator has sought as 'timeless' a language as possible, avoiding both an imitation of nineteenth-century English which can so easily sound like a parody, and the obviously twentieth-century which would give a false modernity to the text" (808–9). This transparency, which nonetheless admits to the existence of a distance between the French and the English texts, is a working in translation of the circulation of a specific cultural capital, a capital whose value determines how the translation is sited. This notion of transparency is quite different from the "bad" transparency described by Tejaswini Niranjana (3). It does not aim to fix a colonized discourse but to show the modernity of Staël's notion of culture as something that should not be fixed by national boundaries.

In specific terms, the passionate, romantic voice of Mirza could have been toned down to adapt to our contemporary mode of writing and to avoid skirting the ridiculous, but its dissident force would have been lost or trivialized. To keep the distance, yet to "familiarize" the text in English (to reuse the well-known Russian formalist notion of "defamiliarization"), I turned to the English romantics for texts of a similar sensibility but also remote in time. Perhaps not unsurprisingly, the most useful parallel text turned out to be Mary Shelley's *Frankenstein*.

For that same "familiarization" effect, Staël's careful feminization of Ximeo, her use of the passive voice to render his lack of agency, had to be kept without the result of pushing her text in the direction of parody. Similarly, the terms used to describe Africans (*Nègre, Nègresse*) had to be carefully thought out, since they now have a negative connotation that was not necessarily present in the original French text.[16] However, since the term *Negro* was endorsed by African Americans until recently, and since the translated text is obviously sited as an older text, not as a modernization, the term was kept.[17] A more ideologically loaded issue was Staël's reference to the African share of responsibilities in the slave trade (in the same way that Aphra Behn had done previously in English). The choice was either to tone down the statement so as to fit our expected audience's ideological expectations (i.e., to focus on the responsibility of the colonizer, not on the complicity of the victims) or to keep it in as an integral part of the liberal antiabolitionist argument of the time. Since Staël also refers again to the African custom of slavery in her later piece on slavery, "Appel aux souverains," the statement was kept as is.

Other syntactic issues such as Ximeo's sudden use of *tu* have been handled in the "margin" of the translation, that is, the introduction, which, like Staël's preface, is a necessary part of the text, since it contextualizes the translated text and brings attention to its status as translation. I noted earlier Staël's valorization of the oral over the written, and I would argue that her whole oeuvre is a valorization of the process of translation over original "pure," "uncontaminated" texts, that she optimistically emphasizes that it is in the retelling of the story in another language or from another point of view that cultures can be revitalized.[18]

CHAPTER 7

Translations of Staël

"MIRZA, OR LETTERS OF A TRAVELER"
Françoise Massardier-Kenney

PREFACE

The reader will readily understand, I think, that the preceding "Essay on Fictions" was written after the three short stories I publish here. None deserves the title of novel; situations are sketched rather than developed, and their only merit lies in the depiction of a few sentiments of the heart. I was barely twenty years old when I wrote them, and the French Revolution had not yet occurred. I should think that, since then, my mind has acquired enough strength to devote itself to more useful works. It is said that misfortunes hasten the development of all moral faculties, but sometimes I fear that it has the opposite effect, that it throws you into a state of melancholy that makes you indifferent both to yourself and to others. The greatness of the events around us makes us feel the emptiness of general thoughts and the impotence of individual feelings to such a degree that, lost in the midst of life, we no longer know what road hope should follow, what motive must arouse our efforts, what principle will henceforth guide public opinion through the mistakes caused by blind allegiance to a party, what principle will mark again, in all carriers, the brilliant aim of true glory.

Allow me, madam, to apprise you of an anecdote from my trip, which you may find interesting. A month ago, in the town of Gorée,[1] I heard that the governor had persuaded a Negro[2] family to come and live a few miles away so as to establish a plantation[3] similar to the one found in Saint Domingue. He had imagined, surely, that such an example would incite Africans to grow sugarcane, and that by drawing to their territory the free trade of this sugar, Europeans would no longer take Africans away from their homeland and make them suffer under the hideous yoke of slavery. In vain have the most eloquent writers attempted to obtain this revolution by appealing to the goodness of men. Thus, the enlightened administrator, despairing to overcome selfish interest, would like to make it stand on the side of humanity, by no longer having this personal interest find its advantage in braving humanity; but the Negroes, who do not think of providing for their own future, are even more incapable of thinking about generations to come, and they refuse a present evil without comparing it to the fate from which it could free them. One single African, freed from slavery through the generosity of the governor, had agreed to take part in his project. A prince in his own country, he had been followed by a few Negroes of a lower station who farmed his land under his orders.

I asked to be taken there. I walked part of the day, and at dusk I arrived near a house that, I was told, had been built in part by French people, but that still had a primitive quality. When I drew near, the Negroes were enjoying their moment of rest: for relaxation they were shooting with bows and arrows, perhaps longing for the times when this pleasure was their only occupation. Ourika, the wife of Ximeo (the Negro who was the head of the settlement), was sitting at some distance away from the games, and she looked distractedly at her two-year-old daughter, who was playing at her feet.

My guide walked up to her and told her that I was seeking shelter for the night in the name of the governor. "Ha-Governor moo koo yooni. Doogoo silwaay da laal jam! Keurgui sa Keuria," she cried.[4] ["The governor sends him! Let him come in, welcome! Everything we have is his."] She came toward me with hurried steps. Her beauty dazzled me; she had the true charm of her sex, that is, everything suggestive of delicacy and gracefulness. "Mo anaa zimeo?" my guide inquired. "He is not back," she replied. "He is taking his evening walk; when the sun is no longer on the horizon, when the very sunset no longer suggests light, he will come back, and it will no longer be night for me." After uttering these words, she let out a sigh, walked away, and when she came back toward us, I could see streaks of tears down her cheeks. We went into the hut; we were served a meal composed of all the local produce. I tasted everything with pleasure, eager that I was to feel new sensations. Someone knocked at the door; startled, Ourika sprang up, opened the door, and threw herself in the arms of Ximeo, who kissed her without seeming to be conscious of what he was doing or seeing. I went up to him. You cannot imagine a more beautiful face; his features had none of the defects of the men of his color. His eyes produced an effect that I had never experienced before: they took hold of your soul, and the melancholy they expressed went directly into the heart of those he beheld. The proportions of the statue of the Apollo Belvedere[5] could not have been more perfect than his: perhaps he could have been considered too thin for a man, but the sorrowful grief that every one of his movements indicated, that his face depicted, was more in keeping with frailty than with strength. He was not surprised to see us; he seemed impervious to any other emotion than his dominant idea. We told him who had sent us and what the aim of our journey was. "The governor earned the right to my gratefulness," he replied. "Can you believe that in my present state I still have a benefactor?" He talked to us for awhile about the reasons that had led him to run a plantation, and I was surprised at how sharp witted and articulate he was. He became aware of my surprise. "You are surprised," said he, "when we are not at the level of sheer brutes, although you treat us as such."

"I am not surprised," I replied, "but even a Frenchman would not speak French better than you do."

"Ah, you are right," he added, "one still retains a few rays when one has lived for a long time near an angel." And his beautiful eyes looked down and ceased to see anything that was outside him. Ourika was crying, and Ximeo finally noticed her. "Baalma," he cried and took her hand. "Baalma! Tay sabisla sa-biis-la vaante maay noo nu fatiikoo." ["Forgive me. The present is yours; bear with my memories."] "Tomorrow," he said, turning toward me, "tomorrow, we shall visit my plantation together; you will see if I can flatter myself that it meets the expectations of the governor. Our best bed will be readied for you; sleep peacefully. I would like you to feel comfortable here. Men whose heart is broken by misery," he told me in a low voice, "do not fear, and even long for, the spectacle of another's happiness."

I went to bed, but I could not sleep. I was full of sadness. Everything I saw carried its stamp. I did not know its cause, but I felt moved as one is when contemplating a painting that depicts melancholy. At dawn, I got up. I found Ximeo even more dejected than the previous day. I asked him what the cause of his sadness was and he answered: "My grief, fixed in my heart, can neither grow nor wither; but the uniformity of life makes it go away faster, and new incidents, whatever they may be, give rise to new thoughts, which always give rise to new tears." He showed me his entire plantation with the utmost care. I was surprised at the order that reigned there. The land yielded at least as much as a like surface farmed in Saint Domingue by as many men, and the happy blacks were not overwhelmed with work. I saw with pleasure that in addition to everything else, cruelty was unnecessary. I asked Ximeo who had advised him about the farming of the land, about the organization of the workers' day.

"I was given little advice," he replied, "but reason can lead to what reason has already discovered: since death was forbidden me, I had to dedicate my life to others; how else could I have lived? I abhorred slavery; I could not understand the barbarous purpose of the men of your color. I sometimes thought that their god, enemy of our god, had ordered them to make us suffer, but when I realized that a product of our country, neglected by us, was the sole cause of the cruel suffering endured by these unfortunate Africans, I accepted the offer to give them the example of growing sugarcane. May free trade be established between the two parts of the world! May my unfortunate compatriots renounce primitive life, devote themselves to work in order to satisfy your greed, and help save a few of them from the most horrible destiny! May those who could flatter themselves that they had avoided slavery apply themselves with an equal zeal to protect their fellow beings from such a fate." As he was talking to me thus, we reached a door that led to a forest on one side of the plantation. I thought that Ximeo was going to open it, but he turned away in order to avoid it.

"Why," I said, "don't you show me?"

"Stop!" he cried. "You seem sensitive—will you be able to hear the long story of my woes? It has been two years since I conversed with anyone. What I usually say is not really speaking. You can see it: I need to confide in someone. You should not be flattered by my trust; but still, it is your kindness that encourages me and makes me count on your pity."

"Ah! have no fear," I replied. "You will not be betrayed."

"I was born in the kingdom of Cayor.[6] My father, of royal blood, was the chief of several tribes that had been committed to his care by the monarch. I was trained early in the art of defending my country, and I had been familiar with archery and javelin throwing since I was a child. At that time I was promised in marriage to Ourika, the daughter of my father's sister. I loved her as soon as I could love, and this faculty developed within me for her and through her. Her beautiful perfection struck me even more when I compared her to other women, and I came back by choice to my first inclination.

"We were often at war against the Jolofs, our neighbors, and as we both had the atrocious custom of selling our prisoners of war to the Europeans, a deeply rooted hate that even peace could not abate allowed no communication between us. One day, while hunting in the mountain, I was led further than I intended; a woman's voice, remarkably beautiful, reached my ears. I listened to her song and I could not recognize the words that our maidens enjoy repeating. The love of freedom and the horror of slavery were the subjects of the noble hymns that filled me with a rapturous admiration. I drew near: a young person rose. Struck by the contrast between her age and the subject of her meditations, I looked in her face for something supernatural that might reveal the inspiration that can be a substitute for the long reflections of old age. She was not beautiful, but her noble and regular stature, her enchanting eyes, her animated countenance left love nothing to wish for in her face. She came forward and spoke to me at length without my being able to answer her. Finally I managed to express my surprise; it became more pronounced when I learned that she had composed the verse I had just heard.

"'There is no need to be surprised,' she said. 'A Frenchman who settled in Senegal, discontented with his lot and unhappy in his own country, retired among us. This old man was so good as to tend to my youthful years, and he gave me what the Europeans have that is worthwhile: the knowledge that they misuse and the philosophy whose lessons they follow so poorly. I learned the language of the French, I read a few of their books, and, for my own delight, I come to these mountains and reflect in solitude.'

"My interest, my curiosity, increased with every word she said. It was no longer a woman that I was hearing; it was a poet. Never had those of my countrymen who devote themselves to the cult of the gods seemed filled with such a noble enthusiasm. When leaving her, I obtained her permission to see her again; her memory followed me everywhere. I left with more admiration than love, and trusting this difference for a long time, I saw Mirza (as this young Jolof was named) without meaning to offend Ourika. One day, at length, I asked Mirza if she had ever loved. I asked this question with trepidation, but her ready wit and open mind made all answers easy for her:

"'No, I have not,' she said. 'I have been loved sometimes; I may have wanted to feel; I wanted to know the feeling that takes over your whole life and rules every instant of the day, but I have reflected too much, I think, to feel this illusion. I feel all the movements of my heart and I can see them all in others. I could not to this day deceive nor be deceived.'

"Her last words troubled me. 'Mirza,' I said, 'how sorry I feel for you! The pleasures of the mind are not all absorbing; only those of the heart satisfy all the faculties of the soul.'

"She taught me all the while with an inexhaustible kindness; in a short time, I learned everything that she knew. When I interrupted her with my praise, she would not listen; as soon as I stopped, she would proceed, and I could see by what she said that while I was praising her I had been the only object of her thoughts. Finally, intoxicated by her charm, her mind, and her eyes, I could feel that I loved her, and I dared tell her: what did I not say to transpose in her heart the exaltation I had found in her mind! I was dying of passion and fear at her feet.

"'Mirza,' I repeated to her, 'bring me into the world by telling me that you love me; open up the heavens for me so that I may soar with you.'

"As she listened to me, she lost her composure and tears filled her beautiful eyes in which, until now, I had only seen the expression of genius. 'Ximeo,' she said, 'I shall answer you tomorrow. Do not expect from me the art of the women of your country. Tomorrow, you will read in my heart; in the meantime, think about yours.' After saying these words, she left me well before sunset, the usual signal of her retreat. I did not attempt to detain her; the power of her personality bound me to her will. Since I had met Mirza, I saw less of Ourika. I deceived her. I invoked trips as pretexts. I delayed the moment of our union. I postponed the future instead of planning it.

"At last, the following day, after what seemed like an eternity, I went to her. Mirza moved first toward me; she looked dejected, because of either foreboding or tender thoughts. She had spent that day in tears.

"'Ximeo,' she said to me with a soft but steady voice, 'are you quite sure that you love me? Is it certain that in your vast country no object has fixed your heart?' I answered with promises. "Ah, I believe you; surrounding nature is the only witness to your promises. Everything that I know about you, you yourself told me. The isolation, the neglect in which I live, provides all my security. What distrust, what obstacle have I opposed to your will? In me, you could only deceive the regard I have for you, Ximeo; you could only avenge yourself of my love. My family, my friends, my fellow citizens, I banished all to depend on you only. To you, I must be sacred as the weak, the young, and the wretched are. No, I have nothing to fear, nothing." I interrupted her: I was at her feet; I thought I was sincere; the force of the present had made me forget past and future. I had deceived; I had convinced her; she believed me.

Gods! What passionate expressions she found! What happiness she felt in loving! Oh, during the two months that passed thus, all that exists of love and happiness met in her heart. My wishes were gratified, but my excitement was fading. How strange is human nature! I was so struck by the pleasure she had seeing me that I soon began going for her sake rather than for my own: I was so sure of her welcome that I no longer trembled when approaching her. Mirza did not realize this; she spoke, she answered, she cried, she brought herself solace, and her active soul acted upon itself. Ashamed of myself, I needed to go away. War broke out in another part of the Cayor kingdom; I resolved to go there directly. I had to tell Mirza. Oh, at that moment I felt again how dear she was to me. Because of her trust and sweet feeling of security, I did not have the strength to reveal my plan to her. She seemed so much to live by my presence that my tongue froze when I attempted to tell her that I was leaving. I resolved to write to her; this art that she had taught me was to be used to bring her misery. Twenty times I left her; twenty times I went back. The unfortunate soul enjoyed this and mistook my pity for love. Finally, I left; I informed her that my duty was forcing me to leave her, but that I would come back at her feet feeling more tender than ever. What response did she give me! Ah, language of love, how charming you become when you are embellished by thought! What a despair at my absence! What passionate desire to see me again! Thinking then of the excesses to which her heart could go in loving made me shudder, but my father would never have called by the name of daughter a woman from the Jolof country. All sorts of obstacles were offered to my thoughts when the veil that hid them was lifted. I saw Ourika again; her beauty, her tears, the power of a first inclination, the entreaties of an entire family, and all sorts of things, everything that seems insurmountable when one no longer draws one's strength from one's heart, made me unfaithful, and my vows with Ourika were taken in the presence of the gods.

"In the meanwhile, the time that I had given to Mirza for my return was drawing near. I wanted to see her again; I hoped to soften the blow that I was going to strike. I thought it was possible. When one no longer feels love, one no longer suspects its effects. One cannot even rely on one's memories. Oh! I was filled with such feelings when walking over the very spot that had been witness to my promises and my happiness! Nothing had changed but my heart, and I could hardly recognize them! As for Mirza, as soon as she saw me I think she experienced in a single moment the happiness that one barely feels at different moments in the whole of one's life, and it was thus the gods repaid her. Ah! How can I tell you through what horrible degrees I led the unfortunate Mirza to know the state of my heart? My trembling lips uttered the word 'friendship.'

"'Your friendship,' she cried out, 'your friendship! You barbarian! Is it to my soul that such a feeling must be offered? Give me death: that is all you can do for me now.' The excess of her grief did seem to lead her to her death; she fell unconscious at my feet. What a monster I was! It was then that I should have deceived her, but it was then that I spoke truth. 'You are without feelings! Go now,' she said to me. 'The old man who took care of me when I was a child and who was a father to me may live longer. I must live for him. I am already dead here,' she said, pointing to her heart with her hand. 'But he needs my care. Go away.'

"'I cannot,' I cried out, 'cannot bear your hatred.'

"'My hatred!' she answered. 'Have no fear, Ximeo. Some hearts can only love and all their passion only turns against themselves. Farewell, Ximeo. You will thus belong to another woman.'

"'No, never, never,' I said.

"'I do not believe you now,' she replied. 'Yesterday your words would have made me doubt the light of day. Ximeo, hold me against you, call me your dearest mistress, let your voice find again the tone of the past, let me hear it again, not to enjoy it, but to remember it again: but it is impossible. Farewell, I will find it again alone, my heart will always hear it. It is the cause of death that I bear and keep in my heart. Ximeo, farewell.'

"The touching sound of this last word, the effort she made when moving away—I remember everything; she is before my eyes. Gods! Make this illusion stronger! Let me see her for an instant so that—if it is still possible—I may feel more strongly what I have lost. For a long time, I remained motionless where she had left, distraught, troubled like a man who has just committed a great crime. Night overtook me before I thought of moving homeward; the remorse, the memory, the sense of Mirza's misery preyed on my soul; her shadow came back to me as if the end of her happiness had been the end of her life.

"War against the Jolofs broke out. I had to fight against Mirza's countrymen. I wanted to shine with glory in her eyes, to justify her choice, and to deserve still the happiness I had given up. I had little fear of dying. I had made of my life such a cruel use that perhaps I risked that life with a secret pleasure. I became seriously wounded. While recovering, I learned that a woman came every day to the threshold of my door. Standing still, she would tremble at the slightest noise. Once I grew worse; she fainted. She was restored to animation and said: 'Do not let him know of the state in which you saw me. I am far from being a stranger to him. My interest will distress him.'

"Finally one day, a horrible day, I was weak still, my family and Ourika were with me. I was calm when I banished the memory of the one whose despair I had caused. I thought I was anyway; fate had driven me. I had acted like a man governed by it, and I feared so much the moment of repentance that I used all my strength to restrain my thoughts, which were all too ready to brood over the past. Our enemies, the Jolofs, struck the village where I lived: we were defenseless. We sustained a fairly long attack, however, although at last they defeated us and took several prisoners. I was among them. What a moment for me when I saw myself in shackles. The cruel Hottentots only reserve death for the vanquished, but we, being more cowardly barbarians, we serve our common enemies and justify their crime by becoming their accomplices. A troop of Jolof soldiers made us walk all night. When day came to give us light, we found ourselves on the bank of the Senegal River. Boats had been readied. I saw some white men, and I became certain of my fate. Soon my drivers began discussing the vile conditions of their heinous exchange: the Europeans checked with curiosity our youth and our strength to find there the hope of making us bear longer the wrongs that they held in store for us. Already I was determined. I was hoping that when passing onto this fateful boat my chains would loosen enough to let me throw myself into the river, and that despite the swift rescue of my greedy owners, the weight of my shackles would drag me to the bottom of the abyss. My eyes were fixed on the ground, my thoughts attached to the terrible thing I was hoping to do. I was detached from the objects around me. All of a sudden, a voice that happiness and sorrow had taught me to recognize made my heart beat faster and shook me out of my immobile meditation: I looked up. I saw Mirza, beautiful, unlike a mortal, but like an angel, for her face was irradiated by the soul within. I heard her ask the Europeans to listen to her: her voice was moved, but it was not fright or emotion that altered it; a supernatural movement transformed her whole appearance.

"'Europeans,' she said, 'it is to cultivate your land that you condemn us to slavery. It is your interest that makes our misfortune necessary; you do not seem to be evil gods, and tormenting us is not the goal of the suffering you will have us bear. Look at this young man weakened by his wounds. He will be able to withstand neither the long march nor the work that you will require of him. Yet look at me, see my strength and my youth. My sex has not sapped my courage; let me be a slave in Ximeo's place. I will live, since it is at this price that you will have granted me Ximeo's freedom. I shall no longer think slavery degrading. I shall respect my masters' power, since I will have given it to them, and their benevolence will have sanctified it. Ximeo must cherish life; Ximeo is loved. I do not love anyone in this world; I may depart from it without leaving any void in a heart that would feel that I no longer exist. I was on the verge of taking my own life; a new happiness makes me outlive my heart. Ah, allow yourselves to be moved and, at a time when your pity is not at odds with your interest, do not resist my plea.' As she finished speaking, this proud Mirza—whom the fear of death would not have forced to kneel before the kings of the earth—humbly bowed her knee. But in this attitude, she still kept all her dignity, and admiration and shame were the lot of those whom she was imploring. For a moment she may have thought I could accept her generosity. I was tongue tied, and it was torture to be thus speechless.

"These Europeans all cried out in unison, 'We accept the exchange. She is beautiful, she is young, she is courageous. We want the Negress, and we let her friend go.'

"I regained my strength. They were going to approach Mirza when I cried, 'Barbarians, slavery is mine. Never, never. Respect her sex, her weakness. Jolof Naax Naanguene Naagoo, weco seen none bu sax ak jigueenoo goxbi?' ['You Jolofs, will you allow a woman of your country to be enslaved in place of your cruelest enemy?']

"'Stop!' cried Mirza. 'Stop being generous. You are accomplishing this act of virtue for your sake only. If you had cared about my happiness, you would not have abandoned me. I prefer you guilty when I know you to be insensitive. Leave me the right to complain when you cannot take my pain away. Don't take away from me the only happiness that I have left, the sweet thought of being bound to you at least by the good I will have done you: I followed your destinies, I shall die if my days are of no use to you. This is your only means of saving my life; dare persist in your refusals.'

"Since then, I have remembered every one of her words, and at the time I thought I did not hear them. I shuddered at Mirza's resolve; I feared that those vile Europeans would approve of it. I dared not declare that nothing separated me from her. These greedy merchants would have taken us both: perhaps, heartless as they were, they already counted on the effects of our hearts; they had even already promised themselves that they would choose for captives those whom love or duty could cause to be bought or followed. They studied our virtues to use them for their vices. But the governor, informed of our struggles, of Mirza's devotion, and of my despair, advanced like an angel of light: who would not have thought that he was bringing us happiness!

"'Be free, both of you,' he said to us. 'I return you to your country and to your love. So much nobility of soul would have shamed the European who would have called you his slaves.' My shackles were removed. I kissed his knees. I blessed his goodness in my heart, as if he had sacrificed legitimate rights. Ah, usurpers may thus attain the rank of benefactors by renouncing their injustices. I stood up. I thought that Mirza was at the feet of the governor like me. I saw her at some distance, leaning against a tree, caught in a deep reverie. I ran toward her. Love, admiration, gratitude—I felt all, I expressed all at once.

"'Ximeo,' she said to me, 'it is too late. My grief is writ too deeply for your hand to even touch it: I can no longer hear your voice without wincing, and your presence freezes in my veins the blood that once flowed impetuously for you. Passionate souls can only know extremes; they cross the distance between the two without ever stopping. When you told me of my fate, I doubted it for a long time: you could still have come back. I would have believed that I had dreamed of your fickleness. But now, to destroy this memory, I have to cut through the heart from which it cannot be erased.'

"As she was speaking thus, the fatal arrow was in her heart. Oh, gods who stopped my life at that moment, did you give it back to me only to avenge Mirza by the long agony of my suffering! The chain of my memories and my thoughts was broken during an entire month. I sometimes think that I am in another world made into hell by the memory of the first one. Ourika made me promise not to attempt suicide. The governor convinced me that I must live in order to serve my unfortunate compatriots, to respect the last wishes of Mirza, who beseeched him, he said, on her deathbed, to look after me, to bring me solace in her name. I obey; I have shut in a tomb the sad remains of the one I love when she no longer is, of the one I failed to appreciate when she lived. There, in solitude, when the sun sets, when all of nature seems to be overcast with my mourning, when universal silence lets me hear my thoughts, then only can I feel, prostrate before this tomb, the enjoyment of grief, the full feeling of its sorrows. My exalted imagination sometimes creates ghosts; I think I see her, but she never appears to me as an angry lover. I hear her consoling me and attending to my grief. Finally, uncertain of the fate awaiting us after life, I respect in my heart the memory of Mirza, and I fear that by ending my life, I would destroy everything that remains of her. You are the only person with whom I have shared my sorrow. I don't expect you to feel pity—should a barbarian who caused the death of the woman he misses be of concern? But I wanted to speak of her. Ah! promise me that you will not forget the name of Mirza, that you will say it to your children, and that you will preserve after my death the memory of this angel of love, this victim of misfortune."

When he finished his story, a dark reverie spread over Ximeo's charming face. My eyes streamed with tears. I tried to speak to him: "Do you think," he said to me, "that you should attempt to console me? Do you think it is possible to have one single thought about my misfortune that my heart would not have already found? I have wanted to tell you my sorrows only because I was quite sure that you could not ease my pain. I would die if it were removed from me. Remorse would take its place; it would occupy my whole heart, and the pains of remorse are barren and burning. Adieu, I thank you for listening to me." His somber calm, his tearless despair, easily convinced me that all my efforts would be pointless. I no longer dared speak to him; misfortune inspires respect. I left him, my heart full of bitterness, and I tell his story to fulfill my promise and sanctify, if I can, the sad name of his Mirza.

"AN APPEAL TO THE SOVEREIGN"
Sharon Bell

Despite the violent crisis in which England has been embroiled for twenty-five years, that nation has never used the dangers she faced as an excuse for neglecting the good that was within her power. Constantly concerned about humanity in the midst of war, and about the common good at the very moment her political existence was under threat, she abolished the slave trade at the time she was waging the most vigorous fight against the doctrine of a perverse liberty.[7] The opposing parties among the English came together for a goal as much moral as it was religious. Mr. Pitt and Mr. Fox collaborated on its behalf with equal ardor, and Mr. Wilberforce, a Christian orator, lent to this great work a perseverance the like of which is usually seen only among those working to further their personal interests.

The abolition of the slave trade, which took place seven years ago, did not affect the prosperity of the English colonies. The Negroes have sufficiently multiplied among themselves to supply the needed labor, and as always happens in the case of an act of justice, the public was ceaselessly alarmed over the possible disadvantages of this measure before it was enacted. But once it was, none of these supposed disadvantages were ever heard of again. Thus, thousands of lives and entire nations were preserved, without the financial interests of commerce having suffered.

Since that time, England, on signing the peace treaty with Denmark, made the abolition of the slave trade one of the articles of the treaty. The same condition was put to Portugal, which, up to now, has conceded only to restrictions. But today, since the confederation of sovereigns has met to enact the treaty and thus confirm the peace it has won with its might, it seems that nothing would be more worthy of the august congress about to open than to consecrate the triumph of Europe through an act of benevolence. The Crusaders of the Middle Ages never left for the Holy Land without binding themselves by some vow on their return. The sovereigns now meeting in France promised the good fortune of Africa to that propitious Heaven from which they obtained Europe's deliverance.

Many political interests will be discussed, but a few hours given to such a great religious interest would not be useless even to the affairs of this world. Thereafter, people would say: "It was at this Paris peace accord that the slave trade was abolished by all of Europe; thus, this accord is blessed, since it follows such an act of thanksgiving to the God of Hosts."

It has been proposed that a monument be raised to consecrate the fall of the oppressor who lay like a pall over the human race. Here we have it, a monument that can be raised with one word: the slave trade abolished by the kings who overthrew the tyranny of the conquest of Europe.

The sufferings these hapless Negroes are made to endure as they are transported from their homeland to the colonies almost make the very slavery that awaits them a relief. We provoke war in the countries of Africa to make the victors surrender their war captives; to be sold into slavery is the accepted punishment along the coasts of Africa for all kinds of misdeeds. The black chiefs who take part in this vile traffic excite the Negroes to crime by inciting them to drunkenness or by any other means, in order to claim the right to have them transported to America. Often, under the ridiculous pretext of sorcery, these unfortunates are exiled forever from the shores where they were born, far from that land even dearer to primitive than to civilized men. "Long coffins," to borrow an expression from a French writer, carry them across the seas; the captives are stacked in the ship in such a way that they would take up more space if they were dead, for their bodies would then at least be stretched out on the wretched plank they are allowed.

In his address against the slave trade, Mr. Pitt said in so many words: "I know of no evil that has ever existed, and I cannot imagine any, worse than 80,000 people annually snatched from their native land by the concerted action of the most civilized nations of Europe." Mr. Pitt's principles were well known, as was the part he played in the present triumph of the allied nations because of his convictions. Should his authority not be counted? And that of the three powers of England, the House of Commons, the House of Lords, and the king: does their authority not confirm the truth of the facts and principles now submitted to the monarchs' attention?

Finally, one cannot hide the fact that Europe owes a great deal to England, which has often resisted alone during the course of these twenty-five years, and nowhere has there been a battle that was not seconded by English soldiers or English aid. How does one repay the richest and most fortunate nation in the universe? A warrior receives from his sovereign a token of honor, but what can be done for an entire nation who has played the warrior's role? The great humanitarian act that England is commending to all the governments of Europe must be adopted: good must be done for its own sake, but also for the sake of the English nation that requests it and to whom it is just to grant this noble token of gratitude.

The same advocate of humanity, Mr. Wilberforce, is in England as head of the society of missionaries who must carry the enlightenment of Christianity into Asia and Africa. But how could one be called Christian if one is cruel? Could not the king of France, that pious heir of St. Louis and of Louis XVI, be asked to agree to the abolition of the slave trade so that this humanitarian act might persuade the hearts of those to whom the Gospel is to be preached? Could one not ask this same agreement of Spain, which awakened national spirit on the continent? of Portugal, which fought like a great state? of Austria, whose sole concern was the well-being of the German Empire? of Prussia, where both nation and king proved so simply heroic? Let us also ask this great gift of the Russian emperor, who limited his own ambition when there was no longer any outside obstacle to check it. An absolute sovereign fought to found the wise principles of political liberty;

the crown of such a monarch should be composed of every kind of glory: the emperor of Russia rules peoples of diverse degrees of civilization within the confines of Asia. He tolerates all religions; he permits all customs; and the scepter, in his hands, is as equitable as law. Asia and Europe bless the name of Alexander. May that name resound as well on the savage shores of Africa! There is no country on earth unworthy of justice.

"PREFACE TO THE TRANSLATION"
Sharon Bell

Mr. Wilberforce is the author of the following essay on the slave trade.

This distinguished orator in the House of Commons, remarkably well versed in everything pertaining to literature and that lofty philosophy based on religion, has devoted thirty years of his life to making Europe ashamed of a great moral outrage and to liberating Africa from a horrible misfortune. When he had amassed all the evidence of the cruelties that worsened the horror of an act of tyranny, when he thought he had the means to convince both great and small, in 1787 he made a motion in Parliament that the slave trade be abolished.

Mr. Pitt, Mr. Fox, Mr. Burke supported him. No truly superior man in England, no matter what his political opinions, would want to lend his support to opinions that would stain his reputation as a thinker and friend of humanity. Mr. Pitt may be suspected of having for some time allowed his followers to support the slave trade, but he held his glory too dear not to separate from his party in this instance. Still, the protests of all those who divide the human species into two groups, one of which, in their opinion, must be sacrificed to the other—these protests prevented Mr. Wilberforce's motion from being carried. The colonists claimed that the abolition of the slave trade would bankrupt them; the English trading cities declared that their prosperity depended on that of the colonists; last, there arose on every side that resistance that is always heard when decent people decide to defend the oppressed against the oppressors.

The excesses of the French Revolution, which caused a certain order of ideas to be viewed with great disfavor, harmed the cause of the poor Negroes. Those who objected to the provocation of war among the peoples of Africa so that their prisoners might be enslaved were called anarchists; those whose actions had no other motives than religion and humanity were called Jacobins. But in a country like England, enlightenment is so widespread, and the circulation of ideas so free, that one can calculate with certainty the very short time required for a truth to become established in public opinion.

Every year Mr. Wilberforce renewed the same motion, which had been defeated the first time, and through this perseverance Reason won new ground each time. The most religious men in England seconded Mr. Wilberforce's efforts; Mr. Clarkson, Mr. Macaulay, and several others must be mentioned in this honorable struggle. A subscription was taken up to establish, in Sierra Leone, all the means proper to civilize the Negroes, and this honorable enterprise cost the individuals who supported it over 200,000 pounds sterling. One can scarcely see how that mercantile spirit for which we reproach the English can explain such sacrifices. The motives that impelled the abolition of the slave trade are every bit as disinterested.

It was in 1807 that this great humanitarian act was realized. Its advantages and its disadvantages had been debated for twenty years. Mr. Fox and his friends were ministers then, but the cabinet changed during the period between the act and its passage into law. Nevertheless, the successors adopted the same principles in this regard, for among the new ministers, Mr. Perceval, Mr. Canning, and Lord Harrowby—all three of them friends of Mr. Pitt—proved to be ardent champions of this admirable cause. As he died, Mr. Fox had committed it to his nephew, Lord Holland, and this noble heir, along with his friends, was allowed to carry the king's sanction to the House of Lords, even though he was no longer minister. "A ray of sunlight," said Clarkson, "broke through the clouds the moment the decree ending the slave trade was proclaimed." Indeed, this act deserved heaven's favor, and at what moment did it take place? At a time when all the colonies were in the hands of the English, and when their self-interest, crudely considered, should have led them to maintain the degrading commerce that they were renouncing.

Today it is widely maintained that the English fear the reestablishment of the colony of Saint Domingue, to the advantage of the French; but in 1807 what chance was there for France to regain mastery of that colony, if indeed that chance exists even today? The party that impelled the abolition of the slave trade in England is that of those zealous Christians commonly called Methodists. In the interests of humanity they display energy, industry, and party spirit; and as they are numerous, they affect public opinion, and public opinion affects the government. Politicians and speculators likely to envy the prosperity of France were by no means neutral parties in the abolition of the trade—they mounted arguments against it similar to those that we see invoked in France today among the colonists and the merchants: they predict the same dire consequences. Yet, in the seven years since England has prohibited the slave trade, the experience has amply proved that all the fears that were manifested in this regard were illusory, that the maritime cities are presently in agreement with the rest of the nation on this subject. We have seen in this instance the same moral phenomenon one always observes under circumstances of a like nature. When it is proposed that some abuse of power be eliminated, those who benefit from that abuse are certain to declare that all the benefits of the social order are attached to it. "This is the keystone," they say, while it is only the keystone to their own advantages, and when at last the progress of enlightenment brings about the long-desired reform, they are astonished at the improvements that result from it. Good sends out its roots everywhere; equilibrium is effortlessly restored; and truth heals the ills of the human species, as does nature, without anyone's intervention.

Some Frenchmen were annoyed that the English ministers had made the abolition of the slave trade one of the conditions of peace, but in this regard the English ministers were nothing more than the interpreters of their nation's will. But the time when nations require humanitarian acts of each other would be a grand age indeed in history. These generous negotiations will meet no obstacle in the heart of a monarch as enlightened by religion as is the king of France, but the prejudices of nations can sometimes act against the very enlightenment of their kings.

Thus, it is the great good fortune of France, of England, and of distant Africa that glory like that of the Duke of Wellington should strengthen the cause he defends. The Marquis of Wellesley, his elder brother, had already suppressed the trade in black slaves in India, where he was governor, even before the decree that abolished it was proclaimed by the Parliament of England. The opinions of this illustrious family are well known. Let us hope, then, that Lord Wellington will triumph through reason in the Negroes' cause, just as he powerfully served the cause of the Spanish with his sword, for it is to this valiant hero that these famous words of Bossuet's should be applied: "His was a name that never appeared except in actions whose justice was unquestionable."

"THE SPIRIT OF TRANSLATION"
Doris Y. Kadish

No loftier service can be rendered to literature than transporting the master-pieces of the human mind from one language to another. There are so few works of the highest order. Genius of any kind is such a rare phenomenon that if each modern nation were reduced to its own riches, it would always be poor. Besides, circulating ideas is the most clearly profitable of all kinds of commerce.

At the time of the Renaissance in literature, scholars and even poets had the idea that they should all write in a single language, Latin, so that they could understand each other without the need for translation. That idea could have been profitable for the sciences, in which the development of ideas does not rely on the charm of style. But the result was that much of the wealth produced by Italians in Latin was unknown to Italians because most readers only knew the vernacular. Besides, to write in Latin on science and philosophy requires creating words that ancient writers never used. Thus scholars used a language that was both dead and artificial, while poets limited themselves to purely classical expressions. It is true that when Latin was still heard on the banks of the Tiber, Italy had writers such as Fra-Castor, Politien, San-nazar, whose style was said to resemble that of Virgil and Horace; but if the reputation of those Italian writers has endured, their works are only read as examples of a period of erudition, and a literary glory based on imitation is a sorry glory indeed. These medieval Latin poets were translated into Italian in their own country, and that proves how natural it is to favor a language that reminds you of the emotions of your own life instead of one that you can only recover through study.

The best way to dispense with translations, I agree, would be to know all the languages in which the works of the greatest poets were written: Greek, Latin, Italian, French, English, Spanish, Portuguese, German. But such work requires a great deal of time and assistance, and one can never be confident that knowledge that is so difficult to acquire will be universally attained. Ultimately, it is the universal to which one must aspire in attempting to do good for the human race. I would go even further: even if one had a good understanding of foreign languages, a successful translation of a work into one's own language would provide a more familiar and intimate pleasure than the original. The imported beauty that a translation brings with it gives the national style new turns of phrase and original expressions. To preserve a country's literature from banality, a sure sign of decadence, there is no more effective means than translating foreign poets.

But to draw a real profit from translation, one should not follow the French, who give their own color to everything they translate. Even if in doing so one were to change everything one touches to gold, it would still be impossible to derive any nourishment or new food for thought; although the finery might be slightly different, one would always see the same face again. This criticism, which the French well deserve, derives from the fact that the art of poetry in their language is invariably kept in shackles. The scarcity of rhyme, the uniformity of verse structure, the difficulty of inversions, all imprison the poet in a fixed circle that necessarily leads back to the same hemistichs, if not the same thoughts, to a certain monotony in French poetic language, which genius escapes when it soars high but from which it cannot free itself in the transitions, in developments—in brief, in everything that leads up to and unites those poetic high points.

It would thus be difficult to find an example in French literature of a good translation of poetry, except for the abbé Delille's translation of Virgil's *Georgics*. There are beautiful imitations, which are conquests that have contributed to the wealth in the nation's coffers, but it would be difficult to name a work of poetry that in any way retained its foreign nature, and I truly doubt whether any such effort could ever succeed. If Delille's *Georgics* has been justifiably admired, it is because the French language has, more than any other language, been capable of assimilating to Latin, from which French derives, and whose pomp and majesty it retains; but modern languages contain so much diversity that French poetry cannot gracefully yield to Latin's rule.

The English, whose language allows for inversion, and whose versification is subject to laws that are far less severe than in French, could have enriched their language by translations both precise and natural; but their great authors did not undertake this labor of translation. Pope, the only one who did, made the *Iliad* and the *Odyssey* into two beautiful poems but failed to retain the ancient simplicity that makes us sense the secret of Homer's superiority.

It is indeed improbable that for three thousand years one man's genius has surpassed that of all other poets; but there was something primitive about traditions, customs, opinions, and the air itself in his time that possessed endless charm. When we read Homer, we have a sense of the beginning of time and the youth of the human race, which renews in our souls the sort of emotion we feel in recalling our own childhood. Because that emotion blends with his dreams of a golden age, we prefer the most ancient poet to all his successors. If you subtract from his composition the simplicity of the first days of the world, it loses its uniqueness.

In Germany, several scholars have claimed that the works of Homer were not composed by a single individual, and that one should consider the *Iliad*, and even the *Odyssey*, a collection of heroic songs that celebrated the Greek conquest of Troy and the return of the victors. It is easy to refute that view, it seems to me, mainly because the unity of the *Iliad* does not allow one to adopt it. Why would several authors have limited themselves to the story of Achilles' anger? Subsequent events culminating in the capture of Troy would normally have formed part of the collection of rhapsodies that supposedly belonged to diverse authors. Only a single person could have conceived a plan focused on one unified event, Achilles' anger. But even without a discussion of the whole theory of multiple authorship, which would require an incredible erudition, it should at least be acknowledged that Homer's principal greatness stems from his century: why else would people believe that Homer's contemporaries, or at least a great number of them, collaborated on the *Iliad?* Here is added proof that this poem is the image of human society at a certain stage of civilization, proof that it bears the imprint of its time even more than that of its author.

The Germans did not limit themselves to these scholarly inquiries into Homer's existence. They attempted to make him come to life again among them, and Voss's translation is recognized as the most exact translation in existence in any language. He used the rhythm of the ancients, and it is said that his German hexameter almost follows the Greek hexameter word for word. Such a translation effectively provides a precise knowledge of the ancient poem, but is it certain that the charm of the original poem, accessible neither through rules nor through erudition, has been thoroughly transported into the German language? The number of syllables has been retained, but the harmony of sounds has not remained the same. When German poetry follows, step by step, the traces of the Greek original, it both loses its natural charm and fails to acquire the beauty of the musical language that was accompanied on the lyre.

Of all the modern languages, Italian is the one that most lends itself to rendering all the sensations produced by the Greek of Homer. It is true that Italian does not have the same rhythm as the original. The hexameter can hardly be introduced into our modern languages, in which long and short syllables are not sufficiently marked to copy the ancient poets. But Italian words have a harmony that can dispense with the symmetry of dactyls and spondees, and the grammatical construction of Italian lends itself to a perfect imitation of Greek inversions. Because the *versi sciolti* stand outside of the rhyme system, they impede the expression of ideas no more so than prose, yet they retain the grace and measure of poetry.

Among all the translations of Homer that exist in Europe, Monti's surely comes closest to producing the same pleasure as the original. It has both pomp and simplicity. The most ordinary practices of daily life such as clothes or dinners are enhanced by the natural dignity of Monti's expressions, and the most solemn events are made accessible to us through the realism of his scenes and the fluency of his style. No one in Italy will ever translate the *Iliad* again. There, Homer will forever be clothed in Monti's apparel, and it seems to me that even in the other European countries, whoever cannot rise to reading Homer in the original will have an idea of the pleasure that he can produce by reading the Italian translation. Translating a poet is not like taking a compass and measuring the dimensions of a building. It is making a different instrument vibrate with the same breath of life as the one we normally hear. A translation should provide as much pleasure as the original, not just duplicate its features.

It seems highly desirable to me for Italians to take the trouble to provide careful translations of various new works of English and German poetry; their compatriots would thus acquire a new genre instead of limiting themselves to images drawn from ancient mythology. Those mythological images are becoming barren; paganism in poetry hardly exists anywhere else in Europe. To make intellectual progress, glorious Italy must often look beyond the Alps, not to borrow, but to know: not to imitate, but to achieve emancipation from those conventional forms that persist, in literature as in society, and prevent the expression of any natural truth.

If poems in translation enrich the arts, the translation of plays can exercise an even greater influence, for theater is truly the executive branch of literature. By joining precision with inspiration, A. W. Schlegel did a translation of Shakespeare that has a truly German flavor. Thus transmitted, English plays are performed on the German stage, and Shakespeare and Schiller have become compatriots. Similar results could be obtained in Italy. French playwrights come as close to the Italian taste as Shakespeare does to the German. It would perhaps be possible to perform *Athalie* successfully on the beautiful stage in Milan, letting the admirable Italian music accompany the chorus. It may be true that Italians go to the theater to talk and meet their friends in the loges rather than to listen; but it is still the case that routinely spending five hours, more or less, every day listening to what Italian operagoers call words is a sure way to diminish the intellectual faculties of a nation. When Casti wrote comic operas, when Métastase wrote musical adaptations filled with charming and elevated thoughts, entertainment lost nothing, and reason gained a great deal. If, in the midst of the habitual frivolity of society, when people rely on others to forget about themselves, you, as artists, could transmit not only pleasure but also a few ideas and feelings; you could train minds to appreciate serious works that give them real value.

Italian literature is now divided between scholars who comb through the ashes of the past, trying to dredge up a few flecks of gold, and writers who rely on the harmony of their language to produce harmonies without ideas, to string together exclamations, declamations, invocations in which not one word either stems from or touches the heart. Would it not be possible to emulate actively the success achieved on the stage, and, thereby, to restore gradually that originality of thought and truth of style without which there is no literature at all, nor perhaps even any of those qualities necessary for literature to exist?

Italian theater has become enthralled with sentimental drama. Instead of the gay, lively spirit that used to exist, instead of those dramatic characters that have been classics throughout Europe, we now see from the very beginning of these plays what I would describe, if I may say so, as the most insipid assassinations it is possible to present on stage. What a poor education the constant repetition of such pleasures gives to a considerable number of people! Italian taste in the arts is as simple as it is noble. But language too is an art, and it too must be treated artistically. Language is integral to our human nature, and we can more easily dispense with paintings and monuments than with those feelings that language should strive to convey.

Italians are extremely enthusiastic about their language. Great writers have shown it to advantage, and intellectual distinction has been the unique pleasure, and often the only consolation, of the Italian nation. If all those capable of thought are to feel motivated to reach their full development, all nations must have an active principle of self-interest. Some countries are militaristic; others are political. Italy's reputation should be based on its literature and its art; otherwise that country will fall into a sort of apathy from which even the sun will not be enough to arouse it.

CHAPTER 8

Black on White: Translation, Race, Class, and Power

Sharon Bell and Françoise Massardier-Kenney

The following dialogue represents an attempt to compensate for the importance of the written in the translation of "Mirza," an importance that goes
against the valorization of orality in the story. This dialogue is also meant to
document the kinds of thought processes that the translator goes through
as he or she is translating, the kinds of "roads not taken" that nonetheless lead to the final version, the kinds of issues that are important for the
translators. The two speakers both translated pieces by Germaine de Staël.
Françoise Massardier-Kenney (identified as *F*) translated "Mirza," and Sharon Bell (identified as *S*) translated the two abolitionist pieces presented in
this volume, "Appel aux souverains" and "Préface pour la traduction d'un
ouvrage de M. Wilberforce." Bell is an African American who has translated
the Haitian writer Jacques-Stéphen Alexis. Massardier-Kenney is a French
native who has translated Lacanian psychoanalytic texts.

The issues the dialogue raises include the influence of the translator's background (be it cultural or racial) on reading and on the translating process,
and power (the superiority/inferiority of the translator over the author, of the
narrator over the characters, of the cultures involved by the translation). This
dialogue is meant more as a mediating ground for asking questions pertinent
to translation than as a place to provide answers.

F: You read my translation of "Mirza." What do you think of the work or
its translation?

S: I thought the translation was very well done. In fact, I was amazed that
in places, you managed to preserve aspects of tone and certain features of
language in the English that I would have thought very difficult to do. But
my reaction to the story itself was very ambivalent. I found the narrator's

comments offensive. If you remember, the narrator of "Mirza" establishes a clear difference between the characters of Ximeo and his wife and those of the blacks who serve them—in fact, between Ximeo and Ourika and the bulk of Africans. These latter are represented as being playful, as having no concept of planning for the future, as being unable to weigh a present evil against a posterior one. Though by the end of the story the narrator is left marveling at the nobility of Ximeo and Mirza, I felt that he looked down on blacks in general (and I myself certainly fall into that category). I had to wonder if Staël had been able to articulate his views so convincingly because she shared them. But I concluded that these comments represented an obvious case of distance between the narrator and the implied author of this story. In any case, whereas it's possible that a nineteenth-century reader could have accepted those initial comments without question, as twenty-first-century readers, we distance ourselves from the things he says. I found that I was so aghast at them that it put me in a position of superiority over him because I could see through his argument. But his comments also tempered my reaction to the rest of the story, in a rather negative way.

F: Absolutely. Yes.

S: And I think that it is interesting that Staël has a male narrator say these things.

F: Yes, he says it to a woman listener, but, again, the narrator might be representing the discourse of the male European who is sympathetic but has those general ideas, like blacks are incapable of providing for their future, but doesn't analyze why it is that they don't plan for their future. It is interesting that there is this distance between the narrator, the author, and the characters.

S: I wonder what the reaction of the public was when it was first published. Did they think like this narrator? Or did they distance themselves from him the way we twenty-first-century readers, especially women, do?

F: It depends on the readers. If the reader is a racist, one who endorses the stereotypes, there probably would be very little distance. The biggest distance might have to do with Ximeo and Mirza. For one thing, they are exceptional characters, and the reader is not. Was I shocked by the narrator's comments? No, I wasn't. It might have to do with the fact that I am white, but within the framework of the story, when the narrator says, "Those people were given a chance to grow sugarcane but they didn't want to do it because they didn't think about the future!" I disagree with his analysis, but

I can see why he would say that. I don't think it says anything about blacks, that it is a statement specifically about blacks.

S: But it appears to be exactly that.

F: True, but all I am saying is that this is a discourse that was used against the working class, that the working class does not plan for the future, that they squander their money, etc. It's a discourse that was current among the middle class in the nineteenth century, at least in France, but we know why the lower class did not plan for the future. They had no future. They had nothing to plan for. So when I hear that, I don't hear it as a statement about race. I hear it as a statement about class—the bourgeois very much in control of his life speaking against the behavior of the lower class. But I do think that in our reactions there is a racial element; you take it personally, whereas I don't. What do you think?

S: Yes, this is the argument I heard all my life, you know: "Blacks are shiftless, lazy, never serious; they're always happy; they don't plan for the future; they squander."

F: Then I have a problem. Since I am not American, I am not quite aware of that discourse. I did not recognize it the way you did. I didn't think, "Oh yeah, the same old thing." What I found most interesting in what Staël was doing is her refusal to endorse essential differences, racial differences, and I think that at the time it was a radical move. And that's where I had a big problem in translating the story. You have a woman at the beginning of the nineteenth century whose main character is a black woman who is extremely articulate and who completely masters language. In the context of the nineteenth century, this is a radical gesture. Then, most people thought that blacks could not do that. To show a character who is the equal, probably the superior, of the reader is a radical gesture, but I have a problem as a translator because that gesture does not work in modern English; to have a black character speak perfect English is not radical. Everybody assumes that there is equality in this regard.

S: Not necessarily. In fact, in the seventies, there were times when I had to go and speak on white campuses to student groups. People would run up to me after my talk and say, "Your English is so beautiful!" And another time at a conference, a man said, "Wow, you speak such good French, and your English is so good too!"

F: So, in thinking that I had not adapted the radical gesture, maybe I was wrong; maybe there is still a need to do that.

S: There is another thing. The lower-class blacks of the story never speak. You don't have to establish a contrast between these two superior individuals and the mass, who is not superior by the way they talk, because the mass never speaks. To have Mirza and Ximeo speak absolutely literate English is, in a way, a gesture. Most blacks don't speak that way with each other in informal contexts. It's more of a gesture than you realize.

F: When I thought about it, I thought that if I really change the way they speak, I am also rewriting Staël, in a way that destroys the project, which is to unearth a tradition of some radicalness, of resistance. Of course, these authors were not all revolutionaries—let's not fool ourselves—but they made that gesture, and it needs to be uncovered, especially in light of the fact that the canonical white male tradition did not do that. So, for historical reasons, I wanted to keep it. But, as you suggest, by keeping it, we are still making that radical claim.

S: What else could you have done?

F: Staël presents a character who is "in translation" because Mirza's native language is not French, yet she speaks in French, so I don't know what I could have done. One thing is to look at some works by contemporary authors from Africa or the West Indies who write in English, or works that have been translated into English and try to follow the rhythms, the metaphors, in a sense to completely rewrite it so as not to give the translation of a translation, but it's very hard to do because it is an early nineteenth-century voice, and we have no idea of what that voice was actually like, and maybe the idea is to emphasize that it is a translation, that that's the only way those voices came to us, in translation. If it hadn't been for translation, they would be silent, or silenced. So the fact that it is in translation might be positive. Because it is only through this project that these texts on race by women will be available. They are not available in their native language at the moment.

S: There's another point too. And it's just this: she has created two characters who have learned French perfectly, who can express poetry, the deepest longings of the soul, in a language that isn't theirs, and we, as teachers of language, know that is a significant accomplishment. Furthermore, Ximeo has learned to speak French from Mirza. She learned from a native speaker; he learned from her. That makes his accomplishment that much greater. But I don't think there is a problem in making them speak perfect English. You don't have to worry about the fact that their French might have been a little foreign. The point is that they completely absorbed a language that was believed at the time to be the language of civilization.

F: But to have characters extremely powerful with language now—but as you say, the situation with blacks may not be as positive as I would like to think—but in the early nineteenth century, that was a radical gesture, which we can assess in the introduction, in the footnotes, but somehow in the text itself, I was unable to do that.

S: There's a tradition in American movies, in several movies where you have a superior black hero who not only speaks absolutely standard English but also listens to classical music, knows fine arts—you know the sort of thing. A class difference, too, is being expressed. But in the sixties, when I saw some of these movies, nobody would have thought of class. The thing that hit you in the face was the racial difference.

F: But I think it is offensive to legitimize a black by the fact that he is only using high culture.

S: Absolutely. In fact, this was part of the motif of the tragic mulatto in black American literature. Often not only was this type of character light skinned, but his or her superiority was seen in the fact that he or she participated in high culture and spoke standard English.

F: So I guess that's what I am fighting against. I thought of a solution for my narrative gesture after seeing the film *Daughters of the Dust,* where people speak English, but a very different kind of English. You understood—well, being French, I did not understand. I didn't recognize some of the words and the sentences, but it was clear to me that it was different from standard English, and I thought if we were doing a movie of "Mirza," that's what we could do, use that kind of language, with subtitles, so that you could get that sense both of extremely high accomplishment and yet of difference, so that you would go to the source language rather than just having the character already speaking in translation.

S: Don't you think that Staël's whole point is that they are not different, or that they are different to the extent that they are superior? It's not a horizontal difference; it's a vertical difference.

F: In terms of the translation of "Mirza," once we tried as an experiment to both translate a part of "Mirza." What is your reaction to the differences?

S: The problems that I had came from a slightly different source, and it was this: I really wanted to reproduce the English of the early nineteenth century.

F: I looked at our translations. I found that there was very little difference. I expected differences; I don't know what. Maybe I am essentializing nationalities or race!

S: Well, I am not an essentialist, and I really wonder if social class in America doesn't wind up having more to do with people's discourse than race does, to a certain extent. As for the two of us as readers, our experience has sensitized us to certain kinds of things, and your observation that this story is about class, to me, makes good sense. I first saw it as being solely about race. The negative comments about blacks made by the narrator apply to blacks of a different class from Mirza and Ximeo, but I saw them as racial, pure and simple. It didn't occur to me that these were things people were also saying about lower-class white people or the lumpen proletariat. But aside from being sensitized to different kinds of issues, and in my case having a vernacular language that's not standard English, aside from that, I really wonder if things like social class and education don't influence the way we think and the way we write more than things like race. And you have lived in America for a number of years—you are becoming bicultural.

F: Then, to go back to "Mirza," are you saying that we need to translate it, to have a text acknowledging, or not even acknowledging but assuming, that there is complete equality?

S: Yes, and in fact, this text assumes that nobility and greatness of spirit can belong to anybody. Black American literature also has this message quite a lot, but, strikingly, not tied to social class. Celie in *The Color Purple* comes immediately to mind. But I think it's fascinating that you find this same message, if you know how to look, how to decode the text, from a woman who lived in eighteenth-century France. I think that's a very interesting addition to the general discourse about race that goes on in America right now.

F: So, my feeling about Staël's contribution was that she refuses to take race as an ultimate difference. She says basically race is a mark of difference that is used against people, but that's all it is. It is something that is used. It is not something that's essential, and that does not disturb you? You endorse that too—is this what you are saying? The question I am trying to ask is: do I think it is a contribution because I am white or a Western intellectual? Did you react differently?

S: See, I didn't pick up that reading. Readers bring to a text their own experiences and their own presuppositions, so I did not read it that way. But when I hear you explain it, I think, "Of course!" Perhaps the fact that I found this text offensive in some ways stopped me from seeing beyond the things that offended me. I think you are absolutely right, that it is a reading where race is not a matter of essential difference, that people are alike everywhere.

She creates these two characters who prove that black people are just like white people, though that's an extremely offensive way to put it.

F: Well, let's put it this way: white people are like black people.

S: Or like this: qualities like intelligence, nobility, goodness, and badness are equally distributed among the human race. Things like genius and stupidity—all these are universal characteristics of human beings.

F: There is no essential difference, but she does recognize some cultural differences, like orality as opposed to writing, and even though this is a written story, it's a written story about somebody who communicates orally. So, because the frame is written, you could say that the power structure is such that the Western tradition (writing) wins. At the same time, the writing is a translation of, a transcription of, the oral. But the oral is present, and that presence, the presence of that voice, is very important. Without Staël, we wouldn't have it. There would be no voice of that Jolof woman, Mirza. At the same time, our reactions were very different, and they seem to be different along racial lines. When you first read the text, you found offensive the passages where the narrator made generalizations about black behavior.

S: And I found offensive the fact that these two were given special status because they were superior. In other words, blacks didn't have any value unless they were superior; nobody considered the mass of blacks at all.

F: But at the same time, it's the same for French workers. In Staël's novels, you don't hear about what the maid thinks. All you have represented is the extremely educated woman. You are right, the lower class is not given a voice. I have another question. You translated the Wilberforce piece, and I would like to speak about it to see if you think that somehow you made certain changes because the issue was race, and you are an African American.

S: There was a place where I very deliberately changed the sentence because she said something I found shocking: she called blacks "savages," or something like that. You also have this thing with *sauvage, primitif, rustique* in French, words whose English cognates have very negative connotations but that are much less emotionally loaded in French. I deliberately softened that one sentence, and yet, because of the difference between what words like *primitif* and *sauvage* mean in French and English, it may be that my refraction would pass unnoticed. I remember that the statement offended me so much, I could not put down what the sentence actually said.

F: My next question is if, in my translation, when you read it, you still have that reaction of distaste, then there is a sense in which I failed because. . . .

S: No, I don't think you, as a translator, failed. I think readers help create texts, and we create them by bringing our baggage, rightly or wrongly, to the text. Scholars are supposed to be able to distance themselves from their own emotional baggage. We are supposed to have the capacity to look at the background out of which a text arose and judge it a little more dispassionately. I'm really talking about two different readings, and in the translation, you translated very much the spirit of the text. But I read it according to my own presuppositions, shaped in part by the racial discourse of America, and by the fact that I've personally been a victim of that discourse.

F: My first reaction to this text, as a naive reader, was that I was a little annoyed by the romantic excesses of Mirza. I must say that in my translation, I tried to soften the excesses and wanted to valorize her speech. I wanted to make sure that people reading only the English would get from the text a sense of the power of that voice, as opposed to the quaint or romantic.

S: I think that the power of the voice comes through. But a lot of times, our reactions to "old" literature are cultural reactions shaped by the fact that cultural values have changed. One example I think of is Dickens's *The Old Curiosity Shop*, where one of the most touching scenes in the novel is the death of Little Nell. All these people came to weep at her bedside for days and days. This is obviously a climactic point in this novel, but for a modern reader it's just embarrassing. We just don't look at death in the same way.

F: But maybe that's where the translator can change things. Is there a voice in English that would allow "Mirza" to come through closer to us, and more effectively?

S: Well, that brings up another concern of mine as I translated. And that was trying to maintain the sound of an early nineteenth-century text. Was it an option not to do that?

F: I think it's always an option. The question is: why are you translating? The reason for translating, for me, was to really reconstitute the tradition of women writing about race, a tradition that is a generous tradition that is not part of the racist discourse. So I was very much pulled to the source text. And again, I thought that some of the options discussed, like using English from an African writer, were as questionable as this one. But I do think that there are other options.

S: I wonder if African writers writing at that time might, except for subject matter, not be indistinguishable from European ones. I don't know the writings of Equiano or Gustavus Africanus, two very early African writers who wrote in English.

F: So that's also a problem. Or choose somebody contemporary—for example, English from the West Indies. But again, who is the audience? The audience will probably not recognize that it's that kind of English. You spoke about the background of the readers. We are basically addressing a middle-class academic readership, so it's very circumscribed by the circumstances. And our readers will be likely to read the discussion or introduction.

S: And another thought occurs to me. If the first gut level of the reading in French is going to be offensive, to what extent do you expect the translation to bring out another reading? When I translated Staël, I wanted my readers in English to get what readers in French got. I don't want to bring out the subtext. If it's there, let them dig for it the way I have to dig for it in French. But it's also valid to translate in such a way that you do bring out alternate readings. In fact, your translation has to bring out some reading.

F: Do you think that the race of the translator is a determining factor in the translation of those kinds of texts, or do you think that an informed translator is what you need, regardless of race?

S: You need an informed translator. But, on the other hand, I think race is intimately tied to culture in this country because of segregation, and culture has everything to do with values you absorb growing up. There is also the fact that translators have to decide what they are going to do with the text. Do we translate this as nineteenth-century English, or do we come up with a really modern translation? Do we soften ideas offensive to modern sensibilities in otherwise sympathetic writers, or do we let them speak freely, for better or worse? A translator has to make those decisions, and again, you almost have to privilege one reading, and the translator chooses which reading to privilege. As a translator, I take the text very seriously, and I don't want deliberately to slant the text in a direction in which I don't feel that it was already going, so I stay close to what the surface meaning of the text appears to be. That means that if other readings exist, maybe a reader who closely analyzes the text can pull them out, but I'm very reluctant to try to do that as part of the act of translation. But you've got to translate one reading or another, so in a way, whether or not to translate these subtexts becomes a false problem. And if a translator arrives at a reading that the text can be seen to support, then it's valid to render that reading in the translation, even if it seems radical, different from what you first perceived when you read the French. When you translated, you didn't think of trying to translate this in very contemporary English?

F: No, I did not think that was an option. But it wasn't an option because my goal was to allow the voice of Staël and Mirza to sound, and if I'd done that there's a sense in which it wouldn't have been Staël's voice. So, that is why I went back to the English romantics, and the most consonant was Mary Shelley, another woman, and the work that helped me the most was *Frankenstein,* the story of the monster.

F: On another topic, does the inclusion of discourses that are opposed to her position in her two abolitionist pieces make you rethink your reaction to "Mirza"? She has listened to the proponents of the slave trade and she addresses their arguments, so their arguments are a part of her discourse, like her references to Christianity. In "Mirza," she does the same. The narrator is not the radical that she is. Therefore, he comes up with those stereotypes about what he expects the Africans to be. I'm just wondering, in terms of your translating those two pieces, whether that affected retrospectively your reaction to "Mirza," or not.

S: It didn't, because I still didn't get it. To look at Mirza and Ximeo in light of what was then current racist discourse never hit me. I looked at it in the light of present-day racist discourse. That's why I couldn't really see what Staël had accomplished in that story.

F: One of the contributions that Staël makes is that she endorses orality rather than justifying black equality or superiority. What do you think of that? Do you think it's significant, or that making her characters express themselves orally is closer to African traditions, although she can't get back to the African voice? Is the fact that she insists on the oral tradition a positive thing, as people like Chamoiseau would argue?

S: The fact that the story is recounted orally didn't really hit me one way or the other. And privileging the oral didn't strike me as harking back to African tradition. Orality turns out to be important in a lot of other cultures, too. I think of the salon in France, for example.

F: But the salon is woman's stuff; compared to the written production of the males, it was considered secondary.

S: And yet the salons were probably the catalyst for the creative output of both men and women in the eighteenth century. And furthermore, the art of conversation was probably raised to a very high level and given a great deal of prestige. Well, that's the connection I made with the oral discourse and the fact that the story is actually presented orally and orality is given such a privileged position.

F: So you tied orality to the salon, that is, to the origin of the white writer, as opposed to tying it to the tradition of a number of African countries where the oral transmission of culture was primary.

S: Yes. I'm wondering what eighteenth- and nineteenth-century Europe even knew about African traditions and orality.

F: Well, they knew they didn't use the written word to transmit their tales, myths, and philosophy.

S: I'm not sure they knew about their tales, myths, and philosophies then.[1] When anthropologists started going to Africa in the mid-nineteenth century, a lot of those things began to be revealed to the rest of the world for the first time. What the discourse we heard here in North America said was that there was no culture. Africans were basically wild people who hunted, who had unbridled sexual mores, and who were incapable of founding families. There was an assumption that there was no culture to be transmitted orally.

F: Even if the French at large didn't know it, showing that their culture privileges the oral would be a fairly advanced gesture, as opposed to saying that the only way to do culture is through the written word.

S: After all, *Bug-Jargal* is oral too. The whole thing is an oral recitation. The oral recitation within a novelistic frame was a device a lot of people used in nineteenth-century fiction.

F: Yes, but in *Bug-Jargal* they don't have the black character going up to the top of a hill and spouting off poetry. Do you see what I'm saying? That there's an insistence here on cultural skills that are oral. These characters know how to write, so it's not that they can't write—it's that they *won't* write. Actually, when Ximeo writes, it's to tell Mirza lies. So writing is devalorized. I stated that the use of pidgin French or pidgin English used by other writers like Maupassant in *Timbouctou* was more racist than what Staël does. Do you agree with that?

S: I think I agree, because Africans were thought not to be able to acquire a language. And so for her to depict these characters as capable of using French to express great depths of feeling with eloquence definitely makes a statement.

F: So you think it's a more racist technique to have black characters use nonstandard English as opposed to standard English?

S: Well, you know, the one example I remember is in *Bug-Jargal*, and I feel that to portray inferiority is absolutely its purpose in *Bug-Jargal*. Although it seems Bug spoke a mixture of French and Spanish, and what you see is command of two languages. But with Jean François, Biassou, and the dwarf, I suspect that their mixture of French, Spanish, and Creole was a manifestation of their inferiority: it's as if they're incapable of learning one language right.

F: I agree. Again, inferiority, and class inferiority as well, because you can't imagine educated people speaking pidgin French or pidgin English.

F: The historical survey in chapter 2 mentions La Place's translation of a text on blacks where he adapts and does something much more radical with the racial elements and completely rewrites it. That's not acceptable nowadays to completely rewrite, to remove some episodes or add some. But if we said it was acceptable at the moment, how would "Mirza" be rewritten through radical translation? As a translator, how would you do it?

S: I really have trouble accepting that liberal a standard. I wouldn't do it.

F: You wouldn't do it? Well, I have the same reaction in a sense. There's a sense in which people can argue that translation of those kinds of texts is being co-opted or used by abolitionists. The question is: can you preserve a nonhegemonic voice when translating literature or expository essays like Staël's? My reaction is that when the translator is a woman there's a sense of deference to the authority of the text. And then you have somebody like La Place, who is the male and is going to come up and make everything right. I find such an attitude offensive.

S: And with the translations of *Bug-Jargal* that we examined, one of the translators did exactly that. But we found another translation that kept very closely to the text, and that was the work of a woman translator.

F: You just reacted the same way when I just asked you how you would do a radical translation, and you said, "Well, I wouldn't." Because there is a sense in which it is a very arrogant position to take something that is radical and say, "It isn't radical enough, let's completely change it." To what?

S: That tends to be my feeling. However, we mentioned the idea that often you have subtexts that perhaps you could bring to the surface, depending on how you translate. I really do believe that different readers, because of their different experiences, preconceptions, and ideals, will legitimately create different texts. So why is it not possible, as these translators work, to produce quite different translations of the same originals but still to operate within limits?

F: When you did your translation of Alexis, you did a radical translation because you used black English very often when the text was in standard French. So, you radicalized it.

S: Actually, it wasn't standard French. In one place that I have just looked at again, the register was very familiar, and it dawns on me now as I'm thinking about this that I don't have that register in standard English myself. But I think, too, that it was a case of trying to bring out a subtext that actually did exist. I know of one white scholar who is translating Alexis, and, in fact, I've seen the Spanish translation of the same work I've translated. The Spanish one was very direct. Whereas I use a lot of the popular register in English, which is black English, the Spanish translator didn't use the vernacular at all. I haven't seen any of the work of the American translator I've mentioned, but I'm very curious to see what he comes up with when his translation comes out.

F: But for "Mirza," how could we do it? I just thought about one way to radicalize it. We could find a person who speaks the language of the Wolof and who could supply us with a translation into Wolof of the passage when the narrator comes to Ximeo's plantation. The guide could then say to the narrator, "Oh, of course you don't speak Wolof, so let me translate this for you."

S: That's wonderful!

F: So that would be a way to radicalize it, to give the characters back their voice, in a sense. Instead of presenting them in translation, you would also have the original language so that your text would contain whatever African language was spoken specifically in that region, plus the French translation. The reader would be put in the position of the French narrator, which is that you understand one thing, but you don't understand the other one. Another thing I thought about, where you wouldn't really need to change the story: near the end, when Mirza speaks to herself, she would speak in another language. In a footnote, you could translate it into French or into English. It would be a way to put the voice back in again.

S: But the idea of having them speak something else in front of the Frenchman and excluding him is a wonderful idea. I thought of other things one can do. In the discourse between Ximeo and Mirza, you could do code mixing with African languages. Why would it be improbable that they had not given each other their own languages, as well as the French? You drop a word here and there. And maybe you don't explain it, or you put it in a footnote. That's a way it could be done too.

F: And that would be a way to bring the issue of translation to the fore, which is a major issue. Even when you have those well-meaning French abolitionists, their black characters are in translation already; their natural language is already lost. So that would be a way to make sure the reader perceives that loss and maybe make the reader reexperience the loss.

S: When we originally began working on this text, we were dealing with ideological translation. And we were considering it fairly negatively. We were considering those instances in *Bug-Jargal* where the translator had changed things around very obviously, deleted things favorable to blacks and added things that weren't in the text that were favorable to whites. From the standard of our times, that's a very obvious misuse of translation. And having started this project discussing incidents like that, that's one of the things that made me especially careful to try not to refract Staël, at least not deliberately.

F: The reason why we've all stayed fairly close to the text was because we were aware of all the negative ideological implications of changing it. If you do it yourself, under another agenda, is it legitimate or not?

S: Well, take the example of the passages in the Staël pieces that I translated, where we deliberately tried to bring out feminist subtexts. I don't know where Staël was coming from as a feminist. And I was very uncomfortable doing some of it, simply because I was so conscious of not changing things ideologically. Yet going from one language to another is complicated because languages are not equal; it's not an algebraic equation. So you take a term like *maîtresse* in "There was no chance France could become mistress of that colony again." It's actually legitimate to say in English, "There was no chance France would regain mastery of that island." That seems to fit with the way we think in English a little bit better. I think translating to bring out subtexts that a reader legitimately sees in a text, in order to bring them out, not to create them where the translator wishes they existed—I don't think that's an illegitimate act of interpretation.

S: Well, I think this brings us back to where we started, considering the quality of the story as well as that of the translation. Your reading of "Mirza" has uncovered some significant subtexts. To propose a different answer to your very first question, I'd say that, while your translation doesn't make them obvious—any more than they are obvious in the French—it definitely preserves them and makes it possible for an informed reader to discover them in English.

Part Four

Abolitionism, 1820–1830

Doris Y. Kadish & Françoise Massardier-Kenney

Translating Slavery vol. I:
Gender & Race in French Abolitionist
Writing, 1780–1830

Kent, OH: The Kent State
University Press, 2009

CHAPTER 9

Translations of Abolitionist Narrative, Poetry, and Theater

SOPHIE DOIN — *Author*

THE BLACK FAMILY (EXCERPT) *1825*
(*Françoise Massardier-Kenney translator*)

A few months had gone by, and Phenor, now the sole consolation of his parents, devoted all his time ensuring the safety of his loved ones. But what can the care of a single man do against thousands of enemies, except delay the moment of its disappearance? That's all.

One night, a thick cloud of smoke rose in the air; its smell awakens Phenor, always quick to flee from the sleep in which he rarely indulges and that never banishes his worries. A muddled sound strikes his ear; he goes out: already the cottages are surrounded by armed men, already the words "pillage," "attack," "fright," and the word, the horrible word, "slavery" are uttered and make him shudder. "It is over for us," he says, hitting his forehead furiously. "Our enemies, perhaps our neighbors, are here; they came in numbers, spurred on by the whites, the whites who today are their allies and tomorrow their masters. It is the end! O my father! I wish I could protect you with my body! O my mother, I wish I could save your life with mine! What am I saying? Ah, let me be a slave if need be so that you can be free! Here they are, here they are! Ah, here comes the end; there are no gods for us."

Soon, in the sinister light of a general conflagration, the unfortunate inhabitants can see their friends dying under the sword, their parents mutilated, their brothers in shackles. Phenor, whose hopeless courage is still an audacious heroism, presses against his chest his faltering mother and at the same time, with all his might, turns away the blows that threaten the old man who gave him life. But the hour of death has tolled for this unfortunate father. He is struck down; he is no longer.

Phenor, surrounded on all sides, makes a heroic effort; opens up a path; and, his mother in his arms, dashes toward a nearby wood.

Among animals, the instinct of conservation gives courage and care to mothers, but the young, whom they protect so well, almost always abandon them as soon as they can manage without their care; hence their young no longer even know who they are. Yet here it is an old, weak, disabled mother who can only be for her son now a source of strain and worries, whom he defends so fearlessly. "Ah," you will say, "it is because this son is a man. You whites, whites, let this word not only strike your ears, but let it penetrate into your souls! Yes, this black is a man; how can he be inferior to you?"

The fugitives are hunted into the wood. Until daylight Phenor can hide his mother there; until daylight he defends himself skillfully. At last, hunted by arrows like a wild animal, and seeing these deathly arrows, these poisonous arrows, fall by the hundreds around the bosom that carried him, he cries out, "Stop, stop, cruel men, will you listen to me? I surrender. I am young, I am strong, I can be of use to you in many ways. Take me, burden me with work, with exhausting and harsh tasks of all kinds, but spare my mother. Look at this poor mother, this poor old woman worn by worries and sorrow! Gaze upon her shivering limbs, her bruise-covered flesh, her withered body; soon she will no longer be. Let her die free! I shall serve you for two; she would only be a useless burden for you. Your interest as well as the cry of pity speak in her favor. Let her be free! As for me, I surrender to you!"

Thus, the good, respectable Phenor is taken away like a wretched slave. Thus in Africa, filial piety, courage, virtue, heroism, and fearlessness, qualities honored among all the people of Europe, qualities rewarded in all classes of society and often respected even by our highway robbers, these virtues only result in enslavement! Who destroyed this natural veneration? Who violated this sacred devotion? It is the Europeans, the whites, who did.

The horrible destiny of the unfortunate black was far from being fulfilled still; he sees the object of his painful distress, his unfortunate mother, being dragged at the rear of the caravan, without regard for her age or for the prayers of her virtuous son. He sees her burdened with heavy loads, broken at last under the weight of so many repeated torments. He sees merciless men bring the hapless creature back to life with heavy blows! It is with sharp cries, heart-breaking tones that he lets out his bitter plaint, that he expresses his just despair. The screams of the maniacs, their odious acts of violence, drown his voice.

Finally, having arrived near an isolated dwelling, he begged his torturers, one more time, to take pity on his mother and to leave her near the shanty. It may be that these cruel and savage men were annoyed by his laments or that they thought they could take advantage of the woman, who was tall and whose size was perhaps advantageous, or that they were driven on by the whites who were escorting them and who wanted to move quickly to the coast where their slave trade ships were awaiting them; they only answered with a violent blow to this wretched woman to make her walk. Unable to hold back his indignation, Phenor leaped to avenge her. At the same time, a young woman who had stepped out of the cottage, struck by Phenor's movement and by the object of his strong interest, cried out, "O God! Thus was my mother! Masters, masters, I am young. I am fifteen, I can endure anything. Leave this poor woman here and take Néala."

O electric movement, soul stirring expression! You then overcame the black man! O poor black! Your eyes, until then burning and dried up, gazed at Néala and filled with tears of gratitude.

The traders moved close to the young woman; they saw that she was by herself. "Come, you, come," they said sharply to her. They got hold of her, tied her up like the others, and similarly burden her head and shoulders.[1]

But to Néala's great surprise, to her great sorrow, they kept dragging along the old Negress with them. Néala filled the air with touching outbursts. She was severely beaten. A deadly shudder overtook Phenor.

At last, the poor Negress has no strength left; she falls. This time, nothing can make her stand back up. "Kill me," she says. They tried to frighten her; they tried to force her still, but in vain. She repeated, "Kill me," and she closed her eyes. They conferred; at the end of a few minutes, a violent blow crushed her head. They removed her effects. Phenor fainted.

There is no need to mention that the most barbarous treatments were used to bring him back to consciousness and to force him to stand back up. "Kill me," he said in turn. "Take me out of my suffering. I will not get up again. I want to follow my mother." They treated him more cruelly yet. Covered with bruises, he repeated, "I want to follow my mother."

The slave drivers' anger then knew no bounds. The most horrible tortures did not cost them anything. The martyr's courage could not move them; it only moved the heavens, the angels who were holding out their arms to him.

Phenor's determination seemed irreversible when the most tender voice uttered these words near him: "O Phenor, live for me, live for Néala. Néala gave herself for your mother."

The black man gave a start. A new day seemed to shine for him, a new life entered him, his eyes gazed upon Néala. Weak, bloody, he gets up, looks at the sky, and walks silently.

O true flash of sympathy, powerful bond shaped by love and misfortune! You are the beneficent dew that cools the plant parched by the burning sun, battered by the storm, crushed under the hooves of the fiery horses.

Here is the fatal slave ship! Here is the building invented by humans where men are mutilated by Christians to the point that they cannot have the little room that one day they will occupy in their coffin. In this coffin, these Christians will feel nothing, and all the sensitive faculties of these men, men like them, are destroyed in the fullness of life. In this place of misery and infamy, in this place of hellish torture, the complete deprivation of movement gives to these unfortunates' limbs the most painful contractions, while the complete lack of air creates for them pestilential infections, fainting fits, suffocations, blood influxes, apoplectic seizures, and all the convulsions of sorrow and rage.[2]

When boarding the ship, Phenor shuddered and became indignant, but it is especially on Néala's account. When he had completely realized all the horrors of his position, he looked to see if there was no way to put an end to so many ills. He looked all around and, taking advantage of a moment when the chain was broken, he seized a knife left on a pile of ropes and rushed toward Néala with the intention of killing her and himself afterward. They tore his weapon away from him, but they could not prevent him from taking away Néala into his arms. He cried out, "Precious creature, unfortunate Negress, can't we at least die together!" They were quickly separated, but their outbursts were so strong, their movements so desperate, their exaltations so frenzied, that the very sight of them was considered too dangerous for the rest of the crew. After being penned up with their fellow slaves for several hours, they were drawn from their prison to receive the punishment that their so-called audacity was to draw upon them from their tormentors.

One moment they thought they would be thrown into the sea; already they were thanking the heavens and looked at each other for what they believed was the last time when—do I dare say it, will it be possible to hear it without shuddering?—when they were locked up into a barrel,[3] yes, a barrel. "So, stay together there," one of the Europeans said to him with a diabolical irony. There, receiving air only every two hours at most, that is, only what was necessary in order not to give out their last breath, they were prey to unimaginable distress during most of the crossing. Finally, unconscious, they were thrown down in the hold until the end of the voyage, and meanwhile on the deck, the sailors, happy to look at the pure blue sky, were singing love songs!

The victims' cries do not interrupt them; they sing, and the ship, lightly rocked by a benevolent breeze, grazes over the tranquil sea and swiftly sails toward the land of misery.

All of you who are reading me with surprise—you who reject what I am saying; you who are indifferent and only feel disgust at this narrative; and you who, in your own climate, are revolted by injustice, who curse slavery and ceaselessly fight prejudices by preaching religion and tolerance—consider that Negroes have souls like you, a soul that is roused by crime, that rebels against injustice and fears being chained; that these are the very Negroes on whom we inflict so much suffering at once!

Open your eyes, you who until now thought that the blacks of Africa were only torn from the bosom of their motherland to be converted to our divine religion; that they were taken to the colonies only to plough the earth like our farmers and to receive the food necessary for them to live, and more plentiful than what they found in their climate; that they are punished only like children who must be disciplined somewhat severely in order to correct their bad inclinations: it is not so, it is not. They are brought there like martyrs; they only eat what is necessary so that they don't die, weakened as they are by exhaustion and torture; they become mad and furious and can only bear life when they have succeeded in killing themselves; finally, they will always refuse heaven as long as they see this sky inhabited by their torturers. I know that some of you will mention slaves who sacrificed themselves to their masters, who followed them in exile, who fed them with the fruit of their labor, but whom are we praising there? Is it the whites? I also admit that other Negroes never complained about their situation; these were probably born in slavery and could only judge by comparison. Could they reason like men of intelligence when they have been dulled since the day they were born? I don't say either that there are no humane masters; there may be some on these burning lands, but should one spread the plague because one can find a few individuals who are never struck by it?

There are sad sights for the man who believes in his noble origin, in his most noble destiny, for instance, these fanatics who, in their terrible zeal, burned the Protestants in Europe because their dogmas differed slightly from their own and who encouraged and protected the thefts, abductions, violence, and assassinations of so many of their black brothers in Africa, whom they thought they could convert by using these odious means. These men strongly believed in the soul; they strongly believed in God but did not know him, these men, excessive in their faith, who turned a religion of peace into a religion of cruelty. Would materialists or atheists have been more barbarous? Fanaticism destroys reason and violates humanity. Some people used to think that blacks could not have souls and were not men like us because their hair, their lips and nose, differed slightly from those of whites. In plying the slave trade, these people only thought about their own personal profit. For them, religion was a convenient excuse; most often they were hypocrites or unbelievers. Those who now engage in the same traffic are also men without honor or faith.

Phenor and Néala, sold to the same plantation owner, saw new hardships ahead of them, but they were together. It was much; it was enough to be able to bear much misery.

"A BLACK WOMAN AND A WHITE MAN"
Doris Y. Kadish and Françoise Massardier-Kenney

A whirlwind of flames rose over the city of Le Cap. Human blood foamed in the streets. Everywhere torrents of vengeance paid for murder with murder, torture with torture. The independence of blacks had just been proclaimed, and degraded creatures, brutish slaves, flocked from everywhere, with hatred in their hearts and weapons in their hands, asking that barbarous masters account for having destroyed their intelligence and crushed their freedom. The sea was already covered with small vessels; several rescue ships were already taking on board the unfortunate fugitives, victims of all the hatred, all the fury let loose on this desolate land. They ran, they rushed, they collapsed as they neared this beacon of hope and salvation. Some, pushed back violently by the crowd, which every minute grew larger, fell and met their death in the sea. Others clung to the ropes, and the air echoed with their desperate cries while their companions, no less unfortunate, were crammed together beneath the feet of those who could still stand up on the deck. In one place, I noticed an unfortunate father tearing out his hair after having seen his son drown before his very eyes; in another, I saw a woman making vain efforts to save her wounded husband, who was about to disappear beneath the waves.

The two arms of this poor woman were wrapped around his and she fought valiantly. But her husband dragged her down; they both would perish.

Arrogant colonists, foolish whites: what honors have you brought forth! what crimes have you wrought! for you, yes you alone, have brought about these bloody disasters, these devastating wars that have led to your destruction. Without your awful despotism, your base desires, your ferocious greed, your execrable vengeance, Saint Domingue would have remained at peace; the unhappy slave would have died a slave. But you wanted to teach him war, and then he demanded war. You put the word "vengeance" in his mouth, and the whole colony resounded against you with this rallying cry: Vengeance! vengeance!

You say you have suffered; you call blacks barbarians and assassins. Ah! why didn't you just leave the child of Africa in the middle of his desert? He would have lived simply, innocently, hospitably. He would have farmed his land. Happiness would have brought him industry, art, enlightenment. Happiness would have produced Christians, and you have produced monsters! How can you complain? Did you think then that the God who punishes all crimes would protect the ones you committed? that this God, who condemns theft, kidnapping, murder, treason, would approve of them when they are committed by whites against blacks? that this God, who said, "All men are brothers," would have wanted to create one species of men who would be the slaves and victims of another species of men? Wretched madmen that you are!

Chaos was at its worst, and deserted houses were being looted. Frightened by the ominous cries coming from all sides, Nelzi drew near the window. She saw the crowd moving in the direction of the coast; she heard the threats coming from blacks, the exclamations of rage, fear, and despair from whites. "Oh my master!" she said. "Can I stand by and watch you massacred before my very eyes? My poor young master, weak, wounded, almost unconscious, how can I carry you from this bed where you lie dying? Alas! all your friends are far away: some in battle, others deceased, still others in flight. All have abandoned you. Your slaves are free and will return as your enemies. The only one who remains is me, just me. Can I, alone, save you? Ah! at least I'll try. Dear God, protect your Nelzi. Oh! how poor Nelzi will love you!"

Her need to do a good deed, to save the one she loved, and her ardent enthusiasm for virtue set her afire with resolution. Nelzi moved rapidly, lifted the victim from what would have been his deathbed, wrapped her arms around him, supported him on her shoulders, descended the stairs as rapidly as the weight of her burden allowed, making her way though a house about to be destroyed by fire at any moment. She arrived at the coast: a rowboat was departing. "Save him!" she cried with a heartrending sound. A white-haired officer heard her voice and signaled the impatient sailors to stop. He reached out to the young black woman. She handed over into his arms the wounded man, who had fainted. She too jumped into the boat. Then, hastening to kneel and raising her wide, tearful eyes toward heaven, she rejoiced, "He is saved! Oh my God, how I love him!"

The old officer's boat soon reached a vessel setting sail for America. When Charles had been revived, when the officer had presented Nelzi to him as the guardian angel who had saved him from the most awful massacre, the young Frenchman held out his hand to his friend, looking at her tenderly. "Oh my Nelzi," he said to her, "I owe everything to you. How will I ever be able to repay you? You are all that's left to me in the world. Ah! may I forget all my woes in caring for your happiness."

Nelzi kissed with rapture the hand that Charles had placed in hers. Then she lovingly answered him: "I am near you, my dear master, I want nothing more."

"I am not your master, Nelzi, You don't belong to me; you belong only to yourself." "Dear God! do you want to abandon me?"

"I shall never abandon you, Nelzi. We will always live together, but I will not be your master. I will be your friend, your father."

"My friend, my father, oh! whatever you wish."

Charles de Méricourt was thirty years old. An orphan since he was very young, heir to a great name, but poor, he owed his brilliant education and social position in the colonies to his uncle, M. de Bellerive. Charles happened to be in Le Cap at that time. Amidst the chaos and hatred that reigned there, even within the parties at war with one another, he had managed to retain his gentleness and moderation until the events that we have just recounted. It was only then that, forced to participate, he was seriously wounded in the general turmoil and was only saved thanks to the devotion of his black slave.

America, that hospitable land, opened its arms to the fugitives. It consoled them, helped them, gave them the means to return to Europe or allowed them to use their talents in the New World. Charles accepted a modest job and established himself in a city in the great state of New York.

Nelzi took care of the household. Charles treated her like a sister, spending all his free time with her. He enjoyed forming this new soul, developing the intelligence that prejudice had repressed until that time. Sometimes he asked himself whether whites hadn't perhaps had some valid reason for treating blacks as a brutish race, A thousand times he had heard rich colonists and beautiful ladies say, with complete conviction: "Blacks are only too happy to be our slaves: what would become of them otherwise? They are really only animals, far beneath monkeys."

"Can I believe," he asked himself, "that for several centuries, a horrible crime has been committed? Or shouldn't I think instead that the intellectual faculties of blacks are, in fact, out of proportion with human intelligence?" Then he would look at Nelzi and notice that fire in her eyes, that mark of a lively intelligence, that expression of deep feeling. He explained to Nelzi the phenomena of nature, the marvels of art, the consolations of virtue, the charms of friendship, and Nelzi understood everything, felt everything, and answered with that eloquence of the soul, with that pure enthusiasm, that is proof of an elevated mind, a noble heart, a deep sensitivity. "How then does this soul differ from mine? How is this interesting being inferior to beings of my species? No, no, it is false, it is impossible. Oh cruel prejudice! No, her body alone has been less favored. . . . But doesn't she have her own beauty? Aren't her eyes beautiful, large, expressive? Aren't her teeth admirable? And what expression in her smile! And her dear voice is so sweet to my ear! Even her color has its glow, its nuances. I see it darken when a reproach passes my lips; it shines when I smile. Her figure is perfect; her curves are grace-ful. Her whole person is endowed with a poise, a piquant beauty. Oh Nelzi, Nelzi, nature has adorned you too with a thousand charms!" Thus spoke Charles, and with each day, Charles cursed ever more European prejudices and colonial cruelty. At first he pitied Nelzi. Soon he admired her: how could he not love her? He was everything for her; she became everything for him. He gave her his heart and his faith before the God of nature.

Nelzi saw nothing above Charles. She had given herself to him from the first day she had known him. She believed that God himself spoke to her though his voice and consented with joy to find a husband in the person who for her gave meaning to the past, the present, and the future. Charles wanted to teach his friend the precepts of our divine religion. The dogma of the immortality of the soul was adopted by her with all the gratitude of a heart full of the immense goodness of the Creator. She admired the pure morality of Christianity, that immutable basis of sound philosophy, tolerance, and freedom. She was touched by the divine order of the divine Redeemer:

love your neighbor like yourself; do unto others as you would have them do unto you. "Your religion must be mine," she said to Charles. "What you love, Nelzi will love. What you admire, how could Nelzi not admire it? But, my beloved, among all your brothers, are you thus the only Christian?"

"What do you mean, Nelzi?"

"Are they Christian, they who took my brothers from their families, from their country? they who repay their thankless work with lashes of the whip? they who have used our blood to irrigate their land of misery? they who answer bitter tears with menace, and just complaints with torture? Is that how Christians treat their neighbors, and is that how they do unto others what they would have done unto them?"

Charles often felt somewhat embarrassed responding to the objections of the innocent black woman, but he made her envision another life where the unjust would be punished, regardless of their color, and the virtuous would triumph, whatever skin covering they might have had on earth. Nelzi was reassured then. She raised her eyes to heaven, thought she saw black legions there crowned as martyrs, and thanked her friend for having opened her heart to this consoling religion.

A letter that arrived from Europe changed their fate. An unknown aunt had sent it to report that M. de Bellerive had lost his son and that his sorrow at this loss, combined with the terrible commotion caused by the events of the French Revolution, had led him too to the grave. The aunt added that having arrived from England two years before M. de Bellerive's death, she had consoled him in his last moments, and that the unfortunate old man had named in his will as his only heirs her daughter and Charles de Méricourt, but on one condition that surely Charles would hasten to accept. The aunt, Mme Darbois, ended her letter with these words: "Come back then, my dear nephew, so that I can embrace you. I know that you have a black woman who has served you faithfully. I know this story. Bring us this heroine of the black race. I assure you that I am ready to treat her more as a friend than as a black."

"I can hesitate no longer," cried Charles. "My country, my country, I shall be able to see you again! You beckon me, ah! who could resist your enchanting voice? . . I lead an aimless life here. I am only employed thanks to the generosity of the American government, which supports me. Oh my Nelzi, I shall possess a little fortune, I shall surround you with the pleasures of a life of ease. I shall show you off with pride as a model of all virtues. You shall help me fight the prejudices that my compatriots hold against your oppressed brothers. Come, my Nelzi, let us go."

Mme Darbois was a good woman. She engaged in good works, but she had kept many of her ancestors' prejudices. Thus, after welcoming her nephew with open arms, she looked at Nelzi with a curiosity typical of a white person; came up to her with a familiar benevolence; then, in appreciation of what she had done for Charles, gave her a kiss, but a patronizing kiss. Mme Darbois put up her nephew as well as she could; as for Nelzi, she was given a small room, tucked away. But she did not dare complain; Charles himself was not complaining.

Charles had read the will: the condition that his uncle had put on the gift of his fortune had quite stunned him. It had to do with his marrying Mlle Darbois; it was a whim of his uncle's, a strange whim, an unthinkable whim, if you will, but still it was on this whim that all of his future affluence depended. Charles was hesitant. He knew Nelzi; he knew that he was the only man she would ever love, and could he think that his beloved, because she was black, would patiently endure the presence of a rival, and a happy rival? He had sworn to make her happy; he had sworn to love her forever. And if he married Mlle Darbois, he would have to give up the intimacy that made Nelzi's happiness and proved to her that she was still loved. But if he refused the marriage, he bid farewell to any hope of wealth. The condition was clear: the one who refused to abide by it gave up his share of the inheritance in favor of the other heir. Then, he would no longer have the means to support Nelzi in a prosperous manner, and what would he do? Apply for a job? What job? And what would Nelzi do, deprived of everything, accused of everything—she who would only have her love to help her fight both misery and dire poverty? Charles was wavering.

Mlle Darbois was very young and very pretty. She seemed to have a sweet and tender disposition; she looked at Charles with pleasure; she smiled at him willingly. Charles could flatter himself that he was not disliked; he could even hope to be happy with this lovely girl. But would Nelzi, Nelzi, ever be happy? Would she not reproach him for his perjury? What shall he do? Whom could he consult? Well, he could ask her. "Yes, yes, that is it. I shall speak to her; she will know my trouble today. No, tomorrow." Tomorrow comes. "No, tomorrow," Charles would say, and tomorrow went by.

Mme Darbois had said a few words. Charles had answered without committing himself, but politely. His good aunt, who wanted the marriage to take place, could see that she would not meet any opposition from her daughter; she did not expect any from the nephew either and was intensifying the development of their intimacy. As she would never have thought on her own that a black woman could be an obstacle to her plans, and as she spoke in her presence the way one speaks in front of a table, a chair, a dog, or a bird, at every moment, she showed her joy, her hope, her impatience, and her wishes. In Nelzi's presence, she would call Charles her son; in her presence she sang the praises of her future son-in-law to her daughter. Nelzi quivered, looked at Charles, did not dare ask him questions in front of other people, never saw him alone, and could not take advantage of the commotion of a large circle, since Mme Darbois had decided to stop entertaining until the marriage was celebrated. At last, enlightened by the aunt's speeches, dismayed by Charles's tenderness when he looked at the young lady, no longer doubting her misfortune, she felt her tears dry in her eyes; her mind clouded, a somber despair took hold of her senses, she escaped in great hurry from the house; she thought she was walking to her death.

An old man, followed by a servant, walked by her; he looked at her insolently, examined her carefully, let her take a few steps, still looked at her from behind, smiled, made a sign to his servant, hastily whispered a few words to his ear, and went away.

The servant kept on following Nelzi; he noticed her nervousness, saw that her gait was uneven, that she stopped, wavered. "What are you looking for, Mademoiselle?" he said with an assiduous politeness.

"Alas! I do not know myself," the unfortunate woman answered, informed about her present condition by this simple question. A stream of tears made its way; her hands covered her burning face.

"Come to my master; he will find a way to alleviate your misfortune."

"Ah, if he is powerful, if he is sensitive, if he is rich, let him give me the means to leave this country, to go back to America. I shall see again the places full of the one I have loved too much. There perhaps. . . ."

The unfortunate girl stopped and, without thinking, followed the stranger who guided her. She came to a magnificent mansion; she climbed a hidden stairway, went through a small waiting room, and found herself in a delightful boudoir. The servant left her. A door opened; a man came forward. His age should have inspired respect, but his affected manners, his piercing eyes, and his impertinent smile only aroused disgust. He made her offers that, at first, she did not understand, but that then soon revolted and frightened her; she moved away indignantly. Then the odious old man took her hand, threatening to take her to the police as if she were a criminal whose flight he had stopped. Nelzi let out a cry, made an effort that knocked down her opponent,

ran toward the first door she saw, found herself on a large stairway, quickly
went up, threw herself in an apartment that was unlocked, went through
several rooms, and fell at the feet of a young and beautiful woman.

"Save me, I beg you, save me," she cried out.

"What do you want from me, child?" answered an extremely soft voice.
Encouraged by this expression of goodness, by the charm of an attractive
face, Nelzi thought she had found a consoling angel. Her ideas were confused, but she felt the need for empathy. With passion and energy she told
her about running away from Mme Darbois and the odious meeting that
followed. At the portrait she drew of the nasty old man, Mme de Senneterre
blushed profusely, and, as a young and beautiful woman may have an old
libertine of a husband and not care for scandals, the charming lady had all
the doors closed; sent away all the servants, who were frightened by the
sudden entrance of the black woman; and, making poor Nelzi sit on a stool
at her feet, sweetly took her hands and wanted to know the smallest details
of her misfortunes.

Nelzi told everything, and she told it with love, with distraction, with
frenzy. The kind woman was moved. "Let them say that blacks do not have
the same feelings as we do. Is this not the eloquence of a burning love? Is it
not the expression of a soul of fire? Poor blacks, poor child. I love you; I love
what suffers; I love what loves." Mme de Senneterre said this with abandon.
Mme de Senneterre was looking for tears; she found them. Several bells were
heard. Mme de Senneterre kissed Nelzi, led her to a bedroom, promised to
take care of her and to spare nothing to bring her back her happiness.

"Happiness," Nelzi answered, looking at her protectress quite sadly and
tenderly. "Ah, without him, without him, it will always be impossible!"

A young man whose entire appearance announced taste and elegance
came in hurriedly; he came up to Mme de Senneterre with the air of the
most flattering attention, but without bowing to her. "Ah, here you are, my
dear Count," she said. "At this time, your presence is more pleasant to me
than ever. Yes, you are going to help me do a good deed. My dear friend,
you see me preoccupied with a very important thing. Here, stay over there,
not so close to me. You are laughing; you do not believe me. You are not
behaving, sir, but I shall prove to you that I want to be serious. First, I forbid
you to move from where you are; my dear, you know that I would be quite
annoyed to be annoyed with you. Listen to me. Imagine the most interesting
creature, a black woman as I did not know there were any, as I am happy to

know there are some, a black woman victim of love, of faithfulness: what an example for us white women—a young black woman who did everything for a white man, who devoted her life to him, who called him her spouse, who loves this spouse as I would have loved mine. . . . If mine had been a man, ah, what a wife I would have been to him then. You know it, Count, you know if ever. . . ."

"I know that you are adorable," answered the Count, kissing her hand softly, "but my dear Eugénie, what can I do for you on this occasion?"

"You are going to figure it out yourself." Then she told him the story of Nelzi's sorrows, suggested to the Count the predicament of the young man. "Perhaps," she said, "the fear of seeing poor Nelzi tormented by contempt, suffering, and poverty is the only reason for his decision to perjure himself."

"I see what my Eugénie expects from me. My uncle is a minister in the government. He can do as he pleases. We shall have a job for your protégé, who will then be free to love his Nelzi all his life." While saying these words with intensity, the Count moved closer and began playing with the beautiful blond curls that covered Eugenie's forehead.

"Yes, my dear!" she exclaimed. "This is wonderful. Oh, what a pleasure for us two to be able to perform a miracle, to ensure the happiness of a black woman. Ah, believe me, dear Count, a little good done by chance will hardly be compensation for all the evil we have heaped upon this unfortunate race! But are you no longer listening to me?" Then the Count was kissing Mme de Senneterre's pretty fingers, one by one. "You do know, my charming friend, that I cannot remain long in your presence without feeling distracted, but I heard you so well that I am only waiting for your order to inform our young friend, who must have been brought near despair by his mistress's absence."

"My dear, go there yourself."

"I agree, right away, but won't I be rewarded for my obedience?"

"You know that I reward you even when you disobey me."

The Count flew to Charles, who thought he had lost his life. Nelzi's flight had enlightened him; he blamed himself for his uncertainties. He was losing his mind. He called himself ungrateful, treacherous. He was not attempting to control his outbursts; on the contrary, in the excess of his sorrow, he threw himself at the feet of Mme Darbois. He apprized her of the oaths he had made to Nelzi, revealed to her the way he had lived with her until then, begged her to put all her friends on the tracks of the beloved girl, adding that he would be a monster if he abandoned her, that he could not live without her, that he happily foreswore his share of the inheritance, not having any other wish than to marry his friend, to go back to America with her or to use his talents anywhere in the world, as long as he was with her, happy if she was happy, without crime or remorse.

At the first sentence spoken by the Count, Charles threw his arms around him, rushed into the carriage, rushed into Mme de Senneterre's sitting room; there, however, respect held him back. His face displayed the strongest emotion. Mme de Senneterre smiled; she quite liked him.

"So I read you correctly, sir? Count, I shall not forget your eagerness to please me; quickly arrange for him to have the position, and I shall give him his friend."

While saying these words, the beautiful Eugénie opened a door, brought in Nelzi. "Do you forgive me?" asked Charles, kneeling in front of the tenderhearted black woman.

"I am only too happy to still belong to you, as long as I am the only one to belong to you, Charles!"

There was such a sensitive and passionate expression of jealousy in these few words that Charles was quite moved. "The man who possesses you," he said lovingly, "cannot want anyone but you Nelzi, there are no charms worth your tears!"

"Such is love, and love without blame," sighed Eugénie, "whether white or black, how pretty that love is."

"A WHITE WOMAN AND A BLACK MAN"
Doris Y. Kadish and Françoise Massardier-Kenney

Domingo lost his father when he was six years old, and his mother died of sorrow at having seen her husband die from his master's ill treatments. All Domingo had ahead of him was tears and slavery when old Marguerite, Mme de Hauteville's trusty servant, saw him cry, learned about his misfortunes, and led him to her mistress. Mme de Hauteville was a good, sympathetic, sensitive woman. She was what every rich colonist's wife should have been. Who can say exactly what spark lights the fire of revolutions? Who can say exactly what drop of water can put out the fire? The balm that provident nature puts in the hands of women to heal so many kinds of wounds is more powerful, more effective than we think, but too often women neglect it or fail to apply it. Perhaps Saint Domingue and many other colonies would still have masters if the owners' wives had not scorned their sweetest power so often. Would it have been a blessing? Fewer horrible events would have ravaged the world, but some poisons are necessary!

Mme de Hauteville took Domingo in, bought him from his master, wished to have him brought up in her household, and obtained permission from her husband to devote him exclusively to her newborn daughter's service. Here was Domingo, who grew up side by side with his little mistress; here he was, having no other duty than to serve her in her games, to guide her steps, to rescue her with all his little boy's strength. Really, Domingo was not ill treated. He was so good, so obliging, he grew so fond of the one who was one day to command him. And, on her side, the young Pauline was by nature so affectionate that the poor little Negro was happy. The idea of slavery did not yet spoil his innocent joy. Domingo did not yet feel his chains.

While growing up, the little black boy attended Pauline's lessons. It was even his mistress's pleasure to have him receive some instruction so as to tempt the little girl to emulate him. Domingo applied himself and learned how to read and write in a short time. He was even given a few drawing lessons. It was a lot for a Negro, and for a Negro like Domingo. Gifted with an ardent soul and a thoughtful character, he very much enjoyed the pleasure of acquiring knowledge and the charms of learning, which were denied to most all his peers.

However, in becoming enlightened, he observed the brutalized blacks, his wretched brothers. Soon he shuddered when beholding the degradation of the species and the fatal effects of a blood-thirsty power. This kind of natural philosophy was quite dangerous at the time, when the arrogance of a caste wanted to crush everything beneath it.

M. de Hauteville was arrogant, haughty, full of prejudices. He was like all the rich colonists of his caste, who would have almost preferred to see the colony burn rather than follow in the steps of the American colonists. One can imagine what was his contempt for the slaves! In his eyes, they were only some kind of animal without souls, whose ears and eyes were made only to see and hear hard work and strict orders. But M. de Hauteville was a father. He loved his daughter, and he happily saw her at twelve shaped like a sixteen-year-old girl is in our climate. Pauline, who was brought up by her mother in perfect innocence with a charming naïveté, had at twelve a mature character, high principles, a steadfast firmness. She had beautiful eyes, a kind demeanor, and a fresh, shapely form. In order to carry out long-standing plans, M. de Hauteville had welcomed into his family young Léopold, the son of one of his childhood friends, whose parents lived in France.

Léopold was eighteen years old; he was charming, witty, subtle, gracious. Nothing was more elegant than his manners, nothing more attractive than his language. He was more learned than most eighteen-year-olds; his conversation was varied, striking, animated. A constant originality embellished his countenance and shined in his speech. His voice had a charm beyond words, and when he was silent, one forgot what one was about to answer in order to think only about what he had said. Léopold was easily moved by generous actions, but for only a moment; soon he moved on to something else, talked, laughed, did a pirouette, felt moved again, and started laughing all over. He was truly a charming young man: many belles had thought so; many eyes had told him so. Léopold had known pleasure but not yet love. He knew of his father's intentions and eagerly came to fulfill them. As soon as he saw Pauline, he congratulated himself on his obedience; as soon as he got to know her, he became quite eager to prove to her that submission was not the only feeling that kept him at her feet.

A storm was brewing in the French Caribbean. Every day clouds were gathering, troubles and disturbances broke out everywhere. For a long time, M. de Hauteville, who was busy attending to his estate, took no part in the seditious and murderous affairs brought on by the hatred among parties and the fatal divergence of opinions. Soon he openly shared the prejudice against men of color. Soon he too, like his peers, made the fatal error of putting into the hands of the blacks the weapons that they would later turn against their masters.

Domingo, devoted through his employment to the personal service of Mlle de Hauteville, kept to the plantation, but he was among the first to have been struck by the electric spark of freedom. The hope or rather the possibility of freedom had come to him as a strange but entrancing dream. Still not able to explain his thoughts himself, the entrancing idea of freedom had made his heart pound. He looked everywhere worriedly, he sought solitude, he gave out long sighs, and became remarkably absent minded. Sometimes he would go near the blacks, ask them questions, pity their fate more bitterly than usual, attempt to impart some energy to them, to pull them away from the state of lethargy into which suffering had thrown them. The overseers watched him with suspicion. They called him an impudent favorite and denounced him to

M. de Hauteville, who frowned, threatened Domingo with the most terrible punishments; and Domingo, when threatened, shook. A secret indignation stirred his blood.

Meanwhile, M. de Hauteville announced his plans regarding the marriage of his daughter. Léopold, authorized by his father, offered his wishes and his hand to Pauline: "Shall I be fortunate enough," he said to her, "to obtain your hand because you wish to give it? Dear Pauline, will you deign respond to all the love of a husband?"

"What is love, my dear Léopold?" Pauline asked, blushing.

"It is an exclusive and delicate feeling. The person who inspires it in us is for our heart the dearest of beings, the joy of our life, and our greatest good."

"Léopold, my father and my mother are dearer to me than you are. I even prefer a few childhood friends to you. I feel friendship for you, of course, but I do not feel love."

"Charming friend, be mine. Your heart is free and pure. My attentions will do the rest."

The education of the mind broadens the soul and extends natural dispositions. Domingo, raised above the common fate of slaves by the circle of his occupations and the knowledge he had acquired, dared to think, and develop within himself all the feelings of a free man. Love, that impetuous feeling, was made for this new and burning soul. It was meant to tear it apart and make it pay dearly for the expansion of his whole being. Although still a slave because of all the institutions, his mind was beginning to lift its chains. He could thus experience the feelings of a free man, without the joys that accompany them.

Love, dearest son of freedom, you who can only bear the chains that you give, you changed your pleasures into a cruel poison for the unfortunate black! You fired him with your devouring flames for an adored mistress. You distressed his eyes with the horrible spectacle of a triumphant rival. Finally, you broke all the faculties of his heart and filled it with a barren despair, an impotent furor.

The news of Pauline's marriage had opened poor Domingo's eyes. He wished he could have escaped from himself. All he could do was make senseless vows and strike his limbs with rage. A convulsive agitation had overcome him.

The threat of major disaster loomed on the horizon, and M. de Hauteville, despite his daughter's extreme youth, wanted to move up the day of her union with Léopold. Suddenly the most sinister news circulated. On all sides great uprisings took place. Blacks advanced with fury. Everywhere massacres and fire followed in their wake. Already numerous properties belonging to M. de Hauteville were burned and destroyed. Fields of sugarcane only offered the spectacle of ashes to terror-stricken eyes. M. de Hauteville's plantation in the middle of his lands could no longer be defended against these destructive torrents. The city of Le Cap offered the only refuge. He hastened to escape there with his family, his slaves, and his whole household.

But self-interest and resentment speak louder than fear. A colonist's arrogance takes nothing into account, not even safety. He becomes even more of a tyrant when he should be making minds more reasonable. He seeks to vanquish by cruelty those whose hearts should be won over and whose souls should be calmed and soothed. From then on the slightest fault that a slave committed was pursued with severity and punished by a barbaric torture. The most inoffensive speech, even the slightest word, was treated as a sign of revolt and silenced by execution.

Domingo himself could no longer claim to be a favorite. Perturbed by his sorrow, he would lose his temper and get carried away. One moment he would appear brazenly before his master; one minute he would look at him haughtily; one second he would stand up to him. . . . It was enough. His punishment was imminent and would be awful! Domingo wouldn't wait for it. This time the orders were given for the next day. A lingering concern for him kept them from putting him in shackles. Knowing all the property inside and out, he stole away at night to Pauline's room and threw himself at her feet: "Until now I was able to adore you as a white and suffer as a black," he said. "I can no longer bear slavery. Its tortures are not made for me. Farewell, my mistress and my idol. Freedom awaits me. In gaining my rights as a man, my right to love and be happy, may I be able to protect you from the furor of the blacks and their attempts at vengeance! Domingo will watch over you." He fled as the new day appeared. Domingo had joined the rebels.

Soon the city of Le Cap would be destroyed with all its riches. Soon the disastrous troubles of the colony would be at their worst! Mme de Hauteville wouldn't live to see them. All the fears, the sorrows experienced by a wife and mother, tore her soul apart. The cruelest agitations completed the ruin of a temperament already withered by the burning climate. She succumbed. With her last glance upward to heaven she asked for her husband to be forgiven and her daughter to find a protector.

There was no more salvation. All the factions were on the scene and broke out with fury. They no longer had allegiance to any country. The rights of France were ignored by all these madmen. There had never been any concessions, nor would there be any compromises. Chaos was at its deepest. The commissioners of the government—enemies among themselves, terrified by so many dangers, uncertain in all the steps they took—finally chose the most decisive and dangerous path: crushing the whites whom they had come to help and losing the colony that they had come to save. The general emancipation of black soldiers was announced, and from all quarters blacks were summoned to come to the aid of a government that soon they would no longer want to recognize. They ransacked the treasures, torched all the properties, assassinated those they had called their assassins. The city of Le Cap was plundered; gunfire covered the congested streets.

M. de Hauteville, fighting at the head of his family, defended himself bravely against a band of blacks hounding him. Léopold used his own body to shield M. de Hauteville, but to no avail. Both were on the brink of defeat.

"Stop," cried a familiar voice. "Have pity on this old man, whose son seeks to rescue him from your blows; stop, I implore you. . . . But watch out: a terrible *ouaga*⁴ protects them from your fury."

Indeed the sky darkened, and the sun disappeared for several instants.⁵ The frightened blacks dispersed. But unfortunate d'Hauteville had received a mortal blow. Domingo lifted him up in his arms and, followed by Léopold, laid him down in a garden adjoining the house in which d'Hauteville had lived until that time. Daylight returned gradually. D'Hauteville recognized his slave. He looked at him with astonishment and shook his hand. Domingo raised his eyes to heaven, and then, looking straight at Pauline's father, he cried: "Oh my master, oh unfortunate old man, can't I save you?"

"No," M. de Hauteville answered with difficulty, "but do not linger. Save my cherished daughter. Run, Domingo, and carry my farewell to her. Go hither. You deserved to be white."

These were the old man's last words. Domingo ran off, crossed courtyards, and arrived at the main plantation. In disarray, Pauline had fled from her slaves and was running desperately, wildly, to come to the aid of her father. She recognized Domingo and fainted in his arms. The brave black man felt his forces redouble in strength. He pressed his precious weight against his beating heart. He wanted to save Léopold too. He found him near the remains of his friend. Together they made their way through the last houses in flames. They went deep into the swamps, they climbed lonely hills. Finally they arrived, breathless, in a thick forest that could protect them from their pursuers. Then, happy to have saved his beloved, Domingo knelt near her and prayed to God. In turn he gave in to his enthusiasm for having gained his freedom, and then to the human feelings that arose in him at the thought of the sorrows that would befall the whites. Like anyone else, perhaps, he could have let himself be led astray by the desire for vengeance. But love lifted him above color prejudice; love taught him clemency.

Domingo then led Léopold to the seaside. From there, small vessels were sailing to neighboring coasts. After exchanging several signals, Léopold finally conceived the hope of fleeing to some friendly land, from whence he could then set sail for France. "Pauline," he said to Mlle de Hauteville, "will you deign to trust yourself to the one whom your father chose to be your husband? I swear to escort you to the heart of my country, and there, at the foot of the altar. . . ."

Pauline interrupted him. "No, Léopold," she said with a firm tone. "No, I shall not compound the rigors of your destiny and the difficulties of your travels. No, I shall not leave this place where so many cruel memories would inevitably bring me back. What would I do in another place? Domingo's honor will be my protection here, where I wish to finish my days. Farewell, Léopold, the ship is leaving. Go, it is my wish; my resolution is unshakable."

The certainty of being unable to bend her resolve or be of use to her settled the question for Léopold. With a torn soul, he left and directed his thoughts to his family. Domingo, kneeling before Pauline, his eyes shining with gratitude and love, swore to himself to live and die for her. "Ah," he cried, "would that I were worthy of being your husband!"

"Domingo, you calmed my father's last moments and saved the life of the one whom my father called his son. You have risen above prejudices. I will follow your example. But I want to flee these scenes of carnage. May a forest be our refuge; may it hide us from the whole universe. Agree to live for me alone, and I will be yours."

For a long time Domingo remained prostrate before his divinity. Twelve years later, when the Republic of Haiti was gloriously established on a solid basis, a carefully built hut was discovered by chance in the heart of a thick forest. A black man and a white woman lived there. They lived by hunting and picking wild fruit. Everyone admired the love and the good character of the couple, but the blacks were unhappy that a black man worshiped a white woman. The object of his adoration was respected, however. "It's too bad," they said longingly. "She deserved to be black."

"THE SLAVE TRADER"[6]
Lisa Van Zwoll

Léon had drawn some liberal and philosophical ideas from his studies, his social encounters, and his family. His joviality, his sweetness, and the generosity of his character made his company desirable; however, he did not have the strength of his convictions. Léon had not studied mankind, nor had he reflected upon the immutable laws of justice enough to always resist the so often cruel influence of prejudice.

As the heir of a considerable sum of money and an orphan at the age of twenty, Léon wanted to invest his capital in Nantes, his birthplace. But shall I reveal the horrible commercial venture that was suggested to the ambitious young man? Slave trading! This infamous traffic was presented to him as the quickest and the surest method to become wealthy. Léon hesitated at first. An internal doubt was bothering him; it was his conscience. To buy and sell men! What a way to make a fortune! To destroy, for these men, all their earthly joys and rip them from the very beings who make their lives livable! To become rich at the price of their pain and tears—what criminal and weighty riches!

A ship captain ready to set sail influenced Léon's decision. This man was reputed to be very fortunate in his business dealings. He had traveled ten times to Africa's coasts and his fortune was already immense. "Come with me," he said to Léon, "what is preventing you? Childish qualms. These blacks that we are going to get, do you believe them to be men? No, they do not feel; they vegetate, like our animals. And further, my friend, if we take them, it is for their own good as much as it is for ours. They barely have enough to eat in their Africa! We bring them to the colonies and they work there, it is true, but they are also fed there. At first they feel out of place and saddened, but soon they grow attached to their masters. Look at our dogs! Once tamed, would they change their situation? Finally, my friend, I doubt that these beings have souls, but if they do, well, good! We will convert them!"

Léon was disgusted in spite of himself by this strange speech; however, he wanted to be rich, so he promised himself he would be humane and he left.

"We have nothing to fear," said the captain, rubbing his hands together. "We have honorary insurance." After a favorable crossing, the barbarians, ready to become thieves of men, approach the African coast. It's there that they will actively work for their cargo, black slaves. Most of the unfortunate blacks crammed in the vessel have been taken in the forests. Tied up for some time to the trees, their limbs are quickly bloodied by the iron shackles forged for them in some French town! "Look at these ebony machines," said the captain to his young companion, who was surprised by all that he saw, and even more surprised by the captain's coldheartedness. "Is there any resemblance between them and us? Are these men?" Léon didn't respond, he didn't even dare answer his own thoughts that murmured against this blasphemy.

Two hundred blacks are piled up in a space two or three feet high, a space where fifty could barely fit. Deprived of air and movement, the unfortunates cry out in horror, despair, and rage. Criminal habits harden man to the spectacle of human suffering. At first Léon trembles at the hardships that burden the blacks, but little by little he grows accustomed to contemplating their lot without trembling. It is for the law to reprimand such crimes; man's heart doesn't know how to sustain a pure sense of justice, and too often he imposes silence upon the touching voice of pity.

A storm is brewing. The criminal ship amidst the foaming plains submits to the wrath of the angry waves. A frightening night envelops the horizon. The poor blacks are locked up in the hold, and a piece of cloth, drenched in tar, covers the hatchway in order to stop the water from leaking into the ship. Can these poor souls breathe? It doesn't matter!

The ship is too full, and it must be immediately lightened. "What should we do?" asks Léon.

"We have no merchandise to throw into the sea," answers the captain. "We can only throw men. Let's go, we must get rid of a few blacks." Following the captain's orders, thirty are thrown into the water!

The storm dies down, the sky clears up, the sea settles, and calm is reborn on the ship. They give a little air to the victims, but a great many were unable to withstand such cruel torture and they perished. "Such a waste," exclaims the captain. "Get rid of them. We will still be able to sell the others." Many of the unfortunates, in their frenzied delirium, bloodied each other and their condition is alarming. "We may as well get rid of them as well," says the barbarian, and the sea takes them into her bosom.

The ship sails in an area dangerous for slave ships, and the sailors notice a boat that might belong to an observation fleet. It does not show its flag to the guilty ship. Whatever its origin, the flag that defends men's freedom is honorable! The slave ship quickly distances itself, seeing itself pursued, but succeeds in escaping the watchers. Soon, the captain commands the dropping of the anchor. "I know this area well," he says. "We will find protection and safety here."

Crime rules this area, and the slave trade takes place here boldly, despite the fact that this region neighbors a free country under the protection of England's laws. But here, chaos, theft, abduction, and violence spread daily in a frightening manner. Léon is led by his new friend to the home of a rich landowner who owes all his wealth to the slave trade. Léon is introduced as someone on the verge of coming into an immense fortune, and since the landowner knows perfectly, and in great detail, the trade that will make Léon wealthy, he welcomes the young man with flattering alacrity and congratulates him in advance on his luck in business. Léon blushes at the compliment, looks away, and meets the eyes of a charming girl. She also blushes and then walks away with an air of sadness and discontent.

Laure was the only daughter of the travelers' host. Along with her naive charm, she had strong moral convictions and profound sensitivity. Raised by her mother, she had a kind and gentle understanding of religion, tolerant and philanthropic beliefs, and a love for justice and freedom. She had never been able to accept the terrible trade that had made her father wealthy and was outraged daily by the evils inflicted upon the slaves. Several times her father had wanted to arrange a marriage for her, but it had always been to one of his fellow slave traders, and Laure had always refused. She had promised herself that she would only marry a man who would alleviate, as much as possible, the sufferings that she had witnessed so many blacks endure.

"Yet another slave trader," Laure said, after having left the room to which Léon had just been brought. "Isn't that too bad? With such an interesting face! . . . A slave trader should always be very ugly and horrify the rest of the world!"

Laura's father asked Léon to stay at his house while the captain took the blacks to the next colony. "Upon his return," he added, "if you consent to it, we can do some business together. I know a fine, skilled man, a very able hunter. We can put our money together to make some good captures at a good price, which we'll sell easily because the captain can find some serious buyers." Léon agreed to everything.

At the end of a beautiful day, Léon breathed with pleasure the flower-infused air. He daydreamed for a few moments and then picked up his guitar, feeling the need to express the emotions from deep within his soul. A thousand confused desires troubled him, and a certain feeling of tenderness and melancholy caused him indescribable pain. Léon started singing. His tone was gentle and penetrating; his big blue eyes became more and more expressive, and his face, a little pale, appeared to be the unmistakable sign of his sincerity.

Laure heard him and she stopped to listen. "He sings so well," she thought. "Such a soft and pure voice! Is it truly the voice of a slave trader?" She approached and saw Léon through the foliage. A strong emotion made her heart beat faster. "Is it possible? Heavens! Is this truly the face of a slave trader?"

The young girl saw Léon on a daily basis, and she found him charming. His conversation was diverse and instructive; he spoke considerably well about the arts. Laure lost track of time when next to this person, who was more than happy to forget everything else in her presence. But her father would arrive and engage Léon in conversation about the advantages of the slave trade. Léon gave the old man his undivided attention, and so the amiable young girl fled from her cruel friend to the other side of the house, where she tried hard to find his many faults. She hated him . . . or at least she wanted to. "If my father offered me Léon as a husband," she often thought, "I would refuse him. Oh! Without a doubt and very quickly. Léon is a barbarian. Léon, why are you so guilty?"

Laure had a little dog. An imprudent person crushed the animal's paw while wheeling a load, and the house was filled with the dog's cries. His compassionate mistress took him in her arms, smothered him with her caresses, and cried over his sufferings. Léon quickly kneeled before Laure, took the dog's paw, and bandaged it. After having bemoaned considerably the unlucky mishap with a deep air of sincerity, he began to kiss alternately the animal's head and his mistress's hand. "So!" whispered softly the young girl. "Léon isn't at all mean—he can't stand to watch a dog suffer! But those poor blacks!"

One day Laure, overcome with suffering, hurried into the room where her father and Léon were sitting. She held the hand of a young black girl about ten years of age. "Father," she said with outrage, "Father, look at this unfortunate child. I never want to abandon her. Like me she had a father, but barbarians just stole him away from her. He is a rich colonist from a neighboring country who had come here to buy goods. In the middle of the countryside, bandits attacked him, and now, without a doubt, a treacherous ship is keeping him hidden from sight. His daughter, this poor creature, frightened, started running aimlessly and shouting for help. I had gone out and I found her on my way. When she told me her story, I promised to help her. Father, is there any way of saving this child's father? You aren't saying anything—he is certainly lost forever then! Come little unfortunate child, I will be your friend, your sister. Come, you are already dear to me, and I want to ease your pains. Near me you will defy those monsters; no slave trader will ever be able to tear you away from me."

Laure burst into tears, her father was embarrassed, and Léon felt violently moved. A new and heartrending emotion caused him to feel an uneasiness he had not felt before.

"So!" continued the young girl, still trembling with rage. "Can you comprehend, Father, can you really comprehend the dreadful torture of that poor man? He lost his fortune and his freedom; he lost his sweet wife, who is calling out for him, and perhaps he will die of fear and pain! He has forever lost the kisses of his little children and the hope of seeing his peaceful fields again. In an instant he lost everything; his remaining refuge is death! Father, look at the crimes you protect! Léon, these are the heartaches you cause!"

Léon trembled; it was not the first time he felt remorse, but then, and from then on, this remorse would haunt him endlessly.

The captain, Léon's travel companion, returned from the colonies and took care of a new load of slaves; it was for this very reason that he had associated himself with Léon and Laure's father. Laure's father judged Léon to have a good path ahead of him, and he was fond of his character; he thus conceived of a plan to unite him with his own daughter.

"Léon," he said, "our investments are prosperous; let us not part ways. I love you like a son and there is a way to strengthen our bond even further. I have but one daughter."

At this, Léon leapt to the old man's neck. "Be my father," he cried out with an effusive and unexpected joy. "I will owe you my life's happiness!"

But when the proposal was made to Laure, she said, "No, father, I do not want to marry Léon."

"Do you hate him, my daughter?"

"No, no, father, sometimes it seems to me that I love him with all my soul, but I will never marry him."

Her father was quite surprised, but Laure remained steadfast, and Léon quite despaired.

One day Léon approached the one he loved. His eyes were full of tears; worry and chagrin had altered his charming face. The young girl noticed it and suffered. . . .

"Mademoiselle," said Léon, "I could have been the happiest of men, but you didn't desire it. I could have been blessed with an adored wife, but you didn't desire it. A man who gives himself to you, who will live for you alone, will he never be able to reach your soul? Mademoiselle, will you hate me forever?"

"Léon," answered Laure, "I don't hate you, I told my father so. You are mistaken and don't know me well. I don't want to hide it from you any longer—I do love you, but I repeat my feelings: I will never ever be the wife of a slave trader. Léon, how could you appreciate the beauty of love when you don't respect the love of these unfortunate blacks? How could you cherish a spouse when you, without pity, rip black men from their spouses? How could you be a gentle father when, every day, you take innocent children from those who gave them life? No, you will always be a treacherous friend, an unfaithful lover, a barbarous spouse, a perverse father! And you want me to be yours! . . . I do love you, it is true, in spite of myself. A feeling leads my heart to you against my will, but reason refuses you, and I obey reason."

Léon was troubled; he didn't know what to bring himself to do, but he sought in vain a victorious solution, an eloquent prayer. "Laure," he said, with a trembling voice, "you know that my fortune depends upon this trade that you curse. If, in order to please you and to obey your heart's desires, I give up this commerce, by what other means will I maintain my wealth? What will I do with all my investments? At this very moment there is an advantageous opportunity before us. Your father wants me to invest all that I have, and I promised to do as he wishes. If suddenly he saw me sacrificing a certain fortune to . . . what he will call your prejudice, will he not accuse me of extravagance? Will he still consent to call me his son-in-law?"

"But," Laure says with emotion, "then I will love you more than anyone in the world and I will tell you so every hour of every day."

"But," responds Léon, "then your father will no longer want me to be your spouse."

Laure sighed, but regaining her energy, she cries out: "Well then, sir, be the father's friend, but forget about his daughter! Do you hear me, sir? Forget about his daughter forever!"

The slave ship was about to set sail, and the cries of pain stifled in its bosom would soon be lost to the open sea. Colonial soil would receive some new victims. The captain, Léon, and Laure's father awaited a happy payoff from the rich cargo they were about to cast into the sea.

Laure is tormented by her grief, her indignation, and her love and cannot sleep. She awakens before sunrise, descends to the garden and encounters Léon, who is also walking, equally restless.

"Oh, Léon," says the young girl. "Look at how much you have made me suffer! What an awful dream you gave me! I saw you being chased, despised, and abandoned by everyone! You were rejected as a ferocious bandit would be! You were infamous and called a cruel slave trader everywhere. Léon, how much you were changed! You no longer had your sweet face, your touching expressiveness, or the penetrating gaze that hides your profession. I have suffered so much because of you! But now, I see you again, and, well, I still shiver. Léon, this ship about to leave, it is the accumulation of the curses that will weigh upon your head. A great many of these poor moaning souls owe their misfortune to you. You deliver them to their torture! Léon, listen to me one last time. You are building between us a wall too high to scale. My friend, there is still time. Free your slaves. We will help them to a free land. The neighboring country, under the protection of English laws, enjoys peace and independence; they will find an asylum and the means to establish themselves. Léon, this expiatory sacrifice will bring peace back into your heart. Don't turn a deaf ear to the voice of she who would like to be able to live for you."

"But your father?"

"My father will be swayed by my prayers and tears, have no doubt upon that. But if I am wrong and my father refuses a lover who has become worthy of me, and refuses to call him his son, Léon, I hereby swear to you that I will follow you anywhere. I will consecrate my entire life to you."

Léon falls to her feet and says, "Is it possible, my beloved? If I lost everything, you would give me everything? You would leave your family, your homeland!"

"Léon, yes, I will do it all for you; my tenderness will compensate for your losses. I will concern myself only with your happiness because I will be proud that I have restored to virtue a heart that was made to be so. Heaven will accept our vows and prayers and bless our union. But don't lose a minute, come, the oppressed are calling you."

Léon finally obeys the orders of his mistress. Love's powerful voice obliges him to be honorable. He is going to free his prisoners and provide them the means to go to the neighboring country. Among these was the father of the little girl whom Laure had taken in. He is returned to his daughter, and his gratitude is touching. Laure sheds tears of joy, and Léon congratulates himself on achieving a happiness he had never before experienced.

It must all be explained to the old man, before whom Léon dares not show himself, but Laure is his daughter and has a virtuous soul and a conscience beyond reproach. She runs and throws herself into the arms of her father, wishing to lead him on the path of noble sentiments. She is ready to show the greatest proof of a daughter's love and tells him the story of what she has convinced Léon to do. "You are rich, father," she adds. "You wanted me to marry Léon, but I could not accept the hand of a slave trader. He is no longer a slave trader, and I beg you to unite us. He is now without fortune, but admire the good deed he has done! Oh! my joy and my happiness will depend solely on him now."

Her father, enraged, scolds her relentlessly and accuses her of being stubborn and foolish. He says he will ban Léon from his home forever.

"Father," Laure answers firmly, "I love you and respect you, but I swore to give myself to Léon if he followed heaven's will. I will keep my promise. If you prevent me from doing so, if you deprive me of my spouse by force, then you shall have another victim, and this time she will be white. After the death of so many, you will be responsible for the death of your own daughter. May such an innocent and devoted victim redeem your crimes and appease the souls of all those who rise up against you!"

At these words, a frightening pallor spread over the face of her father and all his limbs trembled. "My daughter!" he said in a choked voice . . . then he opened his arms to her and to Léon.

MARCELINE DESBORDES-VALMORE

"THE YOUNG SLAVE GIRL" ("LA JEUNE ESCLAVE")
Norman R. Shapiro

Ever does dove yield up her young
Unto the vulture, willingly?
If falls the weakest babe among
Her brood, she cries, flies round the tree;
Never has she the hunstman led
To where her tender fledglings lie;
Never has she, mean spirited,
Let their sweet kisses go awry.

But I a heartless mother know
Who deals her youngest child great ill:
Stifle my weeping, heaven! For, oh!

I bear her pity, and not ill will.
And, when a suffering crone is she,
Remorse will hover—heavy, cold:
Will she not the more piteous be
Than the young child that she has sold!

God! Cast me on that shore where I,
Free, with my sisters, went my way;
Where palm, that counts my years gone by,
Bestows on them its flowers today!
Vile, my luxurious habitat!
I prize my desert climes the more
And seek no crown, save only that
Born of those wastes I loved before.

"CREOLE AWAKENING" ("LE RÉVEIL CRÉOLE")
Norman R. Shapiro

No more sleep cabin, side by you. No more
Me smell nice pretty breath on sweet lips you—
Smell of banana you go eat before:
Smell hot like fire, burn heart me through and through.
    Me want go wake up you.

Come, give nice kiss. Me take? Oh, me no dare!
Me watch, wait you go wake... Too long me moan.
Turn heart by me. Make joy beyond compare!
See? Side by you, dawn fade, leave you alone.
    Too long, too long me moan.

Come. You me lie cool shade banana tree:
Little bird sing when you me chatter love.
Sun jealous. Go hide face in cloud from me.
In eyes you, light more bright than sky above.
    Come. You me chatter love.

No, no more sleep! Share burning flame love make.
Kisses, like honey sucked in flower bouquet.
Soul me on lips, in tears me weep. You wake!
Heart you go sigh. Come, take soul me away.
    Me die in flower bouquet.

"THE BLACK MAN'S VIGIL" ("LA VEILLÉE DU NÈGRE")
Norman R. Shapiro

The night's sun lights the mountain, brightly glowing;
In sandy desert wastes why must we stay?
Come, master! Let me gentle you away;
Awake, good master mine, we must be going.
    For three whole days your eyes you keep
    Shut tight. Will you forever sleep?

The squall has wracked the plantains, cracked in two;
The sail-less boat beneath the waves lies now.
I've washed the band about your bloodied brow:
Come, come... The blacks' poor huts will welcome you.
    For three whole days your eyes you keep
    Shut tight. Will you forever sleep?

Would I knew what long dream you dream today!
Tomorrow will you dream it still? Or, waking,
Will you take, press my hand at dawn's first breaking,
Heeding the call I make: "Awake, I pray!"
    For three whole days your eyes you keep
    Shut tight. Will you forever sleep?

But daylight bathes the shore, and noiselessly
The fisher's bark glides on the water... Come!
Grim is your pallor, cold your brow and numb...
Oh, master! How your voice would hearten me!
    For three whole days your eyes you keep
    Shut tight. Will you forever sleep?

"THE SLAVE" ("L'ESCLAVE")

Norman R. Shapiro

Land of the blacks! Cradle of poor Arsène,
Is it you that send me your memories?
You, Guinea's gentle breeze, that blows again
To ease my heart and calm my agonies?
Bring you the sighs my mother sighs for me?
The song that soothes my father's misery?
　　You, sweet white tots! Play, dance... However,
　　Would you be good? Stay young forever!

O black man lying captive by the shore,
I see you laugh; and, as you muse on death,
Your soul, cloud-borne, will go wafting once more
To where, by fate's decree, you first drew breath.
God-restored shall your mother's kisses be,
And the song taught you at your father's knee!
　　You, sweet white tots! Play, dance... However,
　　Would you be good? Stay young forever!

Never did peaceful black—poor but content—
To snatch you up, set sail over the waves;
Nor, in your land, does the intransigent
Master drone to the moan and sob of slaves!
To scorn and spurn your father's god, did we
Wrench you from mother's kisses, savagely?
　　You, sweet white tots! Play, dance... However,
　　Would you be good? Stay young forever!

"A YOUNG SLAVE'S SONG" ("CHANT D'UNE JEUNE ESCLAVE"): IMITATION OF MOORE
Norman R. Shapiro

There is a darkling wood where hides a rose
And moans the nightingale, mournful to hear;
There is a crystal stream that through it flows:
A stream they called the Peaceful Bendemeer.

My heart goes coursing back to childhood, where,
A lissome reed, I dreamed my reverie,
Slipping betwixt the flowers, listening there
To songs of birds and waters flowing free.

Their murmured music lingering in my head
Would fill the air with its enchanted strain.
Enchained, I thought I heard it again, and said:
"Is that the nightingale moaning again?

"Do those fair blooms yet bow their brows, becrowned,
Over the waters, that I used to hear
Moan low? Ah, no! Time cast them, withered, round,
And they ruffled the Peaceful Bendemeer.

"Their splendor shone, of brilliant charms possessed,
Before they fell to watery grave, stripped bare;
Plumbed were the fragrant tears deep in their breast,
That call to mind the summer's kingdom fair!"

Memory, thus, restores unto my dream
The nightingale's laments I used to hear;
Chained, yet I touch the flowering banks, and seem
To watch flow past the Peaceful Bendemeer.

ABOLITIONIST POEMS

M. DUMESNIL, *SLAVERY* (*L'ESCLAVAGE*)
Norman R. Shapiro

O love of Mankind! Gentle progeny
Of the Eternal, you whose charity
Soothes grief... Cry triumph! Let this song I sing
Ring clear! Come, fill the hearts of man and king.
But, that more touched they be, and better painted
Your pomp and glory, let me trace the tainted
Ways in which Man, spurning the rights of others,
Long treated as vile beasts his human brothers.

Laws themselves scorned his origin divine.
Did he, proud masterpiece of heaven's design,
With brow raised toward celestial heights, born free—
Noble brow blazoned with God's majesty—
Receive his strength, his holy spirit, thus,
Only to let you, ignominious
Races of old, debase them? And, yet worse,
O you, bold masters of the universe,
What did you do for him? Alas! You cast
His flesh in chains, you bound his irons fast...
Citizens trample slaves beneath their feet,
Groaning their pain, to servitude complete
Condemned... Freedom? No more a boon for all!
Rather, it lies usurped in tyrants' thrall.
In Egypt's, Athens's, Rome's bazaars, one can
Buy and sell, for a price, gods' image—Man!
Troubling the peace of honest innocence,
How many the ills this commerce cruel foments!
A patriarch sees his sons willingly
Betray their brother into slavery:
How many the tears this tenderest father sheds
When, to his gaze, a bloodied tunic spreads
The horror of the crime they would keep hidden!

Thus does this vicious scourge reveal, guilt-ridden,
Jealousy's vile excess, with venom rife,
That poisons thus the worthy elder's life.
. . .

[Dumesnil traces slavery through ancient times. Christ announces the end of
slavery. But sullying Christianity, practices of slavery resume. See Appendix.]

But crimes against religion and against
Nature despoiled, with murderous hand, commenced
To sully Christian glory in a tide
Of blood shed in foul traffic's fratricide.[7]

At length, Columbus's new world it was
That much enriched mankind, yet was the cause
Whereby Greed's and Fanaticism's daughter—
Ferocity—spreads wide across the water
Her fulsome horror; monsters twain, they join
Combat's destructive demon to purloin
Glittering Inca gold drenched deep in gore,
Whetting their lust for blood and gold yet more,
Ever more gorging, never glutted, never
Sated, until, at last, their dark endeavor,
Mid rapine's embers, has stripped bare the land
Unpeopled; whence they cast their thieving hand—
In frenzied flight—across the sea to sow
Africa's peace with carnage, pain, and woe.[8]

Children of nature—pure and innocent—
Lived in her image on that continent,
Free of desire, of envy, only paying
Heed to their senses and their needs obeying,
Intent on living well their lives—too short!—
Far from ambition and its foul cohort
Of vices; happy, they, to dwell within
The simple tent or hut, untouched by sin,
Sheltered from wealth of cities' luxury,

Unknown, they lived in sweet equality,
Carefree and tranquil... Such, the happy state
Of Cédar, who, sharing his master's fate,
Was his companion, not his slave, and who
Knew not what humble birth condemned one to.
They trampled underfoot, like common clay,
That gold that, in our climes, holds haughty sway,
Before which, like idolaters, we stand,
Offering honor, glory, fatherland—
Nature itself!—to its proud tyranny.
Nor had sedition, party rivalry,
Made some the victors, some the victims; now
Killers, now killed... Nor did they yet allow
Their souls in burning flames to be devoured;
Souls wherein goodness, pity, wisdom flowered,
Reigning supreme, powerful but benign:
Virtues whereby Man equals the divine.

Thus did these tribes fraternal gently share
Their peaceful life, when lo! now landing there,
Come Europe's monsters! Soon vile Greed would seek
To stain them too, seduce their chieftains, weak
Of head and heart; corrupt their laws; foment
Wars at their pleasure, everywhere they went.[9]
Where do they go, these brigands fury-led?
They slip betwixt the shadows; light their tread
And silent, as the village sleeps—and slay
The old, the feeble wailing their dismay;
Seize husbands, wives, at rest, caught by surprise;
And stuffing shut their mouths, stifle their sighs,
Their frantic cries; push them on, lashed and whipped—
This human chattel from their tent-homes ripped
Unwilling... Over rocks, in desert sun,
Bent by their loads and shackle-bruised, each one
Is shoreward dragged, where, howling loud his pleasure,
The European grips his prey, his treasure,
In avaricious claws... How many were

The wretches that the executioner
Grasped not? How many, in that march of death,
Beneath their weight of woe, gasped their last breath
And thus escaped his clutches? Let us shed
Well-deserved tears, and, among all those dead,
Let us here rescue from oblivion
A certain maid; a young and lovely one
Whose baleful destiny would leave its mark
On the heart of the doughty Mungo-Park.

Aglow with youth and comely grace, the fair
Néala watched with tenderest of care
Over her father, frail and heavy laden
Beneath his years, as she, most loving maiden,
Guided his trembling steps; now by the shore
Of the belovèd stream they both adore;
Now by the fields that, brightly colored, loom
Fair in their sight; often, too, by the tomb—
Flower-spread, strewn with tears—where, dead, the other
Néala lies, who was the beauty's mother.[10]
Her father is her all; never does she
Abandon him, this new Antigone
Of joyful mien... Protect her with your might,
O God; she who, with gentle hands, each night,
Would spin to thread the tufts of down that grow,
Silken and soft, in our fields here below;
Thread that a brother's skill would weave and braid
Into a fabric that, to a fair shade
Of blue, the maid would dye, happy to give
The old man garments. Thus did the pair live
In the contentment of their native hut,
All their needs simply, amply met... Oh, but
Everything changes!... One night, in a flood,
Suddenly spewed, of innocent black blood,
She sees her father, in her arms, attacked.
Néala, horror-rent, quick to react,
Places her body like a living shield

Before him! Ah, what virtue she revealed
In her duress! Awestruck but unaffected
By such devotion, one sees him protected
By her great courage... Passing irritated
That time is fleeting and that they have waited
Even a moment, the fierce enemy—
Burning hot to pursue their villainy,
Their crime—proceed to slay their victim, who
Quivers his last as she clings fast unto
His bloodied body, whence they separate
The pair by force, stifling the shouts of hate
That the fair heroine shrieks out in pain;
Bear her off, hanging from one common chain
Whereon moans many a sufferer now, who could
Rival Néala in her victimhood.
Down she falls to her knees, pleading with those
Who have abducted her: "O woe of woes,"
She cries. "Pray let me bide in this sad place
That witnesses my grief. Let me but grace
My father's last remains. Let me entomb
His bones; that father whom you slew, and whom
Nature would honor. Then back shall I come,
Throw myself at your feet in martyrdom
Straightway." They answered not, but let the lash
Cut, unremitting, many a vicious gash
Into her flesh's pain-wracked loveliness.
Despite the whip, she will not acquiesce
To its blows, pushing, prodding her apace:
"Useless your rage! I will not quit this place
Nor follow you," said she. "Here will I die!
At least by my own death shall I deny
Whatever boon my father's murder wrought."
May heaven avenge sweet innocence distraught!
Strike down those vile assassins to the last!
Three times the sun its veil of night had cast
Upon its light since, through the dust, they would—
Fell villains—drag this model of the good,

The virtuous, in their foul wake... At length,
A cry rings out and, doubtless spent her strength,
Néala is no more... O Europe! Look!
See what a toll your savage traffic took!

As desert groans and blood goes gushing, oh!
Shudder before your scenes of ocean's woe:
Watch as, upon the shores, your agents vile
Into the floating dungeons blithely pile
Hundreds of scores of writhing victims. Gaze
Deep, if you dare, into the dying maze
Of shackled bodies marked for death; stripped bare,
Tighter than coffin-dead, gasping for air...
A putrid air, besmirched with every ill;
And there, abandoned, wallowing until
They meet the fate that some foul god infernal
to those damned to punishment eternal.
This is the fallen angel's dark domain,
Abode where avarice and blood-lust reign
Supreme; where, with his iron scepter, he
Cudgels the wretches in stark misery.
Hideous monsters that hell's precincts spawn
Fight for the right to gnaw and feast upon
The scarcely living flesh... devouring thirst,
Torturous hunger, and, by far the worst:
Contagion, universal scourge, whose breath
Poisons the fetid air... Everywhere death
Spreads like a dirge. Often despair is such
That it grants to the timid arm as much
Strength as it needs to end one's sorry fate;
Even, at times, to rise and immolate
The murderers, and, hero-wise, cast these
Heinous assassins deep beneath the seas.
Ixion on his wheel, and Tantalus
Over the waves, knew not the odious
Pain of this pit, alas! Eyes quake to see
The bloodshed wrought by death and slavery!

Of slavery and death I find still more
When I cross the Atlantic! Gods! Its shore
Teems with the greed and terror that pursue
Those who escape the Ocean's rage, and who
Are fed by sordid hands that measure, weigh
The scraps that nature in the swill would lay,
Unfit... Their bed? Floor of hard clay! A bed
Dug in a dank cell; bed unvisited
By sleep's repose... And planters who will feed,
Minister-like, that horror's every need![11]
In the air, everywhere, bristling all round,
The whistling of the whip's sinister sound,
Lashing, ripping to shreds the skin of poor
African slaves, who cannot long endure
The rigors of their labors; tears will not—
Nor all their cries—allay their grievous lot
A tittle or a jot, not for a trice:
Pity shares not the field where triumphs vice!

Worthy of fairer fate, a poor wretch—young
Son of a chieftain and, himself, among
The ranks of those destined to power—Zamor,
Warrior battle-bred, would fall before
The chattel-slaver and into his chains,
Ocean-borne, far from home... There he remains
On the shore of America, laid low.
Brave hero, he—tilling with heavy hoe
The alien soil; and, in his mind, still fresh,
His willing blade... Enraged to feel his flesh
Harassed, tortured, tormented, "Heavens above!"
He cries. "These? Christians? Theirs, a God of love,
Of kindness? Why, more cruel than tigers, they!
How unlike Him, I vow, in every way,
Whom they vaunt and would fain commend to us!
Goodness He deals; they, daunting death! And thus,
Ferocious beasts, they quell all my desire
To know His love. Little would I aspire

To hold it in my heart! Alas, since I
Would have to join that paradise on high—
His lordly realm—with those abhorred, best we
Renounce that promised happiness, and flee
Our foes' dominion! Let us, rather, keep
Faith with our fathers' gods. Let firm and deep
Be our belief... What difference is there, pray,
Betwixt us and these Christians! They betray
The hospitable greetings I bestow
On them and theirs: a score of times I show
Compassion as they tread our burning sands,
Buffeted by the storms that in our lands
Blow cruel upon the stranger. Harsh and stark
The winds that wrought distress on Mungo-Park,
Who, hopeless, thought his final hour had come
To end the rigors of his martyrdom,
When lo! he sees my tent; my hands reach out
To bid him welcome... He arrives... No doubt
His time is short!... But soon my sisters' care,
Proffered unstinting—with their chants, their prayer—
Like balm divine, restores his life, protected
And safe from harm! Yet I languish, subjected
To the most frightful, baleful pain! Zamor
Was not born but to fall humbly before
This bane! Too long the anguish of the load
I bear! Time now to quit this rank abode
And go console my sisters and my love
In fair Cabinda, by the shore thereof.[12]
And should we die in the attempt, let us
Perish in combat bold and glorious!"
That said, he arms himself. Brothers assemble,
Take heed, march to his voice... The slavers tremble,
Shrink before their assault... Ah me! Ah me!
What vengeance in the wake of tyranny![13]
Need I name all their towns pillaged and sacked?...
The planters' daughters brutally attacked
In blood-soaked shame?... Yesterday's slave now made

The executioner, plunging his blade
Into the master's gaping flanks?... Another,
Slashing the infant that a gasping mother
Holds to her breast?... Husbands, wives—dying, dead—
Clasped in each other's arms?... Need all be said?
Plucking the fruits of its bloodthirstiness,
Alas, oppression dies midst its excess.
Rebellion rises up and, shaking free
Its enchained limbs, brashly and viciously
Crushes the tyrants with the heaped remains—
Now wrenched asunder—of its former chains.
New Spartacuses, risen proud, await
Until another Crassus seals their fate.

But what divinity is this I see
Descending here? She is Philanthropy.
Daughter of the Almighty, she it is
Whose face bespeaks that majesty of his;
Whose kindness reigns in all her august features,
Burning with saintly love of human creatures,
Compassionate, beloved of humankind,
A loving maiden, she; and, close behind,
Charity follows; and, marching beside,
Faith is her good and ever-mindful guide,
Marking her every forward step; Faith, who
Charms hearts into her holy retinue
With heavenly arts and grace divinely blessed
In gentlest tones: Religion sweet-expressed.
Wise men, at length, take up its rights' defense
Before kings' councils with great eloquence.
In vain do passions and sheer greed join force
In favor of the deadly traffic's course;
Religion speaks. Kings listen: "Is it not
Enough that Europe has thrown in her lot—
Willingly, for a full three hundred years,
By greed inspired—to ravage the Zaïre's
Poor children misbegot and desecrated?

Nature watched, trembling; blood flowed unabated;
Heaven moaned low, as God, in His disgust,
Bewailed... Had He not, from one selfsame dust,
Created all Mankind, warmed by one sun?
And had He not, to save us all—each one,
Heathen and pagan too!—from death's thrall, sent
His one begotten Son, with one intent:
To die upon the Cross? Like any others,
Africans are His children and your brothers!
O Christians! Stem the tide of their duress!
Cease to bathe in their blood, transgressionless
And innocent, or live in fear before
God the Almighty's wrath forevermore!
Yes, it is time... Let Greed and Vice lie smashed
Upon their altars; let Turk—unabashed
Follower of the sect that foolishly
Accepts a lying prophet's slavery
Of human flesh—wallow in the chaotic,
Mad brigandage of scorned regime despotic.
Bring to the Africans the arts; bestow
Upon them all their boons and beauties; sow
Peace's voice in their midst; let them hold dear
The Christ and hear His word; let them draw near
His temple. May its portals be flung wide,
And may His saints, grace-blessed, ever abide
By His example: holy their endeavor:
Martyrs, if need be; persecutors, never.
Europe, by Africans too long abhorred,
Will see her glory cherished and adored.
Slavery saps the body and the mind,
Humbling the unstrung soul of humankind;
Ravaging labor of its well-earned treasure,
It dulls enjoyment of the sweetest pleasure;
For man by doleful yoke enslaved, naught is
His own: even his children are not his.
And stripped of everything—of hope as well—
He sees his life a painful living hell;

Railing at heaven, cursing his vile state,
He calls on death to free him from his fate...
Kings! With your royal voices set him free!
Soon all those arms unshackled will you see
Doubling their load, honor-inspired; and you
Will fill with twice the wealth your coffers too.
Liberty—mother wise—fosters Man's hand
To industry; gives him a fatherland
Close to the soil; leads him among his neighbors
In virtue's path; pays rich his earthly labors;
Raises once more his heart's low spirits when
They falter, falling time and time again;
Stirs arts' consoling wonders vast as she
Sweeps clean the vestiges of savagery...
Thanks to her, let the African forget
His pain in all his blood-stained lands, still wet
With tears long shed; and, at last, may he know,
By the work of his own hands' efforts, lo!
Henceforth, the boon of labors salutary,
And taste life's joy under laws tutelary!"
Religion spoke; and, as our kings complied,
Sitting upon their thrones, reigns by their side.

author

VICTOR CHAUVET, *NÉALI, OR THE BLACK SLAVE TRADE*
(*Norman R. Shapiro* _Translator_)

Land of the black inhabitants, of climes
Mysterious, Africa! How many times,
Spurning our eager tread, have you kept dark
The bold adventures of a Mungo-Park—
And more than one! How often, in their wakes,
Have I, hopes high, losing my way, found lakes
Rich-bountied, mountains, flowering woods, concealed
Gifts of the heavens, suddenly revealed
Amid woes pestilential! Howling, here,
The burning north winds of the Atlas, sear
The desert dunes, vast sea of sand; streams flow,

Silvered, bathing cool hamlets spread below;
Banana trees, full, gird the cliffs around
Like headdresses; gazelle, zebra abound
In innocent array, go leaping where
Serpent and tiger lurk in fearsome lair...
And, all the while, the black, trusting in power
Of talismans, defies the threatening glower
Of Moorish foe; dares live his simple life
Among his plow, his offspring, and his wife...
But wait! Already he has towns of sorts—

Here, there—built strong of frond and thatch; and courts,
Poets, and sages too. But ignorance—
Ever the barbarous appurtenance
Of ways uncivilized—still veils his gaze
And clouds his glance. Oh, Niger! If your days
Were but enlightened by our law, our art;
If Europe, culture's heir, would but impart
Her sacred gifts, then... Ah! We waste our breath!
Remorseless, Europe grants but chains and death.

Look! Do you see that ship churning the sea
From Senegal, for those rich isles where we
Reap stalks of nectar sweet? Off will she haul
Her wretched captives into exile's thrall.
Huddled in that dungeon afloat, they need
Less space than in the tomb! Inhuman greed
Smothers them, packed together... As the ship
Rises and falls, their bloody limbs will rip
Against the hold's foul walls... The air groans wild...
A dizziness unknown—tempest's dour child—
Pounds temples, flanks... A love of country now
    Consumes their yearning breast, their fevered brow.

    Each moment, diving into the abyss,
Silent, death marks its victim: That one? This?...
Ah! Pity them not! In their agony
Death is their hope, their longed-for liberty!

Some even tell that, helpless, weaponless,
The slave—brave, dauntless—doubtless must possess
The art to conjure death, open the way
That leads to his eternal rest; they say
That, with the words of human speech, he can
Call on the virtues of his talisman
To summon a merciful death, to come
And soothe the anguish of his martyrdom;
Whence he, attacked by pain, woe-racked, unstrung,
Falls, stifling in his breast his muttering tongue.

In all their less-than-human greed, I see
Shuddering whites wrench from his misery
The African, for whom the cloudless sky
Shines again on his long-beclouded eye;
And the sun, in whose heat these wretches grew,
Prospered... They cheer them, but naught that they do—
Games, happy song that once would charm their ear—
Will rouse them from their chains, transfixed with fear:
Only the lash's furious blows rained on them
Force a pretended dance of joy upon them.

Sucking on pipefuls of a blissful pleasure,
The haughty Slaver, lolling, takes his leisure
Looking with scorn upon his stock-in-trade,
Reflecting: "Black are they. Nature forbade
These vulgar souls to have our wit, our worth,
Our ways! Fit are they to be slaves by birth!
To serve us Christians is what they love best!"
So mused Belmar. Meanwhile, the loveliest
African damsel caught his eye... He fixed
His gaze upon her as she moved betwixt
This weeping slave and that; courageous, calm,
Offering to each one the soothing balm
Of consolation, urging them to be
Brave in the face of their adversity;
Now with a look to heaven, in innocence,
Invoking august power in their defense;

Now cradling on her breast her sleeping child,
Heroically and staunchly reconciled,
As, moaning low a sigh, but tearless-eyed,
Her untamed beauty shone with noble pride.

O you, white European damsels, who,
Flower-like, shine with alabaster hue
Married to roses' pink, forgive, I pray,
The words of praise I am about to say:
Ah! Such her beauty and so fair her face
That ebony would pale in sheer disgrace
Beside her; and her sweet mellifluence's
Accents ring through her soul and charm the senses.
Passion quivers her form, whose graceful lines—
Tight linen-swathed—enchant with love's designs.
What matters if her brow like ebony
Glow dark or lily white? Her heavenly
Features, divinely wrought in beauteous wise,
Bespeak a tender heart; her soul, her eyes
Burn with the flames of that star, beating down,
Blazing afar and bronzing her skin brown.
Time was, the palm before her hut would be
A heartening sign of hospitality
Greeting the traveler spent, who, sore beset,
By rigors of the desert, could forget
His thirst, and find a welcome there. Since then,
Her generous nature, time and time again—
Following in her days of pain—has found
Yet other useful souls, agony-bound,
On whom to lavish tears and tenderness.
Ah yes, that talent to ease the duress
We share—compassion, virtue's sacred duty—
Is your domain, O Woman; your true beauty.

Belmar—the arrogant, impetuous, knave—
Will not debase himself before the slave,
Seeking to woo her. Rather—O dishonor!—
He claims his due, forces himself upon her,

Adding to his disgraceful qualities—
Distasteful and most powerless to please!—
Affront and fear... In vain! For there she stands,
Defiant, meeting his passion's demands
With a disdainful silence. "Ha!" he cries,
"Vile slave! What's this? Will you, before my eyes,
Reject my kindnesses, offend my rights?
Would you greet with such hate and scorn a white's
Advances?" "'Rights and kindnesses'?" she says.
"I pray, do you call 'right and kindnesses'
My devastated land? My home? My mate
Bound in your chains? Our torment? Our harsh fate?
Our exile to a distant, unknown shore?
My breast, fit to feed slavery, and no more?"

"Hush, woman! Ruffle not your hackles! Still
The fury of your wrath. Whatever ill
You think of us, our shackles succor you
From burning desert and vile hovel! Who
Would not be thankful? Bless your fate!" "What? Bless
My fate? Can you know not what bitterness
Your fury casts upon me? What distress?
What grief? You have deprived me of my life,
My freedom! Niger-born—child, mother, wife—
I lived by the Great River, gift that heaven
Had to the blacks alone long ago given,
That yields not to your seas' authority,
But cloaked our tribes in happy secrecy.
Sélim, our warriors' guide, lost traveler's friend—
Valiant and doughty, he who would defend
The wretched—Sélim had made me, of late,
His wife, to share with him his prosperous fate.
I loved, and loved was I. A child I had
Already borne; and gratefully I bade
Our God accept my thanks—he who bestows
On us our days, streams, cooling shade, and those
Moments of tenderest love... Ah! naught I knew

Of your accursèd race, vile through and through,
And the perfidious guile you whites would wreak
Upon us!... Suddenly, we learn you seek
Slaves, and that you, sons of the sea, are come
To gull us with your treasures, and to plumb
Our life itself! 'The Whites! The whites!... ' That shout
Rises up, deathly—far, near, roundabout—
Calling to arms clans, nations, brothers all...
From hill to hill rumbles the tom-tom's call,
Long, low... 'War! War!... ' And crime, to win the day,
Flies forth with joy. And men become men's prey.

"One, fate-betrayed, though worth a hero's death,
Earns servitude. Another, who drew breath
On this war-ravaged soil, is sold by his
Own father, for a scrap of food, and is
Condemned with all his children, judged to be—
By law—his adversary's property;

"That law that you have spread whithersoever,
That knows one word: 'Slavery'! Now, forever!

"Powerful Almoran protected us
Against you; royal father virtuous,
He let us hope we never would fall victim!
Alas! Your emissary came and picked him
To gaze upon your treasures: muskets, swords,
Beads, trinkets of all sorts; fatal rewards
For his cooperation; and those brews
Of flaming fire that you much overuse!
A hundred slaves will be the price: naught less.
And your blood-merchant, joining his caress
To drunkenness poured by your guilt-stained hands,
Exacts the tax on his savage demands.

"Then, at the new moon's gentle light that shone
New life into the evening breeze, soft-blown,

Beneath the ebony-tree's blooms, we dance
As the feathered Bengali coos its chants
And I, Néali, pour unstintingly
The milk and honeyed nectar flowing free,
Inviting each and all to take their pleasure
As the gay tambourine beats out the measure...

"Then, all at once, flames flare... Our roofs catch fire.
From river's bosom; from the hilltops; from the very
Thickets of forest green, the adversary,
Scurrilous, blade in hand, on rapine bent,
Swoops down upon us. Great our wonderment,
Our terror... As saltpeter crackles round us,
As they attack, press on, till they have bound us—
Shackled and chained!—or killed us utterly,
Even our young! O night of infamy!
O mournful our lament! Laden with years,
The old, defenseless, weep and wail their tears,
Flailing their bloody arms... To no avail!
Their throats are cut! For surely one would fail
To sell their like!... Now, exiled from our shore,
We leave but death and fire behind: no more.

"Through endless deserts are we dragged, half dead.
Fatigue, the all-devouring sands, thirst spread
Their racking pains throughout our flanks, and they
Challenge the slaves for any time we may
Have yet to live... At last, we come upon
Your deadly ship, waiting to take us on,
And wrest us from our native soil. At this
Horrendous sight of our life's nemesis,
One and all, with a cry of rage that split
The air, lie down, flat, lest their face be lit
By the whites' flaming sun, begging the earth
To be their grave, she who first gave them birth.
Then you appear, and your barbaric hand
Decides your plunder's fate! Your mere command
Sunders the ties betwixt one and another:

Unmoved by the sweet names of 'husband,' 'brother,'
That hand alone is exile's harvester,
Reaping its due, ripping apart what were
The bonds of love. Ashes and tears shall be
Forever parted by the endless sea!
At least, for me, all is not lost. Here, I
Have those I love, who share my woes. But why,
Oh why drag us to those drear, distant climes?
Kill us! To wait will but prolong your crimes!"

So ends her speech. Her sighs and sobs bespeak—
Stronger and stronger grown—a voice grown weak.
Belmar, were he from our land, might have known
The power and charms of tears; for they alone
Can work most sweet result. He would have faced
Her tears' appeal with a compassion chaste,
And, doubtless, would have blushed a deal at such
Virtuous pleas. But no! Nothing can touch
His ruthless heart: nor pity, nor remorse,
Nor manly duty... Naught will stem his course:
Love reigns supreme! Love? No, mere lust it is
That sends him off into this rage of his.
Drunk on his power, "Enough," he cries, "your vain
Groans of despair. Naught have I but disdain
For your uncivilized, uncouth amours!
Obedience, slave! Mine to command, and yours
But to obey!" "Never! Never, Monsieur!
My husband's will is my command!" "You err,
I fear! Your life is not your own!... Submit!"
His threat falls empty on the air, for it
Troubles her not. "Betray my husband? What?
As in his chains he lies, I should be not
The faithful spouse? Fie! Shame! Rather I pray
Death—angel white—come and wing me away!"

One night, the haughty seaman—passion churning
Within his breast—lay abed, tossing, turning.
The ship was coursing through those waterways

Where burning sun divides the nights from days
In halves, tracing its path. The steaming air,
Dragged in its wake, flamed with its flash and flare
About them, as the thunder, tempest-bred,
Groaned with its flashing growlings overhead.
Beset with tasks, fatigued, our Belmar grows
Disquieted... In vain he seeks repose.
His European blood, seething within
His veins, he rises, yields to his chagrin;
Calls the fair African, yearning, obsessed;
Imagining her pressed, clutched to his breast,
Chest pounding, panting... O illusion!... But
Suddenly, in the thickening shadows, what
Does his gaze now behold, deep in the dark?
How can it be? Good God, I pray you... Hark!
Hear me! Is it a dream?... Néali?... Why
Comes she here in the night... "Speak! Is it my
Love that has brought you to me, amorous
At last, and led your eager footsteps thus?"
Not so! She ventures for her daughter's sake,
Rather, to beg a few drops that might slake
Her murderous thirst; precious draughts that the white
Keeps for himself... Alas! So dire her plight
That you, Belmar, would take advantage of
Her weakness and your strength to force your love
Upon her. Off you drag her... Struggling, she
Resists with tooth and nail... frenzied, breaks free...
Attempts to flee... "Save me! Save me, Sélim!
Avenge our honor!" But her cries to him
And his are vain: their bonds hold fast... The cur,
Belmar—foul wretch—pursues her, seizes her,
In jealous rage fells her, orders his men
To chain her up and pummel her. But when
They seem about to do his woeful will,
Each blow falls harmless: they can do no ill
To such a one, whose fate they much deplore.
One, though, thirsting for blood, comes to the fore,

Eager to strike. Whereat, her daughter falls
To the ground, at his feet, and, begging, calls:
"Please! Spare my mother! Punish me instead!"
Fearless, Néali angered them, and pled
That they make haste and boldly do their duty.
"Ravage my charms! Lay waste my loathsome beauty,
So dear to whites! Destroy it! Let me be
A thing of horror for their eyes to see!"

The captives, in the dismal keep where sound
These cries, shake threatening fists, though stoutly bound
About with ropes... Sélim, raging, despairs
As in his night-black face he glowers, glares,
Wild eyed... "My friends," he shouts. "Who? Which of you
Will join me to face certain peril?" "Who?"
They answer. "Which?... Why, all of us!" Whence he,
Blood gushing from his lips, bites savagely
His hempen ropes... rips... soon undoes the knot...
With a blade frees the bravest of the lot...
Whereat, wielding their chains, they fall upon
Their captor whites, bewildered, woebegone,
And spewing blood!... But oh! Vain their success!
A deadlier art renders them powerless,
As lead whistles about their heads, spreads death,
Destruction, like the tempest's scythe-sharp breath
Cutting down stalks of grain. Their courage serves,
Alas, no purpose. Much though it deserves
Loud shouts of pride—"Martyrs to liberty!"—
Their glory lasts an instant. Blasphemy
Curses their shredded flesh. The timeless waves
Enslave their blood and are their only graves.

Chained to a mast, Néali weeps her pain
And their dire fate and gives her tongue free rein
To voice in plaintive accents her lament,
Begging her noisome captors, torture bent,
To save her from her life and end her days.

But, for a moment, she fixes her gaze
Upon her daughter... hesitates... For yet
Is she a mother! How can she forget
The tie that binds them? And she wonders then
How she would die without regret. But when
Belmar, before her eyes, in victory
Appears, in haughty wise, "What? Can it be?"
Cries she. "O my Sélim! Could I dare deign
Yield up your wife and daughter, victims twain,
To this sin-blighted race? No, no! I can
Yet smite the yoke of this vulgarian,
This deadly beast, this slaughterer reviled!
Be of good cheer! Soon will you see, dear child,
Beneath the palm that stood by at your birth,
Once more the tenderest father on this earth!
And you," turning to Belmar, "who defame
Your human kin, and heap scorn on the name
Of brother... You, whites, who would fain oppress
And shame us, watch and see the steadfastness
With which we die! Slaves in our chains abhorred,
We choose our death! Freedom is our reward!"
So saying, with savage pity she caressed

Her daughter, choked the breath within her breast;
Invoking death, with silent tears she fell
Lifeless, gasped, and gave up the ghost as well.

O fatal vessel! You, who have beheld
Such horrors! May the tempest's winds, unquelled
Unleash on you their fury! May the sea
Join in its depths, in one same destiny,
The killers and the killed! But how? Too vast
The Slaver's realm; too wide his clutches, cast
Hither and yon, crime sullied, reaching for
That blood-strewn treasure and the wealth it bore!
O Frenchmen! Christians all! May you well be
Repelled, revulsed by the iniquity
Of this inhuman trade! And you, O kings,

Senate of Europe, council sage that brings
The world to order! Do you not recall—
When, by the olive tree, you granted all
Our rights, wielding the scepter over laws
To make men free—that you took up the cause
Against the merchants of the flesh, who prey
On innocence? Finish your task! Away
With them and their perversity! Whatever
Colors they fly, whatever flags, they never
More ought be free to ply the sea! What just
And solemn right, what privilege august
Permits their banners thus to represent
Their sacrilegious, murderous intent!
Smite them down! Lay them low! Our land will shed
No tears; and blood, over their pennons spread,
Has quite effaced the colors that were theirs.
Join hands above the waves; borrow the air's
Loud-rumbling thunder, and make it your own!
What holier union—earthly throne to throne—
Shall be more blessed by heaven, and will enshrine
For you the favors of the throne divine?
May Africa, snatched by your rescuing hands,
Gentle her way, repeople ravaged lands,
And gird about her untamed brow, anew,
Bands wrought of art and culture. And may you,
Creoles of European race, beware
The wrath born of her blood, lest, lurking there,
Among you, you may find a Spartacus!
Already... (Ah! You shudder, timorous!)
Or even more than one!... Her progeny
Must be her own! Leave them alone, lest she
Find ways to ravish yours!... As for the many
Raised on your soil, the planter—more than any
Other—surely knows best their worth; and he
Will work to foster their felicity
In holy wedlock; and, joyously, then,
He will lead them, once slaves, now free again—

O liberty!—unto your altars, where
A myriad mortals will love's virtues share.
God will look down, as all good fathers would,
And bless his children's sacred brotherhood.

CHARLES DE RÉMUSAT

L'HABITATION DE SAINT-DOMINGUE (EXCERPTS)
Norman R. Shapiro

Act III

SCENE VIII

Hélène: (*alone*) Too much... It's too much... I haven't the strength to put up with their taunts. They all believe what my Touko believes. How can I prove them wrong? If only he were here, I would make him believe me. (*sighing*) Oh! What would I say? At least he would pity me. At least, not hate me... No, he is too kind, too good. Am I to blame if my arms are too weak? Too weak to defend me?... I called out to him... called his name in my voice choked with sorrow... called out to my friend, my only... My African friend!... If only he had heard me, he would have come to save me. He would have avenged me... Who knows? Perhaps he would have taken me off... off to join his flight... Ah! To be with him, together, in the forests! Just as we were at home, when we were young! Instead of alone, each one of us now... him, in his peril, and me, in my despair! If they catch him, he will die... die, cursing my name... And I will die too, with no pardon, no farewell... Oh Mother! Mother dear... What would you say if you saw her now, your poor Badia, all alone... abandoned by her Touko... alone, without your bosom to comfort her, his arm to protect her... Ah! Too much... It's too much... But the good Lord is good... (*with a desperate sigh*) Now nothing for Badia, poor Badia, but to die... Oh, Touko!... Poor Touko!

SCENE X

Léon: (*upstage, obviously disturbed*) Good God! What can I do? Which way should I turn? So many emotions, so many thoughts... That Frenchman who tries my patience, that woman who breaks my heart!... Racked by

doubts... Bitten by remorse... Can it be that all my principles were nothing but smoke? Perilous dreams... Or can it be that my father and I are
tyrants?... No! No! How could that be? So many have done the same! For
all these years! (*pausing to reflect*) But have they?... The same?... Have
they done what I have done?... That woman... She and I... Oh! That look of
hers... The humiliation... The scorn, the pride... They chill me to the bone
at the slightest thought! And that face, forever before my eyes... And...
(*suddenly noticing Hélène*) God! There... Hélène, it's you... (*as she turns to
leave*) No, please! Don't go... Don't... I beg you—(*He approaches her.*)
Hélène: Stay away, you beast! Stay—
Léon: Hélène...
Hélène: Stay away!
Léon: Hélène... There's no need to be afraid! Please... Don't look at me like
that!
Hélène: You... You...
Léon: What's wrong? What did I do?
Hélène: What did you do? What... (*recoiling as he approaches*) No, no! Stay
away!
Léon: Please! Don't be afraid! It's no longer a master standing before you...
Threatening you... A master, drunk with power and lusting with desire!...
No... Never would I harm you! Never would I dare!... (*stammering*) It's...
I... It's a lover, Hélène!
Hélène: (*fending him off*) Poisonous words, Monsieur! Vicious traps!
Léon: Yes, a lover... a lover who finds you more beautiful even than when
he held you in his arms!
Hélène: Please...
Léon: You're frightened... I understand... Only, tell me you don't hate me!
Hélène: I do! I do!
Léon: Oh! Spare me...
Hélène: (*furiously*) I detest you!
Léon: No! No!... I beg you! Spare me those looks that stun me with grief... that
mortify my pride... If you knew how I suffer... if you knew how humbled,
how crushed I feel... Please! Don't say you hate me! I mean you no harm.
I... Yes, I... I'll say it... I'll say those words that fill me with shame... words
I try to resist, but I cannot... I cannot... Oh, Hélène, I... I love you!
Timur appears suddenly atop the hill, upstage.

Timur: (*aside*) Oh! Jean-Pierre was right! There they are! Together...

Hélène: (*to Léon*) You love me?

Timur: (*pounding his chest, angrily, aside*) Oh, my heart!

Hélène: (*to Léon*) You love me, you say?

Léon: (*pleading*) Hélène...

Hélène: Well, listen to me! You disgust me, you dog!

Timur: (*aside*) What?

Hélène: I loathe you!

Timur: (*sighing*) Ah...

Léon: No! Don't say that! God in heaven! Why can't I find the words?

Timur: (*aside*) She said... She...

Léon: (*continuing*) Why won't you understand? Yes! I love you! I love you! You... so beautiful, so... My heart is yours... My head... My pride, Hélène... My life itself... I... I don't know what I feel. If you have any pity... Oh! Pardon me, Hélène! I'm begging you! Begging... (*He falls to his knees.*)

Timur: (*aside*) On his knees? The white devil...

Hélène: (*to Léon*) Pardon you, you beast!... Why? Why should I believe that same sweet tone, that same gentle look, as when you came to toy with me? When you gave me that foul brew to dull my senses, and...

Timur: (*aside, enraged*) Oh!

Hélène: (*continuing*)... and when you took me... Who knows how?... Dragged me to the banana trees...

Timur: (*aside*) The swine!

Hélène:... struggling, weeping, screaming... And you tied my hands... And you... you... Oh, Touko! Forgive me... (*She collapses on the ground.*)

Timur: (*leaping down from the hill, with a terrifying shout, to Léon*) You're a dead man, you—

Léon: What?... Good God! (*shouting*) Help! Help!... (*He seizes the shotgun, left against the tree by César Julien, and shoots at Timur, who falls to the ground.*)

Hélène: (*jumping, running to Timur, bending over him*) Touko! My Touko!

Léon: Oh! (*As Hélène remains crouched, everyone comes running down left, from the house. Blacks, entering up left, fill the stage.*)

Act V

SCENE V

Timur: (*to Hélène, still hanging back, down right*) You! (*coldly*) Go with the women!

Hélène: Oh, Touko! (*weeping*) I'm afraid...

Timur: Go, I said! I have no need for you here.

Hélène: But my love...

Timur: (*sharply, pointing left*) Out! (*to Venus*) Take her away.

Venus: (*to Hélène*) Come... You can cry your eyes out... (*She pulls her, struggling, left to join the women, as Almanzor, Jean-Jacques, and Telemaque exit, left. The remaining blacks disperse in every direction, leaving Timur alone with Célestine and Léon.*)

Timur: At last... alone... and free... (*coming down right, musing*) How impossible, to be free as long as there is someone else... But now, I am. (*looking at Léon and Célestine*) Except for them... Except for my prey... And now I can devour it, just as I please! Finally, I can be happy! I can do... (*hesitating*)... what I want to do!... Yes, what *I* want... Myself... (*looking off, left*) Not those insolent scoundrels!... Ah! Strange, how much colder my revenge seems now... Now that they try to force me... (*recovering his aplomb*) No! Nonsense, Timur! You're mad! Revenge is revenge, and I swore it! I swore... Come now, be a man! The banana trees, Timur... Remember? (*He approaches Léon.*) Him! And the banana trees... Ah yes, my revenge... (*to Léon*) So? Monsieur? (*scornfully*) Master?... Nothing to say, Léon? Nothing to tell each other, you and I? (*Léon shakes his head.*) You heard their demands? You heard what I promised?

Léon: (*weakly*) No matter... I only want to die... Nothing else...

Timur: Ah yes...

Léon: But at your hands, not theirs... Not those wild, foul beasts... At least you have the right to hate me...

Timur: Oh yes, Léon! I have the right! And I hate more than you know. And you will die, I promise!

Léon: Then strike, Timur! It's time! Only one thing I beg you... I beseech you, Timur... My sister has done nothing to earn your hate. Please... Mercy... Spare her life!

Timur: Your sister?... Yes, I feel no hatred for her. You need not be concerned. (*with a sardonic smile*) Oh yes, she will go free.

Léon: Then kill me and be done with it. The poor thing will never know...

Timur: Be done with it, you say? What? So soon? You think you deserve such an easy death? Your father, yes... What did he do, after all?... But you, Léon? Ah! (*sarcastically*) You deserve better! (*to Célestine*) Come, you... white woman!

Léon: (*suspecting his intent*) What? What are you saying? Please... Tell me...

Timur: Ah, Léon... Léon! The banana trees? You remember?

Léon: Only too well! I would rather die than think about them.

Timur: Ah yes... So would I! If only I might have... But you preferred to torture me! You preferred to fill me with rage and despair!

Léon: Timur...

Timur: Well, what you preferred, I prefer too. Yes! Suffer what I suffered! Yes, Léon! Watch your sister! Watch *us!* Watch *us!*

Léon: (*realizing his intent*) Good God! No! You wouldn't... Oh, barbarian! You beast! A poor, innocent child... And out of her mind... Oh, mercy! Mercy!

Timur: And did you show mercy, on the ground, by the banana trees? Mercy! Ha! (*to Célestine*) Come, white woman! (*He cuts her cords with his hatchet.*) You are free!

Célestine: Oh, the pretty black!

Léon: God above!

Célestine: What game shall we play?

Léon: (*to Timur*) You monster! How can you... Don't touch her!

Timur: Quiet! This slave is mine!

SCENE VI

As he is about to drag her off, Hélène comes running in, left, and throws herself between them.

Hélène: Touko!

Timur: Badia!

Hélène: What are you doing? You... with her...

Léon: Hélène... Stop him... Don't let him—

Hélène: (*to Timur, pointing*) His sister... His... The white devil's sister...

Timur: But...

Hélène: No, Touko! Choose! You must! You must!

Timur: (*to himself*) Oh! What was I thinking... How could I... (*to Hélène*) Badia... My Badia... Please... (*He lets go of Célestine and takes Hélène in his arms, kissing her.*)

Célestine: Oh, black man! Kiss me too!

Timur: (*to Hélène*) Can you forgive me?

Léon: (*heaving a sigh*) Thank God!

Hélène: Touko, dearest! We have no time... They're coming to get you! Your life is in danger!

Timur: My life?

Hélène: Just now, when I left... (*pointing left*) I followed behind them. I listened to them talking. When they found Jean-Pierre, they told him about Juan, and how you killed him. And he flew into a rage, Touko. He swore he would make you pay with your life. He says you're a traitor, and he's arming them all... (*pointing to Léon*) He says that if they find that one alive, they should kill you!

Timur: Oh? Kill me, will they? Do they think I fear their threats? Do they think they are the masters? Do they think I am their slave?

Hélène: Touko...

Timur: Kill me?... Well, we shall see how they kill me! (*to Léon, cutting his bonds*) Live, white man! Let them find you alive! Yes, let them find you! Alive and free!

Léon: What?

Timur: So be it!

Léon: Just when...

Timur: We shall see who is the master!

Léon: I... I don't understand...

Timur: Have no fear, white dog!

Léon: But...

Timur: Oh yes, I hate you! I loathe you still. But your life is sacred to me now... You, my proof against them!... I have had my revenge!

Hélène: Touko?

Timur: (*to Léon*) I shall defend you if I must!

Léon: And I hate you no less, Timur. But I shall defend you as well. Count on me!

Timur: (*shaking his hand*) Count on me!

Célestine: (*looking on*) Come, Brother dear. We have been waiting for you. Papa is wondering what is taking you so long.

Léon: (*shaking his head*) Alas!

Timur: (*looking right, off in the distance*) They are coming... I need your help, Léon. More is at stake than my life and yours. The blacks will be doomed.

They are lost without me... (*with a gesture upstage*) Follow me... (*He takes Hélène by the hand and leads her up the hill.*)

Léon: Yes... Up the hill... We can save ourselves if we must... (*to Célestine*) Come, Sister dear... (*They follow Timur.*)

Timur: I see them!... (*to Léon*) Here! (*Taking a dagger from his belt, he gives it to Léon.*) Take this...

CHAPTER 10

Translating Abolitionist Poetry and Theater

Doris Y. Kadish and Norman R. Shapiro

In 2004, the journal *Nineteenth-Century French Studies* asked Doris Y. Kadish to review Norman R. Shapiro's translation of two five-act plays by the nineteenth-century writer of color Victor Séjour: *The Fortune-Teller* (*La tireuse de cartes*) and *The Jew of Seville* (*Diégarias*). The latter is in verse. Shapiro is a professor of French at Wesleyan University and writer in residence at Adams House, Harvard University. Shapiro had been translating and teaching the literature of Négritude since the early 1970s, when his volume *Négritude: Black Poetry from Africa and the Caribbean* came out. Greatly impressed by Shapiro's talents as a translator, especially of nineteenth-century poetic and theatrical works, as demonstrated in his published editions of Séjour, Kadish contacted him about translating other works, notably the considerable amount of abolitionist writing that she had collected and studied. This material included Charles de Rémusat's *L'habitation de Saint-Domingue*, which they discuss in the interview. Thus began a collaboration that reached fruition with the publication of Rémusat's play, with Kadish's introduction and annotations, as well as the two-volume reedited and expanded version of *Translating Slavery*. Because reflecting about the process of translation is an integral part of the project of *Translating Slavery*, Shapiro and Kadish agreed to reflect upon their experience working together over the past five years.

D: Let me begin by mentioning your literary experience as a translator. You were a forerunner in the field of Francophone studies, having begun working on Léopold Senghor in the late sixties and having published *Négritude: Black Poetry from Africa and the Caribbean* in 1971. Since then, your translations related to both race and gender have been extensive.[1] Has your previous translating experience informed your treatment of the material that you have translated for *Translating Slavery* and, if so, how?

N: Yes. Everything one translates "informs" what one does later. In terms of technique at least... in poetry, the more you deal with formal verse, the more you develop a feel for its demands and how to meet them. The essential, of course, is to develop a technique for addressing the problems posed by rhyme and meter... assuming one chooses to preserve them, that is... Experience teaches... You discover early on that there is no rhyme for *orange*, for example!... Or for the common verb *have*... or, even a more unfortunate lack, for the beautifully poetic word *silver*... ! And you learn the strategy of the indispensable run-on line, while at the same time trying not to overuse it if the original treats it sparingly.

For theater, the more one translates, the more one develops a sense of stagecraft... especially of keeping the text actable—something all too many theater translators seem to forget in their dogged determination to render perfect, antiseptic equivalents... They forget that words have to fit comfortably into the actors' mouths... Above all, you have to preserve, in the dialogue, the general tone of the period being translated. Anachronisms, backward or forward looking, stick out like a sore thumb, except in an out-and-out adaptation. A case in point: whenever I have a chance to watch a theater translation of mine in rehearsal—say a nineteenth-century comedy—I cringe when an actor tosses in a gratuitous "OK," which is very definitely not in my text and just doesn't fit with the "period" dialogue.

So, has my previous translating experience informed my treatment of the material for *Translating Slavery?* Yes, by definition, but I would be hard put to say precisely how or to point to specifics. Except that in translating the plays, it has made me fussy about the externals—decor, stage directions, and such... elements that even the playwrights themselves tended sometimes to treat rather cavalierly.

D: Could you provide examples of how your understanding of Francophone literature and culture has informed your translation of these texts?

N: When I began translating Senghor in the sixties, I was attracted by the refreshing directness of his poetry. A far cry from the often forbiddingly arcane puzzles of many another twentieth-century poet... And when I approached his contemporaries and younger followers—Léon Damas, David Diop, René Dépestre, and others—I was struck by the basic oneness of their inspiration... racial pride, resistance to historical and contemporaneous injustice, positive affirmation in response to negative stereotyping... all the well-known values of the Négritude movement of the thirties, and its development... But I was also struck by the variety of styles and artistry that each of them used to express that inspiration.

It was a challenge for me, a nonblack, to try to crawl into these poets' skins, as it were, to sense both their feeling as blacks and the French heritage that, ironically—as a language of "the master"—provided them with its only means of expression... As Léon Laleau, the dean of Haitian poets, succinctly put it in the thirties,

> . . . sentez-vous cette souffrance
> Et ce désespoir à nul autre égal,
> D'apprivoiser avec des mots de France,
> Ce cœur qui m'est venu du Sénégal?

I hope that my own version of this passage, dating from my beginnings as a translator of black Francophone verse, transmits the same angst at being a victim of racial schizophrenia:

> . . . can you feel that pain
> And that despair—the most intense of all—
> Of using words from France to tame and train
> This heart of mine that came from Senegal?

I say "crawl into [their] skins" advisedly. I guess that's what a translator does, ideally, with any author... without being too mystical... a kind of "let's pretend."... And it's certainly what I would find myself doing later on when translating Baudelaire, Verlaine, Ronsard,... and, above all, La Fontaine... "Today I'll be so-and-so... If he were writing in English, how would he say such-and-such?" In verse, no less... I guess what I'm saying is that we translators are phonies of a sort. Always making believe we're someone else... but always maintaining the objectivity of a critical self-observer, always judging our success... like an actor, always dressed in a different role... Our success depends on how well we can put aside our own selves and be someone else. At least until the end of the poem or the play... or whatever it is we're translating... as *literary* translators, that is... Because our colleagues who toil in the vineyards of technical translation are a very different breed—one that I respect enormously but that I could never join...

My experience trying to feel the passion of a Senghor, a Damas, a Diop...

even a Césaire, who out-puzzled the puzzlers I was originally happy to avoid!... The list is long... Yes, that passion, that empathy, certainly prepared me for confronting the antislavery poets you and I are presenting, even though the literary/poetic quality of ours usually runs a distant second to their impassioned message... As with a number of the twentieth-century poets in my *Négritude*, it is the message that has earned them a place. Ironically, their nineteenth-century predecessors, no less passionate, had proved to be technically more adept, or at least more concerned with traditional verse. Before they knew what "free verse" would be, how "liberating" it would be, they had accepted the figurative "enslavement" of formal metered and rhymed verse to sing their paeans to liberty... not always flawlessly or with great sophistication, but with undeniable conviction...

D: Could you give examples of nuances regarding gender that you had to grapple with in translating these texts?

N: There are several compelling female characters in these texts of ours, in both the poetry and the theater. Besides the ubiquitous, iconic Ourika, who finds herself in both genres, there are the variety of white and black women in *L'habitation de Saint-Domingue,* each with her own defined personality. The sensitively romantic Célestine, intelligent and well lettered, but not overly "liberated"... not a *femme forte*... or a *forte femme,* for that matter... not a heroic Antigone but an emotionally frail victim easily cut down... And Mme de Valombre, devoted mother and dutiful wife, a little naive, not quite sure what she is doing in the tropics, far from Parisian society, forever fanning herself and keeping up appearances... And then there are the several black women in the drama, the "whitest" among them being Marie-Louise, Célestine's long-time nursemaid... It was essential to differentiate, as Rémusat does, between one of those black women—the strong-willed and admirable Badia (Hélène), a main character—and the others of the group, secondary "atmospheric" characters—Venus, Hermone, Clotilde—and even to keep the latter somewhat nuanced among themselves, though in many scenes it would make little difference if a given line were delivered by one of them or another...

As always, the challenge was to make all of Rémusat's women speak an English corresponding to the generally "proper" French that he put into their mouths, without forgetting their occasional lapses. A double suspension of disbelief then... first, that, as blacks, they were speaking "proper" French at all, and, second, that they are now made to speak an English in more or less the same "key."... A delicate balance...

But your question... No, none of our female characters, black or white, really required much "grappling." It was sufficient to follow closely the playwrights' and the poets' own portrayals. The most challenging, and the one who echoed most clearly her own individual angst, was the prototypical Ourika. The twofold Other... woman and black... But I think that, of the two crosses she has to bear, it is her blackness, not her gender, that defines her and defeats her. Which is ironic in that, despite her native intelligence—or should I say "natural" intelligence!—and despite the education she received from her white foster mother, it's a blackness that she never seemed even to notice. At least, not until it confronted her love and brought it down... and with it her very reason for living... Once out of the womb of ignorance, she can't go home again... She can never unlearn that she is black. And that, for her, is far more of an Otherness than simply being a woman...

D: Regarding poetry or rhymed verse in the theater, is it fair to say that you find it "tonally unfaithful"?

N: I have nothing against free verse in the theater, though in English it's not particularly common. Eliot, Christopher Fry..., a few others... And cynics might say that it's really only poetic prose with all the lines starting at the margin and ending wherever the author chooses. In French I don't know many examples. The French are so wedded to the alexandrine... Aimé Césaire does write passages in free verse in his theater when he wants to launch into lyrical "arias" of sorts, in contrast to his more recitative-like prose passages... as in *La tragédie du Roi Christophe*... And no one could accuse his free verse of being unpoetic!...

But in translating a verse play, I would never take the easy way out and render it in English free verse. Or even blank verse, which needs no letters of authenticity in English, surely... This probably came up when we were discussing the two Séjour plays: *Diégarias* in verse and *La tireuse de cartes* in prose. I must have said something like: "In theater I find it more authentic, more tonally faithful, to translate verse by verse and prose by prose..." Each according to the author's intent... and differences between the languages respected, of course... But I, personally, find verse generally easier to work with. And it's not because I think in iambs! It's just that the underlying metrical grid gives the dialogue a substance, a form lacking in the amorphous, total freedom of prose. Not that prose dialogue doesn't have a rhythm... It does—or should. But it's so terribly free... There are so many ways of translating even a character's simplest, most direct statements. Adding a syllable, or deleting one... , indicating a pause, repeating a word for emphasis even if the original doesn't... What is just the "right" way? The slightest change can balance—or unbalance—a line of dialogue and make it more natural—or unnatural—in the actor's mouth. Which is why a theater translation has to be read aloud... and why the translator has to have not only a good knowledge of the source language but also, and especially, a good ear in English. It helps to be a good actor too...

So, as for free verse—prose?—versus formal verse in translating theater, for me it's a matter of fidelity to the author's conception as well as my own predilection. But, strong though the latter is, it would never move me to translate, say, the prose *La tireuse de cartes* into verse! There are limits...

D: You have said that you take certain liberties to tighten up a play dramatically. Could you explain?

N: Basically, there are two extreme philosophies one can adopt when translating a play. You can opt to follow the author as closely as possible and produce an "archival" document that says in English what is said in the original... said, and also done... Because theater—no surprise!—is words and action... But that's another matter. For the moment let's stick to the language, which is, by definition, more the translator's concern.

According to the archival philosophy, then, you say the equivalent of what the original says, as exactly as possible. With some authors no "tightening up" is necessary. Just follow the text... Let me say, parenthetically, that this doesn't mean being slavishly literal and translating word for word, à la typical computer translations or those wonderful Japanese instructions included with electronic products... Take a famous line in Racine's *Phèdre*, for example:

C'est Vénus tout entière à sa proie attachée!

A practitioner of the "I-have-a-dictionary-so-I'm-a-translator" school—one of those who assume that all we need to do is look at the original, take it in, turn a crank, and out it comes—well, such a translator might turn the French alexandrines into iambic pentameter and come up with something literal, like this:

It is all Venus, to her prey attached!

Literal, and even metrical. But poetic? Even so, one can still espouse the philosophy of archival fidelity with taste... One can hew close to the original and still translate quite acceptably. Perhaps something like

Venus it is, entire, clutching her prey!

However, there is the opposite extreme... the philosophy that, as translator, one has carte blanche, no holds barred, to commit whatever mayhem one chooses in order to leave a personal mark... What results is an adaptation rather than a true translation. Not that there's anything wrong in that, unless it becomes a hodgepodge of styles and lexicons... Only that the reader or spectator should know what he or she is getting... Truth in advertising, as it were. . . .

Myself, I try to follow the dictates of good taste—at least my understanding of it. If I were to translate Racine, for example, I would be very sparing in my liberties. None are necessary. No tightening up is required. Or Molière, in the comic theater... But comedy presents another problem. The translator is responsible to the original author and the original text. That's a given. But also to the contemporary spectators... Perhaps less so to contemporary readers, who can make do with footnotes... Responsible, that is, to make them laugh... unless all they want is the archival document again... And to do that, to make them laugh, liberties are not only acceptable but often necessary... A genius like Molière is universal enough not to need much tightening up for today's audiences. A little tweaking here and there can usually do the trick. But not always so with other comic authors... I think, for example, of Labiche... I've translated a lot of him... Much of his humor depends on societal mores that would go over our heads today. But he's hilariously funny all the same and deserves to be translated. What to do? Explanatory footnotes, for the reader, or program notes, for the spectator, aren't very funny! So one takes liberties. Not with his basic plots or characterizations, or with his farcical tangles, but with details... physical action, language, wordplay, for example... An excellent instance of the latter occurs in his one-act *Une fille bien gardée,* in a silly little poem to be recited by a seven-year-old brat when she presents her mother with a bouquet of flowers for her birthday. The original plays—untranslatably—on the debatable grammar of the verse. In my version, rather than struggle to find equivalences in keeping with the tone of the comedy, I chose to rewrite the verse entirely, keeping that tone but changing the details. The result was this bit of suggestive doggerel, properly... improper:

Accept these rosebuds on this special day,
Your birthday, if we listen to the rumors.

> May your day be as lovely, bright, and gay,
> Full of the scents that fill your fragrant bloomers.

The characters then proceed to haggle over the meaning of the word *bloomers*, arguing whether it can or cannot mean "flowers."... The spirit of the original is maintained, even if the details are abandoned. In other words, one collaborates with the author, so to speak, to produce a comedy that is undeniably his, but tightened up here and there... tweaked, to make it work... his, but filtered through my or another translator's prism...

I would never presume to tighten up the work of a sacrosanct playwright... any more than I would dream of "improving" on a poet... a Baudelaire, for example... Perhaps perform a little very minor "adjustment" here or there, to clarify an obscure detail or two... sparingly... But in comedy more is often needed—sometimes even quite a bit more—when the playwright would no longer make *my* audiences or *my* readers laugh without my modest intervention... And, after all, it's with them, *my* audiences, here and now, that I have to be concerned and to whom I have an obligation no less than to the author... not with the abstract, eternal "Audience" that may or may not come along in the future... Besides, who can be sure what they would even find funny?

D: How important to you is the presence or absence of stage directions in translating nineteenth-century plays?

N: An interesting question... Are stage directions necessary?... I might ask you: is it enough, in choreographing a ballet, to indicate a pas de deux without specifying where on stage it is to take place, or with what nuances of gesture and expression? As I said before, theater is words and action. Action among things as well as people... words exchanged against a backdrop of objects, of actions, of interactions...

The French romantics appreciated this. They weren't so prejudiced in favor of the strictly literary component that they neglected the visual, the spatial. Far from it... perhaps thanks, to some extent, to Diderot, for whom facial expression was so paramount in showing the emotions... And they brought to it also their admiration for "local color" as an element in their theater no less than in their poetry. Not only for the spectator actually sitting in the theater, but also for the "armchair spectator" for whom Musset wrote his romantic *proverbes*... or the reader of, say, Hugo's vast drama *Ruy Blas,* whose imagination could seize on the most complicated, exotic sets called for in the text or even imagine more elaborate ones...

Compare *Ruy Blas* or any of Hugo's romantic dramas to Racine, for example. The latter is satisfied with a column or two and characters in togas. Even in a play like *Bérénice,* in which Rome is a virtual character in the action, there is nothing externally, visually Roman called for. A director is free, of course, to fill the set with ornate doors, statues, oil lamps, what have you... though I think it's a mistake to do so. Nothing should detract from the stark and intentional simplicity of the action. But Racine himself calls for nothing of the sort, no such set against which to specify this direction or that... Compare this, again, to Hugo's ultraspecific demands in *Ruy Blas*... details that not only establish the local color but also propel the action... like the chimney in act 4!... Could Don César make his melodramatic entrance by simply walking in the door? Or even climbing in a window—if there were one?... Hardly...

Myself, as a theater translator I cut my teeth on comedy. And, specifically, on farce... And more specifically, on Feydeau... Precise stage directions, and lots of them, were part of my theatrical upbringing. Anyone who has seen or read a typical Feydeau farce knows how essential a part of the play the visual action is. Or "the actions," plural. Because they are legion... and usually minutely detailed... It's a commonplace to call attention to Feydeau's "geometry"... the elaborately constructed machinery in which every element depends on, and influences, every other... the doors that fly open at just the right moment... or just the wrong one, more likely... In this "theater of a thousand slamming doors," as one critic dubbed this genre... with the meshing of gears about to grind down the innocent victim... the "victim"—that common denominator of all true farce, trapped in Feydeau's perverse universe... his "uni*per*verse?... At the mercy of individuals and objects, animate and inanimate... this hostile antagonist or that... but antagonists who don't even realize that they too are the victims of their creator... that their hostility, their antagonism, is imposed on them by him, by his capricious whimsy, as part of the infernal machine that he sets in motion just for the nasty fun of it, watches run its course, and brings to a halt with a charitable twist of the wrist and flip of the switch, and a last loud guffaw... a final affirmation of his own supreme power...

Clearly, such theater needs stage directions—often scenic ones dealing with the set's physical demands and intricacies of plot, but also emotional, "characterizational," situational ones that tell the actor how to stand, where to look, how to react to this or that, what gesture to use, what tone of voice... But the latter kind, whether the author's or my own, should ideally be expendable. Devoted to stage directions as I am—part of the "tightening up" that you spoke of, and that some plays really need—they can be ignored by an intuitive and experienced director. Not so, of course, those that directly determine the action, its boundings and reboundings, and that advance the plot... like "So-and-so lays his umbrella on the armchair"... that sort of direction... Because, as one critic observed in particular reference to Feydeau, when someone puts down an umbrella in one act, you can be sure that he'll be back later to pick it up... and with comical, sometimes nightmarish, consequences...

A skillful director-friend of mine, H. Stuart (Harry) Shifman, tells me that any time he stages one of my Feydeau translations, the first thing he tells his cast is to cross out all the directions of emotions, manner, gesture, and such . . . "With a wry smile," "Furiously," "Utterly puzzled"... that sort of thing... Not because they are wrong, and not because they are useless... but because he wants his actors to arrive at them organically through their own involvement in their characters... If every director were a Harry Shifman, I, as translator, would leave them out myself. As it is, in the real world of theater performance, many directors would be lost without them, and their actors as well.

So, are stage directions all that important? The short answer is yes. Certainly, for those that are an integral part of the plot... those that tell us, for example, in the Rémusat play, that César Julien lays his gun against a tree... the gun that, conveniently, will later be picked up by Léon to shoot Timur... As well as for those that help avoid confusion... those that tell us where so-and-so exits, so that when he or she returns later, the audience doesn't have to wonder how he or she got there... As for those that tell the actor what to think, how to look, what to feel, etc... well, ideally, they shouldn't be necessary. But I bend over backwards, assuming that more is better. In the best of all theater worlds they can always be ignored...

D: How would you characterize the importance of the works you have translated for *Translating Slavery*?

N: Their importance?... It depends on how you mean that. Did any of them change the world? Did any of them play a part in finally bringing down the institution of slavery in the French colonies? Those colonies where, in fact, far more Africans were enslaved to toil in the sugarcane fields than were their kin in the cotton fields of the American South... Much less visible, of course, because they were tucked away in France's possessions rather than in the *métropole* itself, as in the States... And the blacks who did find their way to France in the eighteenth and nineteenth centuries—like Ourika—were treated as exotic curios, not as enslaved *indigènes*...

Curious, isn't it? Today's blacks, impressed by the racial tolerance and artistic freedom of the cosmopolitan Paris of the 1930s, and appalled by the history of American slavery, seldom give a thought to the inhumanity of the French and their role in the slave trade. Or to the inhumanity of African tribesmen themselves... the Bushmen, for example, who were notorious hunters of human bounty,... or to the Arabs, who sold what the Africans reaped... ancestors of the ones who, even today, are enslaving Sudanese blacks... The barbaric history of slavery raises many ironies, and slavery is still alive and well...

But the question... were these works that we present "important"? Yes, but reactively and interactively, not proactively... To answer my own question, I doubt that they had much direct influence in ending the slave trade, but they were certainly symptomatic of its inevitable demise—a demise that, encouraged by Enlightenment thinkers, by religious humanists and revolutionary idealists, was destined to take place in the historic scheme of things... Perhaps a few works—like the several far-reaching *Ourika* texts—may have helped a little to prepare the social terrain for the change... probably not even as much as *Uncle Tom's Cabin,* also a reactive rather than a proactive work, I think...

I really doubt that literary works directly bring about social change much, though they certainly reflect it. But I'm willing to be convinced otherwise...

D: How do you justify translating works such as long abolitionist poems that may not always meet your standards of aesthetically elevated poetry?

N: To answer, I would probably have to say why I translate in the first place... For money? Ha!... For fame and prestige? Double ha!... Even in these days of greater awareness of the importance of the translator's craft—and art?... Even now, in this era of translation studies, "translatology," academic programs in translation and interpretation... No, they're not the same... Even now, most translators, however well respected by the "happy few," tend to remain invisible to the general public and the world at large. Sometimes—shamefully—even unacknowledged... the low men and women on the literary totem pole... As I've said, those who haven't tried their hand at translation think it's easy. Because the more successful a translation, the easier and more convincingly it reads, the easier it looks. The less it calls attention to itself by awkward, contorted syntax or inappropriate tone... And the more transparent it is, like an unblemished pane of glass, the more the translator fades into the background, as if it "just happened."...

So, why do we bother? Do I translate because of some missionary zeal to bring worthwhile literary art before a wider public? Or, as in the particular case of our texts in *Translating Slavery,* to help bring to light forgotten works of social and historic importance?... Works of moral value?... It would be nice to have such a noble motivation. Perhaps some translators really do... Is that why we lay ourselves open to the scorn of critics, who rub their hands, like Uriah Heep, when they think they've spotted a flaw?... Are we masochists, reveling in criticism?... I remember one critic who raked me over the coals of his wit years ago, when I first began translating La Fontaine, because I dared choose to translate *cigale* as "cricket" instead of "cicada," for several defensible reasons... He failed to remember that many have been even more entomologically daring by turning her into a grasshopper.

But I haven't answered my own question or even come close to answering yours. Why I translate? Frankly, for myself. For the satisfaction of meeting the challenge... Because that's what all translation is... a challenge... It's like climbing the proverbial mountain "because it's there," if you'll pardon the cliché... The satisfaction is in the ascent. Negotiating the crags and crevasses, the pitfalls... Reaching the summit is important, but would it be satisfying if there were a ready-made trail and a mule to take us up? I doubt it... The accomplishment is in the doing. If others admire the feat, *tant mieux.* It is only human to find satisfaction in that approval as well.

Challenge... but there are many mountains, and the challenge is greatest when one attacks a writer of stature. When I decided to translate Baudelaire or Verlaine... or La Fontaine or Ronsard... the greats... not to mention others..., I knew each "climb" would be a challenge. And I knew that the challenge would be all the more demanding because those poets were well known, and they had been translated many times before... and no doubt will be again... As Borges said, the more translations of a work, the better. The more one understands it... No translation is "the right one."... Like the cliché about religion, if I may be so bold... each one is a path that leads its own way up the mountain, to heaven, or whatever...

Not only are there many ways up each mountain, but there are also many mountains. Far more than merely the greats... And that very profusion of what you call "less aesthetically elevated poetry" constitutes a challenge in its own right. There are many "elevations" that we can climb if we choose. Works that, by their very less-than-distinguished artistry, throw down the gauntlet... For myself, I have to admit that I take a certain pleasure in confronting such works. Works that ambitious, sincere, little-known authors spent weeks, months, maybe years proudly constructing... works that eventually saw the light of publication between two covers; brought their fifteen minutes of glory to their poets, their playwrights; and then sank back into virtual obscurity, where they have remained until we—you, that is—rescued them from their past... As I say, there is an undeniable satisfaction in translating such escapees from oblivion... collaborating with their authors over decades and decades of silence... treating them almost as our own personal property, because no one else had ever ventured to bring them back to life... And all the better if I can find in them as well the humanitarian message that spoke, at least briefly, to their own generation and that I can help make speak a little to ours...

I wouldn't presume to hope that I have "improved on" these works or given them more literary value than they have. I've tried to approach them on their own terms. After all, not every mountain is in the Himalayas. Modest hills and hillocks can present their challenges too. And trudging through their underbrush to the top, sometimes laboriously, is also fulfilling, even if the view isn't very majestic once we get there...

D: Whom do you picture as the ideal or typical reader of your translations, and how do you want him or her to read them?

N: As I just said, when translating these works, I took them on their own terms. And I would hope that those who read them will take my translations on theirs. They shouldn't expect, simply because these texts have been singled out for the "honor" of translation, that they are masterpieces of literature. Of course, their original authors might have thought so, but that's another matter... Be that as it may, surely they must have felt that, whatever the literary merit of their works, the message was one worth transmitting. On that we agree... So I can answer by saying that I would like for the readers to weigh that message and judge the poets' and playwrights' means of expressing it convincingly. And, of course, my own means of following in that effort... Here again challenge rears its head. If I, hopefully, have met the challenge of translating, have the authors themselves met the challenge of convincing? I think the "ideal or typical reader," as you say, is one who is already predisposed to accepting the validity and the vigor of that antiracist message, and one who needs no convincing that slavery was an abomination, whoever its many culprits were, and that it continues to be so even to this day. No generation has had a monopoly on barbarism, or—thankfully—on those who would fight against it.

As for how I would like these translations to be read... I would hope that they would be read aloud, as all literature should be, ideally. The poems, at least... And that they be read by those sensitive to the flexibility of formal rhymed verse, in which the underlying metrical constraints exist but must not straitjacket the meaning into nursery-rhyme singsong. Unfortunately, not everyone knows how to read a poem effectively, whether a masterpiece or merely a neatly contrived workaday opus... As for the plays, even when not actually read aloud, I hope they will be read dramatically, to bring out their undeniable strengths.

If texts challenge the translator, they also challenge potential readers. I hope I have met my challenge well enough so that they can successfully meet theirs...

D: What do you believe is gained or lost for the readers of your translations who are monolingual or only have access to the translation?

N: I try, of course, to let them lose as little as possible. In the plays, not much at all, I hope... certainly none of the plot... and, I hope, none of the characterizations, which, as I've said, I even tend to flesh out a little here and there... As you know, I keep the essentials of all the dialogues... the tones, the asides, the atmosphere they create, and the perspective they give us on the characters and the situations in which they find themselves... I try, too, by tightening up the stage directions, as we've said, to let the reader visualize the action without losing any of its dramatic effect. If anything, I think I emphasize the characterizations a little more than the author does. In the Rémusat, for example, things like César Julien's absurd pride at being a mulatto, or Monsieur de Tendale's pompous elegance, or Timur's conflicted heroism...

More is bound to be lost in the poetry, by the very nature of the genre. It's not always possible to maintain every nuance of tone between the two languages. But the challenge is to try to compensate... to craft a convincing and faithful whole even where the individual parts vary a little... No translation is expected to be an exact reproduction, after all. This is the great debate among translators. Should poems simply be translated literally, word for word almost, with glosses and notes where necessary to explain the interesting literary, linguistic, rhetorical points at issue? Does insistence on rhyme and meter—where the original uses them—cause the translator to compromise the meaning? Or should they be retained?

You don't want me to get into that debate, I'm sure. Suffice it to say that I defend the latter position, making formal translations of an author's formal verse. If the meaning is sacrificed, I've done a poor job. The trick is to maintain the author's tone—of which meter and rhyme are parts—and to do so, precisely, without causing the reader to lose the meaning and the poem's important rhetorical devices. Without being cynical, I could suggest that those who champion the other point of view, those who find theoretical reasons for pooh-poohing rhymed and metered translations, are the ones who either haven't troubled to try or have found that they can't do it well.

D: You and I have communicated innumerable times about these translations. Now that we are done (at least with this project), could you summarize what either of us might have learned from the other or how our viewpoints may have differed?

N: That's an easy one... I can't speak for you or imagine what you may have learned from me. Except that I'm a stickler for stage directions and that I thrive on the challenge of translation... even the translation of works of dubious "aesthetic elevation," as you put it... But for me, though I've been working in the field of black French literature for some time, and though many of the works were known to me at least perfunctorily, I certainly know them now a lot better. It's a truism that there is nothing like teaching a work to help you to know it. Well, the same can be said of translating it. And these works, strictly literary qualities aside, are well worth knowing. As for the several that I didn't know at all, and that you brought to light for our readers and for me no less,... all of them, as part of the vigorous French abolitionist movement, are welcome revelations of France's "other side of the medal"... a counterpoise to her involvement in *la traite*, the slave trade...

You have expanded my horizon, and for that I thank you.

Appendixes

"LA JEUNE ESCLAVE"

Jamais voyez-vous la colombe
Livrer ses petits au vautour?
Si du nid le plus faible tombe,
Elle vole et pleure à l'entour;
Jamais vers sa tendre couvée
Elle n'a guidé le chasseur;
Jamais elle ne s'est privée
De leurs baisers pleins de douceur.

Et moi je connais une mère
Cruelle à son plus jeune enfant;
Ciel! étouffez ma plainte amère!
Croyez mon cœur qui la défend;
Sur sa vieillesse douleureuse
Un remords sera suspendu:
N'est-elle pas plus malheureuse
Que son enfant qu'elle a vendu!

Dieu! rejetez-moi sur la plage
Où j'errais libre avec mes sœurs,
Où le palmier qui dit mon âge
Leur donne en ce moment ses fleurs!

Le luxe affreux qui m'environne
Me rend mes déserts plus touchants;
Je ne veux pas d'autre couronne
Que celle qui croît dans nos champs.

"LE RÉVEIL CRÉOLE"

N'a plus pouvoir dormir tout près toi dans cabane,
Sentir l'air parfumé courir sur bouche à toi,
Gagner plaisir qui doux passé mangé banane,
Parfum là semblé feu qui brûler cœur à moi,
    Moi vlé z'éveiller toi.

Baï moi baiser si doux, n'oser prend'li moi-même,
Guetter réveil à toi... longtemps trop moi languir.
Tourné côté cœur moi, rend-li bonheur suprême,
Mirez l'aurore aller qui près toi va pâlir,
    Longtemps trop moi languir.

Veni sous bananiers nous va trouvé z'ombrage;
Petits oiseaux chanter quand nous causer d'amour.
Soleil est jaloux moi, li caché sous nuage,
Mais trouvé dans yeux toi l'éclat qui passé jour,
    Veni causer d'amour.

Non, non! toi plus dormier, partager vive flamme,
Baisers toi semblé miel cueilli sur bouquet fleurs.
Cœur à toi soupirer, veni chercher mon âme;
Prends-li sur bouche à moi, li courir dans mes pleurs,
    Moi mourir sous des fleurs.

"LA VEILLÉE DU NÈGRE"

Le soleil de la nuit éclaire la montagne;
Sur le sable désert faut-il encore rester?
Doucement dans mes bras laisse-moi t'emporter;
Bon maître, éveille-toi! marchons vers la campagne.
    Tes yeux sont clos depuis trois jours:
    Maître! dormiras-tu toujours?

L'orage dans son vol a brisé les platanes;
Le navire sans voile a disparu dans l'eau:
De ton front tout sanglant, j'ai lavé le bandeau;
Marchons, les pauvres noirs t'ouvriront leur cabanes.
    Tes yeux sont clos depuis trois jours:
    Maître! dormiras-tu toujours?

Je voudrais deviner ton rêve que j'ignore.
Oh! que ce rêve est long! finira-t-il demain?
Demain, en t'éveillant, presseras-tu ma main?
Oui, je t'appelerai quand j'aurai vu l'aurore.
    Tes yeux sont clos depuis trois jours:
    Maître! dormiras-tu toujours?

Mais la lueuer du jour s'étend sur le rivage,
Le flot porte sans bruit la barque du pêcheur;
Viens!... que ton front est froid! quelle triste blancheur!
Oh! maître! que ta voix me rendrait de courage!
    Tes yeux sont clos depuis trois jours:
    Maître! dormiras-tu toujours?

"L'ESCLAVE"

Pays des noirs! berceau du pauvre Arsène,
Ton souvenir vient-il chercher mon cœur?
Vent de Guinée, est-ce la douce haleine
Qui me caresse et charme ma douleur?
M'apportes-tu les baisers de ma mère,
Ou la chanson qui console mon père?
    Jouez, dansez, beaux petits blancs;
    Pour être bons, restez enfants!

Nègre captif, courbé sur le rivage,
Je te vois rire en rêvant à la mort;
Ton âme libre ira sur un nuage,
Où ta naissance avait fixé ton sort.
Dieu te rendra les baisers de ta mère,
Et la chanson que t'apprenait ton père!...
    Jouez, dansez, beaux petits blancs;
    Pour être bons, restez enfants!

Pauvre et content, jamais le noir paisible,
Pour vous troubler, n'a traversé les flots;
Et parmi nous, sous un maître inflexible,
Jamais d'un homme on n'entend les sanglots.
Pour nous ravir aux baisers d'une mère,
Qu'avons-nous fait au dieu de votre père?...
    Jouez, dansez, beaux petits blancs;
    Pour être bons, restez enfants!

"CHANT D'UNE JEUNE ESCLAVE"

Imité de M. Moore
Il est un bosquet sombre où se cache la rose,
Et le doux rossignol y va souvent gémir;
Il est un fleuve pur dont le cristal l'arrose;
Ce fleuve, on l'a nommé le Calme Bendemir.

Dans ma rêveuse enfance, où mon cœur se replonge,
Lorsque je ressemblais au mobile roseau,
En glissant sous les fleurs comme au travers d'un songe,
J'écoutais l'eau fuyante et les chants de l'oiseau.

Je n'ai pas oublié cette musique tendre,
Qui remplissait les airs d'un murmure enchanté;
Dans ma chaîne souvent il m'a semblé l'entendre:
J'ai dit: le rossignol là-bas a-t-il chanté?

Penchent-elles encore leurs têtes couronnées,
Ces belles fleurs, dans l'eau que j'écoutais gémir?
Non, elles étaient fleurs; le temps les a fanées,
Et leur chute a troublé le Calme Bendemir.

M. DUMESNIL, *SLAVERY* (*L'ESCLAVAGE*) (EXCERPTS)

Greed is the frenzied monster that it bore!
How often, on the terror-stricken shore,
Sowing death's dole, bearing the arms to quell
His burning thirst for gain, did not the fell
Miscreant Arab, crawling to your tent,
Send your blood gushing forth before he rent

From desperate mother's arms, fair maiden, you,
Glory of Colchis's stream—the Phasis—who
Watch as they slash your father, ear to ear!
Your father who, with pious vow, held dear
Your grace, intent on seeing you fulfill
A gentle husband's happiness; yet will
He look on, dying, as you must become
The tiger's prey; you, whose foul martyrdom,
Begetting villains' savage joy, insults
His very death; joy impious, that exults—
Deaf to your pleas—in your most grievous state!

What heart could lie unmoved by your dire fate?
O Aménaïs, virgin fair, the fire
Of marriage was to shine on your desire;
You and Zaïde tomorrow were to wed.
But no! The pleasures he would taste lie dead
Even before they bloomed! Pleasures that would
Have graced your lover with your maidenhood!
There, in the plain, Zaïde—before the day
Has risen—pomp-arrayed, comes, wends his way,
Aflame with love... Into the maiden's tent
He goes, as light glows in the firmament.

But oh! Disaster! Oh! What scene it is
That greets with rending pain that gaze of his!
Her father, murdered, and her mother dying,
Gasping her last and all but lifeless lying;
And she, his heart's love, from that altar-shrine,
Missing, without a trace, without a sign,
Abducted surely... Ah! Ye gods! How might
A mortal's heart not falter at a sight
So unexpected? Is it any wonder
That he, transfixed, as if by heaven's thunder,
Stands dumb! But then, upon his agile steed—
Like fleet gazelle—he gallops off to lead
His quest for Aménaïs, flying whither
He will: to far-flung shores, returning hither
Over the mountaintops and desert sand...
Alas, to no avail! Doleful, unmanned,
Undone, says he: "Let us await her where
Hope springs eternal!" and leaps, then and there,
Into the deadly quicksand, now to keep
Death's vigil in the chill winds' dross, piled deep...
Meanwhile, the brigands have their victim sold.
Oh! If they spared her life after their bold,
Rash crime, it is but thirst for gold that must
Have pent the yearnings of their brutish lust.

In Athens's pomp, where palace tyrant reigns,
Aménaïs groans in brash captors' chains.
O maid afflicted! In your agony,
Your master, charmed, would force you secretly
Into his bed of Tyrian purple dyes...
His fleshly passion scorns your plaintive sighs,
Your cries of virgin innocence, nor hears,
Alas, your bale and bane. Drunk on your tears,
Long will he glut as long you lie tormented,
Nor will his murderous yearnings be contented.
Calling her father's name and her Zaïde's,
The maid, with one last burst of strength, succeeds
In throwing off the brute, seizes the blade
Of steel that he has negligently laid
Aside... Lunges... Plunges it in her breast.
Blood flows free... She swoons, falls, grows pale as death.
Her soul, unblemished, in one final breath,
Wisps heavenward; and, far from earthy sin,
Savors an endless peace amongst her kin.

Look! Do you see that Samos marketplace
Where dimwit citizen, with haughty, base
Design, buys for a pittance—little more—
The genial Aesop, dragged from Phrygia's shore?
How they revile, insult him, who, when free,
Will lay low the republic's enemy
And save it from the despot's wrath; who would,
With pleasing lessons, humble kings; who stood
High in the Grecian courts' esteem for these
Wise fictions, prized even by Socrates!

Everywhere, woe's rights trampled! Heroes bought
As slaves—so many!—for brave exploits wrought,
Yearning for death; but victor scurrilous
Damns them to live the hell of Taenarus.
Ruled by the gods, error's vain progeny,
The world falls prey to scenes of infamy!

At last, amid his mission's blazing light,
The Christ descends to earth from heaven's height.
Confounding disbelief's arrogance, he
Subjects death to his immortality.

As, on the cross, the Savior breathes his last,
The temple quakes; its veil is rent and cast
Asunder... Skies growl thunder... Lightning's blare
Furrows the whirlwind of the cloud-decked air.
The sun, glum and withdrawn, in death-pall laid,
Glowers a dour glance at the fearsome shade;
Earth shudders on its joints; everywhere crowds
Of ghosts, loosed from the tomb, shake from their shrouds
Death's dust upon the living; fear-struck, they
Know that their dim world lives its final day.
But, wresting himself from the black of night,
The Christ rises triumphant, puts to flight
The darkness, and will—mighty god—disperse
Those shadows that engulf the universe.
He casts his azure mantle pure about
The heavens, and his voice's accents flout
The gods Olympian: Rome's panoply,
Swept from the throne of vice, of falsity
And sin, as Jove, frail idol, from the skies'
Divine domain struck down, in ruins lies.
So too all those impostor-gods, now crushed
Beneath his heel; false oracles now hushed

By his strong hand... And, strewing from above
Virtue's soft flames, he steeps with generous love
The souls of men. Truth triumphs, and from high
Above the altars, God proclaims thereby
All mortals equal in their weakness; he
Created all for one same destiny:
The ones who love him and the ones who know
Him not, but who are quick no less to show
Compassion for the tears of those whose lot

Is woe; whose life, alas, lies misbegot,
Ignorance-rife, yet who loathe sin and live
A virtuous life; to those too would he give
His love and tender mercy; for he would
Love equally all who before him stood.
"For all in pain let your good deeds increase,
And heaven is yours." So said this god of peace.
And everywhere his word spreads its sweet reign,
Man will prevail, and earth breathe free again.

Notes

PREFACE

1. We follow Davis in using the terms *abolitionism* and *antislavery* as largely interchangeable (21–22).

2. This definition is based on a number of features highlighted by Terry Eagleton (1–10).

3. Another issue, that of women's special sensitivity to the plight of Africans, will be addressed by Kadish in a forthcoming book. It will take issue with Miller's bold assertion that, other than Behn's influence and a greater proportion of abolitionists among women than men, "no other gender-based specificity can be demonstrated" (*French Atlantic Triangle* 108).

4. Ferguson identifies a number of texts written by English women writers before *Oroonoko* (15–26).

5. In this instance and elsewhere, the authors of this volume have themselves provided the translations of all literary and critical passages unless otherwise indicated.

6. A major change in this revised edition concerns Claire de Duras' *Ourika*, which constituted the focus of part 4 in the 1994 edition. Because of the popularity of *Ourika* and the significant number of new materials it has engendered in recent years, we have chosen to place the original text, our translation of it, and essays related to it in a separate volume. That volume also includes translations of some of the poetic and theatrical versions that *Ourika* inspired at the time of its publication.

1. TRANSLATION THEORY AND PRACTICE

1. See Henry Louis Gates (1–20) for a discussion of that historical turn.

2. For a discussion of translation as a full-fledged critical interpretation of texts, see Hans-Georg Gadamer (chap. 1, 383–405). See also Antoine Berman, where he describes in detail the process of translating as reading.

3. André Lefevere defines refraction as the "process of rewriting a text with a view

to influencing the way the reader reads" and shows that it is an inescapable process. Although his definition may seem too narrow in that it implies that refraction is deliberate, in fact his further discussion makes clear that refraction is for the most part an unconscious process "through which a culture filters potential influences," and "a channel through which the new, both formally and thematically, enters another literature, or is kept out" (139–40).

4. Although the metaphorics of gender and translation have been dissected by Lori Chamberlain, practitioners still rely on the same vocabulary of faithfulness and authority. For example, Anna Livia summarizes the view of translation of Jean Migrenne, the translator of the American feminist poet Marilyn Hacker, thus: "Translation is penetration, he said: when he translated Hacker's work he felt as though he were forcing her to expose herself to him, driving his wedge into her work, the poems themselves a child they had made together" (15–16). The kinds of metaphors used by the translator make clear that this "Jean" is a "John" and that his gender identification expresses an attitude opposite to the one I suggest when I wish to retain the metaphor of reproduction.

5. In his introduction to *Rethinking Translation,* Lawrence Venuti describes the poor status of translation in this country, and the relative lack of works that are actually translated into English. He points out especially translation's lack of recognition by the academic world, although it is largely dependent on translation for its own work. Venuti rightly sees that it is not only an increased number of translations into American English that will be needed to change the situation, but the attitude of translators themselves, or at least of translation critics. They need to cease making casual remarks about translation and turn to rigorous analysis of the work of translation itself. Similarly, the work of reviewing translations needs to be done by professionals who can appraise what a given translator has attempted to do rather than rely on a critical vocabulary composed of one-word judgments, like *fluent, elegant, rough,* or *awkward.* For an extended discussion of this issue, see Venuti's *The Translator's Invisibility.*

6. For a selection of papers focused on issues of power and translation, see Maria Tymoczko and Edwin Gentzler, eds., *Translation and Power.*

7. Staël uses the adjective *Jolof* for both the nationality and the language of what is now Senegal, but the current word for one of the native languages of Senegal is *Wolof.*

8. For an overview of shifts in translation theory in Western Europe, see Susan Bassnett-McGuire.

9. In *White over Black,* historian Winthrop D. Jordan gives a summary of the concept of race in scientific terms: "It is now clear that mankind is a single biological species; that races are neither discrete nor stable units but rather that they are plastic, changing, integral parts of a whole which is itself changing. It is clear, furthermore, that races are best studied as products of a process; and, finally, that racial differences involve the relative frequency of genes and characteristics rather than absolute and mutually exclusive distinctions" (584).

10. Although he is not speaking directly about a third-world situation, Lawrence Venuti's advocacy of what he calls "resistancy," that is, a practice that "preserves the linguistic and cultural difference of the foreign text by producing translations which are strange and estranging, which mark the limits of dominant values in the target-language culture and hinder those values from enacting an imperialistic domestication of a cultural other" (*Rethinking Translation* 13), implies the same kinds of views as those held by Niranjana.

11. Interestingly, the Martiniquan author Patrick Chamoiseau recently made the same point in his novel *Texaco,* which recounts 150 years of history in Martinique from plantation slavery to modern-day squatters.

12. For a discussion of the concept of hybridity, see Homi K. Bhabha.

13. For a discussion of examples of withholding translation, see Gayatri Spivak.

14. For a very successful and authentic use of code mixing, see Chamoiseau's code mixing of Creole and French in *Texaco.*

15. Of course, to say that orality is important in Africa is not to say that it somehow partakes of an African "essence." As Eileen Julien has pointed out, "The dominance of oral language in Africa is obviously a matter of material conditions and not of an 'African nature'" (8). Including orality, as opposed to privileging writing only, is a way to attend to these specific material conditions.

16. On the subject of translating into the "other" tongue, Lotbinière-Harwood, a bilingual Québecoise, offers some interesting comments based on her own experience: "Working into a second language, what comes through (stains) from mother tongue colours other tongue" (150). She views translating from her mother tongue as a "transgression" of accepted translation practices and as allowing her to work in a "freer" space. She might add that translating into the second language is extremely empowering, as one can do what most readers and the author cannot do.

2. TRANSLATION IN CONTEXT

1. My discussion of the history of translation in France is informed by a number of significant articles on the subject: Stephen Bann, "Théorie et pratique de la traduction au sein du groupe de Coppet"; Jacques G. A. Béreaud, "La traduction en France à l'époque romantique"; and José Lambert, "La traduction en France à l'époque romantique."

2. For a fuller discussion of *les belles infidèles,* see Lori Chamberlain (455–58).

3. Behn not only adhered to the same concept of translation but used the same sartorial metaphor to express it in "An Essay on Translated Prose," which serves as a preface to her translation of Fontenelle's *Entretiens sur la pluralité des mondes:* "But as the French do not value a plain suit without a garniture, they are not satisfied with the advantages they have, but confound their own language with needless repetitions and tautologies; and by a certain rhetorical figure, peculiar to themselves, imply twenty lines, to express what an English man would say, with more ease and sense in five; and this is the great misfortune of translating French into English: If

one endeavours to make it English Standard, it is no translation. If one follows their flourishes and embroideries, it is worse than French tinsel" (5–6). The only reason for which her translation of Fontenelle follows the original quite closely, she claims, is that she possessed neither "health nor leisure" enough to "give you the subject changed, and made my own" (20).

4. Jean-François Saint-Lambert, *Ziméo* (1769); Victor Hugo, *Bug-Jargal* (1826); Prosper Mérimée, *Tamango* (1829).

5. Régis Antoine, for example, attributes French literary works about African slaves in the last thirty years of the eighteenth century chiefly to the influence of Saint-Lambert's *Ziméo*, which he singles out as the primary work linking the themes found in Montesquieu to later works about African slaves. He also claims for the character of Ziméo the highly questionable superiority over Oroonoko of being less abstract and more articulate (153).

6. Other important works from this period include "Réflexions sur l'esclavage des nègres," which the Marquis de Condorcet published in Switzerland 1781 under the name of Joachim Schwarz, and Louis-Sébastien Mercier's *L'an 2440*, published in England in 1771.

7. Gouges is among twenty-three individuals whom the translator omits from the list of those identified by Grégoire in his dedication. The name of Claire de Duras' father, Admiral de Kersaint, is also omitted.

8. I am indebted to Simone Balayé for informing me of the existence of Chaumont, whose baptismal certificate lists Juliette Récamier as godmother and Mathieu de Montmorency as godfather, and whose life has apparently remained shrouded in mystery.

9. Norman King analyzes Staël's goals in "Appel" in his response to Berchtold (in Berchtold 216–17).

10. These translations appear in volume 17 of her *Oeuvres complètes*, published by Treuttel and Würtz in 1821.

11. The complete translation of *L'habitation de Saint-Domingue* (*The Saint-Domingue Plantation*) and an expanded version of these introductory remarks are available in the volume published by Louisiana State University Press.

12. For an introduction to Desbordes-Valmore and the novella *Sarah* in French and in translation, see *Sarah*, edited by Deborah Jenson and Doris Y. Kadish.

13. For an introduction to Doin, see Doris Y. Kadish's introduction to Doin's *La famille noire*.

14. One example is Marie-Guillemine Benoist, whose celebrated painting *Portrait d'une négresse* (1800) hangs in the Louvre. Writing under the pseudonym J. Castera, her husband, Pierre-Vincent Benoist, translated Mungo Park's *Voyage in the Interior of Africa* in that same year. Another is Charlotte Dard, the author of *La chaumière africaine*. Her husband was Jean Dard, a linguist and educator in Senegal whose work as a mediator between French and African languages was recognized by the Société de la morale chrétienne.

15. It was Mrs. Clarkson who, with the help of a young French refugee, Benjamin Laroche, translated *Cries of Africa* (Wilson 157–58).

16. It was not unusual for men at the time to bear names that today are viewed as exclusively feminine. A specific case in point is the abolitionist poet Anne Bignan.

17. *Journal de la Société de la morale chrétienne* 3.14 (1824), 77.

18. *Journal de la Société de la morale chrétienne* 2.12 (1823), 351.

19. *Journal de la Société de la morale chrétienne* 3.16 (1824), 235.

20. For an insightful analysis of the limitations in Stowe's descriptions of slave life, see Angela Davis (27–31).

3. OLYMPE DE GOUGES, FEMINISM, THEATER, RACE

1. Writing in 1990, Graham Rodmell underscored the lack of interest in French revolutionary drama on the part of teachers and students of literature in the following way: "The publisher's 'blurb' on the cover of Daniel Hammiche's book *Le Théâtre et la Révolution* accurately defines the impression which is too easily gained by students of French drama: 'The history of the theatre in France seems to drop off to sleep with *Le Mariage de Figaro,* to wake up again with the uproar surrounding *Hernani.* Nothing seems to have happened in between.'" However, one can gauge the extent to which literary critics themselves contributed to this prevailing view by referring to Rodmell again, or more specifically his view that no play produced during the Revolution "can be rated as an incontestably first-rate drama" (205).

2. Critical interest in Olympe de Gouges' literary production was rekindled in the late 1980s as new editions of her work appeared. *Oeuvres,* edited by Benoîte Groult, was published in 1986 by Mercure in Paris, followed by new editions of her plays: *L'esclavage des noirs,* edited by Eléni Varikas; *Théâtre politique,* edited by Gisela Thiele Knobloch; and the first volume of her *Oeuvres complètes,* also devoted to drama, and edited by Félix-Marcel Castan.

3. In support and as illustrations of Thiele Knobloch's assertions, see Marvin Carlson (55, 89, 148). Antoine Court, who provides other examples of the misogyny unleashed against Gouges (68–69), finds him (Carlson) "le plus amusant," a comment that underscores indirectly the influence of feminist criticism in changing perceptions of what is acceptable and what is not acceptable as serious critique.

4. Based on the fact that Gouges employed secretaries who wrote down the texts she dictated to them, some critics have argued that Gouges was illiterate and could not, therefore, have written her plays herself. This argument must be rejected for its selective application to Gouges: using secretaries was a distinguishing practice for the rich and famous not because they were illiterate, but because they shunned anything related to manual labor. One recalls that the hero of Stendhal's 1830 novel *Le rouge et le noir* holds the job of personal secretary to M. de la Mole, a fictional political figure whom no one would think of as illiterate. Thiele Knobloch puts to rest the myth of

Gouges' illiteracy, "a myth imposed by Michelet, Monselet and many others," in a different way: by referring to "the large number of Olympe de Gouges' autographs in the National Archives and the archives of the Comédie-Française" as "proof to the contrary." She also points out that women playwrights' claims to authorship were often ridiculed in prerevolutionary France, that it was "a commonplace expressed by Rousseau and so many others to think that, behind every woman writer, stood a man." Consultation of A. Joannids verifies her claim that "in the registers of the Comédie-Française, women playwrights' names were followed by a man's name precisely for that reason" (Gouges, *Théâtre politique* 9).

5. Gouges, in fact, referred to *L'esclavage des noirs* as a "sentimental drama" ("drame sentimental") in her 1790 pamphlet *Les comédiens démasqués, ou Madame de Gouges ruinée par la Comédie françoise pour se faire jouer* (3).

6. Groult does not try to refute the notion that Olympe de Gouges' style was "inflated, naive, awkward" (see Gouges, *Oeuvres* 41). Instead she points to a few exceptions—showing that "sometimes she knew how to combine brilliant formulas and daring thoughts" (41)—and mostly seeks to excuse Gouges' stylistic "weaknesses" on account of her cultural background by explaining that her roots in an oral meridional culture represented a handicap for her as a playwright.

7. For an analysis of the "conflation, indeed confusion of reality and fiction" (64), between theater and politics during the French Revolution, see Janie Vanpée.

8. René Guilbert de Pixérécourt is considered the father of the genre, and his *Coelina* (1800) the first true French melodrama. Although early nineteenth-century melodrama appropriated many of the characteristic themes of Gouges' revolutionary drama—the persecution of innocence, the recognition of parents and children achieved through the "voice of blood"—*la voix du sang*—the restoration of happiness and unity at the end, as well as many of its dramatic features—three acts, prose instead of poetry, music and dance, mixture of prose—it is nonetheless fundamentally different in its function and outlook. Gouges' drama deals with real ethical concerns and actual social and political issues. They have absolutely no place in Pixérécourt's classical melodrama (1800–1815) and its abstract moral universe.

9. On authorship and copyright, see Marie-Pierre Le Hir, "Authors vs. Playwrights." In light of recent publications that have questioned, directly or indirectly, Gouges' commitment to freedom of expression, her efforts to help dismantle the theater monopoly of the Comédie-Française deserve to be remembered. Making short shrift of the playwrights' universal complaints against the Comédie-Française before the 1791 legislation curtailed its power, several critics have recently recycled the old stereotype of Gouges' pushiness and bad manners and made her vexed relations with an institution that repeatedly postponed the performance of *L'esclavage* the sticking point in their case against her. Convinced of the mediocrity of her plays, Roland Bonnell sides with the Comédiens, arguing that Gouges had no right to expect to be performed (85). Gregory S. Brown elaborates on this theme—her alleged lack of courtesy with the Comédiens, her unjustified insistence on having her play

performed—without considering the stakes that were involved in her struggle and the benefits that resulted from it for playwrights and the public alike.

10. The Comédie-Française was the most prestigious stage in Paris, and it held the monopoly over the repertory of French plays. (It was the only Parisian theater allowed to perform plays in French.) Rodmell writes that "the strength of the position of the Comédie-Française lay in the fact that not only did it possess a monopoly of plays from the golden years of the seventeenth century but also in the fact that the overwhelming majority of playwrights in the eighteenth-century eagerly sought to gain the prestige which derived from having their plays included in the Comédie's repertory" (14). See also Carlson (338).

11. Calling "Reflections" a "postscript," Christopher L. Miller underscores the close relation between the play and the pamphlet (*French Atlantic Triangle* 117). A chapter of Miller's book is devoted to "Olympe de Gouges, 'Earwitness to the Ills of America.'" Since it includes a thorough critique of the previous version of my essay, I want to acknowledge the debt the current one owes to his insightful comments and express my gratitude.

12. The electronic catalog of the Bibliothèque nationale de France (Bn-Opale Plus) lists a book titled *Oeuvres de Madame de Gouges* (FRBNF36061022) that was published in 1786 in Paris by Knapen et fils, but it does not contain *L'esclavage des noirs*—or alternative titles such as *Zamore et Mirza, ou L'heureux naufrage*. Since it is described as *tome deuxième* (volume 2), it is conceivable that volume 1 or 3 contained (if published), or was supposed to contain, an earlier version of the play than the known 1788 editions of *Zamore et Mirza*. Another possibility is that the change of publisher, from Knapen to Cailleau, caused the publication of volumes 1 and 3 to be delayed. A *tome premier* (volume 1) of *Oeuvres de Madame de Gouges* was published by Cailleau in 1788 (FRBNF30526920) as well as a *tome troisième* (volume 3; FRBNF30526954), also in 1788. The latter contains *Zamore et Mirza, ou L'heureux naufrage, drame indien en 3 actes et en prose* as well as "Réflexions sur les hommes nègres." *Zamore et Mirza* was also republished that same year by Cailleau in two other volumes also entitled *Oeuvres de Madame de Gouges* (FRBNF30526919 and FRBNF36061023). An electronic version of *Zamore et Mirza* can be downloaded from the Gallica site of the Bibliothèque nationale de France. Christopher L. Miller, who compared two of the 1788 versions of *Zamore et Mirza,* found them to be identical.

13. Apart from the change of geographical location discussed by Brown and Miller, another major modification is the streamlining of the plot: a subplot concerning a child lost and found, and characters related to that plot, was eliminated in the 1792 version. Although the theme of maternal love is lost in the process, the deletion of this subplot has the merit of avoiding a redundancy—since the theme of recognition was treated twice in *Zamore et Mirza*: Sophie found her child, and her father found her—and of providing a clearer focus on the issue of slavery.

14. Based in part on readings on the black population in France in the eighteenth century, Miller underscores the "unlikeliness" of Gouges' story about her childhood

encounter with a black woman—while conceding that it provides an "intriguing, perhaps fictive, point of origin for her thoughts about race and slavery" (*French Atlantic Triangle* 117). In a section of their introduction to *Black Slavery* entitled "Des noirs plus nombreux," Chalaye and Razgonnikoff make the opposite case: they argue that Gouges' story is likely because there were more blacks in France at the time the encounter is said to have taken place (see x–xii).

15. "Even though most of the basic elements of the two plays are the same, their differences are significant enough to merit attention. I think they should be seen as two distinct works" (Miller, *French Atlantic Triangle* 111).

16. "The scene in the first act is a deserted island; in the second, a large neighboring city in the Indies."

17. "Abolitionism represented for Gouges . . . not a coherent ideology so much as an available social identity, with which to fashion herself publicly as a legitimate and credible public orator—a *femme de lettres*" (216). Paradoxically, Brown also claims that his goal in this article is "not to devalue Gouges as a feminist or abolitionist" (210).

18. Brown adds: "Moreover, in the original version, the non-white characters are all secondary, serving primarily to advance the plot by fostering the reunification and recognition of the Saint-Fremont family" (214). This statement is inaccurate: in both plays, the main protagonists are Zamore (or Zamor) and Mirza, who are "non-white."

19. Brown "sees . . . *what I have called Gouges's retrofitting of abolitionism* as self-promotion. . . . It is true that Gouges's jump-cutting between, on the one hand, promoting her own play, and, on the other, discussing the plight of slaves, is disconcerting. As Brown suggests, it is as if the two issues were of equal importance to Gouges" (Miller, *French Atlantic Triangle* 443 n. 30; emphasis added).

20. Brown "implies, without actually using the word, that Gouges was opportunistic in her 'adoption of the identity of an antislavery writer.' . . . In his interpretation, her abolitionism comes across as much more of a pose than a moral engagement" (Miller, *French Atlantic Triangle* 111).

21. "Of course Gouges was promoting her play in 'Réflexions': she needed to, since the play was being held hostage by the Comédie. And it was, after all, in its fashion, an abolitionist play: performance of the play would advance the cause of abolition (as the reaction of the colonial lobby made clear)" (Miller, *French Atlantic Triangle* 443 n. 30).

22. Miller states that *Zamore et Mirza* was "the play she wrote first," and "Réflexions sur les hommes nègres" "an essay that she authored four years later" (*French Atlantic Triangle* 117).

23. "The play Olympe de Gouges submitted to the Comédiens-Français in 1783 . . . undoubtedly conformed to the prevalent taste for exoticism and the ballet at the end brought an original and lively note; but the Negroes did not sing about their happy lives on the plantation, quite the opposite: they have the bad taste of rebelling against their condition" (Chalaye and Razgonnikoff xvii).

24. Chalaye and Razgonnikoff, quoting Fleury's *Mémoires*, state that when

L'esclavage was initially accepted in 1783 for performance at the Comédie-Française, nine of the thirteen voting members on the admission committee requested changes to Gouges' text: "four voted in favor, none against, nine asked for corrections" (xix).

25. The negotiations between Gouges and the Comédiens on the issue of face paint, as told by the actor Fleury in his *Mémoires*, are thus summarized by Chalaye and Razgonnikoff: "In Fleury's view, . . . 'the philosophical theme' of the play made its staging impossible. They had tried to convince Olympe to give up: 'She was told of the difficulty of smearing the entire Comédie with tar.' But if she understood the objection, she did not resign herself and a few days later, still according to Fleury, she triumphantly brought to the Comédie the recipe of a polish made with liquorice that gave the face the most beautiful copper tones" (xix–x).

26. On the actors' refusal to play the roles of blacks, see also Gouges' "Correspondance avec les Comédiens français."

27. Chalaye and Razgonnikoff, who compared the variants of the play, state that Gouges was "forced to present her play as an 'Indian drama'" (xix) by the Comédie-Française, a modification she objected to and against which she protested in her preface.

28. Gouges' plea to have her play performed as a play on black slavery makes little sense unless one accepts her claim that she "dealt with their [i.e., Negroes'] story in the very first work" she ever wrote, in other words, that the 1783 version of the play was about slavery. Brown and Miller assume otherwise, that the 1788 and 1783 versions of *Zamore and Mirza* were identical, that the play *"had been submitted to the Comédie as an 'Indian drama'"* (Miller, *French Atlantic Triangle* 119; emphasis added). Miller nonetheless notes bizarre inconsistencies in *Zamore et Mirza*—which he attributes, too promptly perhaps, to Gouges' wild imagination and deficient geography: "Much of its discourse would appear to make sense only in reference to the plantation system of the West Indies, with its enslaved Africans, which is not the setting" (124); "the Ballet is to depict the discovery of America" (127); Indians "are now clearly American Indians" (127). Far from representing "an example of the type of 'flaw' in Gouges' writing that has been used in the past to dismiss her work" (128), these inconsistencies are remnants of the original version of the play that Gouges probably retained intentionally to thumb her nose at her censors.

29. A divertissement of dance and music, described in great detail at the end of the play, concluded *Zamore et Mirza* in 1788; a shorter one was apparently performed at the premiere of *L'esclavage des nègres* in 1789; but the divertissement is omitted in *L'esclavage des noirs* (1792).

30. As Catherine Nesci points out: "In *L'Esclavage des noirs*, Olympe de Gouges bases a new society on the freedom of others, which is no longer conceived as a limit or frontier of the subject but as an extension of the abilities of the individual self" (54).

31. For a more recent publication on Gouges' trial, see Vanpée.

32. On Gouges' attachment to the king and on her preference for a constitutional monarchy, see Marie-Thérèse Seguin. For an enlightening discussion of the question raised by Seguin, see Vanpée.

33. On Gouges' commitment to nonviolence, see Catherine Masson.

34. On the desacralization of the king over the course of the eighteenth century, see Roger Chartier (111–35).

35. In "Reflections on Negroes," Gouges offers the following comments on the consequences of emancipation:

> Deadly conspiracies will no longer have to be feared. They will cultivate freely their own land like the farmers in Europe and will not leave their fields to go to foreign Nations.
>
> Their freedom will lead some Negroes to desert their country, but much less than those who leave the French countryside. Young people hardly come of age with the requisite strength and courage before they are on their way to Paris to take up the noble occupation of lackey or porter. There are a hundred servants for one position, whereas our fields lack farmers.
>
> This freedom will produce a large number of idle, unhappy, and bad persons of any kind.

Miller is right to point out that "Gouges allays the primal fears of slaves' revenge and colonial 'blowback'" in this passage (*French Atlantic Triangle* 119). But she also treats freed slaves and free Frenchmen alike: both should stay on their land and cultivate the fields; for both, farming is a "noble" occupation.

36. René Tarin, who also underscores Gouges' "moderation" on the slavery issue—"regarding the colonial question, the author rejects any political extremism" (378)—turns her into an advocate of slavery: "Olympe de Gouges conceives of slavery as the first necessary step in the socialisation of natural man" (378). But Gouges' moderation on the slavery issue has more to do, in my view, with her political pragmatism and, as Masson argues, with her commitment to nonviolence than with philosophical principles.

37. "French people, . . . you want neither liberty nor perfect equality" (Gouges, *Testament politique* 12; also available online on the Gallica server of the Bibliothèque nationale de France).

38. A wealth of historical documents pertaining to the Société des Amis des Noirs is available on Gallica under the title "La révolution française et l'abolition de l'esclavage"—the collection of texts published by Editions d'histoire sociale in 1968. On the Amis des Noirs, see also Claude Perroud, "La Société française des Amis des Noirs"; Valérie Quinney, "Decisions on Slavery, the Slave Trade and Civil Rights for Negroes in the Early French Revolution" and "The Problem of Civil Rights for Free Men of Color in the Early French Revolution"; Daniel P. Resnick, "The Société des Amis des Noirs and the Abolition of Slavery."

39. Gouges' name does not appear among the ninety-five names of the Société des Amis des Noirs' membership roster for 1789 ("Tableau des membres de la Société des Amis des Noirs, Année 1789"), which is available online from Gallica. But neither does Mirabeau's, although he was a founding member; and no names are provided for thirteen people. However, Miller mentions that Olivier Blanc, Gouges' biographer,

"citing Brissot de Warville's unpublished *Memoirs*," claims that she was a member (*French Atlantic Triangle* 111). According to the bylaws, women were allowed in the society, but most of the women whose names appear on the roster were the wives of prominent men: the Marquise de Condorcet, the Marquise de Lafayette, etc. In 1789, the overwhelming majority of the members held a title of nobility (marquis, duc, chevalier) and/or high office in public service or the church (administrateur, fermier général, abbé, évêque). The high society profile of the members—and Gouges' colorful social background by contrast—as well as the selectivity of the admission process (support from five sponsors who were already members was required) make her membership unlikely, in my view. Also to consider is the statement made by Gouges in "Response to the American Champion" (1790), as she was fending off the accusation of being an "agent" of the Amis des Noirs leveled against her by the American Champion, a mouthpiece of the colonists. She declared that she was not personally acquainted with M. de La Fayette, who was a member: "I shall tell you that I do not know this magnanimous hero as you claim."

40. Welschinger writes: "In 1787, Olympe de Gouges had sent Mirabeau her drama *L'Esclavage des Nègres*. Mirabeau answered her on September 12" (407). Mirabeau's letter is reproduced in Gouges, *Théâtre politique* (94–95). It is a short congratulatory, but rather formal, note.

41. Miller states that "she was in fact a close friend of Condorcet's" (*French Atlantic Triangle* 136) but provides no support for his claim. His statement is also subject to caution because it is meant as a refutation of Gouges' claims, in "Response to the American Champion," that she did not know the Amis: "With what do you charge the author? Is it . . . to have been the agent of *men whom I know less than you . . . ?*" Miller interprets this passage and others in this pamphlet as ideological flip-flopping on Gouges' part: "She who was apparently a member of that group and who publicly associated her play with its cause at the time of its premiere, now holds the Amis at arm's length: 'It is not the philosophers' cause, the cause of the Amis des noirs that I undertake to defend; it is my own'" (135). As Miller himself concedes at one point, however, she may or may not have been "a card-carrying member of the Amis" (111). And if she was not, what other option did she have than to refuse to speak on behalf of the Société?

42. The speech given by Jean-Baptiste Mosneron de L'Aunay, a shipowner and trade delegate from Nantes to the National Assembly, on February 1790 at the Société des Amis de la constitution provides insights into the colonists' strategies. Although it is entitled "On the Colonies and the Slave Trade," the speech focuses almost entirely on France's commercial interests. The brief discussion of the slave trade has one goal only: to debunk the alleged misinformation spread by the Amis des Noirs regarding the inhumane treatment of slaves: "No slave trade is conducted with more gentleness than the French slave trade" and "the slaves in our colonies are treated with kindness and humanity." Mosneron concludes with an appeal for the continuation of the slave trade and the non-application of French law, including the *Declaration of the Rights of Man*, to the colonies (14).

43. For a discussion of *L'esclavage des noirs'* reception in the press, see Blanc (73–75).

44. "At last, the battlefield is mine, it is a triumph" (Gouges, *Les comédiens démasqués* 45).

45. Blanc writes that "nearly a thousand people" (73) attended the first performance of *L'esclavage*. The source of this figure, however, is not mentioned.

46. "My play is now buried under the Comédie's insane rulings, it has become its property" (Gouges, *Les comédiens démasqués* 47).

47. "Several men had taken an interest in them [black slaves] and worked to lighten their burden, but no one had thought of presenting them on stage in their costume and their color."

4. TRANSLATIONS OF GOUGES

1. My translation of Olympe de Gouges' "Réflexions sur les hommes nègres" is motivated by the desire to expose contemporary readers to the themes and thoughts of an enlightened and observant writer whose reflections are germane to modern society. I attempt to reconstruct the mood and feeling in her piece, rather than to render a literal translation. My aim, then, is to produce a text that affects the reader in the same powerful way that Gouges did in her own time: to incite readers to question current prejudices that stifle human expression, namely, biases of race and gender.

In order to modernize Gouges' "Réflexions" and make it more accessible to the twenty-first-century reader, I have substantially modified the syntax, with its attendant punctuation, and, to a lesser extent, the lexicon. The following examples should suffice to illustrate my approach. My decision to translate the fairly lengthy single French sentence "Revenons à l'effroyable sort des Nègres; quand s'occupera-t-on de le changer, ou du moins de l'adoucir?" with two sentences in English ("Let us go back to the dreadful lot of the Negroes. When will we turn our attention to changing it, or at least to easing it?") strives to emphasize in a separate phrase Gouges' disapprobation of the condition of the blacks. In another instance, however, I have translated the expression *les hommes nègres* with the word *blacks* because I want to point out the optimism in the situation and feel that the term "Negroes," in current parlance, would have too negative a connotation. In general, though, whenever the term *hommes* was used by Gouges in "Réflexions," I translated it either as "people" or "race," which I perceive to be two neutral terms, in order to avoid masculine specific references. In this way, my translation gives voice to Gouges' political struggle for equality among the sexes as well.

Given that my intent as translator was to have a powerful effect upon the reader, I have solved any difficulties in the translation with this in mind. The French expression *un commerce d'hommes* suggests a number of possible solutions in English, "a commerce of men" being one among them. However, I have opted to use the expression "trading people" to shock the reader with the reprehensible situation created by the juxtaposition of two perfectly acceptable notions: trade and people. Sometimes, I have omitted words in my translation for purposes of effect and clarity: "Why do blonds not claim superiority over brunettes who bear a resemblance to mulattos?" By eliminating the adjective *fade* ("Blonde fade"), I rid the color system that was in place of affective qualifiers and present difference as an objectively observable, rather than a subjectively experienced, phenomenon. Sometimes, I have added words to Gouges' piece for today's reader who would not necessarily understand the theatrical or political context of her day. Gouges' talent for championing human rights needs to be read against her struggle to persist as a dramatist: "This weak sketch would require a poignant group of scenes for it to serve posterity. Painters ambitious enough to paint the tableau would be considered Fathers of the wisest and most worthwhile Humanity, and I am convinced that they would favor the subject of this small Play over its dramatic expression."

2. We have modified the translation of this sentence provided in the 1994 edition of *Translating Slavery*. It was based on an error of punctuation in the original. "Ne nous occupons donc plus de ma pièce" should be separated from "telle qu'elle a été reçue" by a period, not a comma. The comma suggests, wrongly, that the play was received by the public at a time when it had not yet been published or performed.

3. Christopher L. Miller has drawn attention to the omissions at the end of the Groult edition of "Réflexions," from which our translation was originally drawn. For the sake of completion, we have added the missing paragraphs, although they have no special relevance to the subject of slavery.

4. *Noyon's Daughter* was published in volume 3 of Gouges' *Oeuvres de Madame de Gouges* under the title of *The Good Mother*: hence the reference in the last line of "Réflexions."

5. The text of *L'esclavage des noirs* and its preface is a transcription of the original imprint from the Bibliothèque nationale de France. The preface was written at the time of the play's publication in 1792. In *The French Atlantic Triangle: Literature and Culture of the Slave Trade*, Christopher L. Miller refers to two other printed versions of the play: *Zamore et Mirza, ou L'heureux naufrage: Drame indien, en trois actes et en prose*, published Chez l'Auteur et Chez Cailleau in August 1788, and *Zamore et Mirza, ou L'heureux naufrage: Drame indien, en trois actes et en prose* in volume 3 of *Oeuvres de Madame de Gouges*, published Chez l'Auteur et Chez Cailleau in September 1788. Miller states that the second *Zamore et Mirza* appears to be identical to the first, "with the same pagination and typesetting," but that it includes a preface (440 n. 9). Our source for *L'esclavage des noirs* is the microfiche from the Bibliothèque nationale of the 1792 edition; there is no ballet in this version, nor is there one in the Bibliothèque nationale online, as Miller alleges (127). See Sylvie Chalaye and Jacqueline Razgonnikoff for a study of the "manuscrit de souffleur de la représentation du 28 décembre 1789," which is held at the Bibliothèque-Musée de la Comédie-Française.

6. My decision to respect Gouges' use of capitalization in the preface and throughout the play should be seen as a decision to respect the author's originality: Gouges' capitalization of substantives has no apparent system, inasmuch as the same nouns

are not always capitalized, the word *Slave* being a prime example. Furthermore, rendering the inconsistencies in Gouges' use of capitalization points out the unstable practice of punctuation in eighteenth-century English and adds to the general re-creation of that ethos in my translation.

7. Pierre du Terrail, Chevalier de Bayard (c. 1473–1524), "le Chevalier sans peur et sans reproche," a famous captain known for his brave exploits in the Italian wars.

8. The expression "Jean Lorgne" designates a fool, a simpleton, someone abso-lutely mindless. This expression can be found in two forms, as one word or two, in Marivaux's *Le télémaque travesti*. An allusion in Voltaire's *La pucelle d'Orléans* also seems to refer to the expression. (I am indebted to Normand Lalonde at the University of Montreal for this information.)

9. [Gouges' note] Everyone knows that when the Comédiens do not take every possible interest in an author, they grant her only the worst days for the performance of her work, that is, Tuesdays, Thursdays, and Fridays, and furthermore, that her work is most often performed only with hackneyed plays, which are not liable to draw a crowd.

5. ON TRANSLATING OLYMPE DE GOUGES

1. For a discussion of emotional persuasion in France in the eighteenth century, see Sarah Maza (1256).

2. For a discussion of the emergence of a concept of public opinion that increas-ingly served as a surrogate for divine-right authority, see Mona Ozouf, "L'opinion publique" (419–34), qtd. in Maza (1250).

3. Some argue that Gouges' own statements about her lack of culture and literary skill would have been readily dismissed as a mere *topos de modestie* in a man but have been maintained for over two centuries simply because Gouges was a woman (see Gouges, *Théâtre politique* 9).

4. For a discussion of *le droit naturel* and Gouges' fight for the rights of women and blacks, see Varikas (10).

5. There is perhaps another element that can illuminate the ambiguity in Gouges' thoughts on abolitionism. She had a horror of violence, of all violence, be it exerted by noblemen, colonists, black insurgents, or revolutionists (Varikas 24).

6. See Wylie Sypher (106). In *L'esclavage des noirs,* in fact, Gouges confuses Na-tive Americans and Africans. I have retained these inconsistencies in the translation for reasons of historical interest and accurate representation of Gouges' perceptions regarding people of color.

7. For an enlightening discussion of black semantics, see Geneva Smitherman (35–43). See also Serge Daget: "Because *Noir* is neither sullied with prejudices nor already a stereotype, it pleads against alienation and contributes to the foundation of an abolitionist ideology: it thus arises from an innovation" (518).

8. For an intelligent discussion of the use of componential analysis in translation, see Peter Newmark, especially 114–24.

9. One obvious difference between Gouges' and Wollstonecraft's political attitudes can be seen in that "Wollstonecraft makes Marie Antoinette the emblem of what the revolution had to sweep away" (Siebert 104:356), whereas Gouges dedicates *Déclaration des droits de la femme* to the French queen.

10. In the textual introduction to the critical edition of *A Vindication of the Rights of Woman*, Ulrich H. Hardt states: "From the authorities [Wollstonecraft] does cite in *Rights of Woman* we must conclude that she was not familiar with the writings of Mary Astell, 'Sophia,' Olympe de Gouges, or Condorcet, all of whom had fairly recently written about the education of women and women's rights" (Wollstonecraft 7).

6. GERMAINE DE STAËL, TRANSLATION, AND RACE

1. See in particular *Corinne*, edited by Simone Balayé; *Corinne, or Italy*, translated by Avriel Goldberger; Balayé, *Madame de Staël: Lumières et liberté*; Madelyn Gutwirth, *Madame de Staël, Novelist: The Emergence of the Artist as Woman* and "Madame de Staël, Rousseau and the Woman Question"; Charlotte Hogsett, *The Literary Existence of Germaine de Staël*; and John Claiborne Isbell, *The Birth of European Romanticism: Truth and Propaganda in Staël's "De l'Allemagne," 1810–1813*.

2. In this article, Goldberger analyzes previous translations of *Corinne* and describes the strategies she used for her own translation. Although she does not assess Staël's own connection to translation, her own self-consciousness about translating Staël provides useful insights.

3. In "William Shakespeare, Mme de Staël and Politics of Translation," Maddalena Pennacchia describes the impact and the subversive character of Staël's "De l'esprit des traductions" (1816), which, by urging Italian literati to translate Shakespeare into Italian in order to rejuvenate their literature, created a crisis between classicists and emerging romantics.

4. Simon's argument oversimplifies Staël's notion of nation and de-historicizes her struggle against France's cultural hegemony, but the comparison of Staël and Spivak allows us to see how "deconstructivist" indeed Staël's position was at the time. For an insightful discussion of Staël's conception of nation, see Suzanne Guerlac. See, in particular, Guerlac's distinction between a nation-state and nation as a collective identity. Similarly, Spivak's conception of translation as being about "gendered agency in language" could easily be extended to Staël.

5. For an insightful account of the relationship between Germaine Necker and her mother, see Madelyn Gutwirth, *Madame de Staël, Novelist*, chap. 1.

6. In her study of *Corinne*, Jennifer Birkett has shown that for Staël the feminine voice represents "openness, pluralism and the negotiation of change" (397) and is a path to more productive modes of coexistence for individuals, groups, or nations.

7. For a discussion of *Lettres* in relation to Staël's position as a woman, see Gutwirth's "Madame de Staël, Rousseau and the Woman Question."

8. I am using the term *liberal* in its nineteenth-century context of one who follows the philosophical and political system based on individual liberties and equality. The liberalism of Staël is opposed to the despotism of Napoleon or the royalist Restoration that followed him.

9. For a description of her efforts to get Pelasge out of jail, see comtesse Jean de Pange.

10. For a discussion of this concept, see Pierre Bourdieu.

11. For a discussion of the ways in which translation can enrich a culture, see Albrecht Neubert and Gregory M. Shreve (3).

12. Jolof refers to an authentic tribe, but it was a kingdom of which Cayor was a part. Staël has reversed the importance of the two groups.

13. Actually, the Jolofs have no reason not to trade Mirza, since the distinction they make is not between friends and enemies, but between kin and non-kin. Since Mirza is an orphan of unclear origin, she may very well be considered non-kin. For a comprehensive study of slavery in Africa, see Patrick Manning, *Slavery and African Life*, and Paul Lovejoy, *Transformations in Slavery*.

14. For a discussion of the notion of transparency in translation, see chapter 1 of this volume.

15. This is not to say that *Mirza* is completely free of Eurocentrism. After all, Mirza gets her "culture" from a French exile, and the workers on Ximeo's plantation are represented as longing for their former games of bows and arrows, a rather patronizing view of what their culture may have entailed. However, Staël does not represent the topos of "the" African and is careful to distinguish between two West African tribes.

16. For a discussion of the term *nègre*, see chapter 1.

17. For an interesting discussion of the use of the term *nègre* in another context, see A. James Arnold's article on the translation of Aimé Césaire. His discussion shows that a translation may go astray if it does not distance itself from its own ideology.

18. Of course, this hope was in complete opposition to the building of the European colonial empire in the sense that what Europe did in the nineteenth century was attempt to export its values to its colonies and impose them on other cultures.

7. TRANSLATIONS OF STAËL

1. Island off the coast of Senegal.

2. Although the term is now perceived to have a negative connotation in general usage, some historians still use it, and Staël herself uses the word *nègre*, not the word *noir*.

3. The term is used as a synonym for *estate*. Plantations run by blacks existed in the American colonies as well as in Africa.

4. The French text does not use Jolof at all, but the translation does, in an effort to restore the voice of the African characters. See chapter 1 for a discussion of this choice.

5. Famous Greek statue representing the ideal of classic male beauty.

6. Part of the Jolof kingdom.

7. That is, against the Napoleonic perversion of the ideals of the French Revolution.

8. BLACK ON WHITE

1. Eileen Julien provides an answer to this: "According to Ruth Finnegan and Honorat Aguessy, European awareness of African oral literature began with the publication in 1828 of Le Baron J. F. Roger's retelling of Wolof tales, *Fables sénégalaises recueillies de l'ouolof et imitées en vers français*" (11).

9. TRANSLATIONS OF ABOLITIONIST NARRATIVE, POETRY, AND THEATER

1. [Doin's note] The kidnapping of Negroes abducted by surprise is very frequent. See the list of works we have mentioned.

2. [Doin's note] For details on these horrible slave ships, consult the sources we have provided.

3. [Doin's note] Human victims were found piled in barrels on ships caught doing the slave trade. You can check the sources provided.

4. [Doin's note] *Ouaga:* spell, enchantment.

5. [Doin's note] Solar eclipses occurred at the time in the Antilles.

6. [Doin's note] One generally uses this term to mean slave ship; I thought it possible to use it in reference to the person who trades slaves.

7. [Dumesnil's note] "Christian religion and nature rise up against the state of slavery" (Letter from Léon X to the Dominicans). "It is forbidden to enslave Indians or any other nation, even under the pretext of procuring for them the benefits of Christianity, *because slavery is in itself a crime*" (Bull promulgated in 1537 by Pope Paul III).

8. *Flight* captures one of the meanings of the French verb *voler*, which means both "to fly" and "to steal."

9. [Dumesnil's note] Ever since the start of the slave trade, European slave traders resolved to corrupt the morals and primitive laws of Africans, to foment continuous war between different chiefs. These wars benefit the European instigators, who receive the prisoners of both warring parties on board their ships as slaves. See Mungo Park, *Travels in the Interior Districts of Africa*, and Thomas Clarkson, *The Cries of Africa, to the Inhabitants of Europe.*

10. In a series of footnotes that are not translated here, Dumesnil refers to other episodes in Park's and Clarkson's works.

11. [Dumesnil's note] In America, a narrow, unhealthy cabin generally serves as housing for the unfortunate blacks. Their bed is a straw mat more useful for bringing

discomfort than rest. I'm pleased to be able to say that today they are treated with more humanity, especially in the French colonies, where a wise government has resolved to eliminate all pretexts for revolt.

12. Dumesnil identifies Cabinde as "a port and charming place on the coast of Africa." In a footnote, he elaborates on Zamor's actions as follows: "Blacks from the coast of Mina terminate their lives proudly, persuaded that, amidst those they love, they will return to their country, which they believe to be the most beautiful in the world. But some, instead of coldly committing suicide, seek, as Zamor does, to die by avenging themselves."

13. [Dumesnil's note] The terrible reprisals that blacks in the colonies have taken against whites at different times are well known. The history of modern times is full of these atrocities born in turn by oppression and revolt. Both are equally criminal, condemned by the word of Christ. All decent men see these acts with the same fright and sorrow.

10. TRANSLATING ABOLITIONIST POETRY AND THEATER

1. Since then, the University of Illinois Press has published your two translations of plays by the nineteenth-century mulatto author Victor Séjour—the five-act verse drama *The Jew of Seville* (*Diégarias*) and the five-act prose drama *The Fortune-Teller* (*La tireuse de cartes*)—as well as your translations of Louisiana poetry in the bilingual edition *Creole Echoes: The Francophone Poetry of Nineteenth-Century Louisiana* (2004). Regarding gender, your 700-poem, fifty-six-poet collection *French Women Poets of Nine Centuries: The Distaff and the Pen* was published in 2008 by Johns Hopkins University Press, as well as a collection of the child prodigy Sabine Sicaud. A volume devoted to the prolific comtesse de Noailles is in preparation.

Works Cited

PRIMARY SOURCES

Behn, Aphra. "An Essay on Translated Prose." In *Histories, Novels, and Translations*. London: For S. B., 1700.

———. *Oroonoko and Other Prose Narratives*. 1696. Ed. Montague Summers. New York: Benjamin Blom, 1967.

Belloc, Louise, trans. *La case de l'oncle Tom*. By Harriet Beecher Stowe. Paris: Charpentier, 1853.

Bouvet de Cressé, Auguste Jean Baptiste, ed. *Histoire de la catastrophe de Saint-Domingue*. Paris: Librairie de Peytieux, 1824.

Chamoiseau, Patrick. *Texaco*. Paris: Gallimard, 1992.

Chateaubriand, François-René de. *Le génie du christianisme*. 1802. Paris: Ernest Flammarion, 1948.

Chauvet, Victor. *L'abolition de la traite des noirs*. Paris: Firmin Didot, 1823.

Clarkson, Thomas. *Le cri des Africains, contre les Européens*. London: Harvey & Darton, 1822.

———. *The Cries of Africa, to the Inhabitants of Europe*. London: Harvey & Darton, 1822.

Dard, Charlotte-Adélaïde. *La chaumière africaine*. Paris: L'Harmattan, 2005.

Desbordes-Valmore, Marceline. *Sarah*. Ed. and trans. Deborah Jenson and Doris Y. Kadish. New York: MLA, 2008.

Doin, Sophie. *La famille noire: Suivie de trois nouvelles blanches et noires*. Ed. Doris Y. Kadish. Paris: L'Harmattan, 2002.

Dumesnil, *L'esclavage*. Paris: Firmin Didot, 1823.

Flaubert, Gustave. 1887–1893. *Correspondance*. Paris: Gallimard, 1980.

Gouges, Olympe de [Marie Gouze]. *Les comédiens démasqués, ou Madame de Gouges ruinée par la Comédie françoise pour se faire jouer*. Paris: Imprimerie de la Comédie-Française, 1790.

———. "Correspondance avec les Comédiens français." In *Oeuvres de Madame de Gouges*. Paris: Cailleau, 1788.

——. *L'esclavage des noirs, ou L'heureux naufrage.* 1789. Paris: Duchesne, 1792.

——. *Oeuvres.* Ed. Benoîte Groult. Paris: Mercure de France, 1986.

——. "Réflexions sur les hommes nègres." In *Oeuvres de Madame de Gouges.* Paris: Cailleau, 1788. 3:94–99.

——. "Réponse au champion américain ou colon très-aisé à connaître." In *Traite des noirs et esclavage.* Paris: Editions d'histoire sociale, 1968. 4:1–8.

——. *Testament politique d'Olympe de Gouges.* [S.I., 1793]. Fonds Rondel. Rf. 18.231. Paris: Bibliothèque de l'Arsenal.

——. *Théâtre politique.* Ed. Gisela Thiele-Knobloch. Paris: Côté-Femmes, 1991.

——. *Zamor et Mirza.* In *Oeuvres de Madame de Gouges.* Paris: Cailleau, 1788.

Grégoire, Henri. *Considérations sur le mariage et sur le divorce adressées aux citoyens d'Haïti.* Paris: Baudouin, 1823.

——. *De la littérature des nègres.* Paris: Maradan, 1808.

——. *An Enquiry concerning the Intellectual and Moral Faculties and Literature of Negroes.* 1810. Trans. D. B. Warden. College Park, MD: McGrath, 1967.

Holcroft, Thomas. *A Tale of Mystery.* London: R. Phillips, 1802.

Hugo, Victor. *Bug-Jargal.* 1826. Trans. and ed. Chris Bongie. Toronto: Broadview Editions, 2004.

La Bédollière, Emile de, trans. *La case du père Tom.* By Harriet Beecher Stowe. Paris: Gustave Barba, 1853.

La Place, Pierre Antoine de, ed. *Oronoko.* By Aphra Behn. 2 vols. Amsterdam: Aux dépens de la compagnie, 1745.

Mérimée, Prosper. *Tamango.* 1829. In *Romans et nouvelles.* Ed. M. Parturier. Paris: Garnier, 1967. 1:285–307.

Mosneron de L'Aunay, Jean-Baptiste. "Discours sur les colonies et la traite des noirs." In *La société des Jacobins. Recueil de documents pour l'histoire des Jacobins de Paris.* By F.-A. Aulard. Paris: Jouaust, Nollet et Quantin, 1889. 1:9–17.

Park, Mungo. *Travels in the Interior Districts of Africa.* 1799. Durham, NC: Duke University Press, 2000.

——. *Voyage à l'intérieur de l'Afrique fait en 1795, 1796 et 1797.* Paris: Tavernier, 1799.

Phillips, Caryl. *Cambridge.* New York: Knopf, 1991.

Rémusat, Charles de. "De l'influence du dernier ouvrage de Madame de Staël sur la jeune opinion publique." *Archives philosophiques, politiques et littéraires* 5 (1818): 27–47.

——. *The Saint-Domingue Plantation.* Trans. Norman R. Shapiro. Baton Rouge: Louisiana State University Press, 2008.

Renouard, Augustin-Charles. *Traité des droits d'auteurs dans la littérature, les sciences et les beaux-arts.* Paris: Renouard, 1838.

Rushdie, Salman. *Shame.* New York: Vintage International, 1983.

Saint-Lambert, Jean-François. *Ziméo.* 1769. In *Contes de Saint-Lambert.* Paris: Librairie des bibliophiles, 1883. 41–74.

Sand, George. "Harriet Beecher Stowe." 1852. In *Autour de la table.* Paris: Michel Lévy, Librairie nouvelle, 1876. 319–27.

Staël, Germaine de. "Appel aux souverains réunis à Paris pour en obtenir l'abolition de la traite des nègres." 1814. In *Oeuvres complètes*. Geneva: Slatkine, 1967. 2:292–93.

———. *Considérations sur la révolution française*. 1818. In *Oeuvres posthumes*. Geneva: Slatkine, 1967. 55–334.

———. *Corinne*. Ed. Simone Balayé. Paris: Gallimard, 1985.

———. *Corinne, or Italy*. Trans. Avriel H. Goldberger. New Brunswick, NJ: Rutgers University Press, 1987.

———. "De l'esprit des traductions." 1816. In *Oeuvres complètes*. Geneva: Slatkine, 1967. 2:294–97.

———. "Histoire de Pauline." 1795. In *Oeuvres complètes*. Geneva: Slatkine, 1967. 1:88–101.

———. "Mirza." 1795. In *Oeuvres complètes*. Geneva: Slatkine, 1967. 1:72–78.

———. "Préface pour la traduction d'un ouvrage de M. Wiberforce sur la traite des nègres." 1814. In *Oeuvres complètes*. Geneva: Slatkine, 1967. 2:290–91.

Stowe, Harriet Beecher. *Uncle Tom's Cabin*. 1852. New York: New American Library, 1981.

Wilberforce, Robert Isaac, and Samuel Wilberforce. *The Life of William Wilberforce*. London: John Murray, 1838.

Wollstonecraft, Mary. *A Vindication of the Rights of Woman*. Introduction by Ulrich H. Hardt. Troy, NY: Whitston, 1982.

SECONDARY SOURCES

Ambrière, Francis. *Le siècle des Valmore: Marceline Desbordes-Valmore et les siens*. Paris: Seuil, 1987.

Ammons, Elizabeth. "Heroines in *Uncle Tom's Cabin*." In *Critical Essays on Harriet Beecher Stowe*. Ed. Elizabeth Ammons. Boston: G. K. Hall, 1980. 152–65.

Antoine, Régis. *Les écrivains français et les Antilles: Des premiers pères blancs aux surréalistes noirs*. Paris: Maisonneuve et Larose, 1978.

Arnold, A. James. "Translating/Editing 'Race' and 'Culture' from Caribbean French." In *Translating Latin America*. Ed. William Luis and Julio Rodriguez-Luis. Binghamton: SUNY Press, 1991. 215–22.

Balayé, Simone. *Madame de Staël: Lumières et liberté*. Paris: Klincksieck, 1979.

Baldwin, James. *The Price of the Ticket: Collected Nonfiction, 1948–1949*. New York: St. Martin's Press, 1985.

Bann, Stephen. "Théorie et pratique de la traduction au sein du groupe de Coppet." In *Le groupe de Coppet*. Ed. Simone Balayé and Jean-Daniel Candaux. Geneva: Slatkine, 1977. 217–33.

Barbéris, Pierre. "Madame de Staël: Du romantisme, de la littérature et de la France nouvelle." *Europe* 693.94 (1987): 6–22.

Bassnett-McGuire, Susan. "History of Translation Theory." In *Translation Studies*. London: Methuen, 1980. 39–75.

Béreaud, Jacques G. A. "La traduction en France à l'époque romantique." *Compara-tive Literature Studies* 8.3 (1971): 224–44.

Berchtold, Alfred. "Sismondi et le groupe de Coppet face à l'esclavage et au colonialisme." In *Sismondi européen*. Ed. Sven Stelling-Michaud. Geneva: Slatkine, 1973. 169–221.

Berman, Antoine. *Pour une critique des traductions: John Donne*. Paris: Gallimard, 1995.

Bernabé, Jean, Patrick Chamoiseau, and Raphaël Confiant. "In Praise of Creoleness." Trans. Mohamed B. Taleb Khyar. *Callaloo* 13 (1990): 886–909.

Bhabha, Homi K. "The Commitment to Theory." *New Formations* 5 (Summer 1988): 5–23.

Bingham, Alfred Jepson. *Marie-Joseph Chénier: Early Political Life and Ideas*. New York: Privately Printed, 1939.

Birdoff, Harry. *The World's Greatest Hit: Uncle Tom's Cabin*. New York: S. F. Vanni, 1947.

Birkett, Jennifer. "Speech in Action: Language, Society, and Subject in Germaine de Staël's *Corinne*." *Eighteenth-Century Fiction* 7.4 (1995): 393–408.

Blanc, Olivier. *Une femme de libertés: Olympe de Gouges*. Paris: Syros, 1989.

Bonnell, Roland. "Olympe de Gouges et sa carrière dramatique: 'Une passion qui porte jusqu'au delire.'" In *Femmes et pouvoir. Réflexions autour d'Olympe de Gouges*. Ed. Shannon Hartiang, Read McKay, and Marie-Thérèse Seguin. Moncton: Editions d'Acadie, 1995. 65–95.

Bourdieu, Pierre. *Distinction: A Social Critique of Taste*. Trans. Richard Nice. Cambridge, MA: Harvard University Press, 1984.

Brown, Gregory S. "Abolition and Self-Fashioning: Olympe de Gouges and her *Esclavage des noirs*, 1783–1792." *Proceedings of the Western Society for French History* 27 (1999): 210–19.

Brown, Laura. "The Romance of Empire: *Oroonoko* and the Trade in Slaves." In *The New Eighteenth Century: Theory, Politics, English Literature*. Ed. Felicity Nussbaum and Laura Brown. London: Methuen, 1987. 41–61.

Carlson, Marvin. *The Theatre of the French Revolution*. Ithaca, NY: Cornell University Press, 1966.

Casanova, Pascale. *La république mondiale des letters*. Paris: Seuil, 1999.

Chalaye, Sylvie, and Jacqueline Razgonnikoff. Introduction. *L'esclavage des nègres* (*version inédite du 28 décembre 1789*). Paris: L'Harmattan, 2006. vii–xxxvi.

Chamberlain, Lori. "Gender and the Metaphorics of Translation." *Signs* 13.3 (1988): 454–72.

Chartier, Roger. *The Cultural Origins of the French Revolution*. Durham, NC: Duke University Press, 1991.

Clark, Vèvè A. "Haiti's Tragic Overture: (Mis)representations of the Haitian Revolution in World Drama (1796–1975)." In *Representing the French Revolution*. Ed. James A. W. Heffernan. Hanover, NH: University Press of New England, 1992. 237–60.

Cohen, Margaret. *The Sentimental Education of the Novel*. Princeton, NJ: Princeton University Press, 1999.

Cohen, William B. *The French Encounter with Africans: White Responses to Blacks, 1530–1880.* Bloomington: Indiana University Press, 1980.

———. "Literature and Race: Nineteenth Century French Fiction, Blacks and Africa, 1800–1880." *Race and Class* 16.2 (1974): 181–205.

Coulet, Henri. "Révolution et roman selon Madame de Staël." *Revue d'histoire littéraire de la France* 87.4 (1987): 638–60.

Court, Antoine. "Un mélodrame d'Olympe de Gouges ou le noir impossible." In *Mélodrames et romans noirs, 1750–1890.* Ed. Simone Bernard-Griffiths and Jean Sgard. Toulouse: Presses universitaires du Mirail, 2000. 67–82.

Daget, Serge. "Les mots esclave, nègre, noir, et les jugements de valeur sur la traite négrière dans la littérature abolitionniste française de 1770 à 1845." *Revue française d'histoire d'outre-mer* 60.221 (1973): 511–48.

Davis, Angela. *Women, Race and Class.* New York: Random House, 1981.

Davis, David Brion. *The Problem of Slavery in the Age of Revolution, 1770–1823.* Ithaca, NY: Cornell University Press, 1975.

Debien, Gabriel. *Les colons de Saint-Domingue et la révolution. Essai sur le Club Massiac (Août 1789–Août 1792).* Paris: Colin, 1953.

Denby, David. *Sentimental Narrative and the Social Order in France, 1760–1820.* Cambridge: Cambridge University Press, 1994.

Eagleton, Terry. *Ideology.* London: Verso, 1991.

Ferguson, Moira. *Subject to Others: British Women Writers and Colonial Slavery, 1670–1834.* London: Routledge, 1992.

Furneaux, Robin. *William Wilberforce.* London: Hamish Hamilton, 1974.

Gadamer, Hans-Georg. *Truth and Method.* New York: Continuum, 1991.

Gates, Henry Louis. *"Race," Writing, and Difference.* Chicago: University of Chicago Press, 1986.

Goblot, Jean-Jacques. "Genèse et signification de *L'habitation de Saint-Domingue:* Charles de Rémusat et la révolution." *L'habitation de Saint-Domingue, ou L'insurrection.* Paris: CNRS, 1977. xi–xxxiii.

Godard, Barbara. "Theorizing Feminist Discourse/Translation." In *Translation, History, and Culture.* Ed. Susan Bassnett and André Lefevere. London: Pinter, 1990. 87–96.

Goldberger, Avriel. "Germaine de Staël's *Corinne:* Challenges to the Translator in the 1980s." *French Review* 63 (April 1990): 800–809.

Goodman, Dena. "Enlightenment Salons: The Convergence of Female and Philosophic Ambitions." *Eighteenth Century Studies* 22.3 (1989): 329–50.

Gramsci, Antonio. *Selections from the Prison Notebooks.* Ed. and trans. Quentin Hoare and Geoffrey Nowell Smith. New York: International Publishing, 1971.

Guerlac, Suzanne. "Writing the Nation: Madame de Staël." *French Forum* 30.3 (2005): 43–56.

Gutwirth, Madelyn. *Madame de Staël, Novelist: The Emergence of the Artist as Woman.* Urbana: University of Illinois Press, 1978.

———. "Madame de Staël, Rousseau and the Woman Question." *PMLA* 86 (1971): 100–109.

Harth, Erica. *Cartesian Women: Versions and Subversions of Rational Discourse in the Old Regime*. Ithaca, NY: Cornell University Press, 1992.

Hoffmann, Léon-François. *Le nègre romantique*. Paris: Payot, 1973.

Hogsett, Charlotte. *The Literary Existence of Germaine de Staël*. Carbondale: Southern Illinois University Press, 1987.

Howarth, William D. "The Playwright as Preacher: Didactism and Melodrama in the French Theater of the Enlightenment." *Forum for Modern Language Studies* 14 (1978): 97–115.

Isbell, John Claiborne. *The Birth of European Romanticism: Truth and Propaganda in Staël's "De l'Allemagne," 1810–1813*. Cambridge: Cambridge University Press, 1994.

James, C. L. R. *The Black Jacobins*. 1938. New York: Vintage Books, 1989.

Jenson, Deborah, ed. *Yale French Studies: The Haiti Issue* 107 (2005).

Joannides, A. *La Comédie-Française de 1680 à 1900. Dictionnaire général des pièces et des auteurs*. Paris: Plon-Nourrit, 1910.

Jordan, Winthrop D. *White over Black*. New York: Norton, 1977.

Julien, Eileen. *African Novels and the Question of Orality*. Bloomington: Indiana University Press, 1992.

Kale, Steven D. *French Salons: High Society and Political Sociability from the Old Regime to the Revolution of 1848*. Baltimore, MD: Johns Hopkins University Press, 2004.

Lacour, Léopold. *Trois femmes de la révolution*. Paris: Plon-Nourrit, 1900.

Lambert, José. "La traduction en France à l'époque romantique." *Revue de littérature comparée* 49.3 (1975): 396–412.

Leclerc, Lucien. "La politique et l'influence du Club de l'Hotel Massiac." *Annales historiques de la révolution française* 14 (1937): 342–63.

Lefevere, André. "Translations and Other Ways in Which One Literature Refracts Another." *Symposium* 38 (1984): 127–42.

Le Hir, Marie-Pierre. "Authors vs. Playwrights: The Two Authorship Systems of the Old Regime in France and the Repercussions of Their Merger." *Theater Journal* 44.4 (1992): 501–14.

———. *Le romantisme aux enchères: Ducange, Pixerécourt, Hugo*. Amsterdam: John Benjamins, 1992.

Levine, Suzanne Jill. *The Subversive Scribe: Translating Latin American Fiction*. Minneapolis, MN: Greywolf Press, 1991.

Levy, Darline Gay, Harriet Branson Applewhite, and Mary Durham Johnson. "The Trial of a Feminist Revolutionary, Olympe de Gouges." In *Women in Revolutionary Paris, 1789–1795*. Urbana: University Press of Illinois, 1979. 254–59.

Livia, Anna. "Lost in Translation." *Women's Review of Books* 9 (March 1992): 15–16.

Lotbinière-Harwood, Susanne de. *Re-belle et infidèle. La traduction comme pratique de réécriture au féminin/The Body Bilingual: Translation as a Rewriting in the Feminine*. Quebec: Les éditions du remue-ménage/Women's Press, 1991.

Lovejoy, Paul. *Transformations in Slavery*. London: Cambridge University Press, 1990.

Lucas, Edith. *La littérature anti-esclavagiste au dix-neuvième siècle: Etude sur Madame Beecher Stowe et son influence en France*. Paris: Boccard, 1930.

Luzzi, Joseph. "Italy in Translation." *Romanic Review* 97.3–4 (2006): 275–78.

Lynch, Deidre Shauna. "The (Dis)location of Romantic Nationalism: Shelley, Staël, and the Home-Schooling of Monsters." In *The Literary Channel.* Ed. Margaret Cohen and Carolyn Dever. Princeton, NJ: Princeton University Press, 2002. 194–224.

Macherey, Pierre. *A quoi pense la littérature?* Paris: Presses universitaires de France, 1990.

Manning, Patrick. *Slavery and African Life.* London: Cambridge University Press, 1983.

Masson, Catherine. "Olympe de Gouges, anti-esclavagiste et non-violente." *Women in French Studies* 10 (2002): 153–65.

Maza, Sarah. "Domestic Melodrama as Political Ideology: The Case of the Comte de Sanois." *American Historical Review* 94 (1989): 1249–64.

Mercier, Louis-Sébastien. *Du théâtre, ou Nouvel essai sur l'art dramatique.* 1773. Geneva: Slatkine, 1970.

Mercier, Roger. *L'Afrique noire dans la littérature française.* Dakar: Publication de la section de langues et littératures, 1962.

Miller, Christopher L. *Blank Darkness.* Chicago: University of Chicago Press, 1985.

———. *The French Atlantic Triangle: Literature and Culture of the Slave Trade.* Durham, NC: Duke University Press, 2008.

Mueller-Vollmer, Kurt. "On Germany. Germaine de Staël and the Internationalization of Romanticism." In *The Spirit of Poesy: Essays on Jewish German Literature and Thought.* Ed. Richard Block and Peter Fenves. Evanston, IL: Northwestern University Press, 2000. 150–66.

Nesci, Catherine. "La passion de l'impropre: Lien conjugal et lien colonial chez Olympe de Gouges." In *Corps/décors. Femmes, orgie, parodie.* Ed. Catherine Nesci, Gretchen Van Slyke, and Gerald Prince. Amsterdam: Rodopi, 1999. 45–56.

Neubert, Albrecht, and Gregory M. Shreve. *Translation as Text.* Kent, Ohio: Kent State University Press, 1992.

Newmark, Peter. *A Textbook of Translation.* New York: Prentice Hall, 1988.

Niranjana, Tejaswini. *Siting Translation: History, Post-structuralism, and the Colonial Context.* Berkeley: University of California Press, 1992.

Pange, comtesse Jean de. "Madame de Staël et les nègres." *Revue de France* 5 (1934): 425–43.

Papishvily, Helen. *All the Happy Endings.* 1956. Port Washington, NY: Kennikat Press, 1972.

Pennacchia, Maddalena. "William Shakespeare, Mme de Staël and Politics of Translation." *Shakespeare-Genootschap van Nederland in Vlaanderen* 13.1 (2006): 9–20.

Perroud, Claude. "La Société française des Amis des Noirs." *La révolution française* 69 (1916): 122–47.

Quinney, Valerie. "Decisions on Slavery, the Slave Trade and Civil Rights for Negroes in the Early French Revolution." *Journal of Negro History* 55 (1970): 117–30.

———. "The Problem of Civil Rights for Free Men of Color in the Early French Revolution." *French Historical Studies* (1972): 544–58.

Resnick, Daniel P. "The Société des Amis des Noirs and the Abolition of Slavery." *French Historical Studies* (1972): 558–69.

Robinson, Philip. "Traduction ou trahison de *Paul et Virginie?* L'exemple de Helen Maria Williams." *Revue d'histoire littéraire de la France* 89 (1989): 843–55.

Rodmell, Graham E. *French Drama of the Revolutionary Years.* New York: Routledge, 1990.

Schama, Simon. *Citizens: A Chronicle of the French Revolution.* New York: Knopf, 1989.

Scott, Joan Wallach. "French Feminists and the Rights of 'Man': Olympe de Gouges's Declarations." *History Workshop* 28 (1989): 1–21.

———. "'A Woman Who Has Only Paradoxes to Offer': Olympe de Gouges Claims Rights for Women." In *Rebel Daughters: Women and the French Revolution.* Ed. Sara E. Melzer and Leslie Rabine. New York: Oxford University Press, 1992. 102–20.

Seeber, Edward D. *Anti-slavery Opinion in France during the Second Half of the Eighteenth Century.* 1937. New York: Greenwood Press, 1969.

———. "*Oroonoko* in France in the XVIIIth Century." *PMLA* 51 (1936): 953–59.

Seguin, Marie-Thérèse. "Pourquoi les révolutionnaires ont-ils tranché la tête d'Olympe de Gouges, leur compagne?" In *Femmes et pouvoir. Réflexions autour d'Olympe de Gouges.* Ed. Shannon Hartiang, Read McKay, and Marie-Thérèse Seguin. Moncton: Editions d'Acadie, 1995. 17–35.

Siebert, Donald P. *Dictionary of Literary Biography.* Detroit: Gale Research, 1991.

Simon, Sherry. "Germaine de Staël and Gayatri Spivak: Culture Brokers." *Translation and Power.* Ed. Maria Tymoczko and Edwin Gentzler. Amherst: University of Massachusetts Press, 2002. 122–40.

Smitherman, Geneva. *Talkin' and Testifyin': The Language of Black America.* Boston: Houghton Mifflin, 1977.

Spivak, Gayatri Chakravorty. "Acting Bits/Identity Talk." *Critical Inquiry* 18 (Summer 1992): 770–803.

———. "The Politics of Translation." In *Destabilizing Theory.* Ed. Michèle Barrett and Anne Phillips. Stanford, CA: Stanford University Press, 1992. 177–99.

Stackelberg, Jürgen von. "*Oroonoko* et l'abolition de l'esclavage: Le rôle du traducteur." *Revue de littérature comparée* 63.2 (1989): 237–48.

Switzer, Richard. "Madame de Staël, Madame de Duras and the Question of Race." *Kentucky Romance Quarterly* 20 (1973): 303–16.

Sypher, Wylie. *Guinea's Captive Kings.* 1942. New York: Octagon Books, 1969.

Tarin, René. "L'esclavage des noirs ou la mauvaise conscience d'Olympe de Gouges." *Dix-huitième siècle* 30 (1998): 373–81.

Tompkins, Jane. "Sentimental Power: *Uncle Tom's Cabin* and the Politics of Literary History." *Glyph* 8 (1981): 80–102.

Turley, David. *The Culture of English Antislavery, 1780–1860.* London: Routledge, 1991.

Tymoczko, Maria, and Edwin Gentzler, eds. *Translation and Power.* Amherst: University of Massachusetts Press, 2002.

Vanpée, Janie. "Performing Justice: The Trials of Olympe de Gouges." *Theater Journal* 51 (1999): 45–65.

Van Tieghem, Philippe. *Les influences étrangères sur la littérature française.* Paris: Presses universitaires de France, 1961.

Varikas, Eléni, ed. *L'esclavage des noirs.* By Olympe de Gouges. Paris: Côté-Femmes, 1989.

Venuti, Lawrence. *Rethinking Translation.* New York: Routledge, 1992.

———. *The Translator's Invisibility.* New York: Routledge, 1995.

Welschinger, Henri. *Le théâtre de la révolution.* Paris: Charavay frères, 1880.

Wilhelm, Jane Elisabeth. "La traduction, principe de perfectibilité, chez Mme de Staël." *META* 49.3 (2004): 692–705.

Williams, Raymond. *Marxism and Literature.* New York: Oxford University Press, 1977.

Wilson, Ellen Gibson. *Thomas Clarkson: A Biography.* London: Macmillan, 1989.

Index

Bold page numbers denote translated and French texts.